Reading the World

Reading the World

AN INTRODUCTION TO SOCIOLOGICAL CRITIQUE AND ANALYSIS

Rafael F. Narváez

Winona State University

cognella®

SAN DIEGO

Bassim Hamadeh, CEO and Publisher
Carrie Montoya, Manager, Revisions and Author Care
Kaela Martin, Project Editor
Casey Hands, Associate Production Editor
Arielle Lewis, Editorial Assistant
Emely Villavicencio, Senior Graphic Designer
Alexa Lucido, Licensing Manager
Natalie Piccotti, Director of Marketing
Kassie Graves, Vice President of Editorial
Jamie Giganti, Director of Academic Publishing

3970 Sorrento Valley Blvd., Ste. 500, San Diego, CA 92121

Para Marina y Rafael who, Marina says,
"Grew up with the sound of papa's passionate typing."

"At times my life suddenly opens its eyes in the dark."

—Tomas Tranströmer (2001, p. 7)

Contents

Acknowledgments

THIS PROJECT WAS partly supported by Winona State University's Faculty Improvement Funds. Chapter 3 derives from a project funded by the National Endowment for the Humanities (grant # AQ-234985), directed by Rafael F. Narváez. Many thanks also to Karen Coleman for comments and suggestions.

Introduction

IT MAY BE said that the first wisdom of sociology is this—things are not what they seem. [...] Social reality turns out to have many layers of meaning. The discovery of each new layer changes the perception of the whole" (Berger 1963, p. 23). Peter Berger, one of the contemporary masters of sociology, is telling us here that everyday things and events around you hide their true story. The cup of coffee on your desk, the manner in which your acquaintances behave in public, values and norms that are collectively relevant may seem obvious, fully understandable, transparent. Yet these things, Berger argues, are veneers that conceal many meanings. Consider your coffee. Dean Cycon, the founder of Dean's Beans, an organic roaster in Massachusetts, says, "In each cup of coffee the major issues of the twenty-first century—globalization, immigration, women's rights, pollution, indigenous rights and self-determination—are played out" (2007, my italics). Slavoj Žižek, one of the better cultural commentators today, indeed asks, "Are we aware that when we buy a cappuccino we also buy quite a lot of ideology?" (In Fiennes, 2014). Are we aware, that is to say, that when we buy a cappuccino, we also buy into the hidden local and global politics—related to globalization, pollution, self-determination, etc.—that underpin the production of coffee needed to make the cappuccino?

This book will help you uncover these kinds of meanings—meanings veiled by the seeming transparency of things and events in the world. It will help you see that even normal and all-too-familiar aspects of everyday life have unexpected, even startling, dimensions. And it will thus help you understand how, why, and the extent to which everyday things can, in fact, deceive you, precisely inasmuch as they hide certain layers of meaning. This book will thus give you some tools and encourage some habits of thought that can help you gain a fresher access to reality. It will encourage you to open a window into your own mental routines and into the world itself, to look ahead and to let in some light and fresh air.

Scientists working in fields such as physics and biology have uncovered shockingly unfamiliar dimensions right underneath everyday physical reality. Practitioners of disciplines such as psychology and psychoanalysis have similarly rediscovered "ordinary" aspects of consciousness, uncovering an alien psychological world right underneath everyday conscious awareness. Mathematicians are uncovering numerical patterns, hidden codes that underpin and pervade natural forms, endowing them with symmetrical properties, with stability, harmony, and beauty. Geneticists are uncovering the codes of life itself—codes that, when finally deciphered and read, could be edited so that life as such could be rewritten and thus reinvented. The sciences, in general, strive to uncover the secrets of nature and thus allow us to see past what we can normally see and think beyond what we can normally think. Science enables us to imagine what normal habits of thought prevent us from imagining. Similarly, the science of sociology has stripped the veneer of normality from everyday life and can therefore help you rediscover and revisit your familiar world. The sociological approach emphasized in this book will set in motion your ability to read the world around you. It will help you see that your familiar environment is full of unfamiliar, buried stories. As you begin to look underneath the skin of things, as you begin to read these stories, you will also begin to see the extent to which the surrounding world has shaped your own habits of thought, your biography, and your familiar sense of self. Sociology, that is to say, can also help you revisit your internal world. It encourages a self-reflective attitude and a sense of curiosity about the extent to which *you* control, or have controlled thus far, your own process of self-formation.

An Invitation

Many of the readers of this book will have been born at the beginning of the millennium, possibly in the year 2000. Although the first couple of millennial decades have had problems and have borne witness to unspeakable events, beginning with the terrorist attacks of September 11, 2001, your existence has nevertheless unfolded during the most peaceful and prosperous time in human history. Had you been born at the beginning of just the previous century, at your current age, you would have already experienced the First World War, then the largest carnage in human history, responsible for the atrocious and mechanical and lonely deaths of about 18 million persons. You would have seen the rise of fascism. You would have witnessed one of the worst pandemics in history, the Spanish Flu, which added 50 to 100 million deaths to those that resulted from the war (the exact number is not known). You would have been vulnerable to diseases such as smallpox, an unforgiving and disfiguring disease that killed about half a billion people in the 20th century alone—a disease that is now extinct. If you are a woman, you would have not been able to vote in the United States until 1920, when the 19th constitutional amendment eliminated laws specifically designed to disenfranchise women. If you are African American, you would have lived in a country where racist segregation was not only normative, the mainstream and often mob-enforced cultural narrative, but also legal, the very law of the land. To push this historical comparative perspective further, if you had been born at the beginning of the previous millennium and lived like the vast majority of people (namely, peasants bound to a lord), you would have spent most of your life toiling in conditions of semi-slavery. If we consider the average lifespans then and now, your life would have likely been 50 years or so shorter. And your daily existence would have been, in general, devastatingly difficult by your current expectations and standards, as we will discuss in Chapter 1.

It is not that, as pessimists of every era have tediously repeated, the past was better. On the contrary, to insist on a key idea, our era has managed to provide unprecedented possibilities for the growth of science, of art, of music, of medicine, of freedom, of new cuisines—possibilities for the expansion and progress of the human spirit in general. And if we as a society make the right decisions, your children's generation will likely leap into an even brighter future.

Yet if a pessimistic perspective is unwarranted, an overly optimistic attitude—the sort of optimism that is not well researched and thus not well-founded—would be very risky, if not treacherous. We have to acknowledge that, as we will discuss in the following chapters, our epoch is also confronting unmistakable risks. We have to understand that our society also overprioritizes entertainment (Vargas Llosa, 2012); that it faces increasingly professionalized propaganda, neuromarketing, neuropolitics, and fake news; and that it produces self-confirming echo-chambers at an unprecedented scale, which narrowly delimit people's ideas about what is true and indeed what is real. We have to understand that ours is an age when "proof" pertaining to any belief—however absurd, however hateful, however dangerous for the public welfare—is only a click away. And we also have to understand that these developments increasingly limit our capacity to identify and to respond to the risks of our epoch. Above all, we have to see that if on account of these declines we fail to read the world around us, and therefore fail to respond to these threats, our children's generation may inherit instead "an underworld of greed, corruption, and hate," as the noted psychoanalyst Christopher Bollas has argued (2018).

We could indeed argue, with Bollas, that the defective and ugly features of this undesirable future are already hidden in plain sight, obscured precisely by a massive stream of entertainment, propaganda, and fake news, and perhaps also unduly minimized by the victories of our age. Only a generation ago, almost no one would have thought that fascism, which brought so much death, fanaticism, hatred, and poverty to Europe, would ever become a threat to democracy again. And yet, as former secretary of state Madeleine Albright has argued, this cultish ideology has managed to become a more "virulent" threat to democracy today than at any other time period since the end of World War II (Albright, 2018). Or consider the natural environment itself: None other than the United Nations has described current climate events as "a deafening, piercing smoke alarm going off in the kitchen" (IPCC, 2018), and none other than British naturalist Sir David Attenborough has said that if we fail to hear this alarm, "the collapse of our civilization [...] is on the horizon" (Attenborough, 2018). Other such examples could be provided, some of which we discuss subsequently. But for now, let me only suggest that we, as a society, are obligated to be alert and to strive to read our epoch correctly. We are obligated to have a minimum of literacy about the world. Democracy, in any case, cannot function without it. Bear in mind that this political system, as Lincoln noted, necessitates "general intelligence" to function. Jorge Luis Borges said that dictatorships need general idiocy to survive; and the idea is that a simple, credulous, and stereotyped collective imagination is necessary to support authoritarian and dogmatic political systems. By contrast, democracy must be supported by aware, "alert and knowledgeable" citizens, as Eisenhower argued in his farewell address—by publics that, once again, must be literate about the world.

And here we come to another, perhaps the greatest, risk of our age. For all its spectacular accomplishments, ours is also an age when the word "post-truth" is so common that it has made it into the *Oxford English Dictionary*. This is not only the era of fake news but also of deepfake, of deep surveillance, of algorithmic learning, of big data, of microtargeting, and of neuromarketing and its correlate neuropolitics, as noted. It is an era when deception is reaching the state of the art such that it is increasingly difficult to spot it *as* deception. Consider for a moment the implications that this can have for the outcomes of electoral processes, for the way in which political power is allocated, for our relationship with the market, and for how our epoch unfolds in general. In our age, furthermore, deception has become a rather effective mechanism of behavior modification, which as a field of study in its own right, involving disciplines such as mass communication and neuropsychology, is also reaching the state of the art. Although these developments can provide advantages, particularly for marketeers and political operators, they are also hostile to the collective ability to read the world, and they are thus hostile to democracy and to the culture of freedom that has provided unprecedented possibilities for us.

Fortunate such as it is, your generation is thus burdened with a difficult job: protecting truth and reason, and thus protecting the culture of freedom and progress that you have inherited and taken for granted, and protecting it against increasingly smart, systemic, and effective adversaries, internal as well as external. This book is an invitation to this kind of life, the life of the curious and of the free, the proper life for a citizen of a republic.

"Passing Through This Earth like a Log"

Sociologists examine all areas of social life: religious beliefs and practices, sexual beliefs and practices, self-formation as well as state formation, the political economy of sports, the relationship between art and power, cultural narratives that frame racial identities, narratives that frame the ways we experience the body, etc. And given this broad scope, no book can provide a reasonable introduction to all areas of sociological inquiry. (Although, unfortunately, introductory books typically try to cram in all "essentials" and provide choppy surveys with no clear take-home narratives.) This book discusses sociological as well as allied theories that above all can help you see the extent to which things are not what they seem—theories that can help you see your world anew and make you curious about your relationship with it. On the one hand, this will entail getting acquainted with the idea, perhaps the most useful one in the history of thought, that it is very human, very understandable, and very easy to fool ourselves—an all-too-human trait that, although merciful and welcomed sometimes, has caused mental and moral blindness throughout history, much toil, and certainly much suffering. But on the other hand, this book will also help you see that individuals and societies *can* develop a need for cognition, for authenticity, the habit of truth, and a related readiness for the new, for the strange, and for the unexpected—habits of thought that have changed history, liberated us from our own ideas and visions of the world, indeed from our own selves, and that, in doing so, have bettered the human experience.

Beyond being a necessary collective practice, reading the world is also an engrossing individual practice. It engages the mind while also drawing out affects and emotions, anger, at times, or indignation, or empathy, or others. This is so because the world around you is a coded text that encompasses absorbing and entwined stories, some of which may read like a farce, or like a tragedy, or like an epic—like a narrative of sorts, but one that is produced by the social organism itself. When Oscar Wilde noted, "Life imitates art far more than art imitates life" (2008), he provided a fundamentally sociological perspective that, although unrecognized as such, helps us understand the truer, deeper nature of social life. Reflexive sociology, the approach emphasized in this book, can help you see this continuously unfolding imitation of art that is collective life. It can help you decipher the ongoing narratives, the epics, the farces, the tragedies, inherent in the world around you.

Of course, industry and effort will be necessary for developing this kind of literacy, but this effort always pays off and may in fact change and better your life. Ignoring the world around you and turning your attention to entertainment can put a smile on your face, can brighten your day, and sometimes it is the right thing to do. But going about the world with an eye *only* to what comes from the stream of news, entertainment, and infotainment can fundamentally impoverish the way you experience life. A person who cannot see below this light surface will ignore the ideas that have nudged history in this or that direction, that have dissected and marked the human experience, that have helped us see what we are and why we are the way we are. At a personal level, this person will not wonder about the extent to which his world affects his ideas, his mind, his brain, physically, or indeed the very manner in which he experiences his body. This person won't be curious about why she thinks in a certain familiar way, say, about gender, her gender included, or about food, or beauty, or race, or sexuality, or anything else. She will not inquire into the roots of these ideas, which are the roots of her own spirit. This person, that is to say, will never experience a true sense of mystery, the secrecy of nature and of life, everyday life included, the experience that underlies genuine curiosity and wonder. Javier Marías, one of the most lucid commentators today, has this to say about this kind of unidimensional person:

> He is not interested in history at all, that is to say, why things and countries are the way they are and not some other way; neither in history, nor in science, nor in the various discoveries, nor in exploration, nor in the infinite variety of the planet [...]. If he is a believer, he doesn't quite care about why he believes in a particular god, or why he obeys certain laws, or social rules, and not others. He is a primitive in every sense of the word: He accepts, like a simple creature—say, a chicken—, being in a world where he has been thrown in by chance. He accepts passing through this earth like a log, without trying to understand much at all. He eats, plays, has sex, if he can, and that's about it. (2018, p. 37, my translation)

CHAPTER I

"We Must Disenthrall Ourselves"

"And Then We Shall Save Our Country"

About a month before issuing the Emancipation Proclamation, whereby slaves in the United States were declared free, President Abraham Lincoln sent a message to Congress, which included the following, and now famous, paragraph:

> The dogmas of the quiet past are inadequate to the stormy present. The occasion is piled high with difficulty, and we must rise—with the occasion. As our case is new, so *we must think anew, and act anew. We must disenthrall ourselves, and then we shall save our country.* (In Basler and Sandburg, 2001, p. 688, my italics)

Lincoln is here advancing an idea that marked not only the debate of his day and age but also the fate of the United States and, one may argue, the American character itself. He is implicitly suggesting that what we call "common sense" is sometimes a trap—a powerful internal enemy. Although some of our beliefs can, of course, strengthen us, others, particularly those deep-seated beliefs that we take for granted, can imprison us. For, as Mark Twain noted, "It ain't what you don't know that gets you into trouble. It's what you know for sure that just ain't so." Unexamined habits of thought—that is, dogmas—can arrest our imagination, our judgments, the way we go about the world. Dogmas can weaken us and defeat us. And it is, therefore, not enough to simply accept beliefs that seem, and have always seemed, commonsensical. We also have to understand what we believe, what we know, and why—why we believe in certain ideas and ideals and not in others. Lincoln is indeed implying that an unexamined way of thinking is, in reality, a means of not thinking, a justification for irrationality, for the sort of nonsense that people oftentimes grow to love and passionately defend. He, in any case, is urging early legislators to think anew so as to "disenthrall" themselves: to free their minds from limited and limiting assumptions.

Reading the world is likewise a disenthralling process: It is a means, as noted, of gaining fresh access to reality; it helps you think afresh so as to see through taken-for-granted, and therefore invisible, social conventions and practices.

Self-Examination as the Pathway to Progress

Just as sociology helps individuals examine their own biography, and the external pressures that influenced it, this discipline also helps society examine itself and the forces that bring collective values and beliefs into being. In this sense, sociology shares its mission with disciplines in the humanities, including history, philosophy, literature, and poetry, as well as disciplines in the arts, to an extent. For, like sociology, these have also been in the business of holding a mirror to the individual, as well as to society, so as to help us live examined lives—the sort of lives that, as the philosopher Plato argued, are the only kinds of lives worth living. Bear in mind that you can find out whether your beliefs and values are weak or strong only if you examine them; that only if you do so will you be able to see the truths and the falsehoods in your own spirit, and hence correct your course. Likewise, with society itself: It can identify and correct its weaknesses only to the extent to which it can continue to examine its own norms, beliefs, values, and laws. Not by coincidence, the societies that have valued self-knowledge have prospered, have set difficult goals for themselves, have on trend met those goals, and have contributed to the overall advancement of civilization. (We will discuss this soon, but for now, consider the example of ancient Greece—the society that achieved the highest level of development in the ancient Western world. For the Greeks, the injunction "know thyself" was indeed a divine mandate, and for Greek moral philosophers, it was the highest human aspiration.)

To be sure, self-examination is the basic condition for scientific and intellectual progress, in general, and the logic of science actually boils down to this idea.

Unlike dogmatic belief systems, scientific knowledge is, by design, entirely open to criticism. The job of scientists is not limited to producing theoretical models; it also involves continuously scrutinizing their peers' methods and theories, so-called adversarial collaboration. Scientists prefer not the opinion of allies but of opponents, simply because opponents can better test the solidity of their theories, identify weak points, and thus help them to correct their course. Scientific models can be, and often are, weak or entirely wrong, mere conventions shared by individuals and institutions—conventions that sometimes reflect the prejudices of these individuals and institutions. But as these models are, and have to be, systematically dissected and closely inspected for weaknesses and errors, only the good ideas are likely to survive in the end. This is why we have had steady progress in all areas of science. This is why we can cure more illnesses today than at any other period of human history. This is why whereas Galileo's telescope allowed him to see, for the first time in human history, that the moon was "not smooth but [...] full of depressions and protuberances" (1997, my translation), telescopes today would allow him to see *the flickering light of a single candle* if it were lit on the moon. Closer to your own life, it is also thanks to the always self-scrutinizing and hence always improving nature of scientific knowledge that, unlike your grandparents, you have access to such technology as texting. Which means that, unlike them, who had access to the wonders of the "rotatory phone," you are able to send an audiovisual signal to a machine in the stratosphere; a machine that can send it back to a microcomputer in your friend's pocket, a feat of science that in your grandparents' generation would have been seen as science fiction. (Bear in mind that as late as 1986, the songwriter Paul Simon composed an impassioned ballad about these "days of miracle and wonder," which sang the praises of such wild wonders as "the long-distance call.")

It is indeed worth pausing for a moment to see just how far science and the honest scrutiny of our own ideas have actually taken us and how much this particular way of thinking has contributed to your own life.

As noted in the introduction, if you had been born a hundred years ago, your existence would have been impoverished to a significant extent. But if you had been born a thousand years ago and lived the life of about 75% of Europeans—namely, serfs—your life would have been a "continual fear" and in continual danger of violent death, to paraphrase the philosopher Thomas Hobbes. Save occasional respites, your life would have most likely been "poor, nasty, brutish, and short," to borrow an image from Hobbes again (2005). After all, in addition to toiling in conditions of semislavery, you would have had nothing resembling modern pathology or biology or medicine so that you and your contemporaries would have assumed that most diseases were the work of supernatural beings, a comet, witches, or the spooky old lady in the village. And hence your health would have largely depended on breathtakingly stupid notions and procedures, such as exorcisms, the laying on of hands, or invoking saints such as Saint Fiacre whose ghost was somehow gifted with the power to cure hemorrhoids specifically. (The patient should ideally sit on the saint's tomb and, thus positioned, simply ask to be relieved of the condition. Even as late as the 17th century, Cardinal Richelieu reportedly ordered the custodians of the tomb to open it so as to apply a bone directly to the site of discomfort and then took a vertebra with him to reapply as needed [Marius, 2008]. Some medieval medical practices were acceptable, such as the use of some medicinal herbs, but all of them were far less effective, when not inane or directly and even terminally harmful, such as bloodletting.)

A thousand years ago, you would have had no modern dentistry either; no general anesthesia; no vaccines; no electricity; no running, potable, chlorinated water; no shower or shampoo; no flushing toilets; and no toilet paper. Your diet would have been primarily bread and gruel. You would have most likely been smaller. You would have been easy prey to bacteria, wild beasts, and famines. Your chances of dying in childhood would have been about 50%, and if you managed to survive to adulthood, the life span allotted to you would have been about 30 years on average (see Pinker, 2018). And your mind, on the other hand—your mind, which is the center of gravity for your familiar sense of self—would have become twisted beyond recognition. You would have been illiterate and innumerate. You would have seen the forest next to your village as the natural habitat of magical creatures that, in your childlike imagination, would be as real as foxes and trees. You would have believed that diseases, storms, and natural disasters were the work of witches, perhaps one of your neighbors, creatures that were able to fly, to kill by means of magic, to have sex with Satan, to summon plagues. You would have believed in omens and in unicorns, in astrology and werewolves, in the divine rights of your semiliterate and despotic king. Your intelligence quotient (IQ) would have been far lower (an issue addressed in Chapter 8).

The obvious idea, here, is that science has decisively contributed to eliminating these problems, particularly among the peoples that embraced it first (while also giving us such new marvels as telescopes, antibiotics, Paul Simon's wild ability to make "the long-distance call," and your own wild ability to have a microcomputer in your pocket that allows you to communicate with an intelligent machine in the sky). Less obviously, these things have been made possible largely because, at some point in history known as the Enlightenment, discussed next, some folks finally gathered the courage to open their own ideas to scrutiny, to systematic, honest, and methodical criticism. This was a period when some men and women decided to consult not the old and often ghastly mistaken sages, but the world itself, according to a standardized method. This was a time when people began to read the world, hesitantly and secretively at first, one observation at a time, one wonder and one mystery at a time.

Closed Societies

In contrast to this scientific logic—*in contrast to the idea that self-examination is the pathway to progress*—all forms of dogmatism reject self-examination, do not allow for either scrutiny or criticism, and constantly struggle against dissenting ideas. Let us consider a couple of historically significant examples.

Up to the 13th century, the Islamic civilization was perhaps the most advanced. It was a source, in any case, of exceptional philosophy, farming practices, techniques of musical composition, techniques of navigation, and optics. They excelled in architecture: The palaces that Muslims left in Spain are among the most spectacular architectural achievements extant in the Western world. They excelled in mathematics: Words such as *algebra* and *algorithm* are of Arab origin; we use Arabic, rather than Roman, numbers; we owe the decimal system largely to Muslim scholars. Muslims excelled in astronomy: About two-thirds of the stars that have names have names with Arabic origin. They excelled in art. The West discovered abstract art arguably in 1914 when artist Piet Mondrian proclaimed that "art is higher than reality" and therefore must not be limited to realistic representations. Muslims, on the other hand, had already produced some of the greatest abstract masterpieces in the 9th century, about a thousand years before Mondrian made his supposed discovery. Muslims excelled in medicine: While many Europeans were using incantations or torturing old ladies (witches) to cure diseases, Muslims were already relying on biological testing. For example, they tested the level of sugar in the urine of patients by mixing it with dirt and exposing ants to it to see if the insects swarmed around it or not, thereby determining higher or lower sugar content.

It is interesting to note that these Muslims indeed saw Europe as a barbaric continent. For Europe, after all, was mostly disintegrated, generally ghastly poor, easy prey to superstition, to famine, and to diseases that ravaged the continent from time to time. As noted, the life of most Europeans was "a continual fear": fear of diseases, of witches, of hunger, of bandits, of despotic lords, of the afterlife, of the evil eye, of bad omens, of black cats. And save all the exceptions, European lords and clergy were themselves dogmatists who were not above such practices as torturing or burning alleged wrongdoers alive, often for frivolous reasons—the type of social control that today we associate with the barbaric Islamic State. And beyond these already gruesome practices, most Europeans would have simply fit the definition of a barbarian. As suggested by German philosopher Friedrich Schiller, a barbarian is merely a slave to dogma, no more and no less than that. This is a person who can cause senseless suffering, barbarically, simply because he or she cannot question the commandments of a master narrative—commandments that, in his or her imagination, issue from an ancestral, mysterious, and potentially dangerous power, from a dark authority that a barbarian obeys even when its judgments seem pointless and cruel.

But from the 13th century on, the impressive Muslim world, which in many ways fulfilled the role of a civilizing force in a barbaric Western world, itself began to experience the progressive encroachment of dogmatism. Clerics began to grow suspicious of their own scholars, partly because scholars were open to any source of knowledge, be it Muslim or Greek or Hindu or any other, and partly because scholars began to question ancient dogmas: the resurrection of dead bodies, the physical existence of paradise or hell, etc. Clerics, for these reasons, began to think of scholars as uncommitted to the faith and then as heretics. These increasingly nervous stewards of the faith began to ban books and, eventually, to demand that "unholy" books be publicly burned, an incalculable loss to the cultural patrimony of humanity. They began to maintain that algebra—algebra of all things—was nothing less than the work of the devil. And they thus began to demand a return to "the truth." To borrow the phrase from Lincoln again, they longed for a return to the dogmas of the quiet past.

If the closing of the Islamic tradition could be traced to one person, that person would be Abu Hamid al-Ghazali, arguably the most influential Muslim theologian of the High Middle Ages. In contrast to the leading Muslim philosophers of his era—the forward-thinking folks who had taken this tradition to its highest point—al-Ghazali argued that nature is *not* governed by observable principles or laws. And he added, darkly, menacingly, that even positing the existence of such laws would be like trying to chain God's hands, a view that, in contrast to the preceding Muslim scholarship, was explicitly hostile to science. For the natural sciences, in particular, are built on the elemental idea that natural phenomena (e.g., rain) predictably occur when certain underlying conditions are met (e.g., heat, evaporation, cooling of vapor at a higher altitude, condensation, which results in precipitation). This is simply the idea that the natural order is governed by these kinds of observable patterns—patterns that, when well-understood, can be formulated as principles or laws: the laws of motion, the laws of thermodynamics—the laws of nature.

In addition to arguing against the idea of observable principles or laws in nature, al-Ghazali provided his own, alternative, nonscientific, and non-natural explanation for, of all things, natural phenomena. He noted that the ultimate cause of any natural event is Ala. He explained, for example, that if a piece of cotton placed over a fire begins to smolder, this does *not* occur because, as we would say today, cotton is a form of fuel that combusts when its temperature reaches a point of ignition if there is enough oxygen for it to happen, etc. No. For him, this piece of fabric begins to burn simply because Ala decides that it should be so (perhaps enlisting a couple of angels to take care of the mechanics of this process). And, furthermore, Ala, al-Ghazali teaches, can decide otherwise if He pleases. Which is why we should readily accept the possibility of miracles; for instance, the idea that a piece of dry cloth may *not* smolder when placed over a fire, or the idea that a piece of wood may instantaneously become a snake, or the idea that a man can, and did, ride a horse to the moon to split our natural satellite in half. Al-Ghazali's position, let us add, thus claimed to know the cause of any and every natural event (namely, God). And one of the problems with this idea is that scientific research can begin only when people realize that they *do not know* what causes a certain outcome, only when people *accept their ignorance about the way the world works*.

Thus the process whereby al-Ghazali's ideas gained a place of preeminence within the Muslim world discouraged scientific work in general. His theological position, which was eventually accepted by almost all subsequent Muslim theologians, made scientific research ungodly, if not heretic—guilty precisely of attempting to chain God's hands. To be sure, he plainly said that those philosophers who were trying to understand the operations of the natural order were heretics. And he then explained, unpromisingly, that heresy is, of course, a crime punishable by death (al-Ghazali, 1963).

Thus Muslim scholarship began to decline. And the Muslim world, in general, began to decline as well, such that today we can no longer say that it is the center of the production of knowledge, exactly. Spain, a country not notable for its scientific output, nevertheless produces more scientific literature than 46 Muslim countries combined, and, reportedly, each year, more books are translated in Spain than all the books that have been translated in all Muslim countries in the past 1,000 years, ever since the Muslim world began to take the al-Ghazalian road (Ofek, 2011). Of the top 200 universities in the world, zero are located in Muslim countries, according to the *Times Higher Education* 2018 ranking. Steven Weinberg, Nobel Laureate in physics, has noted that "for forty years I have not seen a single paper by a physicist or an astronomer working in a Muslim country that was worth reading" (Weinberg, 2007). As reported by *Nature*, one of the most prestigious scientific journals in the world, Muslim countries do produce significant research, but only in three fields: desalination, falconry, and camel breeding (Masood, 2002). Yet beyond these minor areas of study, "whatever indicator one looks at, the status of science in most Muslim countries is bleak," as reported by Syrian-American researcher, Wasim Maziak (2017).

This decline has also had consequences from the point of view of economic development: "Muslim-majority countries are appreciably poorer than the world's economically advanced countries, even the rest of the world" (Kuran, 2018); and Muslim-majority countries also lag behind on other economic indexes such as adult literacy and life expectancy (Kuran, 2018).

Perhaps more significantly, this decline has also had very serious consequences in terms of civil rights and freedoms. Some Muslim countries do provide freedoms (and living standards) comparable to those enjoyed in advanced democracies. But these are the most secular ones—the most open and less dogmatic ones—arguably Tunisia, Indonesia, and Turkey, in particular. (Although even in Turkey, a country that is nominally democratic and entirely ruled by constitutional law, incarceration of investigative journalists, judges, and police officers who antagonize the regime is rather common. "Many are persecuted and detained, many are tortured," as reported by Diego Garcia-Sayan, United Nations special rapporteur on human rights [2019, my translation]). On the other hand, Muslim countries that, still following ancient dogma, are more orthodox and less open to self-scrutiny are also less free and less democratic (not to mention poorer). This is the case of Malaysia, Pakistan, Sudan, and Afghanistan, for example—cases that are worth considering in detail.

In Malaysia, in 2018, two women were condemned by a local sharia court, which rules according to ancient Quranic laws, to be publicly caned for having had a lesbian relationship (and meanwhile, the Disney film *Beauty and the Beast* was banned until its "homosexual" contents were edited out). In Pakistan, "blasphemy" (e.g., expressing an opinion contrary to religious dogmas, which is elsewhere protected by free speech laws) is a crime punishable by death. A Pakistani woman named Asia Bibi spent 8 years on death row simply for having made comments that her neighbors considered offensive to Islam; comments made after her neighbors refused to let her drink water from a cup they were using, a scene that brings to mind the "white only" water fountains of the Jim Crow era. In Sudan, an even more orthodox country, about 65.5% of girls under 12 years of age undergo genital mutilation, the removal of the clitoris, "normally done without anesthesia," such that "some young girls die from the shock and pain caused by the mutilation" (UN Human Rights Council, 2016). In this country, according to the UN Human Rights Council, "in situations of poverty and *as accepted social practice*, parents perceive a girl child as a source of wealth and income, which further contributes to the practice of [early marriage]" (2016, my italics). Such practice, according to the Sudanese Personal Status Law for Muslims, can be legally justified, even if the girl in question is 10 years of age, and a court can "allow for justifications that do not take into consideration the best interests of the girl child" (UN Human Rights Council, 2016). In this country, the Criminal Code makes execution mandatory for crimes such as apostasy and adultery, and execution in such cases may include stoning followed by crucifixion. The Sudanese Criminal Code punishes homosexuality ("sodomy") with flogging and incarceration, and with death after the third offense (UN Human Rights Council, 2018, pp. 3–5). According to the Encyclopedia Britannica, "modern-day slave markets" still exist in Sudan (Jacobs 2000).

Let us focus on Afghanistan, perhaps the most dogmatic Islamic country and, along with North Korea, one of the most dogmatic countries in the world. The literacy rate in Afghanistan is *17% for women* and *45% for men* (UN Human Rights Council, 2015). A United Nations special rapporteur on human rights has noted that Afghani girls, like their Sudanese counterparts, are also often regarded as "an asset exchangeable for money or goods owing to the practice of the bride price" (UN Human Rights Council, 2015). Some victims of this practice of early and/or forced marriage

> often resort to committing self-immolation. Although not all women and girls who take this action intend to kill themselves, they inflict severe injuries upon themselves, which in some cases results in their death. The Afghanistan Independent Human Rights Commission recorded a total of 133 cases of self-immolation from March to November 2011. (UN Human Rights Council, 2015)

"Self-immolation" includes burning oneself alive. Furthermore,

> the Afghanistan Independent Human Rights Commission registered more than
> 280 women who had been killed by family members during 2011 and 2012. Most
> of these killings had been carried out on women and girls who had refused to enter
> into an arranged marriage or had been accused of having a relationship that the
> family considered to be inappropriate. (UN Human Rights Council, 2015b)

Note as well that sharia law, which largely rules civil life in these countries, also allows for, and may require in some cases, such punishments as stoning to death (for example, for adultery, as noted) and public flogging, as well as mutilation and dismembering. Importantly, this law also forbids the enactment of ideas, principles, or norms that are deemed antithetical to Islam and is hence entirely hostile to the idea of a culture open to scrutiny, self-analysis, and change. The most extreme expression of this kind of religious legalism is the Islamic State, which sees itself as the only defender of God-given and thus eternal and unappealable laws, and of mysterious, hence unknowable, and yet unquestionable truths (e.g., the idea that the Prophet rode a horse to the moon to split it in half).

Indeed, attempting to uphold a 7th-century ideology, which they regard as the only true form of Islamism, these terrorists regard any dissenting voice, however hesitant, as a mortal enemy, literally as a legitimate military target. And the problem is that any normal human being would oppose the fact that they burn prisoners alive or bury them alive, or the fact that they crucify dissenters, that they punish homosexuality by throwing accused men off rooftops, or that they distribute kidnapped girls as sexual slaves among themselves, or that they sell them in open markets, or that they display the mutilated bodies of dissenters in public, or that they conduct executions and amputations in public. Hence, eliciting revulsion from almost everyone, these dogmatists in turn regard almost everyone as a mortal enemy of what they see as the only true faith. This includes, to begin with, most other Muslim groups, such as Shi-ites. And, of course, it includes all Christians; all Buddhists; all Hinduists, Shintoists, and Zoroastrians; and all agnostics and atheists. It includes Republicans and Democrats. It includes women who believe that women should have civil rights, people who like "decadent" music, people who like wine, and so on. They even see invaluable cultural treasures, such as Roman ruins in "Islamic territories," as military targets. Should the Islamic State take over the world (which will never happen, but is what they devotedly pray for), we would see the largest carnage in human history, as only these dogmatists and their converts and slaves would survive.

Again, this is the most extreme example of dogmatism today. But it can, nevertheless, help us see what can happen, and *has* happened in this case, when a *closed belief system* is taken to its logical and final conclusion—namely, violent fanaticism. Such a process generates mental and moral blindness, worldviews that are as asinine as they are intense, and intensely polarized in terms of "us versus them"—worldviews that throughout history have claimed the lion's share of human suffering. In contrast, when groups, or generations, or nations that uphold a system of meaning become curious about the nature and origin of their ideas, and begin to invite honest scrutiny, they tend to produce useful knowledge; they tend to enjoy higher degrees of freedom—political, artistic, academic, sexual, religious—and their members or citizens tend to prosper. It goes without saying that other factors can contribute to progress or a lack thereof: natural resources, natural disasters, war, etc.; and it also goes without saying that the openness of a society is not a magic bullet of progress. But all other factors being equal, the open or closed character of a society significantly contributes to how the society in question fares and to the quality of life of its citizens.

Open Societies

As the once splendorous Muslim world began to decline, the so-called Western world began to leave the High Middle Ages behind (the period from the 11th to the 13th century, roughly; this is the barbaric epoch that, as noted, was ruled mostly by dogma and therefore by fear[1]). And then the West began to open up and to evolve, very slowly at first, until it managed to reach the era known as the Age of Enlightenment in the 18th century—a process that, like the decline of the Muslim world, provides important historical lessons of its own.

Let us begin with the embryonic and eventually history-changing contributions of a 13th-century priest named Tommaso d'Aquino, aka Thomas of Aquinas, as he is known in the anglophone world. This Italian friar was a characteristically medieval saint and in this sense a dogmatist who had visions of the Virgin Mary, who believed in levitation, who thought that visions could be granted by divine revelation, who worried about the nature of angels, how smart they were, how dangerous. And yet he also saw himself as a philosopher. And as such, he tried to open Christianity to the rule of reason by proposing the fateful and at the time outrageous idea that the universe operates not only according to a God-given "eternal law" but also according to "natural law." A couple of centuries after al-Ghazali denied the existence of natural laws, Aquinas argued that this kind of law must be studied and understood, and *not* by means of theology, *not* by means of prayer, but through the rational methods of natural philosophy. Aquinas indeed argued that this form of reasoning, even if not Christian, matters *in its own right—irrespective of the religious affiliation of the reasoner*. And he thus opened Christianity to theories about nature that came from other traditions. About a century after the books of important Islamic philosophers, such as Averroes and Avicenna, were publicly burned by Muslims themselves, Aquinas began to enthusiastically promote these very same books, as well as those of the pagan Aristotle, among others.

Thus risking his safety and freedom (not to mention the comfortable social position that his family enjoyed), Aquinas opened some cracks in the otherwise hermetically closed belief system that dominated the Christian Middle Ages. And, to borrow an image from Leonard Cohen, that's how light began to get in. Initially, this light came from ancient Greece, as well as from the Islamic world that al-Ghazali had censured and that Aquinas had commended. But soon enough, it began to issue from locally grown expressions of natural philosophy, which were made possible by these openings. Thus this largely illiterate, barbaric, and stagnant European epoch finally managed to move forward, clumsily at first, leaving the "Dark Ages" far behind (the period between the 5th and the 11th century). Fed by a growing curiosity about the newly uncovered machinery of the world, the emerging natural philosophers, also risking life and freedom, eventually managed to illuminate the long path precisely to the Enlightenment, an age of curiosity and wonder, an age of change, and hence also an age of turmoil, the birth pangs of modernity, our own era.

Although with roots in Aquinas's ideas, this new and tumultuous time period, also known as the "century of lights" in Romance languages, was more directly influenced by modern philosophers, beginning with René Descartes. Already in the 17th century, this French polymath had argued that the path of progress entailed *doubting the truth of any given proposition* until it becomes no longer reasonable to doubt it anymore—that is, until the proposition in question becomes *demonstrably* true.

---

1   The concept of "the Western world" is widely contested and yet widely used as well. It is contested in part because no such culturally, historically, or linguistically homogenous world actually exists. But this term is also widely used simply as a shorthand to denote the array of cultures that, their differences notwithstanding, have their main roots in the Greek and Hebrew traditions, Europe and her heirs, in particular. This is, in any case, how we will use this term in this book.

"Demonstrably" being, in this 17th-century context, *not* the run-of-the-mill term that it is today, but a new and, for some, confusing technical term—a term that, when uttered outside the small circle of natural philosophers, kindled gossip about heresy in its wake, with heresy being a crime that could result in the heretic being burned alive.

The Enlightenment was also rooted in the hypothetico-deductive method. This is the scientific method proper that, proposed by the English philosopher Sir Francis Bacon in the 17th century, stressed above all demonstrability through empirical evidence. Bacon's ideas were historically important in their own right, but also because they set the foundations for none other than the Royal Society, the English academy of sciences that in turn provided the foundations for much of modern science. The goal of this group was to establish the most effective ways of mapping, empirically and demonstrably, the operations, the mechanics, and the dynamics of the natural order. Its motto, importantly, was *Nullius in verba*, typically translated as "take no one's word for it," but which could be also be translated, perhaps more accurately, as "there is nothing in mere words." This was the war cry of these newly fanged natural philosophers. Any claim to truth made by any of the fellows of the society had to be factually verifiable for it to be accepted. Any claim to truth had to withstand the pressure of adversarial scrutiny. The coat of arms of these daring and spirited folks had three hounds as its only motif, and the idea was that the fellows had to have the drive of a hound to discover hidden things. In practice, they also had to have the nose of a hound to sniff out claims that were weak or unverifiable.

Bacon's method was refined in the context of this truly heroic group of individuals, particularly by Sir Isaac Newton, the man who, in the 18th century, provided the mathematical models for the fundamental laws of nature, such as the law of gravity. This newly refined and newly refueled approach to scientific inquiry now began to illuminate the secrets of the world at an unprecedented speed, thus setting free, one discovery at a time, this new and unstoppable era, precisely the century of lights.

Of course, the historical process that saw the rise of the Enlightenment was far more complex than what the earlier outline conveys. But, for our purposes, it may be summarized as a time when a few committed, clearheaded, and exceptionally smart radicals, taking their cues from people like Bacon and Descartes, and sometimes risking their lives, decided to open the given system of beliefs to scrutiny. It was a time when, as a result of this remarkable revolution in human consciousness, ideas thereto unthought, things thereto unseen, musical procedures thereto unheard, political principles thereto untried, and cures and therapies that defied the prevailing wisdom began to emerge. Thus, and along with other factors outside our focus, Western modern science, modern humanism, modern democracy, and modernity itself were set in motion. Your ability to elect your representatives, your ability to text, your ability to use antibiotics—your everyday freedoms and material comforts—have roots in these historical upheavals and the consciousness-altering books that Enlighteners produced. Although veiled by their seeming ordinariness, by their seeming lack of history, the Enlightenment is present in these everyday wonders: in the phones, in the medicines, in the freedoms, etc., that you take for granted. The enlighteners themselves are present in these real-life miracles that constantly come to your aid to make your life easier than that of your forbearers. As noted in the introduction, ordinary things sometimes hide an epic story.

As also noted, the closing of the Islamic tradition could be arguably traced to Abu Hamid al-Ghazali, who, in contrast to Thomas of Aquinas, argued against the existence of the laws of nature and thus discouraged the study of natural phenomena. What would have happened if, in the stead of al-Ghazali, the Islamic world had seen the rise of an equally influential *reformist*, the equivalent of Aquinas, and then experienced a process of even greater cultural opening? It is impossible to answer this question, of course. And yet one cannot help but wonder whether this already advanced civilization would have thus become the one that ended up taking us to the moon and giving us modern democracy. Would that kind of open Muslim world have continued to be the centrifugal force for the production of knowledge and art as it was a thousand years ago before it faced its most capable and relentless internal enemy, dogmatism?

When Open Societies Fail

The idea is not that the Western world thus became good while the Islamic world became bad, or that the West is somehow free of failures or blame. The point of the foregoing historical outline is not to cheer for "the West" uncritically but to underscore the concrete benefits of an idea at the root of the Western tradition: the idea that openness and self-examination are sources of knowledge, of truth, and of progress.

To extend the foregoing historical perspective and to deepen the lessons that it teaches us, it is also important to underscore that the modern West has, of course, experienced barbaric lapses of its own and that it indeed has been responsible for the largest genocides in human history, far greater, numerically, than those perpetrated even by the Islamic State. These include six million Jews killed by the Nazis and 9.5 million Soviets killed by the communists in the Soviet Union, to name only the most notorious acts of modern Western barbarism. Yet catastrophic failures of a tradition that began with the Enlightenment also help us to see the importance of Enlightenment ideals, particularly the importance that openness and self-examination have in societies. These and other such crimes against humanity (e.g., those perpetrated by Franco in Spain, by Mussolini in Italy, and by Leopold II in the Congo, together responsible for millions of murders as well) were committed by dogmatists who rejected this Enlightenment ideal. The aforementioned genocides were perpetrated by Hitler and by Stalin, who arrogated for themselves the role of defenders of final axiomatic truths. Truths that, they thought, had to be protected against any dissenter, against any book, against any work of art, at any cost. Hitler upheld dogmatic beliefs about "Aryan superiority" and contended that a German culture opened to external influences—say, in physics, or in music, or in psychology—would be a contaminated culture. (Great masters, such as Albert Einstein in physics, Gustave Mahler in music, and Vincent van Gogh in painting, were demonized by the Nazis.) Like the medieval fanatics discussed earlier, Hitler also burned books that did not cater to his stereotyped view of the world, about 25,000 of them, including masterpieces by Nobel Prize Laureates Ernest Hemingway and Thomas Mann. And he denounced the Enlightenment as decadent, blamed it for having produced a corrupt "bourgeois morality" that was overly concerned with such things as democracy and human rights. Similarly, Joseph Stalin, another slave to a dogma who, like Hitler, thought that *he* was the instrument of history, the servant of the spirit of history itself, and thus responsible for the final destiny of humanity. These grandiose views gave Hitler and Stalin permission to destroy, exile, or torture mere dissenters, or even their family members. Both men craved a closed society. Their dogmas were not separated from the state but became the very spirit of the state.

These Western failures not only suggest that openness is a source of progress, as noted, but that it can also protect a society, even a continent, against the barbaric excesses of dogmas and of dogmatists. These Western failures, that is to say, validate the idea that when a system of meaning begins to reject scrutiny, closes up unto itself, and is hence regarded as final and unquestionable, people begin to suffer, and the people who embrace these meanings tend to decline or to become morally corrupt.

But on the other hand, and perhaps more importantly, the *successes* of the Western world also support the Enlightenment idea that openness and self-examination are sources of progress. These successes indeed stem from this very idea (see Pinker, 2018). And what successes are those? To begin with, Enlightenment-derived advances in the natural and human sciences, in medicine, and pathology, for example, which *have saved billions of lives and have alleviated the suffering of billions of persons the world over, including, in all likelihood, your own suffering.* Likewise, with Western advances in the physical sciences, which have also given billions of persons such conveniences as a phone and then a smartphone, a car and then a far safer car, an electrical typewriter and then a laptop. Beyond the sciences, Western contributions to the humanities, to the arts, and to the culture of freedom that is expanding across the world have likewise bettered the lives of billions of people the world over. Indeed, its failures notwithstanding, it is right and proper to commend the Western world for its decisive role in expanding civil rights and freedoms throughout modern history, including the freedoms that you yourself enjoy as a matter of course. These include the freedom of expression, of opinion, of religion, of assembly, of thought, of movement; sexual freedoms; academic, scientific, and artistic freedom; freedom to marry by choice; economic freedoms; freedom to elect representatives; freedom to elect them regardless of gender, or religious preference, or race, or ethnicity, or class position; freedom of having ideas that do not coincide with the official doctrine; and the freedom, above all, of cultivating your own mind.

Many cultures have contributed, in greater or lesser degrees, to human welfare. The main contribution of Western culture, in summary, has been the idea that openness illuminates the pathway to material as well as to cultural progress. This is the idea that the *human mind cannot reach its potential if it does not have a minimum of freedom, and that lacking this minimum freedom, the human mind will eventually produce not only overly conforming persons but also creeps and monsters*: Stalin, ISIS, and so on.

Here is a final point of clarification, which might be useful for some readers: All cultures, the freest included, have, of course, fostered, and foster today, at least some dogmatic meanings. And some of these meanings may well be benign, or even beneficial for individuals and groups, as we will see later on. But the idea to keep in mind is that neither the everyday life nor the form of government of the cultures that have prospered in freedom has been, or could have been, *ruled* by dogmas. Democracies, of course, protect religious freedom and, in this sense, religious dogma so that even the opinions of dogmatists are protected under free speech laws, which is proper and right. But religious freedom, which falls under freedom of thought, also includes the freedom of being unreligious, and precisely by permitting a plurality of theological views and opinions, including agnostic views, these political systems also allow for exchange or confrontation or questioning of religious tenets. So that related dogmas, rather than ruling everyday life, are likely to end up serving deliberative principles. Democracies, that is to say, respect and yet also delimit the sphere of influence of religious doctrines, including through laws that separate church from state.[2]

---

2   Let us credit Austro-British philosopher Karl Popper for coining the concept of *open societies*. His *The Open Society and Its Enemies* is a critique of what he calls "historicism," the notion that (a) history follows immutable laws, God-given or secular, that can be discovered; (b) that experts who discover these laws thereby discover how to engineer the historical course of a nation and can therefore design an undisputable and long-term social and economic program; and (c) that it must be enforced by them, by experts, by elites, religious or secular, regardless of the ideas and wants of citizens. *The Open Society and Its Enemies* shows that this kind of long-term social engineering approach, the approach of all closed and dictatorial regimes, has not been the road to progress. On the contrary, it has diminished freedom, social and historical literacy, artistic expression, civil rights, hope, and quality of life in general. Against this historicists approach, Popper proposed a trial and error, short-term, *ad hoc* form of social engineering. This is a little-by-little approach that strongly relies on constant scrutiny and on deliberative, vigilant, and creative citizens, not just on experts but also on regular and sovereign individuals who feel responsible for their own existences and their own futures, people who generally prefer not to outsource this responsibility to the bureaucrats of a political party, to a dictator, to a "strongman," to a group of clerics.

CHAPTER II

"Government by the People"

Openness and Democracy

In radical contrast to dogmatic ideologies, the disciplines in the social sciences and the humanities have striven to hold a mirror not only to the individual but also to society itself, as noted, to help us deliberatively consider our own collective beliefs and attitudes, and the mechanisms that bring them into being. For these reasons, these disciplines are allies of progress as well as of democracy, a political system that, like science, is also designed to examine itself constantly. In contrast, people under dictatorial and dogmatic regimes are expected to quietly internalize a belief system and to simply accept the given dogmas without ado, without a sense of curiosity about their origin, validity, or moral implications. They are discouraged from living reflective and examined lives.

Beyond the examples provided in Chapter 1, it is important to consider current ones, what happens today—in the midst of the Modern Era—in countries such as a North Korea or in fundamentalist societies, such as those envisioned by the Taliban. These political systems also punish dissenting ideas and actions, often horribly, even nauseatingly. Taliban gunmen shot a 12-year-old Pakistani girl in the head, on the bus from school, merely for going against an official dictate that banned girls from schools. (And this particular girl, Malala Yousafzai, survived, decided to dedicate her life to the rights of children, and was eventually awarded nothing less than the Nobel Prize for Peace at the age of 17. The Nobel Committee underscored her "struggle against the suppression of children and young people and for the right of all children to education.") In North Korea, according to articles 194 and 195 of the country's 2009 Criminal Code, "watching or listening to music, dance, drawings, photos, books, video-recordings or electronic media that reflects decadent [...] contents" is punishable with reform through labor for up to five years (HRC, 2014). And exposure to "decadent contents," for the North Korean authorities, can involve, for example, watching a foreign movie that doesn't reinforce the closed, idiotic, pompous, and deaf narrative of the regime. A 31-year-old woman and her brother, as we read in a UN Human Rights Council report,

> were caught watching South Korean movies and were tortured. She was
> detained for one month, during which she was deprived of sleep and beaten.

She had to write a long apology for days on end [...]. The woman's brother was beaten so badly that he could not walk for a while. (HRC, 2014)

To underscore the central idea here: These siblings were imprisoned and tortured for the crime of watching a mainstream movie.

These examples show that these kinds of dictatorial regimes enforce, rather than question, the dogmas of the past (even as they rely on applied science and its spirit of openness to survive). In contrast, true democracies must not only question unexamined ideas to sort out and discard those that are no longer adequate for the "stormy present" but must also constantly foster new ideas that are truer, in synchrony with the present, and more helpful for the future. True democracies are *not* limited to allowing citizens to vote periodically, so-called spectator democracies. Truly democratic systems feed from *deliberative* social and political processes, and can hardly survive when citizens become unable to engage in meaningful and deliberative discussion, in open, honest, and *informed* argumentation and debate. Citizens of true democracies are expected, for example, to consider whether the country should go to war, whether drugs such as alcohol or marijuana should be legal or illegal and why, how and why society should extract and protect environmental resources, and so on. Democratic systems thrive on the ongoing "public use of reason," to borrow an idea from the philosopher Immanuel Kant. Democracies are *not* designed to rely primarily on the expertise or the will of elites. Dictatorships do that. Remember that a democracy is a "government of the people, by the people, and for the people," as Lincoln noted in the Gettysburg Address, and that, as a government *by* the people, it necessitates "general intelligence," as Lincoln also noted. Indeed, in a democracy *citizens are to be blamed when things go wrong*.

Democratic citizens, in other words, must be willing and able to read the world. They must be literate about power, what sustains it, and why. They must be literate about what passes off as "common sense" and why. They must be capable of examining, ongoingly, the ideas, values, and beliefs that are accepted as normal, often without a second thought. They must know where, historically, these ideas come from. Charles-Louis de Secondat, Baron de la Brede et de Montesquieu, a key political commentator of the 17th century, said that despotisms have to rely on fear. To function, these regimes must instill fear in people's hearts in an effort to keep them firmly in line. The North Korean regime, the Taliban, the Islamic State, the government of Nicolás Maduro in Venezuela, for example, are unfree and deplorable regimes that fundamentally rely on fear as a political tool and weapon. As you recall from the introduction, Jorge Luis Borges said that dictatorships need idiocy. Dictators need a credulous, dogmatic population, cheering and cheerful dupes, because informed and deliberative citizens scrutinize official truths, interrogate power, and examine the nature and purposes of the regime. In contrast, neither fearful nor dogmatic nor gullible citizens can sustain a truly democratic system. Without "alert and knowledgeable citizens," to borrow a phrase from Dwight Eisenhower again, democracies begin to resemble dictatorships.

"Group Lunacy"

As suggested in the previous chapter, the darkest and most brutish periods of the Middle Ages, Nazism, fascisms, dictatorships, and fundamentalisms of all kinds have all promoted, and depended on, a public inability to read the world. These kinds of regimes have historically depended on a collective inability to see that the beliefs that the regime mandates are only dogmatic beliefs and not the axiomatic truths these beliefs purport to be. Let us add that these regimes have also promoted irrationality in the citizenry and that they have often succeeded in achieving this strange goal.

The standard textbook mechanisms for reaching this goal have included propaganda and slogan agitation, silencing of dissidents, controlling schooling and curricula, overseeing the production of art and literature, banning of books, and manipulation of media in general. One of the modern masters of these kinds of strategies was Joseph Goebbels, the baleful minister of propaganda of the German Third Reich. He famously argued that a lie that is constantly repeated, constantly agitated according to the principles of political propaganda, will eventually become accepted by a majority in the population. And, he added, there are therefore virtually no limits to what the general public may accept as truth and hence no limits either to what a regime may effectively propagandize. For our part, we have to soberly recognize that in this sense, baleful Joseph Goebbels was mostly correct, and that, as the case of Germany illustrates, most people did come to accept grotesque and preposterous propaganda notions—for example, the idea that "Jews are contaminants." To be sure, these kinds of notions also provided *ideals* for many Germans, who in fact fought for them, and who, in doing so, sacrificed others, the "contaminants," and even themselves. (And it goes without saying that many Germans also devoted their lives, facing great risks, to combat these kinds of dogmatic notions, often from places of exile.)

This is the sort of collective phenomenon that Nobel Laureate in literature Doris Lessing calls "group lunacy" (1987). It involves irrational and yet passionate collective beliefs that are often promoted by these kinds of authoritarian regimes. Usually coming hand in hand with group self-righteousness, these kinds of collective dispositions have coincided with periods in history that allow people to put "stupid and murderous ideas into practice," as Lessing says (e.g., Nazism, terrorism). To be sure, the publics of these (effective) dictatorial systems—publics for whom the official truths become mere acts of faith—have tended to identify enemies avidly: enemies of the truth, of "the people," enemies of the faith, enemies of the leader. This is partly why six million "contaminant" Jews were killed while many average Germans applauded the actions of the Reich. This is also why suicide bombers today—encouraged also by preposterous ideas, such as the image of waking up in Heaven surrounded by virgins tendered by God—do in the end push the button, to indiscriminately kill passersby, students, tourists, merchants, beggars, people who simply happen to be around, all of them "infidels," all of them "contaminants," all of them mortal enemies.

The case of Germany noted earlier can also help us see another important feature of dogmatism—namely, that dogma is not a problem that can be simply and entirely superseded by the overall advancement of civilization, like a terrible old disease that is now curable. Dogma is resilient and resistant, and, when vanquished, it can easily return to reclaim its place in history. Germany was a democracy. It was a very important center for the production of knowledge, of science, of art, of glorious music. And yet like the medieval Islamic world, it also fell to the same internal enemy: dogmatism. Literacy about the world, in other words, is an *ongoing* necessity, when not an ongoing struggle, as it is today. There is no final victory against dogmatism, only ongoing battles. Hence the importance of an also ongoing collective ability to read the world and the importance, today, of the ongoing struggles to support it.

Before concluding this first part of the chapter, it is also worth underscoring that today we are seeing a misinformation warfare among countries that utilize political propaganda and slogan agitation as their weapons of choice, but to target the populations of *other* countries. These strategies are designed to move the hearts and minds of foreign populations, so as to encourage collective beliefs and behaviors that, in the long run, undermine the targeted country. In the past, bombs were deployed for such purposes. Today, tweets, posts, "news," "scientific reports"—misinformation—are deployed. According to investigative journalist Oren Dorell of *USA Today*, Russia alone has launched misinformation campaigns in 27 countries since 2004 (2017). Consider one of the many available examples, a pioneering one: The old idea that the human immunodeficiency virus (HIV) was created in and by the United States as a biological weapon to exterminate Africans and gay men. This was a notion that periodically made the news in the United States and around the world during the late 1980s and early 1990s. As recognized by the head of the Russian government, Mikhail Gorbachev, who issued an official public apology to the United States, this malicious fabrication was part of an ongoing and far larger Soviet operation designed, precisely, to undermine, internally and externally, the credibility of the United States.

Of course, misinformation has always been a garden variety weapon used by countries, even in ancient times. But the relevance of this kind of weapon has increased in proportion to the increased possibility of quick and large-scale dissemination allowed by the Internet. For this reason, this kind of misinformation needs to be combated *not* primarily by governments, from above, but primarily by citizens themselves, from below. After all, average citizens are the targets of these "investigative news" and "scientific reports," which are only malicious propaganda. Average citizens themselves, therefore, have to be able to sort out propaganda from actual news, propaganda from actual historical research, propaganda from actual science. Otherwise, they won't be able to defend their country against this highly professionalized and increasingly important form of political warfare.

The Defects of Democracy

Although I have emphasized the defects of dictatorships, these kinds of political systems do not have the monopoly on defects. While democracy is the best political system human beings have invented, it is also error prone and fragile, because it depends on the people, and we, human beings that we are, are error prone and fragile. To be sure, democracies not only have defects of their own but also hold potentially ruinous risks which we need to examine.

Note, first, that these are *representative* political systems and that, as such, democratic governments will necessarily represent the citizens *regardless of whether citizens are politically, culturally, or historically literate or not.* In a democracy, a completely uninformed person and a world-expert can equally decide who should be president. A person who still believes that the United States created HIV to destroy innocent people and, on the other hand, the scientist who discovered this retrovirus can both vote for policies and laws pertaining to acquired immunodeficiency syndrome (AIDS) treatment, prevention, and research. In a democracy, the ignorant, the corrupt, the thoughtless, the irresponsible, etc., are all entitled to vote. And hence "a government of and by the people," to recall Lincoln's Gettysburg Address, can either be a "government of and by good and sufficiently informed people" or a "government of and by the misinformed and the thoughtless." And for this reason, as well, democracies must try to maximize literacy, to produce a sharp citizenry. Otherwise, unaware persons, if they become the majority, will also become the decision makers. Democracy is literally not foolproof.

Second, in a democracy, you have the right to make bad choices, as long as you are not infringing on the rights of others. You have the right, for example, to eat mostly bad calories and thus eat yourself into a protracted and painful illness. Likewise, with the system itself: It can also make bad choices without infringing on its own legal principles. And historically, democracies have done just that from time to time. They have democratically deprived women of their right to vote; they have incarcerated persons for sitting in the wrong side of the bus (the case of Rosa Parks); Hitler was democratically elected in Germany; Maduro initially clambered the political ladder through democratic channels. Furthermore, democratic systems can legally and democratically cause harm. They can damage the environment, for example. They can democratically and legally ruin the economy. They can weaken the rights of legitimate groups that do not have political representation: future generations, workers in foreign countries, animals, etc. And, hence, just as an individual can make better decisions if better informed, and thus have better control over his or her life, citizens of democracies need to be informed, as well; otherwise, they will have little control over their own history. Informed voters, after all, are more likely to vote for informed policies; they are more likely to elect, and to be represented by, competent political classes, and, hence, they are more likely to steer a reasonable and humane historical course.

Here is a third potential problem inherent to democracy: The strengths of this system can become its weaknesses. Freedom of expression, for example, has historically been one of the gifts of democracy to the world. And yet, precisely because anyone is free to express an opinion, it is difficult for the system to control the diffusion of propaganda and of falsehoods. In our day and age, freedom of expression permits excesses such as fake news. Even though it is perfectly well established that the United States did not create HIV to kill innocent people, for instance, anyone can go to a public forum, a radio show, a blog, or a TV show and maintain that, in his or her opinion, the United States committed just that crime. Any well-established fact, any reputed scientist, any legitimate research institution with legitimate data that are important for the public welfare can be "discredited" by an individual who lacks the most elemental expertise, or by an industry whose interests are contrary to science, or by a religious fanatic, or by a tweet.

Consider the following example. Noted American novelist Philip Roth wrote a story, *The Human Stain*, with a main character named Coleman Silk. A Wikipedia editor decided that Coleman Silk was based on an actual person named Anatole Broyard, which Roth, the creator of the character, denied. Roth said, "The entry contains a serious misstatement that I would like to have removed. This item entered Wikipedia not from the world of truthfulness but from the babble of literary gossip—there is no truth in it at all" (2012). But amazingly, the Wikipedia folk repeatedly dismissed *Roth's own input about his own work*. And in the end, the author reported, "My interlocutor [agent] was told by the 'English Wikipedia Administrator'—in a letter dated August 25 and addressed to my interlocutor—that I, Roth, was not a credible source: 'I understand your point that the author is the greatest authority on their own work,' writes the Wikipedia Administrator—'but we require secondary sources'" (2012). In a democracy, in other words, "the babble of gossip" and misinformation have a fighting chance of prevailing against "the world of truthfulness."

Today, this is a worrisome problem, because ours is also an era when misinformation, as suggested, can spread at unprecedented speed—virally, as we say—via your phone, via your Facebook account, and via a global and all-pervading network. As also noted, ours is not only the era of fake news but indeed the era of "deepfake." This is a widely available technology that allows a forger to create an utterly realistic audiovisual document of any well-known person—for example, a politician running for office—saying or doing things they never said or did at all. Recent news about pornographic videos featuring well-known actresses such as Scarlett Johansson have raised alerts in this regard. But the real concern is that heads of rogue states, or corporations, or religious sects, or fanatics, or dictators may now disseminate incriminatory videos of persons or organizations that threaten their interests, and only experts would be able to determine the inauthenticity of the document in question.

Today, in any case, political classes the world over do not have to rely on truth if they so choose. They can rely primarily, or even exclusively, on their ability to control the flow and spread of "post-truths," an increasingly effective way of targeting certain clusters of voters. These are also increasingly professionalized and predictable public relations strategies that rely on advanced scientific models pertaining to behavior modification, as noted. (Consider "neuromarketing" and its correlate "neuropolitics," for example. Primarily via analyses of brain imaging obtained from research participants exposed to advertisements, these techniques attempt to measure the reactions *not* of the aware and awake person, but of the brain itself. Books with titles such as *Unconscious Branding* [van Praet, 2014] and *How to Talk and Sell to the Brain* [Georges et al., 2013] are revealing in this sense. At present, the actual efficacy of these mechanisms is not fully established. But these researchers work to design campaigns that can bypass the conscious awareness of targeted publics and directly recruit the reward networks of the brain. Although these techniques could arguably serve legitimate purposes, for example, helping a targeted group to have a better diet, it is also easy to see that they could serve illegitimate and propagandistic, if not entirely undemocratic and malevolent, purposes as well.)

From Democracy to Kakistocracy

For these reasons, democracy in general—and democracies in our era, in particular—truly require literate citizens, people able to figure out what is true and what is merely a "post-truth." The risk, otherwise, is that the freedoms our democracies have historically fought for *and achieved* may become "negative freedoms": the freedom, precisely, to make bad choices; the freedom to spread (mis)information; the freedom to elect incompetent, or self-interested, or corrupt political classes; the freedom to spiral into demagoguery; the freedom to cause harm. Here is an odd word worth keeping in mind: kakistocracy, "the rule of the incompetent," or more literally, "the rule of the worst." If we fail to maximize our ability to read the world, we are likely to end up with a kakistocratic class clumsily crowding the halls of power, one that, worse still, will be able to claim legitimately that it is the legal and democratic representative of the people. Democratic systems do not come fully finished and already equipped with standard checks and balances that prevent this sort of thing from happening. Democracy is constantly made and made yet again by individuals with higher or lower degrees of knowledge, commitment, ability, and honesty. And let us keep in mind that there are real-world examples of blatant democratic missteps.

Consider the most glaring one. A former bus driver named Nicolás Maduro was democratically elected to lead a country with enough oil reserves to be one of the richest in the world. Under his leadership, Venezuela has become one of the poorest countries in the world. "Families are having to search for food in rubbish bins. By some measures, 87 per cent of the population of Venezuela is affected by poverty, with extreme poverty at 61.2 per cent," as reported by the UN Office of the High Commissioner for Human Rights (OHCHR, 2018a). The international charity organization, Caritas, has calculated that from April to August 2017, 55% of Venezuelans in three monitored states were forced to obtain food from "nonconventional" places, a euphemism for garbage (Caritas Venezuela, 2018). As I write this, about three million Venezuelans have fled their country since 2015 simply to survive, often *walking* for days and weeks to cross their borders, typically without proper documentation (OHCHR, 2018b). This immigration process, the highest recorded worldwide, is caused by misery and desperation. The minimum monthly salary, which represents the income of about 70% of the formally employed Venezuelan workers, cannot cover, at the time of writing this, half a bar of nougat (Manetto, 2018). Not unusually, a medical doctor may earn only one dollar per day (Lozano, 2018). Women giving birth are very likely to find medical facilities that have no water, gloves, soap, or food, let alone medication (Lozano, 2019). Diseases formerly under control, such as malaria, have become epidemic (Lozano, 2019). This is the country with the highest hyperinflation in the world and the longest lasting hyperinflation in the region (International Monetary Fund, 2018). The International Monetary Fund (2018) prognosticated that, should it continue to enforce the same out-of-control economic policies, Venezuela will face an inflation rate of nothing less than *10,000,000%* for the year 2019. (The expected 2019 inflation rates for regional economies such as those of Chile, Peru, and Ecuador are 3.0%, 2.0%, and 0.5%, respectively [2018].) Venezuela has one of the highest levels of criminality. In it, political protesters may face extrajudicial executions. According to the Organization of American States' secretary general, Luis Almagro, 6,300 Venezuelans have been extrajudicially killed by the regime (although it is unclear how many of them were murdered for political reasons) (in Palomino, 2018). Political prisoners in this country are routinely tortured (ABC International, 2018). This includes beatings; electrical shocks; affixation with plastic bags, with gas, and with toxic chemicals; starvation; simulations of executions; rape; sodomization with broomsticks, etc. (OHCHR, 2018b).

And, as if to add the finishing touches to this kakistocratic nightmare, governmental corruption is unchecked. According to Transparency International (2018), Venezuela is the most corrupt country in the hemisphere and one of the most corrupt countries in the world, occupying the 168th position out of 180 countries listed. Venezuela's own (former) military intelligence chief, Hugo Carvajal, has denounced the regime's ties with regional drug-trafficking cartels (Herrero & Casey, 2019). And Luis Almagro has defined the Maduro regime as a "drug-dealing state" (in Palomino, 2018).

Yet the mob that rules Venezuela boasts having been democratically elected, not once but many times, and it thus claims the legitimacy granted by its own people. The last presidential election of May 2018 was widely denounced as fraudulent. And yet, although it has been impossible to determine the extent to which each of the other electoral processes were rigged to the advantage of the regime, it is nevertheless clear that because this regime controls a vast propaganda apparatus and falsely promises food and medical subsidies to voters desperate for food and medicine, a significant percentage of Venezuelans have voted for it. These are folks who, as a result of their own political choices, are sometimes forced to eat only what they can find in garbage bins, an unkind image that, nevertheless, reminds us that collective literacy—about politics, about economics, about power—is essential in the context of a political system designed to depend precisely on people's choices.

"A Small Group of Thoughtful and Committed Citizens"

Collective knowledge and awareness can prevent tragedies like the one that has befallen Venezuelans. This is so especially in the context of a democracy, where citizens, after all, are expected to stop and to evaluate, to compare and to analyze, and then chose the better representatives and policies while filtering out the bad ones, the unprepared ones, the inane, and the reckless. (Although, in the case of Venezuela, the regime's constant and massive deployment of misinformation has made this process difficult, at least initially.)

Let us add that knowledge and awareness can also help ordinary individuals become the social change they themselves want to see, even if these changes are initially small and involve only their immediate worlds. Jim Henson, the American puppeteer who created many of the Sesame Street characters, stated his life ambition as follows: He wanted to live in such a manner, he said, that after his death, the world would be a tiny bit better, only because he had lived in it (in River, 2014). It is, of course, very difficult to make the world a better place. But even a glance at history can show us that single, average individuals do promote much of the positive social change we have seen in the world (provided, of course, that they are able to read society correctly and identify the changes that it needs).

This is an important idea that we will develop subsequently, but for now consider a deliberately small example, the work of another young woman, McKenna Pope. When she was only 13 years of age, this

American girl thought that one of the world's largest producers of toys, Hasbro, should change its cooking toys to make them gender neutral rather than branding them as girl toys. Unlike the Hasbro folks, and unlike most people, McKenna was able to see that there was no objective reason for, say, a toy oven to be sold to girls only. And that was the social change she wanted to see. Hence, she went online, collected signatures (45,502 of them), ignored the haters, and, eventually, Hasbro happily changed its line. Social and historical literacy help citizens see not only problems but also possible solutions, which can accumulate and over time account for significant social changes. As cultural anthropologist Margaret Mead has noted, "a small group of thoughtful committed citizens can change the world," and "indeed it is the only thing that ever has" (in Seager, 2009). This is precisely why dictatorships discourage the public's ability to read the world: Because this ability—in a scientist, in a 13-year-old kid, *in a student such as yourself*—can foster social change.

CHAPTER III

Sociology as a Platonic Science

"A Series of Footnotes to Plato"

It is difficult, perhaps impossible, to think of a writer who has had a more profound impact on the entire Western tradition than Plato, the ancient Athenian philosopher who lived around the 4th century before the Christian Era. Alfred Whitehead, one of the greatest philosophers and mathematicians of the 20th century, half-jokingly said that Western philosophy has been merely "a series of footnotes to Plato." As we will see next, sociological theory has also added important footnotes to the line of thinking that was set in motion by this truly vital philosopher.

Plato, in fact, gave the initial push to some of the ideas that have marked our collective memory, our imagination, indeed our self-regard. Consider, for example, the idea that human beings are endowed with a mortal body and an immortal soul. Although this image is typically associated with the Bible, particularly with the Apostle Paul, it is fundamentally platonic. Paul actually believed that human nature encompassed not a mortal body and an immortal soul but a body (*soma*), a soul (*psyche*), the flesh (*sarx*, the seat of appetites, lust included), and spirit (*pneuma*: in short, the divine breath of life). And he thought that death destroyed not only the body but also the flesh *as well as the soul itself* (Martin, 1995; Wright, 2011). Indeed, death for him was the beginning of a waiting period to end on a final day of reckoning and judgment when "the last enemy of Christ," Death, would be vanquished, a time when therefore dead *bodies*, rather than living and ethereal souls, would arise.[1] Paul's biblical narrative, in other words, is very different from the commonly held Christian idea about an immortal soul that lives in a mortal body. Why did this biblical idea eventually change among mainstream Christians? Above

---

1   What Paul says, more precisely, is that the resurrected body will no longer be *soma psychikon*, ensouled corporeality; it will be *soma pneumatikos*, materiality moved by the Divine Breath, not by an individual soul (Martin, 1995). This resurrected body would be de-souled (as well as de-fleshed so that cleansed from the flesh, it would leave its gender behind, and hence men and women who ascend to Heaven would be, much like angels, uncorrupted and therefore equal). *Soma pneumatikos* will be, in fact, so different from the pre-mortal one as to be visually distinguished by its luminosity, a halo-like pneumatic glimmer, a soft breath of light, often depicted in religious paintings as gilded radiance, a notion that Paul likely inherited from the older Greco-Roman idea that radiant heavenly bodies may well be alive, perhaps eternally so (Martin, 1995).

all, because it was not sustainable. What if my body is eaten by a beast, or rent and rotten by leprosy, or destroyed by fire? Could it then be recomposed and brought back to life? And would this radically recomposed body still be *me*? If death also destroys my soul, will death therefore destroy my person? Who, in fact, will receive my postmortem reward or punishment? Enter now an African Bishop, Saint Augustine, who, in the 4th century AC, came to remove this vulnerability from the theological system bequeathed by Paul. To do so, Augustine enlisted, precisely, the theories of Plato. He borrowed, in particular, the more sustainable platonic idea of an immortal soul that, bearing my personhood, exits my body to then ascend unto an eternal order. Like Paul, Augustine was also concerned with questions about bodily resurrection, and he did provide a theory pertaining to the ways in which dead bodies can be reconstituted. But also drawing from Plato, he emphasized above all the *immortality of the soul*. And this was the mostly platonic model of life and death that, via the African Bishop, eventually became dominant, first among medieval friars; then, from the 13th century on, among philosophers, poets, and artists; and then simply "commonsensical" in Christian culture up to the present day.

Perhaps you yourself believe in, or have considered at some point in your life, the idea of an immortal soul inhabiting your mortal body. Perhaps you have wondered about the fate of your postmortem soul. If so, this is why we say that Plato has influenced our culture and our imagination. His ideas are *not* just in books stowed away in silent libraries. They are alive in a literal rather than a metaphorical sense: They are part of people's worldview; they live in and with us, even in people who have never read a word written by Plato.

The Sixth Sense

Here is another platonic idea that is more in tune with the argument that concerns us: Without knowledge, Plato noted, we can only see the "surface" of reality, the "appearance of reality." To see beyond the skin of things, to see a deeper, more interesting, and indeed a more *real* domain of reality, you need your mind's eye, Plato implies, not your naked eyes. Implicit in his broader argument is the idea that the naked eye, as we will discuss next, doesn't and in fact *cannot* see beyond the surface of reality. The naked eye is blind to what Plato calls "presence": the higher plane of reality—the sort of reality that really matters.

A few examples are needed to illustrate this important and perhaps counterintuitive platonic view. Let us begin with a simple question: Could a young child who doesn't know her ABCs be able to see the letter A? To respond in a platonic fashion, let us argue that this child would be able to see merely a pile of lines—but not, of course, the letter A as such. Only as a bearer of knowledge—namely, the knowledge of the ABCs, would this child be able to see the A as an A and not as a pile of lines and shapes. The child could see the A only eventually—with her mind's eye—and not merely with her naked eye. The naked eye of our preliterate child is blind to what Plato may call the "presence" of the A. The A is completely *absent* to her.

To be sure, reality in general is, in this sense, mostly absent from this child's point of view. Although she has a model of reality in her head, this model is largely removed from reality as it actually is. The child experiences only the surface aspects of reality and is blind to its deeper aspects, which a physicist, a biologist, or a poet may easily see. These deeper layers can become gradually present, in different ways and degrees, only insofar as the child develops cognitively: only as she learns to gradually open her mind's eye.

Plato, I should clarify, never provided such an example, although, perhaps, he might have been amenable to its use. But here is an example a bit closer to his teachings: Consider the figure of a triangle with a 90-degree angle (△), and let us now ask a seemingly absurd question: Is this a triangle? The first and ostensibly obvious answer is that it is, of course, a triangle. What else could it possibly be? But we might also answer, after Plato, that this is *not* a triangle at all but the mere *representation* of a triangle, much like the lines of an A merely represent the concept of an A. The actual triangle, Plato would say, is a mathematical construct, not a drawing, not a physical construct. You can see it only if $A^2 + B^2 = C^2$ has a clear meaning in your mind. The child in the earlier example merely sees a pile of lines and not the letter A. Similarly, if $A^2 + B^2 = C^2$ holds no real meaning for you, you are like a child who, when considering the figure of a triangle, merely sees a pile of lines and not the actual triangle—namely, the invisible mathematical reality that underlies these lines, this drawing, this material and visible *representation*. Without knowledge, the mathematical construct, the real triangle, is absent. Once again, its presence unfolds itself only to the bearer of knowledge, in this case, knowledge of mathematics.

What Plato wants us to consider is the idea that although the mathematical dimension of the triangle is invisible, its invisibility does not make it less real. You cannot see mathematics, but this doesn't make mathematics less real. Many things are real while also being invisible, untouchable, soundless, tasteless—completely beyond the reach of the senses. Time, for example, cannot be seen, touched, heard, tasted, smelled—but time is real, nonetheless. Likewise, light itself is invisible: You can see objects touched by light but not light itself; you cannot touch, smell, or hear light either, but this, of course, does not make light less real. Dark matter is pervasive in the universe and is around you; it has an enormous gravitational pull and in this sense is very heavy, outweighing visible matter by a factor of six to one, and yet it is utterly inapprehensible by our senses, as are the thoughts in someone else's head, consciousness, in general, or the past. These and many other aspects of reality are beyond the reach of the senses. But this does not make them unreal. Plato, that is to say, invites us to consider the idea that, because reality extends beyond what we can perceive, it can never be fully grasped if we limit our ideas about reality, our model of reality, to the information provided by the senses.

What follows is that the especial characteristic of human beings is that we are the only animal species that can render such invisible realities visible—*present*—as we are the only species that can see them through the eyes of the mind. All other species, in contrast, will be forever trapped in a small bubble of reality delimited by their particular kind of sensorial input.

Animals, of course, may have a far more powerful sensorium than ours, as TED speaker David Eagleman has reminded us. We are nearly blind, for example, if compared to an eagle, an animal that can spot a rabbit three miles away. We are mostly deaf in comparison to a bat. We hear from about 20 hertz, a low sound frequency, to about 20,000 hertz, and a bat can hear up to 110,000 hertz. Our sense of smell, in comparison with your dog's, is extremely poor. The only portion of the electromagnetic spectrum that we can actually see, from red to violet, is infinitesimally narrow, about a 10 trillionth of this spectrum. And this is not because the other portions are invisible, but because we just don't have the right detectors. A snake, on the other hand, can see "below" red—namely, infrared. As far as this animal is concerned, we are glow-in-the-dark, bioluminescent creatures (bioluminescence is the capacity of living organisms to emit light, like a firefly). This is so because we emit heat, which this snake "sees" as infrared glow. In contrast, we are blind to our own bioluminescence. Many other examples could be provided, but the idea is that, although we have comparatively deficient senses and depend on a very weak sensory signal to construct our model of reality, we also have a sixth sense of sorts—the power of which no other animal can possibly match. This "third eye," to use a mystic-sounding expression, is *knowledge*, which can allow us to see infinitely beyond what any other species can possibly see and allow us to model aspects of reality that could never possibly enter into the scope of any other species' imagination. (Think of, say, the nature of time within a black hole: unlike any other known organism, human beings alone can try to model it more or less successfully in our minds.)

Furthermore, unlike any of the sensing organs of any other species, our sixth sense can become exponentially better very quickly if we only follow its rules: the rules of logic and of science. Hence, this remarkable extra sense can allow us to see higher and higher, and deeper and deeper layers of reality. And to be sure, the question for us is whether human knowledge has a limit, whether there are aspects of reality that are not only stranger than we presently imagine but also stranger than we can possibly imagine. Does nature have "perfect mysteries," to use Plato's term? Mysteries that will always remain beyond what we may possibly comprehend? Or will nature eventually run out of secrets so that the human mind will then become a perfect model and mirror of it?

Higher- and Lower-Grade Reality

For Plato, the abstract mathematical reality represented by $A^2 + B^2 = C^2$ is far *superior* to its material representation. $A^2 + B^2 = C^2$ is superior, for example, to a drawing of a triangle, to a cutout of a triangle, etc. Why?

Note, first, that the drawing, *the representation* of a triangle, can be easily destroyed. It can be erased, for example. It is perishable, flimsy. It is fated to eventually decay. In contrast, $A^2 + B^2 = C^2$ cannot be erased. Pythagoras died; you and I will eventually die; the world will be encompassed and crushed by the sun at some point in time, but even then, *$A^2 + B^2$ will still be equal to C^2*. This "ideal"—*that is to say, non-material*—form of the triangle is hence eternal, Plato says. English author Ian Fleming has a book titled *Diamonds Are Forever*. Actually, no material object, neither the earth itself, nor the sun, nor our galaxy, are forever. For Plato, the domain of *forever* is not material but immaterial. $A^2 + B^2 = C^2$ is forever. No hammer, no cataclysm can destroy it. Mathematical theorems, rather than diamonds, are forever. (And hence the playful recommendation of mathematician Eduardo Sáenz to guys out there: If you become engaged, he says, and if you therefore wish to pledge something like everlasting love, forget the diamond, and "give her a theorem" instead. Give her the everlasting $A^2 + B^2 = C^2$.)

For Plato, mathematics is indeed the eternal language of the cosmos itself. An atom, a galaxy, the book you have in your hands, any material thing exists because certain physical principles, which are in principle "mathemathizable," endow it with consistency and stability. All matter obeys some kind of law, the laws of motion, of gravity, etc., and these can be in principle modeled mathematically. Matter is not, and cannot be, chaotic, lawless. If it were, we would not have physics, the study of the laws, of the mathematics, that govern the material order. For Plato, this sense of cosmic lawfulness—this grand and all-pervading systemic logic—is evidence of a cosmic intelligence of sorts, underpinning material reality. And indeed, he postulated the existence of nothing less than a "cosmic soul": an all-perfect, eternal form of reason, the seat of principles or laws that make all material reality possible. Plato imagined this cosmic soul as an omnipresent and eternal "animal" from which everything emanates.

And he thought that any form of intelligence has to have the ability to express itself and thus has to have some sort of a language. Hence, as reality itself is endowed with an inherent form of intelligence, it must be endowed with a language as well. But what kind of language would a cosmic soul speak? Precisely, the language of mathematics. But note that, unlike any human language, which imperfect speakers create and recreate one word at a time, this mathematical language is not created but discovered. We discover it as we dig deeper into the logic that sustains reality itself.

Mathematics, in other words, is a universal system of meaning. $A^2 + B^2$ equals C^2 in the United States and in China, as well as in Andromeda, the neighboring galaxy. So that if you were to imagine a high school in Andromeda, those students, with their green scales, slanted black eyes—and entirely different mental circuitry—would, nevertheless, be learning that $A^2 + B^2 = C^2$, simply because this is the case in this and in any other part of the universe. (And for the same reason, these alien students would be eventually learning about the relativity of time, discovered by their own version of Einstein, about entropy, about gravity, and so on.) The Pythagorean theorem, in other words, reflects an aspect of reality. It is like a phrase of a language that emanates from reality itself; it is a phrase of the cosmic soul, of the universe itself—a phrase that Pythagoras managed to decipher for us. (And to clarify, the first to propose that mathematics is the language of reality was not Plato but Pythagoras, from whom Plato got some of his key ideas.) Pythagoras's students, for this reason, literally worshiped their master. They wondered whether he was, in fact, a demigod, rather than a mere mortal. How else, they reasoned, could he have learned the language of the cosmos itself?

Beauty and the "Cosmic Soul"

For Plato, the particular characteristic of human beings is that we are able to decode this cosmic language, that we can attempt to learn it ourselves. And to the extent to which we do, we are able to read not only the world but also the cosmos itself. (As Galileo likewise noted, the universe "is written in a mathematical language" without the knowledge of which our relation to the cosmos would be "a pointless wandering through a dark labyrinth" [1997, my translation]). So that if you were to, let us say, watch the night sky armed with this ability, you would see that it is perpetually sending signals, and that, in this sense, the night sky is constantly speaking. But you would also see that it is not expressing any sort of human language, fraught with human ideas and concerns. You would see that the night sky expresses, instead, the language of numbers. And yet, you would also see that this language *does not consist of mere numerical patterns*, for it ultimately speaks the language of order and of harmony, which, for Plato, are inherent to the logic of mathematics. ("Harmony," to be sure, is a musical as well as a mathematical concept. When listening to music, your ears are, so to speak, unconsciously doing mathematics, decoding how different sound frequencies, measured in hertz, come together to form certain ratios that human ears typically find musical, harmonious; ratios that are not expressed by what we call *noise*. Incidentally, this is an old idea. Drawing from Pythagoras, Saint Augustine already believed that God himself had a mathematical mind from which these harmonic ratios emanated. So for Augustine, music expressed, in a limited and all-too-human form, the eternal harmony inherent in God's creation.)

For Plato, then, as the cosmos expresses a grand harmonic structure, it therefore expresses the language of Beauty itself. This is not the mundane, this-worldly beauty of, say, a well-formed horse, that of a flower, that of a statue. It is infinitely grander. It is a sort of cosmic and eternal beauty, which, inherent in *presence*, can only be seen with the eye of the mind, through the filter of knowledge. For Plato, the ultimate quest of the philosopher is, in fact, "to attain to that Science which is no other than that of the Beautiful Itself, and so at last to know what Beauty is" (1936). At its very highest, knowledge is knowledge of beauty, for Plato. (And let us add, borrowing the phrase from biologist Richard Dawkins, that at its very highest, science "is the poetry of reality.")

To summarize, $A^2 + B^2 = C^2$, eternal such as it is, exists on a "higher" plane of reality, for Plato. It exists as though in a "heaven of ideas," he says, or a "heaven or forms," the domain and the source of this eternal harmony and beauty. In contrast, the material drawing of the triangle, perishable such as it is, is thus a "lower" form of reality. *Material* representations, for Plato, exist merely as part of the transient and constantly decaying world of matter. Indeed, he wants us to consider the idea that *all* material representations are like *shadows* cast by invisible and yet eternal and thus superior realities so that the material figure of a triangle, for instance, is like a shadow cast by the invisible mathematical reality represented by $A^2 + B^2 = C^2$. Material figures of triangles—drawings, cutouts, and so on—are like shadows that, cast by the invisible domain of mathematics, fall on the visible and transient physical world, the surface world, the imperfect world that our imperfect senses can imperfectly grasp. For Plato, everything material in fact owes its existence to the cosmic soul, this eternal "animal" that speaks the language of mathematics and what we today call physics, the set of principles and laws that make the existence of the material order possible. For him, an invisible and eternal world thus lies beyond the visible and transient world. The world that the naked eye sees is only a shadow of a deeper, invisible, and more real and far more beautiful domain.

The Extent to Which the Senses Convey Inaccurate Information

Consider the wall next to you. The naked eye tells you that the wall is still and solid. But what happens if you see it with your mind's eye, armed with even elemental knowledge of physics, particularly of particle physics, the subfield that studies the very small? Let us imagine that you extract one of the atoms that form the wall and enlarge that atom to the size of a football field. If you were to do so, you would *not* see a large sphere the size of the stadium. Instead, you would see, in the middle of the field, a little ball the size of a blueberry, which would be the nucleus of the atom, and somewhere around the goal area there would be the nearest electron, which would look like a still invisibly small speck of dust perpetually spinning around the blueberry. In between the blueberry and the speck of dust, there would be empty space. The next atom in the wall would be in the next stadium (see Dawkins, 2005). Armed with knowledge of physics, that is to say, you would see the wall *not* as solid but as a container of mostly empty space, space that from time to time is broken by tiny, buzzing particles that congregate so as to be perceived, by someone of your size, as solid and as one and the same (Dawkins, 2005). Hence, seeing the wall with your mind's eye would also help you see that it is not still, but dynamic, precisely a swarm of atoms buzzing in perpetual movement.

Incidentally, the emptiness that you would now see in the wall explains why massive quantities of very small particles, such as neutrinos, go through it constantly and effortlessly.

Let us add, furthermore, that this also applies to your own body, which in this sense is a container of mostly empty space, as well. Space that is also broken from time to time by very small and buzzing particles that swarm together to become you. At bottom, this swarm is atomic and therefore inorganic or, more precisely, not yet organic, with a foot in the inorganic world. And yet this cloud of not-yet-organic things—namely, your atomic body—is endowed with consciousness, including consciousness of its own existence. Some of these atoms come from the air you breathe and the water you drink. Thus, through your breathing and drinking, the inorganic world emerges within the organic world, and the inert world comes to partake from the world of consciousness. Other atoms in your body come from the food you absorb and transform into tissue. And all of them have their origins in stars that had to massively explode, that had to die in order to release the elements that eventually endowed you with life (Krauss, 2013). The particles in your body, like those in the wall, are also constantly being traversed by smaller particles such as neutrinos. Think of, say, your right eye. About 60 billion neutrinos go through it and through every square inch of your body every second (Cox, 2008). Note, as well, that this swarm of particles and the cells that make you, *you* are constantly decaying, dying, and constantly being replaced by new ones such that you today are entirely different, atom by atom, from you as a child. This changing and fluid arrangement of particles that endow you with life, with a mind, and that confer consistency to your body also hosts a vast microbial cloud, far more microbes than people on earth, a microbiome that allows your body to perform some of its basic functions. This vast army of living things in and on you can also affect your behavior, how much you eat, and possibly aspects of your social and sexual response. In this sense, this bacterial swarm is part not only of your body but also part of your mind.

What this strange set of facts illustrates is the also platonic idea that only your mind's eye can allow you to see your own existential reality. The naked, prescientific eye will never have a hint of these things. It will be blind to its own nature, to its own reality. And, of course, neither the wall nor your body are unusual. The bigger platonic idea is that the nature of *all* physical reality is likewise largely absent to the naked eye. The idea is that what you see around, what you experience as reality, is, so to speak, an *interface* for a different and more fundamental reality. To be sure, the digital interfaces you use every day can provide a good analogy for the way you perceive the world. The videos on your phone, for example, depict a familiar world that is at bottom very unfamiliar, as these videos can be reduced to a numerical code (made of zeros and ones) that can only be seen by the eye of the mind. This is a code that, hidden in plain sight, confers movement, sound—life—to the space and time that these videos convey. Similarly, the space and time you perceive, the familiar world around you, is also like the surface of an invisible, abstract, and utterly unfamiliar world.

It is also worth noting that, as Richard Dawkins has argued, if you were very small, if you were the size of a subatomic particle, it would be natural for you *not* to perceive the world that you do perceive, the reality that is so familiar to you. If you were the size of a subatomic particle, you would not perceive, for example, the seeming solidity or stillness of the wall at all (Dawkins, 2005). You would see, instead, a constellation of bigger things: atoms. So that if someone were to suggest that this wall in front of you is somehow solid and still, such a notion would strike you as obviously absurd. If we, as a species, were as small as a neutrino, our ideas about matter, defined by such properties as solidity and stillness, would have not arisen in our imagination at all. But given our human size, we perceive a sense of solidity and stillness in nature, this "useful fiction," as Dawkins says (2005). Dawkins, in fact, tells us that we perceive such things as solidity and stillness on account of our perceptual and, relatedly, *conceptual* limitations—and only because it is useful for our species to see the wall and other such objects *mistakenly*, as solid. Such visible and seemingly "obvious" properties as stillness and solidity are *useful misperceptions*, mistakes that, however, enable us to navigate the world in an efficient manner, given the needs of our particular life-form. Dawkins suggests that if we were the size of a neutrino, the "reality" that we normally perceive would not have arisen at all, and a radically different sense of reality would have arisen instead. Plato would agree. And he would probably add that what we call reality, our human-all-too-human version of reality, in fact comprises a set of superficial habits of thought, a *domain of meaning that can change and that has changed throughout human history, precisely because we can produce and have produced different meanings.*

The Extent to Which the Senses Deceive You

The example of the wall suggests that sensory information tends to be not only superficial but also *deceptive* (even if useful). Let us turn to a couple of examples that bespeak, precisely, the *deceptive powers of the senses*.

For thousands of years most people thought that the earth was flat. The image of a round planet didn't make sense because, during this pre-Newtonian era, the senses had tricked us into believing that things on the bottom of a sphere always fall off. Thus we thought that people on the bottom of an impossibly round earth would fall off and be devoured by the monsters that lurked at the bottom of the abyss where Hell begins. As Columbus's sailors hear the roar of the sea, the "mother sea, the hoarse voice answering the wind with phrases of eternal condemnation, mysterious drums resounding in the depths;

they cross themselves and want to pray and stammer, 'Tonight we'll fall off the world, tonight we'll fall off the world'" (in Galeano, 1985, p. 45). Closer to our own experience, we tend to assume that the sun rises in the east to set eventually in the west. But because the sun is relatively still with respect to the earth, it neither rises nor sets. To the naked eye, the sun does appear to set every day at its appointed hour, but this is also an illusion. In this sense, there has never been a sunset, ever. The sun that you see setting, furthermore, is actually not there in your line of sight, as astrophysicist Neil deGrasse Tyson has reminded us. It is already below the horizon, and what you see is only its refracted light (the earth's atmosphere "bends" the light of our star, much as the water in a glass seems to bend a straw). Moreover, you don't see the actual sun in real time either. You only see the light that our star emitted about eight minutes ago, the time it rays take to travel to your eyes, as deGrasse Tyson also notes. The horizon, finally, is not there either; for there is no actual edge, no actual horizontal line. If it were an edge, you could travel toward it and reach it. But, of course, the horizon will always retreat as you move toward it.

Perhaps these examples are obvious and we need to consider more nuanced ones. Think again of the visible spectrum, the colors of the rainbow, violet to red. To say that we *see* the colors within this spectrum is inaccurate. This implies that these electromagnetic waves are themselves color-coded, that colors are inherent and objective properties of the world out there, and that we simply register them with our eyes. But these waves do not have intrinsic or inherent colors. They only generate a biochemical reaction, beginning in the rods and cones in your eyes and ending in a little electrical storm in your visual cortex, which generates the subjective sense that you are seeing colors inherent to the external world. Hence, a different arrangement of these cones and rods would generate a different range of colors in your mind, or no colors at all with the exception of black and white, an extreme version of an actual condition known as *achromatopsia*. (The opposite of which is *tetrachromacy*, the capacity to detect more colors than those detected by persons with "normal" sight. Indeed, tetrachromacy is the capacity to see *several* colors where normal percipients see only *one*.) If our species had a different visual apparatus, we would also have different beliefs about the "real" colors seemingly inherent to the world. In this sense, colors are in our consciousness, not in the world itself. Let's return to the sunset. The sense of beauty that you might derive from its reds, and blues, and pinks is, in this sense, an illusion as well. The sweetness of an apple is, likewise, not an intrinsic property of the apple. It is our particular interpretation of the apple's objective properties. Hence, a lion, for example, having a different sensorium, would not experience the sense of sweetness that we do (felines, in general, do not have the genetic equipment to perceive what we call sweetness). Sweetness and colorfulness are in our consciousness, not exactly in reality itself.

Yet our senses tell us that sweetness and colorfulness are intrinsic aspects of reality, that they have an existence of their own, independent from us.

Because the senses often lie, scientists—physicists, in particular—have to learn to think beyond raw perceptual information in order to understand reality. Steven Weinberg, Nobel Laureate in physics, and one of the most profoundly gifted minds of the 20th century, argued that our everyday life requires a set of ideas and intuitions that, although useful for navigating our everyday world, are nonetheless useless when it comes to understanding the deeper structures of reality. He asks, "How can we get the ideas we need to describe a realm where all intuitions derived from life in space-time become inapplicable?" To describe this realm, scientists have to learn to see beyond the raw information provided by the senses, beyond their habits of thought, and beyond the version of reality that they have inherited from their culture and internalized one day at a time. Learning science, in this sense, is a form of unlearning, of thinking oneself away. This is what allows scientists to discover new realities underlying what Plato called "the appearance of reality." Only inasmuch as we learn to see through the seeming obviousness of the world, can we discover a world beneath the world. Only in this way are we able to free ourselves from the tricks constantly conveyed by the senses and emancipate ourselves from the limits of "common sense." This is perhaps the main platonic lesson. And this is also why we think that Plato was one of the first to set in motion our history of thought. It took us more than 2,000 years to fully understand this idea, but eventually we did. And today, we have finally and fully realized that raw perceptual information is not only limited and limiting but that it can be imprisoning as well.

Prisoners in a Cave

Plato wrote a story to convey these ideas to his students. We are born, this story goes, in ignorance and thus in darkness, unable to see real presence. We are born as though in a dark cave, and if we remain in ignorance as we grow up, we live like prisoners in a cave. Plato asks us to imagine a group of prisoners who have spent their lives chained inside such a cave. In front of them there is a wall, we are told. And the prisoners are chained in such a manner that they can see only that wall and nothing else. Behind them there is a great bonfire, which is always lit and thus always casting shadows on the wall that the prisoners have always gazed at. In front of the fire, and behind the prisoners, a menagerie of animals and people cross by every day, thus casting their shadows upon the only wall that the prisoners can see.

The prisoners, therefore, grow up seeing only these shadows, of animals, of statues carried by beasts of burden, shadows of men and women. The prisoners have never seen actual animals but only the shadows of animals. They have never seen statues but only the shadows of statues. And as they have never seen anything but shadows, they believe that the shadows of the things are the things themselves. Such is their hapless existence. One day, one of the prisoners escapes. Out of the cave he confronts the at first searing, painful light of the sun, which represents knowledge, much as darkness represents ignorance. He is dazzled, confused, and believes at first that the light is an illusion, maybe a bad dream. Having always believed that the shadows are real, he now thinks, as he approaches the exit of the cave, that the things that he is now seeing—real horses, real things—are actually illusions, nightmarish apparitions, bizarre impersonations of reality. Eventually, he becomes used to the light and comes to discover, to his growing amazement, that the shadows that he always took for reality were in fact only shadows. Real horses, he now realizes, are infinitely more interesting than their shadows. An actual tree, a woman, a statue, are much more impressive, more beautiful than their shadows. Reality, actual reality, begins to take his breath away.

Plato tells us that the duty of such a person is to go back to the cave to try to en*light*en those who were left behind, to try to fill this inhuman cave with light, the light of knowledge. And we thus imagine that our hero eventually goes back to the cave to announce his discovery to the other prisoners. Perhaps he is motivated by pity for them. But as these pitiful creatures have never seen any other form of reality, they are unable to understand that there is an entirely new world just beyond their perceived world. They hear him but cannot listen to him. They don't understand him. Some of them begin to suspect that he has become insane. Being pitiful creatures themselves, they pity him. As for our hero, he is now unaccustomed to the darkness and therefore cannot quite distinguish each shadow in the cave from the next. Hence, the others begin to see him as foolish. They eventually see him as a dangerous idiot trying to subvert the order that governs the cave.

This, Plato implies, is often the fate of those who speak on behalf of aspects of reality that are not immediately apparent, that are more profound, that really matter. Purveyors of unknown truths are often misunderstood, Plato implies. They are ridiculed, or feared, and they often pay the price. This is true, as even the briefest glance into the history of knowledge shows. Consider, for example, the story of Giordano Bruno, a 16th-century Dominican friar. Against the "commonsense" of his time, he argued that the earth revolves around the sun and that the universe is infinite and populated by intelligent beings. Today, we know that the earth revolves around the sun and that islands of intelligent life are likely to exist in the universe. But his contemporaries could not believe him. They mocked him; they eventually regarded him as a heretic, and he was asked to recant, to confess that he was wrong to claim such heretical ideas. He bowed to some of his accusers' demands (the Catholic Church) but attempted to preserve the basic ideas of his theories and discoveries. Thus under the charges of blasphemy, heresy, and immoral conduct, and after eight years of imprisonment punctuated by vicious torture, he was finally burned alive in a public square before a loud mob. His books were forbidden. The fate of those who speak on behalf of what Plato calls "presence" has often been cruel. The case of Giordano Bruno is not an exception. On the contrary, throughout history, new ideas have often been seen as dangerous and as punishable, at least initially.

The Life of the Theoros

The allegory of the cave also suggests that without knowledge, we not only remain prisoners, prisoners of our own ideas, but also, in fact, lead a life that is not worth living (while perhaps pitying those who tell us that there is a brighter, more interesting world outside). Implied by Plato is the idea that the prisoners of the cave are in fact not fully human. Bear in mind, again, that for him, the special characteristic of human beings is that, unlike any other animal species, we can develop the capacity to see the *presence* that rises beyond the raw input of the senses. In the cave, the prisoners remain, as it were, prehuman. Darkness dehumanizes them. Ignorance debases them. We would fear blindness, but ignorance is already a deeper form of blindness.

Note as well that for Plato, knowledge seems to be a longing, almost a form of love (from the Greek *philos* and *sophos*, philosophy simply means "love of wisdom" and arguably "love of knowledge"). Inasmuch as it connects us to a higher plane of reality, knowledge, according to ancient Greek tradition, is in fact governed by Eros, the spirit that governs *connection*, the spirit of "the between." Eros governs, for example, the relations between lovers (called "erotic" for this reason). He governs the transactions between mortals and immortals—or the connection between the human mind and presence, the higher plane of reality discussed earlier. When found, when discovered, when therefore the philosopher experiences a sense of connection with presence, he or she experiences, above all, an affect, not a simple cognitive event. And this affect is potent. Eros, in fact, represented the most potent and transformative force that could possibly pass through the human spirit, always taking momentary possession of it, sometimes with catastrophic and long-lasting consequences. When Giordano Bruno intuited that the universe is infinite, he described the vison as "falling in love," and he argued that knowledge can allow us to experience a form of love that is far higher than "ordinary love." This is "heroic love," which Bruno described as both a "divine" and a "frenzied" affect (he uses the Italian word "furore," which I have translated as "frenzied" but may also denote "maniacal"). Nobel Laureate in literature Pablo Neruda says that true love makes you "pace around hungrily," "sniffing the twilight," like a hunting animal consigned to a barren land, an image that could also describe the experience of true knowledge, as Plato and Bruno may agree. Plato would add, perhaps, that knowledge is sometimes a form of fatal attraction that arises to claim the lover's life, as the story of Giordano Bruno, and many others like it, unmistakably illustrate.

Knowledge, in any case, is not a pile of facts; it is not mere information. Information is like dead knowledge. But information can nevertheless become alive—if and only to the extent to which it begins to move you. When and if it claims your sleep and draws you forward—if, to use Plato's language, it gets you "higher"—information thereby gives way to knowledge.

Let's return to the story of the cave. Knowledge is the path that leads out of the cave—the path that eventually allows our hero to become a *theoros,* literally "a seer," someone who begins to see. The prisoner who escapes becomes a *theoros* so that, after a lifetime of darkness, he can now finally see. In fact, he eventually is able to behold the sun itself, Plato says. He is a *theoros* because he becomes the bearer of *theoria,* the origin of the word "theory," which is, precisely, the ability to see a richer reality beneath the appearance of reality, a new world beneath the world. *Theoria* is also the origin of the word "theater": The *theoros* becomes a spectator of the world; the world becomes a spectacle for him. *Theoria* opens his mind's eye to reveal the inherent beauty of presence. The man who escapes the cave is amazed, transported by the new reality that he now sees—a new reality that becomes alive before his eyes and that begins to unfold precisely like a spectacle. Reality, as he now sees it, is no longer shadowy, ghostly, inert, devoid of a spirit. Returning to the example of the wall, as a bearer of knowledge, a physicist sees the wall not just as a blank wall, as we colloquially say, but as an economy of forces that is supported by a logical, mathematical, and, thus, harmonious structure, a stage where energies—from protons, electrons, etc.—are organized in an almost choreographic manner. The Einsteins of the world thus see the otherwise invisible dramatic tension and the beauty inherent in the world. They see reality as the spectacle that is invisible to most of us. A physicist sees at least glimpses of the cosmic soul and, hence, glimpses of an eternal and universal beauty. It is not a coincidence that physicists, and scientists in general, often describe some theories as "elegant" or as "beautiful." It is not a coincidence either that for these scientists, the beauty of a theory is a strong indication of whether the theory in question will turn out to be true and demonstrable empirically. And it is not a coincidence, finally, that theories that are found convoluted, "inelegant," or "ugly" often turn out to be, strangely enough, inaccurate models of reality.

Theoria, importantly, not only casts light on the invisible dimensions of the external world. It also casts light on formerly invisible aspects of your own self, of your own internal world. The *theoros* who escapes the cave comes to see not only the external reality but also his potential as a human being, which was formerly hidden from himself, buried by ignorance. Thus he sees not only the world but also *himself* as though for the first time. *Theoria* makes him aware of his own ignorance. The prisoners in the cave are not only ignorant of the world outside; they are also ignorant about their own ignorance; they are blind to their blindness. This, as Plato may agree, is the most dangerous, the most primitive and elemental modality of ignorance. This type of ignorance robs you of the very motivation to know. Why would you try to know anything if you cannot possibly think that there are meanings hidden from you? Why would you try to escape if you believe that you are already free? Plato, let me repeat, says that such an arrested life is simply not worth living.

Ignorance about one's ignorance not only keeps us in darkness but also makes darkness normal. The prisoners of the cave have never seen light, and therefore their dark surroundings are entirely normal for them. They regard the announcement of a new reality with pity because they see their ignorance as knowledge. Plato says that those who grew up in the cave perhaps developed a science and a philosophy that speak on behalf of their world, the world of shadows, of errors and illusions. Therefore, those who are most used to these errors, those deeper in ignorance, may have become the philosophers of the cave, the high priests, the smart ones. Consider this: The cretins who figured that it would be a good idea to burn alive an intellectual giant like Giordano Bruno were convinced that they, of all people, were the true guardians of knowledge. These kinds of folks tend to see the announcement of a new reality as a dangerous act of subversion, as a form of treason, as heresy. Their mind, to paraphrase jurist Oliver Wendell Holmes, "is like the pupil of the eye; the more light you pour upon it the more it will contract." Their mind is a prison they choose to live in because they cannot see it as a prison. And they invite others in.

The Life of the Free

The examples provided in the foregoing about North Korea, the Islamic State, and the regime of Nicolás Maduro illustrate the parable of the cave rather well. These kinds of regimes regard new ideas as treason and revelations of a richer reality as delusion. They contract, like the pupil of the eye, when confronted with light. Plato, for this reason, would agree with Immanuel Kant, the 18th-century German philosopher who argued that one has to "dare to understand," that one has to have the "courage," the "audacity" to know, partly because true knowledge is regarded, precisely, as dangerous by the self-appointed guardians of "the truth" and of "commonsense" (and partly because true knowledge, as we will discuss soon, can do violence to our own cherished beliefs and illusions).

For Kant, incidentally, having the courage and audacity to know is, in the end, having the courage and audacity to be free. For you may be free, he implied, only to the extent to which you have true understanding, only if you are able to use reason. A blind choice cannot be a free choice. If, like the average North Korean citizen, for example, you hear only North Korean propaganda and are therefore blind to the atrocities of the regime and convinced of its greatness, your support is not freely given. It is conned out. This regime curtails the freedom of its citizens not only through dictatorial laws. Its systematic censorship and propaganda, and its systematic sponsorship of social and historical illiteracy also curtail freedom. To a lesser extent, this applies to democratic life as well: In a democracy, choices that derive from fake news, from propaganda, neuromarketing, and neuropolitics, and choices that result from the application of deep surveillance technologies are likewise not really free. In a democracy, on the other hand, an illiterate person cannot really enjoy democratic freedoms either, such as a free press or the freedom of thought necessary to conduct scientific research. Indeed, if you are literate but have no knowledge of the world, your freedom is restricted as well so that, if you don't know the risks of certain foods, for example, you are not freely choosing to eat them if you do. Only if you know these risks will you be able to think, compare, analyze, and then freely decide what to do. A child cannot be free to choose whatever lifestyle she pleases precisely because she doesn't have enough knowledge about the world yet. Her truest sovereignty will be eventually given not by a law that guarantees her civil rights but, above all, by knowledge. Not her legislators but above all her teachers, if they are able to open her mind's eye, will allow her to experience freedom.

Freedom emerges from classrooms and libraries, not only from the halls of power. Ignorance, fake news, post-truths not only blind you but also threaten your freedom, as Kant argues. They are a threat, more generally, to the ideal of a "land of the free."

Sociology as a Platonic Science

It is evident that Plato's ideas apply to the physical order, as the example of the wall illustrates. But can these ideas help us understand the social order? Let us go back to Peter Berger: "The first wisdom of sociology is [that] things are not what they seem. [Social] reality turns out to have many layers of meaning" (1963). This statement is clearly platonic. The first wisdom of sociology is that you can see the social world only with your mind's eye, not with your naked eye.

Let us again recall the world of coffee, which can illustrate this idea. As noted, coffee is more than just a drink. You go to your favorite coffee shop and buy your daily cup of coffee, but this time, you are curious about how many people have worked on it. One? Ten? Perhaps thousands: farmers in, say, Guatemala, who sowed, tended, and harvested the beans; people who work on the transportation network—from mules to trucks to ships to vans; perhaps workers in Brazil who chopped down trees that were then processed into coffee filters, etc. The point does not need belaboring: Your cup of coffee encloses a global economy. Leonard Read, a 20th-century American writer, noted that not one person in the world is actually able to make a pencil. Not one of the seven billion people in the world knows how to harvest the cedar for the pencil *and* the volcanic rock and oil needed to make the eraser, *and* to produce the lacquer to paint the pencil *and* the graphite to write with, *and* mine and process the zinc and the other metals needed to make the brass ferule to hold the eraser, etc. Similarly with coffee, we assume that anyone can make coffee, but adding the filter, the two scoops, the water, and then pushing the button merely involves the last couple of seconds of a large process that, controlled by no one in particular, typically necessitates the input of many organizations, financial institutions, governments of thousands of people, you, the consumer, included.

Furthermore, these processes involve not only the mechanical aspects of production but also political and ethical dimensions as well. Rigoberta Menchú Tum, a Nobel Peace Prize Laureate, has said that coffee is about "survival" (2010). Menchú spent much of her childhood working on coffee plantations in Guatemala, in conditions of semislavery, places where "suffering," she says, "was everywhere" (2010). The owners of these plantations abused workers, exploited children, corrupted officials, and cruelly punished dissenters, sometimes with death. And, meanwhile, they marketed their product as a pastoral fantasy, complete with quaint peasants happily working on sunny plantations. Menchú notes that her consciousness "was born" in these plantations. This happened when she realized that *a hidden world* of poverty—a largely invisible world of misery and violence—was needed to sustain the visible world of coffee. Depending on what type you drink, your coffee may well be a veneer in this sense as well. A veneer designed, precisely, to hide the suffering that Menchú describes—suffering that may well be part of the cup of coffee itself. If and inasmuch as it conceals underlying meanings, your coffee may thus be deceiving you—unless you see it armed with knowledge, of sociology, of economics, of political economy, of environmental science. Only then can you see the hidden "layers of meaning" that Berger alludes to.

Berger also says that seeing these kinds of hidden layers of meaning changes your "initial perception of the whole." Again, the ability to see beyond the surface of things reveals the forces that shape the world, the dramatic tension inherent in social life, the way the machinery of history works. And it thus gives you a glimpse into the political structures you support, perhaps unknowingly, with your everyday actions. When this happens, when you see the social machine at work, and if you don't like what you see, you may then decide to do things differently. If you can see, for example, the world of suffering within your cup of coffee, you may decide to buy another kind of coffee. And when other people begin to read the same features of the world—if the collective consciousness is thus raised, as it sometimes happens—social change is likely to occur. Today, for example, more people around the world are aware of the political and ethical issues surrounding coffee. Menchú's writings have been very influential in this regard. And as a result, the politics, ethics, and economics of coffee have changed: New markets have been opened for organic farmers and roasters; a global demand for fair-trade coffee has emerged, which has changed older farming and trading practices. Menchú is an awareness specialist who has helped us see the world a little better and who has thus helped change this aspect of the global economy, one of the most important industries of the modern era. And she has also helped improve the lives of many workers. Through her eyes, coffee workers have come to see that their lives and their rights matter to many people in the world. They now see that those rights are achievable, that their lives can improve, and that positive historical changes, in general, are achievable.

As noted, coffee is not exceptional. The larger point is that the world in general is sustained by certain processes and structures that, often unseen, can be brought to light and then changed when people begin to understand them. Again, any glimpse into history will show you that social change is often brought about by changes in the collective mind, as a result of the collective ability to see a world formerly out of sight. The civil right movements that shook the legal and cultural foundations of countries like the United States, for example, are unthinkable without newly emerging forms of collective consciousness about how the world works and why it works in that way and not in some other way. Or consider current problems, say, the current environmental crisis—massive pollution of the ocean, the air, large-scale disappearance of animal and plant species—or the manner in which the information on the Internet is regulated, the ways in which fake news affect political processes, etc. The future of any such issues will also largely depend on the public ability to read the world.

Let us finish this chapter with a couple of (deliberately unrelated) examples pertaining to these kinds of social problems and the extent to which their fate hinges, or has hinged on, public literacy.

The Financial World

One of the most demoralizing economic crises in history reached a high point in 2007–2008. It started in the United States, but it soon became a global crisis that contributed to the destabilization of economies in countries around the world. In the United States, this crisis can be partly explained as a series of failures in the economic model itself, including a near collapse of the housing market and a dramatic financial crisis that forced the government to "bail out" the banking system by injecting it with a multibillion-dollar rescue package. There were other causes for this crisis, as well, including, in particular, widespread corruption in the financial system itself. William Black (2014), a bank regulator with firsthand knowledge of the banking system, has said that fraudulent banking practices cost us $11 *trillion* (i.e., $11,000,000,000,000) in loss of wealth experienced by the economic system overall. These practices have been "weapons of mass destruction," Black has noted (2014). Although they increased the wealth of particular operators, including fraudsters, they also resulted in the impoverishment of the middle and lower classes, and they threatened the banking system itself. For this reason, the banks that had deployed these "weapons of mass destruction" against the public had to be rescued precisely by means of a massive injection of public moneys. And, hence, the victims of these practices in the end had to rescue those organizations that had victimized them.

Here is another important factor that facilitated this crisis: a depressing lack of public literacy about the economy and about the attendant corruption in the system itself, an irresponsible public indifference and passivity that provided a fertile terrain for these practices and this crisis to grow. Experts such as Black foresaw the impending problems, but their messages were ignored. Judging by the amount of TV coverage devoted to trivia, the public seemed more interested in inconsequential matters, the petty misadventures of celebrities, etc., until it eventually awoke already shaken by the economic crisis itself. This kind of public illiteracy contributed to the public's impoverishment and, in this sense, to its disenfranchisement. A more literate and vigilant citizenry, as Black says, would have been better able to advocate for its own interests, thus advocating, indirectly, on behalf of a more balanced and democratic economic system. Black suggests that the financial system contributes massively to both dominant political parties in the United States so that the political classes, generally and save honorable exceptions, tend to avoid interfering with it. Hence, Black says, it is up to us. It is up to the public—a public that must be knowledgeable to be effectively mobilized; for, if you don't know the issues at stake, there would not be a reason for you to protest against them. If you don't know what "financial regulation" entails, for example, you will not be able to ask your representatives to work toward financial regulation.

In Europe, there seems to be significant public awareness about potential risks associated with an unregulated financial system. The banking system, in any case, is more closely monitored, not only by the European Banking Authority but also by powerful organizations that represent the civil society: Transparency International and Anticor, in particular. These organizations have worked hard, and arguably effectively, to raise public awareness about corruption in, and the risks inherent to, an unregulated financial market. The United States has not produced these kinds of outfits. Save perhaps Americans who were shaken by this crisis directly, it would be difficult to argue that we did learn our lesson from the 2008 crisis and that folks are now aware that a completely unregulated financial system, as proven by this global problem, is potentially dangerous for their own interests and for the economy as a whole. If this is the case, if we in fact have forgotten our own history, we may therefore be condemned to passively repeat it (to paraphrase Jorge Santayana's famous phrase).

The Food System

Here is another (deliberately unrelated) aspect of our society: food. Let us first acknowledge that the food system has provided many benefits and that, in some ways, we owe a debt of gratitude to some of the captains of industry who have toiled to create it and to strengthen it. This industry has made food much cheaper and massively available; it has amplified the job market; it has thus contributed to economic development. Yet this industry is also at the root of significant problems that have grown on the fertile terrain of public illiteracy (about food in this case). To identify these problems, let us right away quote one of the most important scientists in public health, Collin Campbell, professor emeritus of nutritional biochemistry at Cornell University.

> By any numbers of measures, America's health is failing. We spend far more, per capita on health care than any other society in the world, and yet two thirds of Americans are overweight, and over 15 million Americans have diabetes, a number that has been rising rapidly. We fall prey to heart disease as often as we did thirty years ago, and the War on Cancer, launched in the 1970s, has been a miserable failure. Half of Americans have a health problem that requires taking a prescription drug every week, and over 100 million Americans have high cholesterol [...]. To make matters worse, we are leading our youth down a path of disease earlier and earlier in their lives. One third of the young people in this country are overweight or at risk of becoming overweight. Increasingly, there are falling prey to a form of diabetes that use to be seen only in adults, and these young people now take more prescription drugs than ever before [...]. These issues come down to three things: breakfast, lunch and dinner. (Campbell, 2006, p. 3)

Indeed, problems associated with the food that we typically consume also involve "various cancers, autoimmune diseases, bone health, kidney health, vision and brain disorders (like cognitive dysfunction in Alzheimer's disease)," all of which "are convincingly influenced by diet" (Campbell, 2006, p. 7). Bear in mind that the food system, which is largely controlled by a group of multinational corporations, is skewed toward (profitable) bad calories, as Campbell has also noted. And that it is a system that, ultimately encompassing the "government, science, medicine, industry, and media—promotes profit over health, technology over food and confusion over clarity" (2006, p. 250). Beyond the ailments considered earlier, let us also consider some numbers pertaining to toxicity in food. The Centers for Disease Control and Prevention (CDC) have determined that approximately *93%* of Americans six years of age and older have detectable levels of Bisphenol A (BPA), a toxicant that, often present in canned and packaged food and beverages, is associated with reproductive and neurological problems (Calafat et al., 2008). Although it is true that research also suggests that not all detectable levels of BPA are dangerous, we, nevertheless, have legitimate reasons for concern. Rat models do suggest that "developmental exposure [...] to BPA may disrupt aspects of spatial navigational learning and memory" (Johnson et al., 2016).

Here is another problematic aspect of the food industry, related this time to animal welfare and to the factory farms that largely sustain food production in the United States. It is also true that, as people who support eating meat maintain, human beings have been eating meat ever since we climbed down from trees. It is true that people throughout history have eaten meat in order to survive. And it is true that the killing of animals, and in this sense their suffering, is a fundamental aspect of the natural order itself. (Even the briefest glimpse at a tiger, for example, will reveal at once that nature itself has designed this animal above all to kill. Its claws and fangs unmistakably signal that the life system itself has been designed to feed literally from life and, in this sense, from suffering.) And yet the perspective of the animal welfare activist must be considered as well, particularly the idea that the food system, in general and save exceptions, deals *unnecessary* and indeed unimaginable suffering to billions of animals each year. Consider the typical "battery cage" for chickens, for example. It measures 18 by 24 inches, and it is stuffed with seven to 10 chickens who typically spend their lives in it, unable to move and stretch, covered in feces, never seeing the light of day. And consider the manner in which many of these chickens are slaughtered. As reported by Princeton researcher Peter Singer, about three million of them are boiled alive each year in the United States alone (2007, p. 26).

These are the problems that, causing suffering to animals and to humans, have grown on the fertile terrain of public illiteracy about food.

But back to Campbell, he implies that this sense of illiteracy is not simply a matter of intellectual laziness in the public. There are other factors that contribute to it, related, again, to "government, science, medicine, industry, and media." Let us focus on the role of the media, in particular. Robert Kenner (2009), an American filmmaker and investigative journalist, has noted that a "deliberate veil" has been placed between the food system and the average consumer of food. If you were surprised by the image of three million chickens being boiled alive in the United States, that would be an example of this deliberate veil. If you don't know that the "annual medical cost of obesity in the United States was $147 billion in 2018" (CDC, 2018), a bigger figure than the 2017 gross domestic product of Hungary (Trading Economics, 2018), that would be another example. If you don't know that the average American apple spends 11 months in cold storage so that at the point of consumption, it has lost about 90% of its antioxidants, that would be yet another example. There is a "curtain," Kenner says, "between us and where our food is coming from." When you go to the supermarket, he notes, you see no traces of how this system works, as it advertises itself as a "pastoral fantasy" reliant not on a factory system and factory farms, but on caring farmers fond of their green grass, their white picket fences, their pampered animals. And when you turn on the TV, a constant stream of advertisements purveys the notion that the bad calories that this system massively produces are sure to increase *not* health problems but the fun factor in life. Even when you turn to science, you might also come across a version of this "veil" that Kenner has in mind. Industries are funding seemingly legitimate research studies, not in an effort to pursue the truth and convey it to the public, but above all to protect their own interests. As researcher Alice Fabri and her colleagues have noted, "Publications resulting from Coca-Cola and Mars-sponsored research," for example, "appear to skew the evidence toward solutions that favour industry interests by focusing on food components that can be manipulated and marketed by food companies" (Fabri, Holand, & Bero, 2018).

Let's return to Robert Kenner. He notes that the mainstream industry in general "doesn't want you to know what you are eating" (or drinking), or indeed why, "because if you knew, you might not want to eat it." And, of course, for our part, we, the public, often tend to accept the dominant "common sense" mechanically—the successfully marketed fantasy about American food. And thus we ourselves have enormously contributed to our own public health problems noted earlier and to problems with animal welfare—problems that would likely drop in an inverse proportion to increased public literacy about the food system. Let us consider the history of lead regulation, which is instructive in this regard.

Regulation of Lead Production

Although already regarded as a powerful toxicant at least since 1900 (arguably since the times of ancient Rome), lead was nevertheless a key ingredient of many household products, paint, gasoline, and others, and it was thus an important ingredient of the economy itself. The industry justified the use of lead by arguing that the public was only facing harmless exposure levels that already occurred naturally and that the production and commercialization of lead was not increasing these levels in a significant way. But in the 1920s, a scientist named Clair Patterson discovered that exposure to lead was rapidly and dangerously increasing and that these increases were directly tied to the activities of the also rapidly growing industry. Yet instead of accepting the painstaking evidence that Peterson and others had provided, and thus yielding to regulation, lead producers decided to defend their own interests. And they did so very successfully—for decades—in part by investing, precisely, in "science" that validated their utterly irresponsible legalistic arguments (recall that lead exposure can result in severe mental retardation in children, depending on the level of exposure).

Eventually, however, this industry was forced into submission, and lead production became increasingly regulated. Many individuals and organizations contributed to this process, universities, the press, the U.S. Congress and others. But regulation was also facilitated by a progressively aware public that, informed by the scientific community and by the press, began to understand the alarming nature of the situation and to be revolted by the practices of the industry. The public hence began to ask for regulatory policies simply because folks knew about the dangers and wanted to protect their children, their communities, and their country. Today, arguably, every child in the United States already has a minimal degree of literacy about this toxicant. And any average American adult would be adamantly unwilling to permit the unregulated use of lead because we have, as a society, the necessary degree of literacy about this product and this industry.

Power is the ability of someone to have various degrees of control over someone else's ideas and behavior. A parent, for example, has power over a child; the law can have power over a citizen. Public knowledge is a key regulatory mechanism of power in society. This is so because when public literacy increases, it becomes more difficult for, say, the market, or for an industry, or for an ideologue, or for a dictator, etc., to control the ideas and behaviors of the public. That is why not only dictatorships but also some industries and some organizations have striven to "lower a curtain," as Kenner says, between the public and the surrounding world. This curtain has historically been—and is today—an essential ingredient of their power.

The World of Religion

It is not necessary to explore the earlier examples in detail, as these are only passing illustrations pertaining to the problems associated with illiteracy about society. Let us turn to a final and very different aspect of society—namely, religion—and, approaching religion sociologically, let us try to read this aspect of the world. This switch is important for the following reason: This subfield of sociological studies, the sociology of religion, is often resisted or even resented sometimes. This is not because the analysis of religious ideas is inherently difficult or offensive, but because religious narratives and images tend to be invested with a sense of the eternal, regarded as immutable, and therefore seen as beyond scrutiny and analysis. Yet, as we already saw when we discussed the origin of our ideas about body and soul, it is easy to trace these narratives and images historically—an exercise that, importantly, rather than offending the faith of the believer can allow her to have a better understanding, a much better reading of the objects of her own worship.

Let us consider the typical depictions of Jesus of Nazareth. Jesus was an ancient Judaean or Semite. As the Apostle Paul writes in his Letter to the Hebrews, "it is clear that our Lord was descended from Judah." Ancient Semites were not blond. They were not light skinned. They were dark skinned. Jesus could not have possibly looked like the blond man often depicted today, particularly in the United States. He was dark skinned, phenotypically close to the peoples of Western Asia and North Africa. The *image* of a blond Jesus, and the images of the European-looking Sacred Family that many people worship today, conceal many layers of meaning—namely, the social-historical processes that brought these particular images into being. Once again, this is not an attack on Christianity; on the contrary, it is an attempt to cast a clearer light on this important religion. The point of this historical exercise is simply to recognize that these racialized characterizations of God, the angels, and archangels as European—natural as it might appear to be—occurred as a result of historical processes that are typically hidden from worshipers themselves, worshipers that, in mechanically assuming the seeming whiteness of the Celestial Order, are therefore not fully able to read basic aspects of their own religion. Hence, if you are a Christian, your ability to read this aspect of the world can help you see through the veils and coverings that history has placed on these early images. And, to insist on the key idea, this ability can thus help you understand your religion's most original symbols and meanings.

This form of literacy can also help you better see the history of your religion, particularly the fact that the creation of a European-looking Celestial Order served political and economic purposes well beyond this religion's original ethical commitments. Implied by these images, for example, was the idea that European colonists were the natural heirs of the Celestial Order, a notion that validated the colonists' professed moral authority, helping them to justify their often ruthless and economically motivated colonial expansion. There is a dark irony in the fact that the image of Jesus, the dark-complexioned Nazarene whose central message was "love thy neighbor" was recast and used as a weapon of European colonial expansion. There is a lesson in the fact that the image of this Nazarene man was recast and used as the coat of arms of racist genocide during colonial times.

The Manifest and Latent Functions of Beliefs

More generally and abstractly, let us finally note that all belief systems have manifest functions—explicit, visible, professed functions—but also latent functions that are implicit and hidden from most believers (Merton, 1957). When some colonists appropriated Christianity for their own benefit, for example, they manifestly upheld such Christian doctrines as "love thy neighbor," but the latent and hidden function of their version of Christianity was actually that of exploiting their neighbors.

Adherents to any belief system easily recognize the explicit functions of their beliefs (e.g., love thy neighbor), precisely because these are explicit. But it is often hard for them to recognize the implicit, and yet actual historical functions (e.g., colonial expansion), precisely because these are latent and therefore hard to see. When this happens—that is, when we cannot see the discrepancies between the explicit and the latent functions of our own ideals—it is difficult for us to align our ideals with their actual historical manifestations. For this reason, rather than mechanically assuming that (our) good values will automatically result in good deeds, we ought to be prepared to identify the latent functions of these values. And we have to be able to recognize the possible bad deeds and the bad outcomes that good values may very well produce. Only such a community can manage to steer a historical trajectory that is in fact consistent with its own ideals. Only such a community can be true to itself.

Note also that all social systems—for example, the food system in the United States or, more generally, the economic system—also have manifest and thus evident functions (e.g., production of food) but also latent and thus hard to see functions (e.g., public health problems, unnecessary surplus of animal suffering). So as a society, we have to be able to identify the latter as well, not only to avoid these problems but also to be true to our own ideals—ideals such as, for example, preventing preventable diseases (associated with food) or preventing preventable suffering (associated with animal welfare).

The ability to read the world, let us finally note, helps you to better see through the array of beliefs, products, and institutions that sustain your world. This ability can allow you to see how the world is constituted and why. It helps you to be more conscious and deliberative. It helps you to think with higher degrees of freedom. Public knowledge about the world can make the world a bit freer, more harmonious, less ugly, or even more beautiful. For Plato, knowledge, at its highest, is the knowledge of beauty. At its highest, knowledge of the world is about the conditions needed to create harmony and beauty in the world.

CHAPTER IV

A Sociological View of Deception

Passion for Unreason

It is the 1950s. A housewife in a suburb of Chicago has gotten the idea that, among the billions of human beings on earth, she herself had been especially appointed by a powerful alien civilization to deliver a message to humanity about nothing less than the world's impending destruction (like the Disney character Buzz Lightyear). The plain absurdity of the idea notwithstanding, Dorothy Martin, nevertheless, managed to convince a cadre of folks that she was right—folks who, like herself, also claimed the role of messengers to, and saviors of, humanity. An MIT psychologist, Leon Festinger, saw in this odd event a unique opportunity to test a hunch: the idea that psychologically average persons who hold a strong and erroneous belief may very well cling to the patently irrational idea, even after facing obviously disconfirming evidence. What would these suburbanite saviors of humanity do when, against Ms. Martin's prophecy, the world actually didn't come to an end on December 21, 1954? Would they then take a step back and wonder if, perhaps, Savior Dorothy might not have been appointed by concerned and English-speaking aliens after all? Would this unmistakable level of (disconfirming) evidence be enough to persuade them of their error? Or would they, instead, seek reasons to still cling to the now evidently false narrative? The world, it turned out, was not destroyed in 1954. But regardless, these enthusiasts of the occult avidly sought out reasons not only for clinging to their narrative but also for strengthening their belief in it. It was because of their righteous actions that God Himself had taken pity on humanity and saved us all. Dorothy was not a simple and obvious fraudster but a global hero.

Festinger and colleagues (1956) argued that, rather than being a fluke, an oddity of human psychology confined to this small group of UFO believers in an American suburb, their reaction said something crucial about human psychology in general. For these investigators, the main lesson was that, as they had predicted, psychologically normal adults who hold a strong belief easily resist plainly disconfirming evidence. And this claim (initially resisted by other researchers, ironically) was eventually supported by hundreds of subsequent research studies, particularly in the area of social psychology. So today, we know that human beings can indeed develop an all-too-human passion for ignorance, rather than for logic, for evidence, for knowledge—an insight that, in the era of fake news, is all the more evident and relevant, not to mention alarming. Knowledge, after all, is harder and far more demanding than simple belief. Plus, simple beliefs and fantasies can easily feed grand illusions and dreams. In contrast, actual knowledge often intrudes in the domain of daydreams and goes against cherished fantasies. For example, the awesome notion that I am a member of the chosen and destined to deliver a crucial message to humanity about a day of reckoning and destruction (a fantasy often found among the peoples of the world, incidentally) will be immediately spoiled by knowledge (Buzz's initial predicament, as you may recall).

This idea, that human beings easily develop a passion for ignorance, can be traced to ancient times. Plato's teacher, Socrates, was already keen to demonstrate to anyone who cared to listen that human beings had a tendency to pander to "*doxa*," mere belief or opinion, while also having a tendency to avoid, when not to denounce, actual knowledge. But the first to provide a proper theory about this phenomenon was arguably Sigmund Freud, the founding father of psychoanalysis, whose ideas are worth examining in detail.

Unreason in Everyday Behaviors

The 20th century is sometimes called "the Freudian century," an acknowledgment of the vast influence that, for better and for worse, Freud had on an array of fields: medicine, the humanities, the social sciences, and the arts. (He left a deep mark in disciplines ranging from pediatric medicine to history, from psychology to philosophy, from linguistics to sociology, from poetry to painting, to music, to film, to theater—to, indeed, the everyday language that we employ.) Like any other pioneer, Freud made mistakes, even egregious ones, and although some regard him as a genius, others regard him as a fraud. This perspective, Freud as a failed theoretician, is important, but we can only note it in passing, as an analysis of the broader implications of the theory is not needed for our purposes. We will focus, instead, on the good and, in the end, enduring Freudian ideas, particularly the ones that can help us better understand, precisely, how and why we may fool ourselves.

Freud helped us see, first, the extent to which human beings are motivated by emotional, irrational, and, in fact, potentially dangerous animalistic instincts— which are mostly outside our conscious knowledge or control. These hidden motives, Freud argued, often operate behind our backs, and they push us to do things that our conscious awareness may very well reject or disavow. That is why rational persons sometimes do things that don't make rational sense, things that are harmful to them, that make their lives harder—behaviors that, precisely because they have causes beyond the reach of consciousness, are hard to control, let alone prevent. Psychotherapists often see patients who, knowing that their own behaviors negatively affect their lives, are nevertheless incapable of avoiding them. These are patients who need to be saved from themselves, and who typically ask themselves, "Why do I continue to do this or that even though I do know that in doing so I am harming myself, or belittling myself, or making my life more difficult." These kinds of conducts, Freud argued, often reveal a darker human side and indeed bespeak the motives of, metaphorically speaking, a hidden agent within us. An agent that, if unchecked, can elude our awareness and burden our life. Psychopathology, for Freud, means that these hidden motives dominate our lives, rather than simply nudging us from time to time to engage in irrational and potentially harmful behaviors. This form of psychopathology involves unconscious and therefore invisible motives that nevertheless play a determinant role in the way our lives unfold.

Although by the end of his life, witnessing the seemingly inexorable advance of the Nazis, he felt pessimistic about our actual ability to rein in these darker agencies, Freud, nevertheless, devoted his life to identifying precisely these agencies hidden within the human spirit. His main goal was allowing the individual, as well as society, in general, to have better control over them.

And he began this quest by first disabusing us of our formerly naïve self-regard. Before him, and under the influence of ideals from the Enlightenment, we generally believed that the fundamental difference between us and any other animal species is that, unlike them, we go about the world motivated above all by our God-given capacity to reason. Shakespeare's Prince Hamlet said it well: "What a piece of work is man! How noble in reason! How infinite in faculty! In form and moving how express and admirable! In action how like an angel! In apprehension how like a god!" We also believed that, unlike "the primitive," who was ruled by magic, instinct, and unreason, "civilized man" was ruled fundamentally by science and reason, so that his behavior was always motivated by a rational assessment of the situation at hand. Of course, we do have the capacity to reason, and we can indeed develop a craving for knowledge, as Plato wanted it (the vast scientific apparatus human beings have built already proves that unmistakably), and civilization does involve the advancement of reason, and reason is indeed a noble Hamletian faculty. But as Freud showed us, human beings, civilized or not, all too often embrace fantasy. Indeed, we often prefer ignorance over knowledge, like Plato's prisoners, even when confronted with unambiguous evidence that disconfirms our beliefs, like the UFO enthusiasts in the foregoing example.

Importantly, let us now add that, for Freud, this fondness for fantasy and ignorance—although it can be very destructive—can sometimes be merciful, necessary, or even beneficial (that is why we choose it, when we do). This is a revealing insight that we have to examine in detail.

A Useful Psychoanalytical Insight

Freud approached questions about the role of unreason and fantasy in human behavior in part by studying the nature of sexual fantasies as well as sexual pathologies, what laypeople sometimes call "sexual perversions."

One of his patients, Freud said, liked to couple the "mucus terminal ends" of his digestive system to other persons' mucus terminal ends of their own digestive systems. What kind of bizarre sexual perversion is Freud describing? A kiss. Objectively, a kiss is that. What Freud is illustrating, here, is that, as noted, hiding some layers of reality from conscious awareness is sometimes desirable: Some objective meanings have to remain concealed —"known but unthought," psychoanalysts would say—for a kiss to become desirable, for it to be glamorized in romantic narratives, for it to be a kiss proper. It is true that a kiss is a coupling of the mucus terminal ends of the digestive apparatus, but this is a grim truth, unromantic, and in the end pointless. Incidentally, Freud also helped us see that just as some truths are helpful, even dazzling, as Plato's allegory of the cave suggests, other truths can be useless. We used to think, after Plato, that truth is by definition good and beautiful. But Freud helped us understand that there are, so to speak, species of truths, ranging from the universal, luminous, and heroic Platonic truths to the lesser truths, that are a bit grim, a bit dour, a bit ugly. (And by the same token, not all forms of unreason or fantasy are pernicious. A review of mystic poetry and surrealist art would reveal that fantasy, unreason, and, in this specific sense, falsehood may well be a source of beauty and indeed of insight. Although unreason *is always the enemy of science and of politics*, it is not always the enemy of beauty.)

Freud, let us clarify, used the example of the kiss to explain the nature of human sexuality in general. He argued that for any person to find sexuality desirable, he or she has to approach sexuality with some such filter that, as this example suggests, conceals the crude biological implications of the sexual act. Of course, human sexuality involves a crude physiological dimension, the input of hormones and the mechanics of biology. But, unlike the sexuality of animals, human sexuality is not limited to the operations of a biological machine. For animals, the sexual act is primarily a question of discharge and thus not very different from eating and excretion. In contrast, human sexuality involves physiological and, in a sense, animalistic processes that are, however, mediated by meanings, and by a necessary degree of fantasy without which it would be no different from animal sexuality. A Martian may wonder, for example, why human feet, or indeed shoes, which in no way are involved in the reproductive process, sometimes become fetishized and sexually charged. The answer is that human sexuality can encompass, precisely, nonreproductive organs or even things, as long as these become invested with (mostly unconscious) *meanings* that cater to the sexual drive. And here *meanings* is the operational word. Human sexuality encompasses physiological processes whose aims are reproductive—but also *mental process*, fantasies, and attendant acts, all of which have no reproductive aims at all but that are, nevertheless, involved in sexual gratification. Indeed, sometimes, these are the most significant aspects of human sexual gratification.

Human sexuality, for Freud, is thus "polymorphic": Because human sexuality is related to meanings and fantasies that can change, its nature is to take various forms. (The sexuality of animals is generally not polymorphic; animals are born with a sexual template that simply unfolds as they mature.) And because human sexuality is polymorphic, what we may call a "sexual perversion" may well be a manifestation of sexuality that simply clashes against our varying and largely arbitrary social conventions. For this reason, what for one culture will be a manifestation of unnatural sexuality for others will be natural. The ancient Greeks, and many ancient warrior societies, celebrated homosexuality, for example. In contrast, Hebrew-derived cultures tended to regard homosexuality as unnatural and punishable.

This is not to say, importantly, that every culture is, in its own way, entirely right and morally correct, and that, therefore, we cannot judge other cultural standards or beliefs. On the contrary, if we define ethics as the search for universal values, this definition already implies that we have *the ethical mandate to judge any culture* to the extent to which the culture in question fails to meet universally valid principles, such as those related to human and civil rights. Freud was not encouraging a vapid, misguided, and naïve form of cultural relativism (precisely the idea that all cultures are right in their own way). Instead, he simply helped us see the following:

a. Although the seeming unnaturalness that people attribute to some expressions of human sexuality can be pathological, its perceived unnaturalness is not necessarily *intrinsic* to the sexual act in question. Instead, it can be *extrinsic*, a mere *decision* of this or that culture. "Perversion," "deviance," even "crime," as he implied, are not always *intrinsically* perverted, deviant, or criminal. Up until 2003, oral sex was considered a crime in 13 U.S. states; and then it was a crime no more. For some cultures, drinking alcohol is sinful, and others celebrate their religious rituals with alcohol. What Freud implied is that, because some behaviors can be made deviant or not by this or that culture—cultures, in this sense, *create* much of the deviance, or the perversion, or the crimes punished by the culture in question. In agreement with this Freudian perspective, sociologist Howard Becker (1963) has argued that the act of smoking marijuana, for example, is not *in itself* deviant, as many people see it. Its seemingly deviant and criminal nature, Becker argued, is in the culturally filtered eyes of a beholder. That is why some persons, communities, or countries regard it as deviant or criminal, while others regard it as normal and legal. While marijuana possession is legally sold in Holland, it can carry the death penalty in Singapore, a country that has created this form of deviance.

b. Wrongfulness as well as normality are thus cultural constructs to an extent, an idea that, also implied by Freud's polemic, is especially helpful for us. For if we believe that all forms of wrongfulness, as defined by our culture, are *intrinsically* wrong, we will neither question our moral standards nor our laws. But if, in contrast, we are able to see that wrongfulness can be a mere cultural construct, we will be able to establish a dialogue with the moral standards of our culture, as well as with our laws. And, hence, we would be able to scrutinize—*and therefore change and improve*—not only our moral standards, norms, and laws but also our culture and our country.

c. We can also infer from Freud that it is difficult for a society to establish a dialogue with its own morality and laws. This is so precisely because human beings often prefer to embrace ignorance instead of knowledge, fantasy instead of reality, which makes it easy for us to build, to enthrone, and to revere a fiction about what is good and what is bad or evil, a fiction about what is normal and what is perverted. It follows that it takes effort, audacity, and daring to improve our moral standards, our laws, and our culture, in general. This is not a task for passive but for active citizens committed to anchoring their lives and their country in truth.

The "Unthought Known"

Freud's view that fantasy is what makes the human sexual experience *human* has broader implications outside the sexual domain. This idea also helps us understand the way we experience reality, in general.

We already saw the extent to which important layers of physical reality are veiled from our view, and how human beings tend to perceive only the surface of reality, as Plato and Richard Dawkins imply. But Freud adds that we often unconsciously *strive* to filter aspects of everyday reality—for example, those that threaten our self-image, our habits of thought, the balance of the emotional sphere we inhabit, our "comfort zone," as we colloquially say. For him, just as we veil the raw biological aspects of sexuality, we also tend to veil various aspects of reality, in general—various uncomfortable truths. We saw that, sometimes, interested groups (some politicians and marketeers, for example) try to hide layers of meaning from people. Freud, in turn, helps us see that people often spontaneously conceal such layers of meaning from themselves, that human beings unconsciously, and sometimes for good reasons, hide aspects of their own reality.

At a basic level, this is a simple and easy idea to understand. Bear in mind that for most of us, it is hard to see our deficits directly; those of people we love; those of our country, if we have an emotional investment in it; or those of our religion, etc. It is easy for us to deny potentially distressing aspects of reality and to consign them to what psychoanalysts call "the unthought known," so that these potentially distressing facts remain *known* to us at *some unconscious or semiconscious level* while also being unthought, excluded from our conscious, explicit thoughts. Here is an extreme but easy to understand example. Oftentimes, alcoholics don't like to think. This is *not* because they are unintelligent, but because thinking is sometimes injurious to their ego. Some truths are painful for many of them—truths related, perhaps, to a personal failure or to memories of abuse, etc., and alcohol provides the "perfect" drug, as it numbs thinking itself. But healthy persons often find some truths uncomfortable as well, or injurious to their ego. And rather than drowning the thinking signal with the noise of alcohol, we devise other unconscious defensive strategies and often succeed in consigning these truths to the unthought known. Healthy persons also often fool themselves.

As this process unfolds, this part of the psychical apparatus, the unthought known, tends to become a repository of material that is problematic, embarrassing, painful to acknowledge, or even pathological. This includes repressed anxieties and fears that we cannot easily and consciously name or identify, and that are nevertheless still within us, pushing us to do certain things, to avoid doing other things, motivating some of our likes and dislikes, supporting some of our inclinations and phobias. (Hence, psychoanalytical therapy is primarily about acquainting the patient with his or her own unconscious, with these otherwise hidden elements, to thereby help him understand why he does some things that don't seem concordant with his conscious wishes or designs.) Thus, to the extent to which we hide aspects of reality from ourselves, we cling *not to reality itself* but to a comforting *version* of reality that we ourselves create. Of course, this does not mean that we live in a fictive bubble entirely detached from reality. It means that replacing aspects of reality with a reassuring fiction can, sometimes, make our lives easier, at least seemingly so. The old adage that applies here is that ignorance is *sometimes* bliss. Bear in mind that reality is, of course, under no obligation to cater to our wishes. We wish that our loved ones never suffer, for example, and yet, as the Buddha discovered, the reality is that suffering is an inevitable aspect of the human condition (and as noted, it is an inevitable aspect of the life system itself). We do not wish for trauma to visit our lives, and yet the reality is that trauma will affect a relatively predicable number of people, perhaps ourselves included. People often dread the idea of dying, and yet, we will all die. Hence, as there is a gap between our wishes and the offerings of reality, human beings have to either face these painful, or ugly, or embarrassing dimensions of reality—or defensively and unconsciously repress them. The first option is by definition painful or embarrassing or unappetizing, and therefore, we often default to the second option and thus feed the unthought known.

To insist on the key idea: Human beings thus avoid aspects of reality and replace them with various fictions so that *the human perception of reality is not fully and purely real, as it is often distorted by a human-all-too-human taste for fantasy.*

Our Tendency to Mask Reality

We will explore the sociological implications of this idea soon. But let us begin with initial examples that illustrate how normal and healthy persons go about the world masking and avoiding aspects of the external reality. Think of food, again (not a Freudian example, by the way). A perfect steak may be brought to a dinner table, cooked to celebrate special occasions, become part of good family memories—only if people mask, much as we do with a kiss, aspects of the event; for instance, the fact that, objectively, it is a piece of a dead animal likely slaughtered by a system with no reverence for suffering. In contrast, a vegetarian who feels viscerally revolted by the idea of eating "a piece of a dead animal," does not see this event through these filters. He or she sees these layers of reality more directly and more literally. The old adage that applies now is that to enjoy a sausage, you must not peek into the sausage factory, as this literal blood bath would make the sausage inedible for most people. Importantly, this is not because you do not know how a sausage is made. You do. But, nevertheless, looking into the factory would make it difficult to remove this potentially disturbing aspect of reality from full conscious awareness and to consign it to lower levels of awareness so as to avoid the cognitive or affective conflict that the full conscious awareness would generate.

But yet again, this easy example is only the beginning of a larger and less obvious story. Let us add that Freud also helps us see the extent to which we avoid seeing *ourselves* directly and objectively.

Consider, first, the elemental aspects of our existence: the biological mechanics, the fluids, the organs, the buzzing bacterial cloud that pervades our system, the swarm of cells constantly dying and being born—think of "the human being under the skin," as German philosopher Friedrich Nietzsche would say. It is unpleasant, if not traumatizing, to see vivisections or examinations of cadavers, because, save physicians who train themselves to regard human corpses as "subjects," we are not at home in this layer of reality. We are threatened by it. Of course, we do know that this is an intrinsic aspect of our existence, just as we know the intrinsic aspects of a kiss or how a sausage is made. Yet, these uncanny aspects of our own nature must also be removed from full conscious awareness, protectively. It is not a coincidence that the word "person," which originated in the Latin *per-sonare*, literally means "to speak through a mask," the idea being that in the mirror we see a person in this sense: a mask that allows us to gain our familiar sense of self. If it is unpleasant to directly see the internal human organism, it would be distressing to directly observe our own internal system. This experience would disconnect us from our normal, familiar self-image, just as failing to filter the raw mechanics of a kiss would lead to an awkward disconnection that would destroy the constructed reality of the kiss. Hence, we tend to avoid this visceral aspect of our own corporeal reality, and we consign it to the unthought known; hence, we tend to construct a version of reality that includes our own "person." We construct our own mask to hide aspects of ourselves from our own selves.

We also tend to mask impulses and desires that are socially unacceptable or dangerous for us or for society if experienced and expressed directly. Animals experience and express aggressive or sexual impulses directly without masking them under a veneer of politeness or civility, but we have to filter such impulses, and mask them from our own selves as well. When these elemental impulses are committed to the unthought known, we don't experience them directly. But as also noted, they remain inhibited or latent within us, ready to pounce when the rules of civility, which require that we censor these impulses, break down. This happens during extreme social situations, such as war, a fight, a riot, a famine, a sexual encounter, for example. Or it can happen when our capacity for impulse control is inhibited; for instance, as a result of using alcohol or other drugs that inhibit impulse control, or during a dream, or when we "slip" (as in "a slip of the tongue"), or when we "lose control of ourselves": when we lose control over these otherwise inhibited, censored, arrested impulses.

For these reasons, the mechanisms that censor these egotistical impulses can be very helpful for us and for society. And, indeed, society is possible only inasmuch as these instincts and urges are inhibited, as this makes social coordination and unity possible. In agreement with Freud, Emile Durkheim (1995), the founder of the French sociological tradition, described human beings as bearers of two natures: *Homo sapiens* is also *"Homo duplex"*: We are the "dual man" or the dual creature, as Durkheim argued. One part of us is, precisely, impulsive, "lower," animalistic, and, in this sense, "presocial," not attuned to social norms that make societies possible. This is the part of our nature that, because it is animalistic and potentially disruptive and dangerous, must fall "under the empire of culture," Durkheim adds. Culture, that is to say, must install a self-judging, censoring, and, thus, norm-obeying part of our selves. He called this portion of our psychical apparatus "the higher pole of the self." This is the part of us that is attuned to social conventions and practices; it is the part of us that works to repress the instincts, whims, urges, or impulses that can threaten these practices, these rules of social life.

This higher pole, for Durkheim, as it inhibits the "lower pole," allows us to establish a social contract: It makes it possible for human groups to abide by more or less predictable norms and rules of social engagement; and it thus makes human societies possible. Hence, the cost of the human social contract, for Durkheim and for Freud, is repression. The cost of society is the inhibition of these presocial, and often antisocial, aspects inherent in our own nature. The cost of social life is hiding and disavowing an important part of our humanness. Again, to be a person is to wear a mask *even when dealing with our own selves*. Although this can be alienating (because we thus establish a distance from the deeper aspects of ourselves, from desires, impulses, needs), it can also be beneficial. A society in which people cannot rein in these impulses would be normless, unstable, chaotic. War, breaking the social contract, thus lifting otherwise needed social masks, unbridles these kinds of ferocious forces latent within the human spirit. War gives people permission to set their rancor and prejudices, their predatory instincts and their resentments loose—so that at war human beings may seem "inhuman" (invading armies are often described in this way). By having a lower degree of control over our own nature, we seem "animalistic," so people also often say that those who act cruelly and uncontrollably act "like animals." Not unusually, people think that war is about heroic and epic exploits (indeed, some Romantic artists and philosophers argued that war is the most genuine aesthetic experience). But war involves the collapse of culture, the collapse of the higher pole and, hence, the rule of instinct, the empire of the lower, animalistic pole.

To summarize this chapter thus far, Freud showed that human beings *spontaneously, instinctively* tend to avoid direct contact with this kind of internal and potentially injurious psychical reality. More generally, he also helped us see that we instinctively, and to an extent unconsciously, tend to replace portions of the broader reality with *versions* of it. Let us now add that he thus helped us understand why, for much of human history, we have been seduced by, and have often espoused, the strangest fantasies, even when they go headfirst against elemental reason and against reality itself. These include, for example, the notion that a suburban housewife was chosen by an alien civilization to save humanity, as we saw; or the notion the Prophet rode a horse to the moon to split it in half, as believed by some Muslims; or the idea that human beings are only two days older than the stars, as believed by some Christians; or the notion that Jews are contaminants, as believed by the Nazis, and so on. The idea is not that only the individual, isolated, replaces portions of reality but also that human societies in general tend to do that.

The Importance of Deception in Society

Irving Goffman, one of the most important sociologists of the 20th century, was the writer who first reminded us that the word "person" literally means "to speak through a mask." He was the first to argue that this is not just a strange coincidence but a recognition of the fact that a minimal amount of masking, *a minimal amount of deception and duplicity is indispensable for the human experience to be properly human.* Goffman has also shown that the social order is possible only inasmuch as people *continuously* hide not only raw impulses and emotions, as Freud argued, but also, depending on the occasion, some of their ideas and beliefs (that others reject), aspects of their character, parts of their bodies, natural functions—many and central aspects of who we are. Again, human beings typically encounter one another wearing a mask. For Goffman, this means that we generally present an idealized version of ourselves to others—a version that is appropriate for the situation that frames the encounter: a job interview, a first date, meeting someone for the first time, a class presentation, a party, a church service, etc. For Goffman, deception is a normal and, as we will soon see, a necessary aspect of social life.

To understand this idea, it is worth providing some background knowledge pertaining to the significance that deception has for social animals in general, humans included. Media researcher Pamela Meyer has studied the importance of lying in everyday life. And she has noted that average Americans face 10 to 200 lies each day (some of which are, of course, "white lies": "great sweater," "wonderful to meet you," etc.). Meyer shows that when meeting one another, strangers deploy an average of three lies within the first 10 minutes and that even married couples, on trend and save exceptions, lie to their spouses during *one of every 10 interactions*, sometimes "protectively" so as to not to inflict ego injuries on their partners: "nice haircut," "great meal," etc. As Meyer notes, although we are overtly against lying, covertly we rely, and must rely, on lying to function as normal social beings. Indeed, deception seems to be important for other social animals, as suggested, and might be an important aspect of sociality in general.

Consider Koko, the amazing gorilla who, trained to use a version of sign language, managed to develop a vocabulary more or less equivalent to that of a 2-year-old child. Koko adopted a kitten. And there are few things more charming than seeing a massive gorilla tenderly caring for a playful, blue-eyed kitten. One day, Koko got upset for some reason or another and, as Mayer also reports, expressed her anger by ripping off a sink from her enclosure and tossing it to the side. When confronted by her handler, Koko seemed regretful, even embarrassed. She hesitated. And then she explained, in sign language, what had happened: "The kitten did it." This was a lie; it was a candid camera moment, and it was also a significant scientific tip. Koko was seemingly able to lie spontaneously (no one had taught her to do so), which prompted scientists to wonder if lying might therefore be innate in social animals. Indeed, we do suspect that social animals in general need to deploy a minimal degree of deception to form social groups. Now, human beings are the most exquisitely social of all animals, and, perhaps for this reason, we have an exquisitely developed capacity for deception. Indeed, we are able to engage in deception even before we have the concept or the word for it. Consider, for example, the "fake cry" that young babies often deploy, even before, let me insist, being able to articulate the concept of deception. We are also able to lie to our own selves, as follows also from the discussion about Freud, which is seemingly a uniquely human trait that has huge implications for the human experience, as we will soon see.

Importantly, neither Meyer nor Goffman nor Freud nor Festinger are saying that we are all phonies. Of course, some people wear a cynical and purposefully deceptive mask: a con artist, a snobbish person, a corrupt politician, etc. But human beings, in general, wear a mask simply to have a normal, predictable, nonconflicting encounter with others. And sometimes this is the *morally correct* course of action. A doctor, for example, may be exhausted, ready to go home, and may thus not feel particularly concerned about the next patient's predicament. Yet she must, as professional duty demands, present an appropriate *version* of herself as a concerned and caring provider to contribute to her patient's well-being. Sometimes, wearing a mask is something we do on behalf of our fellow human beings.

Comedian Ricky Gervais has imagined a sort of anti-Goffmanian, utterly truthful and transparent world, where people always and inevitably show their true selves. This is a world where no one wears a mask, where no one knows how to deceive, or even what a lie is. This society, depicted in the film *The Invention of Lying*, is not a society of saints; it is a disaster, instead, and the everyday situations that people encounter are fodder for comedy. The movie's hero, for instance—a clumsy, plump, socially hesitant man played by Gervais himself— goes out on a blind date. As soon as his date spots him, she, a tall and beautiful woman, instantly tells him what she thinks: It is too late to regret having accepted going on a date with him, she announces, so in an effort to cut her losses, she will go with him to a restaurant to at least have free food and free drinks. Of course, having sex afterward is out of the question, she adds, as she is in no way attracted to such a man. To be sure, such comic situations could also be fodder for tragedy, as this or any utterly truthful world would be impossibly unpleasant and asphyxiating.

Naturally, we often drop the social mask when, for example, in the company of intimate friends, partners, or when alone, or when impulse control is inhibited (again, as a result of consuming alcohol, etc.). But even in these circumstances, there is usually a minimal and necessary amount of "impression management," as Goffman calls it, pertaining perhaps to bodily functions, socially unacceptable impulses or desires, etc.

Social Life as a Vast Theatrical Operation

Goffman has provided a masterful sociological narrative that helps us better see how society works and the important role that deception plays, and must play, in our private lives, in our communities, in the unfolding of history itself. Goffman has helped us see that social life has many things in common with the theater, as social life occurs mostly in what he calls frontstages (as opposed to backstages, as we will soon see). Frontstages, also called "front regions," are precisely those areas of everyday life where we tend to perform according to social rules or cues: for example, when dealing with customers, when in class, when first meeting an acquaintance or a date. On such occasions, our actions, our manners, what we tend to wear, what we tend to say and how we say it, become more or less scripted. These aspects of the presentation of the self are more or less coded and standardized so as to be socially and culturally acceptable. In frontstages, we tend to follow certain models of behavior that we have inherited from our culture and our traditions (as opposed to standards of behavior created by ourselves). And these models of behavior are transmitted through institutions, including those of the family, the educational system, or the media.

Note that these kinds of *scripted* behaviors do not question cultural norms and conventions, of course; on the contrary, they reaffirm and legitimize them. So as we go about the world performing these social roles, and acting according to convention, we thus contribute precisely to legitimize and reaffirm the meanings, values, and norms that are important in our culture. We thus enact and reproduce the values of tradition (and, in this sense, the imaginations and some of the values of the dead generations), and we thus generate a sense of continuity between the past and the present.

Such scripted and inherited models of behavior tend to govern not only how we act but also our very perception of the situation at hand. They provide guidelines for how we should think of, and approach, such situations as, for example, a class, a date, a party, a formal dinner, meeting a new acquittance, a doctor, or a boss. Thus the frontstage is, as in the theater, an area of performance, and for this reason, it is an area of concealment, because in these situations, we wear the appropriate masks: the appropriate manners, clothes, language that befit the various social *roles* that we semiconsciously play as we partake in social life. Performing these social roles can be very useful. First, they allow us to fit in. And they also protect us against the retributions and petty punishments that our communities deliver to infractors simply because communities expect that members comply with their norms and values, however arbitrary they might be. But frontstage behavior can be damaging to us as well. It can steal a measure of spontaneity and freedom from us. So that, to the extent to which our lives become primarily governed by "scripts" (i.e., by unexamined and taken-for-granted rules of conduct), we compromise our capacity to be true to our own selves. To the extent to which this happens, we thereby become mere extensions of a culture or tradition and lose the ability recognize the self as self in its own right. You might have come upon the following quote from Shakespeare's *As You Like It*:

> All the world's a stage
> And all the men and women merely players;
> They have their exits and their entrances;
> And one man in his time plays many parts.

If frontstage conventions overdetermine a person's everyday life, he or she may become "merely a player." This is a person who unthinkingly follows convention and the scripts of a culture: those of fashion, of peers, of a religion, of a social class, of a fraternity, cultural narratives about masculinity or femininity, etc. This is someone who unreflectively goes with the "entrances and exits" that convention imposes on him or her, someone who doesn't make the crucial decisions about his or her place in the world, who plays a secondary role in his or her own life. And this kind of existence may go on, as Shakespeare adds, until the day when the person finds him or herself playing the

> last scene of all,
> That ends this strange and eventful history,
> [The scene that] is second childishness and mere oblivion;
> Sans teeth, sans eyes, sans taste, sans everything.

The Backstages of Social Life

In contrast to the frontstage, in the backstages, we exclude ourselves from role-playing. Also as in the theater, in the backstages, we are, in a certain sense, more ourselves. Here we are more natural, less affected, less constrained by social expectations. Our behavior is less scripted and less coded because it is not under the scrutiny of others, of society. Examples of backstage situations include interactions with very intimate friends when we feel entirely free to be ourselves. (Not by coincidence, the words *friendship* and *freedom* have the same origin, the Old English word *freo*.) Other examples of backstage scenarios include coming out of some closet or, again, when we are by ourselves, or when we are, more generally, outside the range of the social gaze. Our backstage *persona* is precisely what we tend to mask, in different ways and degrees, in the frontstage—unconsciously, for the most part, without fully intending or strategizing our frontstage role. (And, of course, the behavior of some people is much more "backstaged" than others, much less concerned with performing according to social demands and conventions. And other people are much more "frontstaged," more overdetermined by social expectations.)

A backstage-oriented attitude can be good, precisely because it allows us to be our natural selves. A true friend is someone who doesn't elicit a frontstage performance from us, someone who allows us to be, precisely, our natural selves. But backstage behavior can be problematic as well. Not concerned with convention, it may limit our degree of social integration and social acceptance, because society generally rejects an unfiltered and entirely truthful presentation of the self. Consider the autistic spectrum. It is often difficult or even impossible for some persons within this spectrum to abide by societal conventions, which they see—correctly, as it turns out—as arbitrary. (Why, for example, on some occasions we must wear a tie, a knot on our neck, as convention demands? Why not wear another type of garment? There is no natural reason. This is merely cultural convention or script. It is, precisely, an arbitrary cultural rule.) For this reason, persons within this spectrum often dismiss cultural norms. They may regard them as not binding, or they may indeed reject them as absurd. And it is therefore difficult for them to cultivate "a front," in Goffmanian terms, which involves, precisely, the enactment of convention. The behavior of these persons tends to be backstaged when the occasion requires that it be frontstaged. Hence their predicament, which may be expressed as the strange *ability to see* the arbitrary and often absurd nature of social conventions and prescriptions or, in Goffmanian terms, of cultural scripts. Scripts that "normal" folks tend to unreflectively accept, because it is generally very difficult for us to see the arbitrary or even the absurd aspects of convention, the already scripted and ritualized nature of many of our behaviors. And yet this relative blindness to the arbitrary and scripted aspects of social life, which makes it easier for us to follow arbitrary conventions, also makes it easier for us to fit in and to partake in communal life, something that is generally difficult for individuals within the autistic spectrum.

"The Me" and "The I"

George Herbert Mead, an early 20th-century scholar who provided the basis for Goffman's theory, can help us amplify and conclude the foregoing discussion about the theatrical aspects inherent to social life. (And brace yourself: Mead was a sociologist, a social psychologist, and a philosopher of the first order, and some of his ideas require that we leave aside presuppositions about ourselves.)

Mead argued that the self hosts two psychical structures or "phases of the self," which he called "the me" and "the I." If we were to trace the origin of the "me" first, it would ultimately stem from our need to be accepted by some sort of group: by a family, by community, by a clan. The "me" stems from a deep-seated need to satisfy our social instinct—an instinct that is critical for the survival of any social animal, as these animals are not designed to survive by themselves and are therefore instinctually driven, precisely, to form part of a group. The "me," Mead implied, is the part of human psychology that is attuned to social norms and traditions, because inasmuch as we comply with these social expectations, we can be allowed in the group that abides by them, and we may, therefore, satisfy our hardwired need to belong to something bigger than ourselves, again, a tribe, a nation, a clan, a group of peers. The "me" is the part of our psychological structure that helps us gain a sense of membership in these kinds of social groups and in society in general.

This morning, you got ready to face the world, perhaps took a shower, perhaps applied gel or makeup, chose clothes that were at least minimally appropriate for appearing in public, and, when in public, you behaved in a way that was also at least minimally attuned to the rules that govern social life. Socially, this can be defined as a backstage event (before your appearance in public) in preparation for the frontstage (public life). Psychologically, this was a preparation to enter into a "me" phase, to turn on the socially abiding "me" that is elicited by frontstages. The "me" is the part of us that is attuned to, and in synchrony with, the expectations of others. (Going beyond Mead's theory, let us add that the "me" is the aspect of human psychology that is typically compromised in persons within the autistic spectrum—persons that, for the reasons expressed earlier, have to formally learn, often with great difficulty, at least the broad mechanics of regular social interactions; they have to learn the social mechanics that for "normal" folks emerge naturally, as the expected result of their process of socialization. Autistic persons who have to be taught how to navigate social interactions often end up managing a rigid, mechanical, and monotonous interactive style, which in "normal" folks is fluid and not exempt, sometimes, of what we call "gracefulness": gracefulness involving not only saying the right and polite stock phrases that are socially expected, but also deploying a bodily language that fluently and half-consciously enacts the traditional norms of civility.)

The "me," in summary, is the part of you that is elicited by the nature of the social world. Its marching orders are given by the norms and expectations that govern normal social interactions.

But, importantly, the "me" is never fully conscious of its behavior or what ultimately motivates it. This morning, as you were getting ready to face the frontstages of the immediate world, you were not telling yourself, "I'm doing this mostly to comply with the roles and requirements of a cultural tradition assigned to me at birth," something that an autistic person might need to be explicitly told. It is difficult for us to be fully aware of the extent to which our actions are indeed governed by a constellation of inherited norms—norms that whir with life, particularly when we interact with others in frontstage situations. Norms that regulate, and that have always regulated, how we act, including what we are likely to say to others, what we do not say, how we generally dress, how we tend to greet and eat, our gestures, including linguistic gestures, voice modulation—our frontstage persona in summary. Norms that hence regulate *how* we are when in public and *what* we become as a result of growing up partaking from a certain tradition or normative order. Bear in mind that all human beings are, and have to be, socialized to function in their culture and that this involves a sort of daily training that helps us recognize, accept, and deploy cultural norms, normally, naturally, and without being fully aware that we are enacting and deploying these norms. Norms that we tend to internalize and that, to the extent to which they thus become second nature to us, also become part and parcel of what we are.

It is only upon reflection, only to the extent to which we draw our conscious attention to our behavior, that we may have more control over the norms that tend to govern the way we act. It is only to the extent to which we stop to see ourselves as though from an outsider perspective—in the act of enacting a social role—that we may thereby control the process that molds our social persona and aspects of our familiar sense of self. For Mead, your familiar sense of self was not simply given at birth. It has been largely acquired within a cultural context. But the self can also be achieved or accomplished, and it can be a personal accomplishment, perhaps the most significant accomplishment of one's life, derived particularly from self-reflection, from the ability to think about how and why culture molds our behavior and our persona. The word "radical" comes from the Latin *radice,* "root," and *a radical* is simply a person who goes to the root of things. The act of objectively contemplating our own behavior provides a radical perspective for us, as this allows us to see the cultural roots of this important phase of ourselves, the "me."

This external and self-objectivizing vantage point is the perspective of the "I." Whereas the "me" is the immediate, unreflective, automatic experience of being in the world, the "I" is our capacity to reflect about this experience. Save the backstages of social life, we go about the social world in a rather performative "me" mode. But if and when we stop and ask ourselves *"why do I abide by these standards of conduct and not by some other ones? Or why do I behave according to these familiar ideas and not others?"* we then switch to an "I" mode. We hence become aware of the roles we play. We are now curious about the social scripts assigned to us. Who wrote them? Why? To borrow again from Goffman, we thus become aware of the masks that characterize our "person" (remember: from the Latin *per* and *sonare,* person means "speaking through a mask")—masks that otherwise are not evident to us at all.

The "I" is thus the part of us that does not wear this mask of social acceptability. The "I" is less determined by, and less concerned with, social convention. The "I" is less scripted and more spontaneous. And it can give way to more instinctive, more visceral, less predictable, but also less civil, reactions. The "I" can break through the veneer of norms and civility and disrupt the normality of social interactions. It is "the response of the organism [itself] to the attitudes of the others," Mead says (1934). And in this particular sense, it is also the part of us that is freer: freer than the "me," precisely because the "I" is not constrained by prescriptions or by norms or by expectations or traditions.

A Balanced Self and a Balanced Society

Psychological health, Mead implies, involves a sense of balance between these phases, the "me" and the "I." When this balance is achieved, we are able to be ourselves, we are able to act spontaneously and in this sense freely. The "I" is active in this situation. We can reflect about our role in the world. We are able to put distance between ourselves and the roles assigned to us. But the socially inclined "me" is also active, balancing out the activity of the impulsive "I." And thanks to the activity of the "me," we are also inserted within our group, within our culture, as citizens who are willing to abide by norms and customs, as long as these do not demand that we entirely censor our more impulsive, spontaneous, and freer part of ourselves, the "I." In contrast to this healthy self, the unbalanced self is overdetermined either by the "me" or by the "I." When the "me" comes to dominate the way we think and relate to the world, our attitudes and dispositions become overly scripted. We become, in a sense, "tools" of a culture, of a group, of a tribe, of a fraternity, of the current narrative about our gender, about sexuality, about success, etc. We unreflectively enact the related scripts. On the other hand, when the "I" dominates, we become socially irresponsive, perhaps childishly egotistical, either annoying to others, or problematic, or detrimental to social harmony or even a menace to the social order.

Similarly, regarding society itself, a healthy society is likewise balanced, Mead would argue. This kind of good society allows for spontaneous, I-oriented self-expression. It allows us, even encourages us, to ask, "Why is it that I have to think and behave according to this set of prescriptions and not others?" And yet this society also provides clear norms and prescriptions for us to internalize and to adopt as our own self-regulating, self-guiding principles of conduct. A democracy has the tools to become this kind of healthy social system. A true democracy allows the individual to express himself or herself, for example, by guaranteeing freedom of thought and expression so that, say, non-normative sexual or religious identities may be freely expressed. This kind of political system also allows people to interrogate their own behavior, as well as the cultural norms and traditions that underpin it. And yet a democracy does not encourage unregulated and anarchic expressions of individual wants and desires. Instead, it clearly defines social obligations. It tells us that we are free, but not free to the point of disregarding the welfare of others, and it therefore expects adherence to rules and conventions that guarantee a normal social interaction and a balanced and predictable "social contract."

In contrast, a fundamentalist society—which by definition revolves around fundamentally abiding codes of conduct—does not allow for the spontaneous expression of the "I." It does not allow for the expression of the innermost and freest inclinations and questions of the individual. A fundamentalist society strives to prevent an individual from questioning his or her "normal" behaviors, his or her "normal" persona, or his or her "normal" roles in life. This kind of society caters, above all, to the "me," the socially abiding part of the self, and represses the more spontaneous and freer "I." This kind of system is thus overly repressive. It is unbalanced, unfree, and, in this sense, unhealthy. George Orwell's famous novel *1984* opened a window into the most extremely repressive social order, where the "thought police" were charged with eliminating every trace of individuality and spontaneity in everyone. This was a regime that—bent on eliminating the "I" and thus bent on transforming the person into a vacant mask, a completely socially abiding "me"—is the most pathological imaginable. Save exceptions investigated by the thought police, all other "brothers and sisters" in this pathological society were entirely unable to question the roots of their ideas, the roots of their beliefs, the roots of their behaviors and of their personas, or why they thought in certain ways and not others, why they acted according to some standards and not others.

CHAPTER V

Engineering Reality

As follows from the previous chapters, social life has, must have, and has always had, hidden layers of meaning. In some ways, this is useful and desirable, and to be sure, social life is viable *only* when aided by a minimal measure of concealment, deception, and, indeed, lying. In this sense, our everyday perception of reality is, in various ways and degrees, socially *constructed* and thus includes a measure of deception and, as Freud would argue, of fantasy. This means that we don't always perceive reality itself, but a version of reality that simply works well enough for us—a version that is typically conveyed by a tradition, by inherited and socially relevant narratives. Such a version of reality is not created by anyone in particular. It is the more or less spontaneous creation of our culture, of the collective imagination, present and past.

But, as we will see next, sometimes aspects of reality become concealed not spontaneously but intentionally, methodically, and systematically, not for good reasons but for dubious reasons. In this chapter, we will try to answer the following questions: Can the public perception of reality be at least partially constructed so as to fulfill the interests of groups, of a government, of a dictatorship, of a religious sect, of the market, etc.? If so, to what extent and with what consequences for individuals and for society? Can your own perception of reality be engineered? If so, to what extent has it already been engineered?

Capitalism: "A Gift from God"

A glimpse at the dominant economic system in the world, free markets, will help us answer some of these questions. Let us begin by outlining the logic and the philosophy underpinning this kind of economic model, focusing on the work of the father of the idea, 18th-century Scottish economist and philosopher Adam Smith.

Think of, say, an 18th-century shoemaker, the sort of worker who would be a familiar figure to Adam Smith. If our shoemaker is the only one in town, chances are his shoes will not be the best they can be, because they only need to be good enough to be bought by potential customers who, after all, don't have other options. And so, as long as he is the only one in town, our shoemaker lives without worrying too much about his income or the quality of his shoes. But one day, a second shoemaker sets up shop. Our first guy now has a reason to worry, because if he doesn't improve the quality and the prices of his product, shoppers will go to Second Guy. Thus, as if by magic, the quality of our guy's products begins to improve while his prices remain affordable, simply because he needs his job and therefore needs to be competitive. Hence, Adam Smith argued, *as these conditions of competition arise*, the self-interest of First Guy ends up benefiting not only him but also society as a whole. Folks in town now have access to better shoes at affordable prices. To insist: Although First Guy is *not* in business for the sake of his fellow human beings, his self-interested activities will, nevertheless, benefit his fellow human beings. Smith said, "It is not from the benevolence of the butcher, the brewer, or the baker that we expect our dinner, but from their regard to their own self-interest" (1994, p. 15).

The bigger idea is that a system of free and fair competition, full of people who are pursuing, above all, their self-interests, will end up contributing to society in general. Smith claims that that self-interest, and in this sense selfishness, can, under these conditions of fair competition, become "a gift from God." Note as well that, beyond products and prices, our shoemakers will also demand better technology, say, better hammers, nails, and so on, in order to make better shoes. And again, the larger point is that a free market needs, demands, and achieves technological progress. So a society that embraces this kind of economic system will also be interested in science, which is necessary for technological advancement. This society will, therefore, demand better research, better education, will likely have better schools, and will, in the end, foster human ingenuity and imagination. For Smith, therefore, capitalism is not only an economic model that creates wealth. In addition, it can also improve the human spirit itself. For this to happen, a society needs to understand and embrace the truest principles of this mode of production.

Adam Smith was not a monger of ruthless capitalism as his detractors generally tell us. He thought of himself as, above all, a humanist, someone concerned with the advancement of the human spirit, and in this sense, he was of the same ilk as poets, philosophers, composers, and artists. His contemporaries generally saw him in this light as well. (And they also saw him as the quintessentially well-mannered, rather shy, wise, and absent-minded professor.)

Importantly, Smith was speaking on behalf of a despised group, merchants, who were often regarded as contemptible and inferior by the still dominant, and often ruthless, land-owning aristocrats. Against this grain, Smith was arguing that this despised class of individuals was destined, in the end, to serve the interest of humanity itself. This was neither because of their intrinsic humanism, nor because they were learned and sensible academics or politicians, but because the economic system they were half-consciously creating was destined to mine the egotism and selfishness of society—in order to feed the rise of the human spirit. Smith also wanted his contemporaries to see and begin to appreciate the new "virtues" that these despised merchants were developing, particularly their audacity, their willingness to embrace risk. In contrast, he said, the supposedly superior aristocrats, who were a little too tied to the land and to the centuries-old narratives and myths about their superiority, had thus developed an aversion to change, to innovation, and to progress. They were dinosaurs. And they were frivolous. They were far more likely to spend their money on nonproductive and sumptuary things like gold and ornaments—the kind of commerce that benefited them and their egos but not society as a whole. They were not invested in the welfare of society.

Hence the *new* individuals, the risk-taking and audacious merchants, were right in claiming, against the interests of the oldish and rancid aristocrats, their central role in the business of conducting the affairs of society. This, to be sure, was a radical idea.

Indeed, our shy and absent-minded humanist was a radical in many other important ways. Siding scandalously with David Hume, the Atheist with a capital A and 18th-century version of a rockstar philosopher, Smith became a bit of a scandal himself, nonchalantly ruffling all the feathers of the dominant classes. Publishing Hume's posthumous work, with an added critique of his own pertaining to religious institutions, including Oxford University itself, Smith also showed, unwantedly, that he was not one to be cowed into submission by mere condemnation or scandal. He was shy in person only. In print he was bold, audacious, and not above taking personal risks. He was thus a sort of merchant for the new and, as he saw it, emerging economic humanism—namely, capitalism.

His theory is, of course, far more complex than the previous couple of pages can possibly convey. Smith might have devoted several pages, for example, to discussing the role of international tariffs and yet another couple of pages to discussing whether there are more or less drunkards in wine-producing countries, such as Italy, France, and Spain, and why, or he would discuss the benefits of these or other specific taxation practices, etc. And I am providing only the most basic and the broad aspects of his polemic. Yet these basic aspects should be enough to see that the main predictions of his theory turned out to be true. We will discuss the risks and problems of capitalism soon. But let us presently underscore that this system can and did improve aspects of life, as Smith had accurately predicted. Free markets have been very good at amplifying job opportunities, creating economic growth (even if skewed toward wealthier individuals), and motivating the development of science, technology, and, in this particular sense, amplifying the human imagination. We may plausibly argue that the process of industrialization, in fact, has resulted in improvements in aspects of human nature itself. Industrialized and capitalistic societies have, for example, seen steady and massive gains in health, longevity, and, indeed, gains in aspects of intelligence as measured by IQ testing, particularly related to people's ability to think abstractly, partly because the market has generated technologies that force more abstract thinking (e.g., digital media). The process of industrialization has also resulted in unprecedented improvements in various other areas of life: It has increased literacy; it has amplified transportation and communication systems around the world. Together with the ideas and methods of the Enlightenment, industrialization has also contributed to extending the human lifespan; it has encouraged medical advancements, and it has thereby helped to conjure away much of the pain and fear that constantly haunted human beings in previous eras.

In part, these have been the intended goals embraced by the heirs of the Enlightenment but, on the other hand, these have also been the unintended consequences of the egotistical search for profit that Smith presciently described.

"Dark, Satanic Mills"

Yet as bold and smart as he was, Adam Smith was nevertheless unable to see other and potentially problematic, if not immoral, facets of capitalism, which are important to point out to provide a full view.

Initially, the factory system that Smith analyzed was almost entirely unregulated. Virtually no laws governed work in the emerging system, and it is indeed difficult for us to understand or even imagine the everyday lives of workers under it. If you find a job today, you expect as a matter of course that laws and regulations will guarantee your rights as a worker, sanitary conditions, minimal wages, safety standards, number of hours of work per day, and so on. Your employer may fail to meet these minimum requirements, but you have legal recourses that allow you to defend your taken-for-granted rights. In an unregulated system, in contrast, you don't have these recourses because the system is not governed by the same laws. And hence your choices under such a system are (a) not taking these jobs, which, however, is only a choice in theory because in practice you need to eat, or (b) accepting a you-have-virtually-no-rights deal, the only real choice for most workers.

The audacious merchants that Smith describes were, in general and save exceptions, exploitative and ruthless as well. They filled their textile factories, their mills, and their coal mines with children as young as 5 years of age. In fact, children were often the preferred workers because they were more easily beaten into submission, literally so. A rather common managerial practice consisted of beating the child who finished his or her task last to motivate him or her to work as fast as possible. Not uncommonly, children worked in conditions of semislavery, and, indeed, the practice of forcing orphans into "internships" meant that these children, who were taken from orphanages to factories literally by the cartful, had to live in factory barracks. It meant that they were often worked from five in the morning to nine at night, with no benefits and no safety standards, and that they could get paid with food only (they were generally paid with the "knowledge" that they supposedly obtained from their "internships," as the hypocritical defenders of this system argued). These children were often referred to as "white slaves," because their masters virtually owned their time and their labor, and because, like slaves, they had no legal recourse against any of these miserable conditions of existence.

When this kind of brutality against workers, children and adults, began to enrage the general public, the House of Commons of the English Parliament began to make inquiries and to interview both the captains of industry and the workers to assess the situation. Elizabeth Bentley was one of these workers. Here is her testimony:

What age are you?
–Elizabeth: 23.
Where to you live?
–Leeds.
What time did you begin work at the factory?
–When I was six years old.
At whose factory did you work?
–Mr. Busk's.
What kind of mill is it?
–Flax-mill.
What was your business in that mill?
–I was a little doffer.
What were your hours of labor in that mill?
–From 5 in the morning until 9 at night, when they were thronged
For how long a time together have you worked that excessive length of time?
–For about half a year.
What were your usual hours when you were not thronged?
–From 6 in the morning till 7 at night.
What time were you allowed for meals?
–40 minutes at noon.
Had you any time to get your breakfast or drinking?
–No, we got it as we could.
And when your work was bad, you had hardly any time to eat it at all?

–No; we were obliged to leave it or take it home, and when we did not take it, the overlooker took it, and gave it to the pigs.
Do you consider doffing a laborious employment?
Yes. [...]
Does [it] keep you constantly on your feet?
–Yes, there are so many frames and they run so quick.
Your labor is very excessive?
–Yes, you have no time for anything
Supposed you flagged a little, or were late, what would they do?
–Strap us.
Constantly?
–Yes.
Girls and boys?
–Yes.
Have you ever been strapped?
–Yes.
Severely?
–Yes.
Could you eat your food well in that factory?
–No, indeed I had not much to eat, and the little I had could not eat it, my appetite was so poor, and being covered with dust; and it was no use to take it home, I could not eat it, and the overlooker took it and gave it to the pigs.

(In Miles-Morillo and Morillo, 2013)

All this for a penny an hour. The interview continues; the life of 18th-century workers continues as well, but we may only summarize it as generally dismal, as warped by an abusive system. English poet William Blake, perhaps the most important of all Romantic poets, described these mills as "satanic." The self-interest of these captains of industry was not a "gift from God" as far as Blake was concerned. Many of the audacious merchants that Smith extolled were also creeps who took advantage of children who, like Elizabeth Bentley, could not possibly defend themselves.

Karl Marx

Marx was another revered, as well as despised, 19th-century figure, a man who pioneered some of the ideas that dominated the 20th century, a theorist who got some things right while also making some egregious mistakes. Perhaps more clearly than anyone else, Blake included, he saw the problems of the economic system that Smith had so lavishly eulogized and provided a partly useful perspective that we must now consider.

But let us begin with a couple of facts about Marx's life, which will help us understand his worldview and theories. He came from a relatively wealthy family who had converted from Judaism to Protestantism, not out of religious conviction, necessarily, but particularly because being a Jewish person in 19th-century Europe made life harder for you (you could not marry freely; your academic and economic prospects were curtailed; your social life was limited). The conversion to the Protestant faith worked well for the Marxes. They prospered. And young Karl, like many of the educated and well-off kids of his generation, in fact, grew up nourishing grand aspirations, indeed, the idea that he had some role to play in the world at large (an impulse, incidentally, that was rather common in the more chivalrous 19th century, particularly among the well-off, and that has virtually disappeared from our mainstream and entertainment-oriented worldviews today).

Although the Marxes were not particularly devout Protestants, it is nevertheless clear that the adolescent Karl had a sense of Christian devotion, a curious beginning for a man who would become one the most formidable enemies of the institutions of Christianity. In particular, the younger Marx believed that sacrificing one's life on behalf of others was the heart and soul of the Christian doctrine, and so he thought as a young man that a desirable and proper fate involved both grand ambitions and a grand sacrifice.

Thus life went on for the young Marx. As a grown man, he got accepted into the University of Bonn, and then to the prestigious University of Berlin, which offered him a constellation of the greatest European intellectuals of the time; it was a place that forever transformed him. This was the school that set him onto a path that fulfilled his grand ambitions and grand notions of personal sacrifice—a process that ended up having very profound consequences, for better and for worse, for the entire world, for the entire 20th century. In the end, Marx indeed ended up sacrificing his advantageous social position (and eventually the social position that would otherwise have befallen his family) and traversed the world as a critic and eventually the most important enemy, of capitalism. Like the Romantic poet, William Blake, Marx also denounced this system as exploitative (it "oozes blood from every pore," he said). But rather than describing it poetically, he constructed a theory that, drawing from economics, philosophy, history, and sociology, questioned the foundations of this system—a theory that was entirely against that provided by Smith and that in the end marked lives of about one-third of *the world population* profoundly, as it provided the foundation for Marxist countries the world over, including China and Russia, a theory for which millions of men and women, deluded and lucid, sacrificed their lives.

Let us discuss some of the main features of this world-changing sociological perspective. Marx asserted that capitalism, because it generated unprecedented concentrations of wealth, also generated its own internal contradictions; for such a society, where the majority were exploited, would not forever sit on the sides of history to witness its own exploitation passively. Hence, Marx argued, this kind of economic model was destined to implode eventually, to destroy itself, because these masses of exploited workers that the system itself generated would eventually realize the fact of their oppression, would rebel, and would lead an epic battle to destroy this system. In this, Marx was utterly mistaken. Capitalism obviously never imploded. It is here to stay, for better or for worse. As Commentator Slavoj Zizek has noted, it is in fact easier for us to imagine life on Mars than life on Earth without capitalism.

Marx also thought that the alternative to capitalism was an economic system that, in essence, gave control of the entire apparatus of production to the workers themselves. The revolution of the workers outlined earlier would result in their taking over the control of the means of production, farms, factories, businesses. But this process, Marx thought, necessitated a first step, a transitional historical stage—namely, the transference of all economic assets, factories, farms, etc., to the state. The idea was that the state bureaucracy would become a sort of regent of the workers for a while, stabilize the apparatus of production, train workers to lead society, and then hand over the management of the means of production to the workers themselves. Hence, the state would create the conditions under which workers would become the rightful owners of all productive forces. This would be a sort of economy of the people, for the people, and by the people. In this, Marx was dreadfully wrong as well. The countries that have tried to move forward in this way, Russia and China, for example, have generally run into unsurmountable obstacles, have become economically unsustainable, and have turned to some version of capitalism. China, in particular, gave up this Marxist economic model to wholeheartedly embrace a particularly savage, all-out version of capitalism. And the Chinese state bureaucracy, rather than creating a transition into a worker-run economy and society, became a rigid autocracy that arrogated for itself the right to run the country and to minutely and often despotically control the lives of individual citizens.

Let us underscore as well that Marxist countries, such as the former Soviet Union and, today, North Korea, saw a rapid descent into barbarism, into state-sponsored brutality. They became utterly neglectful of even the most minimal version of human rights. And, in this sense, life in these countries became, all things considered, even worse than life under the ruthless exploitative system perpetrated by the "audacious" and sometimes "satanic" captains of industry that Smith and Blake, respectively, described. Recall once again that, under Stalin, in the Soviet Union, about 9.5 million men and women, many of whom were either peasants or workers, were murdered by the regime. And I have already described the North Korean government, the last Stalinist government in the world, as brutal, preposterous, impoverished, barbaric, and utterly unfree—a regime that, as reported by the United Nations 2014 Commission of Inquiry on Human Rights in North Korea, engages in systematic and widespread crimes against humanity, including murder, imprisonment, enslavement, torture, forced abortion, and rape, perpetrated particularly against persons in detention centers.

Yet these have been failures of Marxists regimes, not necessarily failures of Marx's theory. He, in any case, never advocated for the sort of terroristic regimes dreamt by people like Stalin. For instance, although Stalin was responsible for genocide, Marx was against the death penalty (in times of peace; his revolutionary program embraced violence, of course). If it is important to recognize the mistakes in his theory, as we have done, it is also important not to confuse the theory with the various applications of it, by various and sometimes genocidal groups. Marx was not a Marxist.

Alienation

On the other hand, it is also critical to see that Marx also got some things right. In particular, he provided a social-psychological theory about capitalism that has resisted the test of time and that can help us see the dangers within capitalism today, a mode of production that, as also noted, dominates almost the entire planet and that could, therefore, if unchecked, jeopardize the lives of people the world over.

Let us go back to Elizabeth Bentley. How would you be if you changed places with her at birth? How would you yourself be if, instead of going to kindergarten and to school, for example, you would have been forced to work at the mill where she spent most of her life? Let us consider, first, the obvious differences between you and this changeling you. This changeling would not have had even the basic education that you have already obtained. She would have had a radically different understanding of life and the world: that of someone who, beyond having no education, never had any opportunities either, including the opportunity to make choices about her own existence and her own worldview. Your childhood, adolescence, and adulthood would have been radically different. Your emotional style would have been different as well. As a matter of survival, you would have had to be at least more stoic and resigned, for example, if not depressed, and you would be less at home with sentiments of trust in, and love for, the world. You would be physically different. You would likely be shorter. Your chronically undernourished body would be adapted to, molded by, the routine of, and the automation inherent to, the factory. William Blake tried to see the world through the eyes of children like Elizabeth, and he described the vision thusly: These mills, these factories, these mines were taking "my infinite brain," he said (infinite in that a human brain has infinite possibilities of thought) and "enclosing into a narrow circle." Your changeling brain would have likewise grown enclosed into a narrow circle so that its "infinite" possibilities would have been reduced to those few that aligned with the needs of the factory system.

Again, it is obvious that you-as-Elizabeth would not be entirely you. Less obviously, the only question that remains is whether you would be in fact so different as to make it impossible to still speak of *you*. How much could we change about, and remove from, you without also removing your familiar sense of self? It could be argued that your familiar sense of self could have been taken away by an abusive and obviously exploitative factory system. At the very least, this system would have seized not only your time and labor but also your potential and, in this sense, your fate. Marx argued that, beyond economic exploitation, the deeper problem with the then emerging form of capitalism was that this system was designed, precisely, to take away not only the time and labor of workers like Elizabeth but also their spirit. What he saw in this early version of capitalism was a kind of body-snatcher situation (obviously not Marx's words): a system that, precisely, feeds from the human spirit. Marx thus argued that capitalism is fundamentally alienating. The you-as-Elizabeth example suggests that capitalism would have alienated you from your very own self, that this system would have removed you, estranged you from your truer self. Elizabeth never realizes her potential. She could have been a doctor, a painter, a physicist, but the factory system took away these possible fates, and she was therefore fated to never become acquainted with her truer self.

But let us not simply trust Marx. Instead, let us see what the captains of industry themselves, and their allies, were telling the English parliamentarians who also interviewed them along with the workers. One Andrew Ure argued,

> The main difficulty lay [...] above all in training human beings to renounce their desultory habit of work and to identify themselves with the unswerving regularity of complex automation [...] Even at the present day, when the system is perfectly

organized, and its labor lightened to the utmost, it is found nearly impossible to convert persons past the age of puberty into useful factory hands. (In Lazonick, 1990)

It is easy to read in this paragraph, as Marx did, that these defenders of capitalism did not see workers like Elizabeth as persons—persons with this or that potential, talent, or dream. Folks like Andrew Ure were explicit about their objectives: They wanted to take a worker like Elizabeth—before puberty, before she had had a chance of developing a mind of her own—and "convert" her into an effective piece of machinery, one that identifies with the "unswerving regularity of complex automation." Marx, therefore, argued that this system regarded workers as means, not as ends in themselves. He argued that this system expected that *life itself* would cater above all to the system's needs, not to its own needs, which are the needs of the human spirit. And Marx finally implied, more abstractly and lastingly, that *the way a society designs its economy will affect the ways in which regular people think, feel, daydream, and desire, as well as their identities and self-regard*. So changes in the economic model, Marx also thought, can change these aspects of the collective spirit, weakening or strengthening them, weakening or strengthening us.

For Marx, the historical development of the human spirit, thus defined, therefore depends to a large extent on the decisions that we as a society make about the economy. The way we design an economic model, the ways we regulate it or not, how we guide economic production and distribution will guide the history of the human spirit. This is one of Marx's enduring insights. And it is one the most important ones for our day and age, as we will presently discuss.

Engineering Desires

For Marx, your desires, aspirations, ideals—if emerging through a capitalistic economic model—will tend to reflect *not* only your particular needs and reflections but also impersonal systemic needs. Needs that, in the last account, boil down to the interests of the owners of the means of production. Let me insist: Marx wanted us to see that the fuel for the growth of this emergent economic system was the human spirit itself, your spirit included. Which is a big claim. So big, indeed, that it may seem exaggerated and may, therefore, necessitate a closer analysis. To begin this analysis, let us first go back to the defenders of capitalism to see what these theorists themselves have to say about the relation between (modern) capitalism and human psychology. Let us consider, in particular, the theories of one of the most ardent and influential advocates for this mode of economic production, a man who in fact provided the necessary theoretical conditions for the global spread of capitalism today.

Edward Bernays was the founding father of marketing and "public relations" (PR) (i.e., political and commercial propaganda) and one of theorists who helped expand the free-market model particularly during the second half of the 20th century (although he established this new, in the end triumphant, discipline in the 1920s). He was Sigmund Freud's nephew. And he knew that, as Uncle Sigmund had shown, human beings tend to replace aspects of reality with fictional accounts of reality. He knew that we spontaneously consign some desires and impulses to the unconscious, and that we thus hide these impulses from others and, again, from ourselves—indeed, particularly from ourselves. He knew, furthermore, that these impulses do not, for this reason, disappear, that they remain within us, motivating some of our behaviors, without our knowledge or control. He knew that normal human beings are often motivated by forces that, in this sense, operate behind their backs. Bernays knew as well that these hidden impulses remain latent under the socially acceptable mask, the mask of civility, that we all have to wear to make society possible.

But he went far beyond the theories propounded by his uncle. His big breakthrough—and the idea that set modern marketing in motion—was that marketers could perhaps manipulate this hidden reservoir of unconscious desires, these hidden pressures within us that motivate many of our behaviors. Perhaps, Bernays thought, captains of industry may be able to control and direct such latent motivations. Perhaps they may be able to use these hidden motivations to spur consumers into buying products. Perhaps they may be able to have at least some control over the ways we perceive reality. Could marketers, he wondered, "engineer" the very desires, and thus the actions, of consumers? Could marketers thus control at least some aspects of our behavior? This would be great, he thought, because then industries would be able to have better control over the purchasing behaviors of their customers and thus sell their products more effectively. Could marketers manipulate, at least to an extent, how *you* think, what you want, how you prioritize your life? If so, with what consequences for you and for society as a whole?

It was the 1920s, and captains of industry were only beginning to realize that people, as Freud was arguing, had powerful drives that escape their own conscious knowledge or control. Prior to the Freudian revolution, old-school marketers were in the business of addressing the consumers' *conscious needs* and *conscious, rational motives*. These marketers generally highlighted the actual *reasons* why you would want to buy their product. They appealed to your capacity to reason about the pros and cons of their goods. But after this Freudian-Bernaysian revolution, commercial propaganda, guided now by Bernays, began to target *not* people's ability to reason, but primarily their emotions, including latent negative emotions: fears, envies, deficits—the irrational, potentially threatening, and unconscious portions of the psychical apparatus.

"Engineers of Souls"

Perhaps the most famous example of Bernays' new approach involved the tobacco industry, which hired him to extend the tobacco market to women, who were generally not smoking, largely because smoking was seen as unfeminine and thus as undesirable. But before discussing Bernays' groundbreaking marketing strategy, let us first recall that the 1920s saw the rise of the first wave of feminism in the United States, a movement that fought for equal civil rights for women, such as the elemental right to vote. And women, influenced by this political movement, had become keenly cognizant of the fact that they were literally disenfranchised and clearly deprived of power in general. Clever Bernays capitalized on this newfound hunger for freedom and power among women. And his marketing campaign centered on the idea that this cultural taboo against smoking was yet another patriarchal ploy against women. He campaigned the notion that cigarettes were "torches of freedom," symbols of women's independence so that not smoking meant, for women, depriving themselves of their freedom to choose any lifestyle they wanted.

In the end, Bernays was unambiguously successful, and the happy tobacco industry managed, as they wanted, to amplify their market to the other half of the public: women.

Of course, tobacco is not really able to give you a lot of freedom and independence. First, it is an addictive drug, and addiction is not exactly equal to freedom, and, second, if smoking gives you cancer, and chances of this outcome are high among smokers, it will take away even your freedom to breathe. The notion that smoking will amplify your freedom makes no sense. It is darkly ironic. It presupposes that the targeted audience comprises at least a minimum number of suckers. But what Bernays discovered was, precisely, that marketing campaigns could be irrational, even wildly ludicrous, while also being wildly successful. He discovered that the public could be easily taken for a ride and that it all depended on applying basic scientific principles, particularly those of psychology, to bypass the customer's rational defenses. This customer, Bernays soundly demonstrated, could be easily nudged not only into happily buying things that he or she didn't need but also things that were harmful for him or her.

The idea that Bernays bequeathed to modern marketers, and to many contemporary politicians, is that it is not only okay to strive to manipulate "the masses" (*us*), deploying, for this purpose, the most advanced psychological techniques, the most advance behavior-modification protocols. He argued—unintentionally reminding us of Marx's critique of capitalism—that manipulation is in fact *necessary* in any free-market society. Indeed, he implied that it was necessary because "the masses," to begin with, were generally too uniformed and in fact too stupid to be able to decide—*or even desire* for themselves. Walter Lippmann, a very influential American writer who also had a decisive influence in Bernays' theories, had already argued that the American public often seems to comprise a "bewildered herd" that needs to be tamed, trained, and guided by ideological pastors (see Rositer & Lane, 1963). In the eyes of economic and political elites of the time, this was generally seen as a sensible idea, and Bernays, in particular, was an early champion of this kind of worldview. And, indeed, he strove to provide the first scientific methods and techniques whereby these economic and political elites in the United States could, precisely, control the "bewildered herd." How? Primarily by using psychological protocols to "manufacture" motives for us, by thus creating ideas, values, and choices for us—key aspects of the communal belief system—as well as the appropriate attendant emotions experienced by "the mass" of consumers.

Up until the 1920s, the U.S. economy was primarily a "need-based economy," where people generally bought products that fulfilled actual needs. Bernays thought that the goal of marketers should be to transform this need-based economy into a "desire-based economy." This would involve transforming culture, as well, for it to become desire based. Consumers in this brave new world that Bernays envisioned would not be limited in their purchasing potential by what they actually needed. They would not be limited by reason. Bernays proposed that marketers could engineer superfluous, inexistent "needs" *for* consumers so that, as the market would then sell not only the products that people actually needed, the economy would therefore grow and profits would increase.

The new science Bernays created should be conceived of precisely as a kind of *engineering*. But what is engineered by it is not, say, a computer or a bridge, but aspects of the consumer's way of thinking, feeling, and behaving, your fantasies, dreams, and aspirations. In this sense, his theories were oddly resonant with the goal that Joseph Stalin had for his totalitarian communist regime, at least in that Stalin also wanted, above all, to create an army of "engineers of souls" (which would include communist novelists) —souls that would be manufactured to be perfectly aligned with the objectives of the system itself. On the other hand, it is also strange that Bernays' theories were *not* resonant with some of the key and original principles of liberal capitalism. His theories contradicted, in particular, the idea that any form of social engineering was antithetical to the principles of a free market, a concept postulated by one of the fathers of modern capitalism, Friedrich von Hayek. For Hayek, the "free" in "free market" referred not only to freedom of commerce but also to free, as opposed to "engineered," citizens. For him, the humanistic potential of capitalism could be realized only if the products that a market produces are regulated by sovereign, vigilant, and knowledgeable citizens. These are citizens able to think about products freely, deliberatively, and intelligently, not citizens whose ideas and desires, as Bernays proposed, were engineered for them.

Let's return to Marx. His idea that capitalism uses our dreams, values, fantasies as means to fuel its own growth seems now prophetic. Again, we only need to read what the creators of modern marketing had to say about market growth. Bernays himself said, "If we understand the mechanism and motives of the group mind, is it not possible to control and regiment the masses according to our will without their knowing about it?" (1928, p. 71). Furthermore,

> the conscious and intelligent manipulation of the organized habits and opinions of the masses is an important element in democratic society. Those who manipulate this unseen mechanism of society constitute an invisible government which is the true ruling power of our country. [...] We are governed, our minds are molded, our tastes formed, our ideas suggested, largely by men we have never heard of. This is a logical result of the way in which our democratic society is organized. Vast numbers of human beings must cooperate in this manner if they are to live together as a smoothly functioning society. [...] In almost every act of our daily lives, whether in the sphere of politics or business, in our social conduct or our ethical thinking, we are dominated by the relatively small number of persons ... who understand the mental processes and social patterns of the masses. It is they who pull the wires which control the public mind. (1928, p. 37)

Paul Mazur, a Wall Street banker and one of the first to promote these sorts of marketing and political strategies, argued, "We must shift America from a needs to desires culture. People must be trained to desire, to want new things, even before the old have been entirely consumed [...] We must shape a new mentality. Man's desires must overshadow his needs" (in Gore, 2008, p. 94).

Engineering Reality

What Mazur and Bernays argued, in summary, is that the market can and should decide what we desire and, in this sense, how we think, while also convincing us that these are our own private desires and ideas. The goal was that marketers should be able to train people to, let us say, desire shoes with bright colors such that people would think that this was their own wish, their own idea, not a calculated marketing strategy, simply expressed by their desire for these kinds of shoes.

Bernays, in many important ways, won the battle for the collective imagination. Freud called the discipline he created "psychoanalysis," from the Greek, *psyche* (soul) and *ana-lyein* (to free, to unchain, to acquit). Freud thought that psychoanalysis could unchain the human soul. Bernays, in contrast, wished to "regiment" it. And as he proposed, in our society, many personal motives are, in various ways and degrees, in fact regimented and indeed manufactured by market forces, for better or for worse. Today, we take for granted that to grow, free-market economies must continuously create layers of prefabricated meaning and, in this sense, a reality *for* consumers. This economic system manufactures a world where these particular kinds of desires and motives seem to make sense. In this commercially managed world, TV commercials, billboards, and digital advertisements must purvey a reality that the average consumer sees as plausible, acceptable, and desirable. And to do so, the market must also continuously conceal inconvenient truths. For example, branches of the tobacco industry have systematically encouraged the notion that their product increases the manly score of consumers, while systematically concealing the fact it causes cancer, as established by an American court, the decision of which we cite next. In this commercially managed world, expected levels of profit often hinge precisely on the construction of artificial realities for consumers, and in this sense, this kind of market growth hinges on controlled deception.

In this society, products are typically invested with "brand identities": precisely, symbolic, moral, and affective auras, which are added to products. But the market strives to create not only brand identities but also aspects of the identity of consumers themselves: thoughts, emotions, ways of being. Inasmuch as it does so, free-market forces thereby create aspects of the consumer himself or herself. And the "ideal consumer" that Bernays envisioned and wanted to engineer is a person whose aspirations, as Marx predicted, are not ends in themselves, but means for market growth. Furthermore, this "ideal consumer" is a "docile" creature, in Bernays's eyes, someone who can be manipulated, simply because a manipulable person is an easy sell. (In contrast, someone who is knowledgeable and aware is a hard sell, because this person is more likely to stop and think for himself or herself about a product without concern for the marketing hype. It would be difficult, for example, to convince this aware person that if he or she starts smoking, his or her freedom will be somehow enhanced.)

Importantly, this is not to say that free markets are always devious and fraudulent. As noted, *capitalism can and has indeed provided many critical benefits to humankind in general and in this particular sense has fulfilled the function that Adam Smith ascribed to it.* But if it is important to acknowledge fully the desirable potential of this system, it is also important to recognize its negative potential. In particular, it is critical for us to see the simple fact that, ever since mass marketing was set in motion, marketers have always striven precisely to "control and regiment the masses," as Bernays says, "according to our will [the will of industries] without their knowing it" (1928). And that marketers have learnt, and have had to learn, that their success largely depends on this ability, which is the ability to create aspects of reality for consumers, often by filtering and hiding other aspects. We have to understand, that the success of *this* kind of free market has depended on its ability to engineer at least some of our desires, ideas, values— *regardless of whether these are good or bad for us.* Indeed, we must see that marketers—using increasingly complex techniques that include advanced psychological, psychosocial, and neuroscientific models and methods, as noted—have become very good at creating a reality that is often deceptive and sometimes harmful for those who accept it (e.g., cigarettes are empowering).

But why should we as a society care about these developments? Simply to be able to protect our interests, our health, our friends, our children, our country. We as a society also have to see that this new and triumphant form of modern capitalism has been in conflict with basic democratic ideals. Bernays honestly believed that the new science that he had created would help democracy. As noted, he thought that the average citizen was neither informed nor intelligent enough to make meaningful and effective decisions. And so, Bernays thought, this new science would finally allow those who knew better to simply engineer the correct ideas, values, and desires for these average folks. As you recall, the U.S. Declaration of Independence proclaimed that a just government derives from "the consent of the governed," and Bernays thought that such consent could and in fact must be "manufactured" or "engineered" by those who knew better than the governed (2013, 157). Hence, he called for the "conscious engineering of public opinion" (2013, p. 38) and of "good will" (2013, p. 93). But in creating the new science to accomplish this goal, he delivered a blow to a basic democratic goal: that of forming literate and active citizens, folks able to read the world, folks able to grant their deliberative consent, and thus able to be the stewards of their own interests. Of course, there were irrational, emotion-driven, docile consumers and citizens before Bernays, but the model he successfully championed systematically and systemically encouraged these tendencies.

Risks of Consumerism

It is critical to underscore that Bernays opened up not only the modern field of marketing but also, more broadly, the field of PR and that this field is not limited to clever and sometimes funny and charming commercial advertisements. This field is today an important, effective, and central political, sociopsychological, and economic force. Although, of course, in the business of spinning propaganda, it does not operate primarily via overt commercial advertisements or via overtly propagandistic means because the best propaganda is *not* seen as propaganda. This industry often strives to pass its propaganda off as "news," "science," "patriotism," and legitimate "public interests." And the best PR "spins," as the industry calls them, are, in fact, absorbed by the public as mere common sense, even when these spins make no sense at all, as we will presently discuss. To do so, this industry often uses visually sophisticated, seductively dramatic, neuroimaging derived, emotionally effective material, often "news," for example, that perhaps might have moved your own spirit.

PR experts have sometimes deployed their considerable knowledge on behalf of the public good. For example, during the AIDS/HIV epidemic, public health officials were worried that men were not using condoms. Men were often reluctant to do so, and this reluctance was costing lives and taxpayer dollars. And it was in part thanks to PR operators, who cleverly convinced many men that wearing condoms was desirable, that lives and public moneys were saved. Other such examples could be provided. But these propagandistic systems can be, and have been, dangerous as well. Investigative journalists John Stauber and Sheldom Rampton (2002) have reported on the role that PR industries have had in effectively "spinning" information pertaining, for example, to toxic waste, presence of cancerogenic (cancer-inducing) toxicants in food, including food marketed primarily to children. Stauber and Rampton have shown that PR industries, sometimes hired by outfits that operate on the fringes of the law (industries known to be heavy polluters, for example), have successfully masked critical layers of meaning from us, thus exposing us to unnecessary and even grievous risks. Recall, for example, our discussion of the lead industry. In our own day and age, we can consider the role of the tobacco industry to provide one of the most glaring examples. Indeed, let us turn our attention to this particular portion of the market, its actual effects, and its PR strategy.

Unsurprisingly, the PR experts of the tobacco industry also have gone to great pains to purvey the notion that consumers are buying more than tobacco, nicotine, and tar. Like others in the business of branding and spinning, they have also tried to purvey the feeling that the consumer is actually buying a cool factor of sorts, perhaps a measure of popularity, sophistication, masculinity, or femininity, if not "freedom," as the earliest propaganda for cigarettes put it. Pall Mall used an image of Santa Claus to sell its cigarettes as "guards against throat scratch." Lucky Strike deployed thousands of "endorsements" by doctors, claiming the purported medical benefits of smoking, and Camel, likewise, branded itself as a doctor-recommended product (Eliot, 2008). Yet this is a product that has resulted in terminal, catastrophic consequences for many consumers and their families. About 480,000 men and women die every year in the United States alone as a result of tobacco-related problems. The tobacco industry kills about six million people in the world every year, a statistic comparable to that of the victims of the holocaust. And death by lung cancer is a form of drowning, a long and desperate struggle for air. In 1999, the U.S. Department of Justice filed a lawsuit against this industry on charges of conspiracy to deceive the American public. U.S. District Court Judge Gladys Kessler, who presided over the case, came to the following conclusions after hearing the arguments from both sides. This case, she wrote,

> is about an industry [...] that survives, and profits, from selling a highly addictive product which causes diseases that lead to a staggering number of deaths per year, an immeasurable amount of human suffering and economic loss, and a profound burden on our national health care system. Defendants have known many of these facts for at least 50 years or more. [...] Despite that knowledge, they have consistently, repeatedly and with enormous skill and sophistication, denied these facts to the public, the Government, and to the public health community [...] Defendants have marketed and sold their lethal products with zeal, with deception, with a singleminded focus on their financial success, and

without regard for the human tragedy or social costs that success exacted [...] Over the course of more than 50 years, Defendants lied, misrepresented and deceived the American public, including smokers and the young people they avidly sought as "replacement" smokers about the devastating health effects of smoking and environmental tobacco smoke.

The evidence in this case clearly establishes that Defendants have not ceased engaging in unlawful activity ... For example, most Defendants continue to fraudulently deny the adverse health effects of secondhand smoke which they recognized internally; all Defendants continue to market "low tar" cigarettes to consumers seeking to reduce their health risks or quit; all Defendants continue to fraudulently deny that they manipulate the nicotine delivery of their cigarettes in order to create and sustain addiction; some Defendants continue to deny that they market to youth in publications with significant youth readership and with imagery that targets youth; and some Defendants continue to suppress and conceal information which might undermine their public or litigation position. ... Their continuing conduct misleads consumers in order to maximize Defendants' revenues by recruiting new smokers (the majority of whom are under the age of 18), preventing current smokers from quitting, and thereby sustaining the industry. (Kessler, Gladys, *U.S. v. Philip Morris*, 2006)

This industry, let us add in passing, also deployed well-researched and well-funded marketing campaigns to sell sugary drinks to children, by means of cartoon characters, toys, clothing, wristwatches—"total marketing," as the marketeers called it. It thus also contributed to the obesity epidemic and to related cardiometabolic disease, with all the personal and social cost, in suffering and in money, that this implied (see Nguyen, Glantz, Palmer, & Schmidt, 2019).

Commodities Versus Products

Let us imagine how absurd it would be for, let us say, soda advertisements to merely issue objective public notices about their products, with all the pertinent information about price, third-party research about potential benefits and risks, etc. They, of course, cannot afford to rely on that kind of advertising strategy. Instead, this industry invests effort and money purveying the idea that when you buy their product you are somehow buying more than just a beverage with caffeine, sugar, and salt. They tell you that life has to have a "Coke side" to it and that this sugary drink is "it." They strive to purvey the *feeling* that you are buying a fun factor somehow added to the carbonated drink itself. They strive to link their product to a whole affective and symbolic universe. They, that is to say, do not purvey merely products for consumption. They purvey "commodities."

Now, let's return to Marx. He argued that commodities are things that, although ordinary, make us feel that, by consuming them or by owning them, we can somehow transcend our ordinary lives. Commodities are generally ordinary things that pass themselves off as special or even as extraordinary in the eyes of a consumer. Consumers buy them not necessarily because they need to use these things, but because these things allow them to feel a bit extraordinary themselves, perhaps more "successful," or more popular, or more masculine, or more feminine, etc. If you purchase a product, instead of a commodity, you pay mostly for the "use value" of the thing in question. That is to say, you pay for the direct and tangible and practical benefit that the thing provides. Bread is the textbook example of a product. You don't buy bread to feel, say, more masculine, or more feminine, or cooler, or more successful, or somehow special, or sophisticated. You buy bread to eat it. You pay for its use value. When you buy a commodity, on the other hand, you are paying primarily for its symbolic value (also known as "exchange value"). That is to say, you are paying primarily for the *feeling* that the thing confers upon you; again, the feeling, for example, of manliness.

But, importantly, it is not the case that such a commodity, which in our example momentarily grants you the wish of manliness, will, in fact, make you manlier. It is not the case, for example, that cigarettes such Marlboro, whose campaigns associated users with "stallions," will objectively make you more of a man. There is a peculiar irony in the fact that the folks who have marketed this commodity have tried to associate it with sexual potency, because tobacco is associated with erectile dysfunction, which may lead to impotence. Plus, diseases such as cancer and emphysema, also associated with smoking, will not increase your manly score that much. Hence, guys who started using this brand name with an ear to its marketing—the targeted consumers who felt that, yes, the product somehow added to their masculinity—were paying for the fantasy, for the illusion, for the clever deception devised by the industry. This industry has made its money largely from these consumers, who semiconsciously buy a feeling, rather than the product itself (and if they eventually develop an addiction to nicotine, they will then pay for the use value of the product, the fact that nicotine assuages the craving associated with addiction). The industry has made its money largely from commodities rather than from products.

Here is another angle to commodities. You have to cross the desert, and you have no water; then someone offers you a choice between a bucket of water and a bucket of gold. Of course, the smart choice is the bucket of water, unless you prefer to die with a swollen tongue while clinging to your gold. Water has use value, which in the desert is the only true value. In this scenario, gold has no value at all because symbolic value doesn't count—outside *some sort of social agreement*, outside socially constructed meanings about, precisely, what has value and what hasn't. For this reason, symbolic value can be created, can be changed, and can be created anew. Some folks will accept the symbolic value ascribed to a thing, while others may laugh at the idea. Wine has symbolic value in countries such as the United States and Japan, where you can easily find people who drink it to feel sophisticated. But it has far more *use value* in countries such as Spain, where it would be difficult to find people who drink this traditional and largely working-class product to feel sophisticated. Again, symbolic value is created. And the free market that Bernays envisioned is a machine for creating this kind of value and for adding it to a maximal number of things. This marketing model successfully commoditized the economy, and economic growth has hinged on commoditization to a large extent. These modern industries have made a lot of their money from the thin air of this kind of value: from the feelings that they learned to sprinkle on top of their products.

Hypercommodities

This tendency toward commoditization has continued. And, in fact, modern capitalism has begun to generate profit from "hypercommodities." As noted, plain old commodities are attached to products—products that generally grant some sort of use value to the user, even if minimal. So our guy who pays for the feeling of masculinity when buying cigarettes may also like, perhaps, the smell of the product and is hence paying for this kind of use value as well. In contrast, we will define hypercommodities as goods that have neither a tangible product associated with them nor a definable use value. If you could sell, for example, just the feeling of masculinity—detached from an actual, tangible product—that would be a hypercommodity in our definition (which, incidentally, will *not* be shared by all sociologists). A hypercommoditized market can pull off just that sort of trick, as we will presently discuss. This market is the logical extension of the idea, proposed by Bernays, that there is money in people's unconscious, in this repository of emotion, irrationality, unfulfilled wishes, fears, instincts, and frustrations, which elude our own awareness. The new market has learned to mine this collective unconscious directly. This means that it has also become much better at overpassing the conscious awareness of the consumer (to thus "regiment [them] according to our will without their knowing about it," as Bernays said). And this new market is thus getting better at eliciting not only emotions but also related irrational behaviors from consumers—behaviors that captains of industry increasingly see as sources of profit. Consider the following examples.

Introduced in 2009, *FarmVille* became a widely successful computer game, perhaps one of the most popular in the world, according to some metrics. You get a plot of land, a cow, virtual tokens, and your job is to click on a virtual patch on your computer and to keep on clicking and clicking to tend the farm, to milk your cows, to seed, to plow, and so on. If you seed, you then wait for hours for your plantings to grow. And then you click, and click, and click yet again to harvest the fruits of your labor. Eventually, you find yourself spending a chunk of your life clicking on a computer screen and getting more and more things for your farm—things that, of course, require more clicking, which gives you more coins, for more things, and so on and so forth. At this point, you are likely paying actual money to the makers of this thing to buy the extra-premium, super-fun things that, however, require, yes, more clicking. Above all, you don't want to stop all this because if you do, your plants die, your cows die, your farm dies. Others might see this as a very desirable outcome, to free you from this tedious activity. But, of course, you want to avoid this sad end to a farm that has already exacted much of your time, tedium, and, perhaps, money. And so you carry on with this strange behavior, which an external observer may see as not too different from that of a low-grade robot designed to click on various parts of a screen simply to keep a timer from expiring (i.e., cows dying).

Perhaps the question is whether all this is that fun and whether this thing is a game at all. Is this merely a senseless activity whose sole purpose is to generate the transfer of money to a couple of folks? These folks, the makers of *FarmVille*, don't seem to think that their game (so to speak) is that fun. They themselves described it as "fun pain," as reported by investigative journalist Charles Seife (2015). It would seem, then, that their strategy was not to entertain, exactly, but to mine the capacity that tedium has to engage a percentage of the population and to engage them to the point that these folks would then pay money to be increasingly occupied in the odd activity. If so, their strategy was unambiguously successful. Also, according to Seife, the makers of this game earned in 2011, "roughly a billion dollars from online gaming—about a quarter of it from *FarmVille* and the rest from similar games in their portfolio" (Seife, 2015, p. 180).

Ian Bogost, a professor of interactive computing at the Georgia Institute of Technology, was interested in this phenomenon. He decided to bring the logic of these kinds of games to its final conclusion, so he designed a game called, appropriately enough, *Cow Clicker*. You get a cow, and you have to click on it at a certain rate or else the cow dies. You can pay actual money for goodies that allow you to keep on clicking. The game started partly as a satire, Bogost says, as an ironic commentary on this emerging social and economic phenomenon. But soon enough, folks were playing in earnest. And they were paying money in earnest. And they earnestly failed to see the satirical and protest-oriented intent of the game. Eventually, Bogost had enough, it seems, and all *Cow Clicker* cows died a programmed death ("cowpocalypse," he says). And then something even more interesting, or perhaps alarming, happened. "To this day [the cows] remain disappeared, although some devoted players still click where the cow used to be" (Bogost, 2018).

FarmVille is not a unique invention. The market in general is becoming increasingly "gamified" and commodity producers such as Coca-Cola, for example, are beginning to use the same logic—namely, compensating gamers/consumers with virtual tokens to encourage mechanical behaviors and "fun pain." Coca-Cola has created the *Happiness Quest* game, described by the online magazine *TechinAsia* as follows:

Users are motivated to scan the QR code on their favorite vending machine and create its virtual identity. This entails naming the machine and choosing its avatar from a library of 20 designs. Users can scan multiple machines and create each machine's unique identity as a sort of catalogue of check-ins and a rolodex of virtual friends. Each user is asked to designate a single machine to be "my machine" which will communicate with the user on a more personal level. This communication includes campaign news [...] and other relevant news. (Halcomb, 2011)

Think about this "quest for happiness" for a moment and about what the industry is telling us. Vending machines of sugary drinks become your "virtual friends." And "your machine," the most special of these friends, communicates with you "at a more personal level." How? By sending you Coca-Cola "news" as well as other news equally "relevant" for your life.

To insist, this is not a unique invention. It seems to be a new phase of capitalistic economic growth—a phase that is increasingly reliant on hypercommoditization, which entails dispensing with use value and making profit from nonproducts and symbolic value primarily. And to clarify, this is not a critique of games in general. Games can be smart, edgy, educational, and even artistic, which in my mind is the highest compliment. I have only provided an argument pertaining to hypercommodities. The idea is that the market that Bernays envisioned appears to have entered a "higher" phase. We noted that this system has learned to mine the social unconscious and to bypass the "higher faculties" of average consumers—faculties such as reflection, analysis, and comparison. Let us now add that the market is hence encouraging, it seems, habits of thought, attitudes, and dispositions in consumers, which are the opposite of those reliant on higher faculties. Bernays envisioned an "ideal" consumer—namely, a docile person. But it would be fair to suppose that not even he managed to imagine the hypercommoditized scenario that seems to be emerging or the consumers who are now happy to transfer their money to folks who only have "fun pain" to sell, such things as the bizarre fantasy of a tedious "farm" or the friendship of a vending machine. This market, in any case, is not in the business of helping you to rationally assess the pros and cons of consuming products (e.g., beverages with caffeine and sugar and salt—bear in mind that excessive sugar is directly related to the obesity epidemic and to attendant diseases, such as diabetes and depression). Marketers, in fact, sell much more than products: Again, they sometimes purvey varying levels of ignorance; they sell motives; they sell emotions; they sell emotional styles; they sell lifestyles. And in this sense, they also sell prefabricated and mass-distributed layers of reality for folks to consume.

Perhaps the pertinent questions are these: Can you, if fully inserted within this version of capitalism, be entirely free of these interested and prefabricated notions and fantasies? Would that be desirable? If so, what could you do to free your heart and mind from these ready-made dispositions? Adam Smith thought that capitalism was a humanizing and a humanistic force: To what extent it is or can become one? (More about this at the end of the chapter.) Recall that, as Immanuel Kant implied, making a free choice implies *knowledge* of what we are choosing and the ability to stop and think about the advantages and disadvantages of our decision (a blind choice is not and cannot be a free choice; a choice made in ignorance is not freely made either). And consider now choices and behaviors derived from propaganda: To what extent are these free? Is this system increasing your freedom or reducing it?

Hyperreality

To insist and to summarize: Free markets have provided many and very important advantages. But this type of economic system, as Bernays envisioned it, strives to "pull the wires that control the public mind [and to] harness old social forces and contrive new ways to bind and guide the world" (1928, 38).

French sociologist Jean Baudrillard (1995) coined the term "hyperreality" to describe processes whereby premade, manufactured narratives and ideologies are enacted, lived, and, thus, experienced as reality itself. Baudrillard wants us to see that this kind of capitalistic market has become a "machine for making emptiness": a machine for emptying reality of many of its true contents and for replacing these with fictive meanings, with fictive ways of thinking and feeling and living, *with fictive realities*. He uses the example of the First Gulf War to illustrate this idea. This was the first war that was systematically reduced to routine 30-second bits dissolved in a massive and constant media stream—a war that, in this sense, many audiences experienced primarily as a spectacle. CNN correspondents, for example, "acted much like radio reporters, since they were unable to transmit pictures of what they saw. 'Now there's a huger fire that we've just seen' [...] 'And we just heard—whoa. Holy cow. That was a large air burst that we saw. It was filling the sky'" (Encyclopedia of the New American Nation, 2015). Another reporter compared this bombing with Independence Day fireworks. But this kind of reporting, and these kinds of comparisons that equalize such things as the bombing of a city with the festivities of a city, are inadequate at best. For, as Nobel Laureate in literature Harold Pinter has noted, these military attacks have resulted in "hundreds of thousands of deaths," in horrors for civilians, men, women, and children, that were nevertheless emptied by these sorts of narratives and images—horrors that, therefore, "never happened," as Pinter also notes. "Nothing ever happened. Even while it was happening it wasn't happening. It didn't matter. It was of no interest" (2016, pp. 7–8).

This tendency toward "making emptiness" has become normative today. If you open, say, a Snapchat piece of news about a current war, the ugly and ghastly spirit of war that Pinter has in mind will be already emptied from the 10-second piece as well. This mini piece of news will also be quickly diluted in an even more massive stream of images and bits of information—a stream where this piece of news is mixed with banalities and thus equalized with them and banalized itself. This stream thus flattens moral hierarchies instead of highlighting the moral failures of the system to encourage audiences to correct these failures. It tends to empty the actual significance of events. Baudrillard would argue that the constant stream of images we see passing through our screens are, for these reasons, like the shadows that Plato mentions in his allegory of the cave. You recall that the chained prisoners in this platonic story confuse the shadows of the things they see with the things themselves. Baudrillard would say that the constant flow of images in our screens, likewise, tends to provide the mere illusion of reality, and that, in this sense, we also tend to confuse the shadows of things with the things themselves.

Hyperreal Persons?

Furthermore, Baudrillard implies that a hyperreal society creates, in a sense, hyperreal persons. Let us go back to the beer industry and its narrative about manliness. You might have seen beer commercials that make fun of guys who scream "like a girl" when on a roller-coaster ride, or that make fun of guys who are grossed out by fish, or who cry when their girlfriends leave them. These kinds of commercials, you might have noticed as well, thus give targeted consumers (young men, primarily) a ready-made and mass-distributed narrative about masculinity. And they purvey the sense that the consumers' masculinity somehow hinges on their capacity to buy the advertiser's product.

Of course, the notion that manhood hinges on buying beer is as ideological as the notion that manhood hinges on smoking. But it ceases to be merely ideological when guys actually experience their gender more or less in accordance to this ideology. When guys enact the narrative suggested by the marketers—when guys act in a manner that brings the *logic* of these commercials to life—they thus bring to life the constructed reality purveyed by the industry. Of course, not all men exposed to this sort of propaganda buy into it, or act in a manner concordant with the interests of the industry (and beer itself, as a product, not as a commodity, can be a very good thing as well). But even a glimpse into the statistics pertaining to the use of alcohol among young men does suggest that alcohol has become an aspect of their worldview about masculinity (see, e.g., Iwamoto et al., 2011). And, hence, there is a degree of correspondence between the interests of the alcohol industry and the way many young men understand—*and enact*—their masculinity (Iwamoto et al., 2011). For Baudrillard, these kinds of fictive realities are, therefore, not limited to branding and marketing commodities. Inasmuch as our thoughts, identities, values, and desires (and even our memories, as we will see later on) become aligned with the objectives and narratives of the industry, the *consumer himself* is the creation of this economic process. (And recall that Marx had argued that capitalism feeds from the human spirit itself.) If, and to the extent to which, this happens,

a. our ability to read the surrounding world, therefore, becomes compromised, as our relation to the world is filtered by the interests of the market, and

b. our relation to our own selves also becomes compromised: If a guy judges his masculinity according to a metric provided by an industry, or if a woman judges her body according to a metric of a commercial advertisement, or if a child derives a sense of self-worth from commodities and PR strategies that target children, then their self-regard is filtered, and in this sense distorted and created, by external interests.

Hyperreality is the natural habitat of these kinds of malleable consumers—consumers who, in our emerging socioeconomic system, have become indispensable for economic growth. Hyperreality is sustained by prefabricated mcfantasies that, although dystopian at times, nevertheless seem plausible and desirable for these consumers. And *dystopian* is not an exaggerated word in this context. How else could we describe the notion that a "happiness quest" can help you befriend vending machines that communicate with you "on a more personal level"? Uruguayan writer Eduardo Galeano has provided a "delirant" idea, as he says, that may help us wrap up this discussion and introduce the chapter's conclusion. We are at a point in history, Galeano argues, where we have to begin imagining a different society, one where "folks will neither be driven by cars, nor programmed by computers, nor bought by supermarkets, nor watched by TVs" (1996, my translation).

Finishing with Adam Smith

As noted, Smith predicted some of the possible benefits of capitalism accurately: This economic system did contribute in some important ways to human progress. But it would be absurd and dangerous to assume dogmatically that this model of economic production will simply unfold as a civilizing force—a force that will just have as its ultimate goal the improvement of human life. For, as Marx accurately predicted, capitalism, in fact, has the potential to transform human life into a means of its economic development, rather than serving human life as an end in itself. And it is up to us to prevent this from happening. What can we do to prevent this outcome while at the same time harnessing the benefits that capitalism can offer?

Smith thought that the fundamental characteristic of this system, capitalism, is that it does not need an external arbiter or external laws to succeed, because it has its own internal arbiters and laws, which, when present, push this system toward the realization of its desirable potential. For Smith, the key arbiter and lawgiver of this system is the consumer: us. For it is the consumer, he argued, who decides what to buy and why. So that if a product is bad, or dangerous, or inefficient, or ugly, or stupid, we would then decide not to buy it and would thus guide the system, one purchase at a time, toward ends that *we* like and value. In this view, human beings are, therefore, the ends of this system, rather than its mere means of growth, because we constantly direct and redirect the system's output toward our own interests. Indeed, some of the early economists thought that capitalism is, in this sense, a system of natural selection, not so different from nature itself. So if left alone, a free market would systematically and automatically select the "fittest" products, where "fittest" means better: products that cater to human needs, to human values, and to human progress.

But this view is partly mistaken. A capitalist market does, in a sense, select the "fittest" products, like nature itself. But one has to bear in mind that, in nature, "fitness"—as in "survival of the fittest"—does not mean better, or prettier, or smarter, or more humane, or more compassionate. Sometimes the very opposite is the case. In nature, sometimes the "fittest" species are—if judged according to our human scale of values—the lowest, ugliest, and most brainless animal species. Indeed, one of the longest living animal species (or more properly, the longest living subphyla of animals) is the jelly fish, which is not bad for a brainless animal, one literally without a brain. Or consider the species that are more likely to outlive others. These super-survivors would *not* include, say, the mighty lion, or the cute panda, or the graceful gazelle, or even the brainy human. Insects such as the cockroach, as well as bacteria, are far more likely to outcompete those magnificent animal species. And what makes the cockroach so fit and so competitive? It eats its own offspring, its own dead, and its own feces. These are not characteristics that we value. You don't want, say, your roommates to boast these abilities. And yet life itself does value them very highly, because these capacities make each cockroach a highly autonomous biological machine that doesn't depend too much on external conditions. (In contrast, the cute panda, for example, is a specialized eater that completely depends on bamboo to survive so that when bamboo forests suffer the species suffer with them.) Let's go back to capitalism. This system can easily promote, like nature itself, this kind of ugly and yet effective form of fitness. Some capitalistic products can, of course, be genuinely beautiful and useful. But sometimes, the products and commodities that are more likely to survive and outcompete others can be the equivalent of the cockroach: ugly, or dangerous, or inane, as discussed earlier. When successfully commoditized, these kinds of things can be easily, even eagerly and massively, bought. Their ugliness and inanity notwithstanding, they can have an excellent fitness score in our modern markets.

Here is another way of stating this: A free market can fulfill its humanizing potential *when consumers actually do become good arbiters*. Capitalism can benefit humanity but only to the extent to which we can, in fact, develop the ability to discriminate against the bad, inane, or dangerous products, the agendas of the industries that produce them, and the politics that support them, when and if they exist. This is an ability that, as we saw, doesn't seem to be thriving in our day and age, largely because it goes against the interest of *this* kind of modern, Bernaysian, hypercommoditized capitalism, which has become triumphant. But again, the free market in principle can fulfill its humanizing promise, as Smith wanted it, inasmuch as the public, all of us, develop a sense of literacy about its output, how it affects us, how it affects society, how it affects the environment, and how it affects our future and the future generations. Capitalism can become a humanizing and humanistic force but only to the extent to which human beings themselves become humanized and humanistic. Today, this involves going against the modern grain that Bernays and others like him so cleverly and successfully championed.

CHAPTER VI

Conformity and Deviance

Advantages and Disadvantages

Human Beings Tend to Adapt to Social Circumstances

Even the most democratic societies constantly nudge people to conform to certain standards, ideas, values, fashion styles, and appropriate emotional styles (e.g., "boys don't cry"), often regardless of whether these habits are good or bad for us, or for our society, or for the future. In this chapter, we study why people tend to comply, in different ways and by different degrees, with the broader demands of culture. We will examine important studies pertaining to how and why our decisions and aspects of our lifestyles may become manufactured *by the broader array of social and cultural forces*, not only by the market. And, relatedly, we will also see why we say in sociology that, unlike any other animal species, human beings are, in fact, largely created by culture and history.

Let us begin by discussing some of the classic studies pertaining to the phenomena of conformity, studies that let us see why we generally tend to follow the will of a group. Solomon Asch (1951), one of the prominent social psychologists of the 20th century, was the person who pioneered research pertaining, precisely, to how and why people conform to the norms and expectations of groups. Let us outline one of his most illustrative experiments, which took place in the 1950s. Asch recruited 123 male study participants who were told that they were going to participate in an experiment about visual acuity. One by one, these subjects entered a room where they encountered five or seven males who also seemed to be participants in the experiment, although in reality, they were confederates working for Asch. The experimenter showed the participant and the confederates two large cards, A and B, and asked the group to compare the contents of these cards. Card A had three perpendicular and parallel lines, marked as lines 1, 2, and 3. And card B featured only one perpendicular line, which was the exact size one of the lines on card A. All A and B cards in a stack were designed so as to make it immediately and unambiguously obvious that the single line on the B cards matched in length *only with one* of the three lines on the A cards.

One by one, the confederates and the real study participants were shown pairs of A and B cards drawn from the stack, and they were asked to state which of the three lines on card A matched in length with the line on card B. For the first couple of trials, the confederates gave the obviously correct answer, but after the fourth trial, the confederates began to give obviously incorrect answers. Let us say that the single line on card B matched in length with line *two* on card A, and yet the confederates were all in agreement that the line on card B matched with line *three* on card A. At this point, something interesting began to happen. Save some exceptions, the actual participants also began to provide the obviously incorrect answers, following the cue of the confederates, even if the confederates were wrong. Some participants went along with the wrong assessments of the group simply because they didn't want to rock the boat; they didn't want to stand out. Asch called this "normative conformity to the group." But others, importantly, went along with the group *by first denying the visual evidence provided by their own eyes*. It was easier for them to think that their own eyes were conveying the wrong information, rather than thinking that *the group* was conveying the wrong information. Solomon Asch called this phenomenon "informational conformity." This means that participants became blind to obvious aspects of reality merely to go along with a group of strangers.

Asch's research suggests that human beings are, in general, strongly motivated by a will to conform. Human beings generally avoid transgressing the norms that govern their social surroundings. Although we are a predatory species (responsible, in fact, for the massive disappearance of other species), we also often act like members of a herd species and bow to the will of the group. Asch and many others have shown that individuals, in fact, often strive to dissolve themselves within the group, even if in doing so these individuals may be causing at least some harm to themselves (examples will be provided soon).

Cultures That Encourage Individualism

All societies and all social groups elicit a degree of conformity from most social actors (save young children or people with socialization deficits, such as sociopaths). Indeed, without a minimal degree of conformity, no society can exist, as we will also see next.

Yet the idea that individuals normally tend to adapt to external demands is difficult to accept for many people, particularly for members of cultures that outwardly encourage self-reliance, self-determination, and a sense of uniqueness in citizens. So, beyond the laboratory conditions that frame Asch's research, let us presently consider everyday examples pertaining to the phenomena of conformity and adaptation. Consider such occasions as weddings, funerals, parties, church functions, classrooms, your place of work, elevators—circumstances that demand a degree of conformity from all of us. It is clear that, in these environments, people generally tend to abide by the expectations of the group; for example, dress codes, codes of conduct, and rules of speech, as noted. As many researchers have shown, we dress, behave, speak, and even gesture in ways that are more or less appropriate for the particular occasion. We tend to carry ourselves so as to signal a degree of agreement with the norms governing the interaction. In an elevator, for instance, people typically try to avoid displays of emotion and speak with an "appropriate" tone of voice, with appropriate manners and gestures. At a funeral, we generally broadcast appropriate signals; at a job interview, as we saw when we discussed the work of Goffman, we tend to act and behave in a manner that befits the expectations of interviewers; when meeting acquaintances for the first time, we yet again tend to display the version of ourselves that facilitates and eases the encounter, etc.

To be sure, even members of groups who profess nonconformity—for instance, those who defy mainstream standards, values, or tastes—also tend to conform to the standards that govern their particular subcultures. Punks, hippies, gang members, the Amish, and many other communities contest mainstream social norms. But members of these groups very much adhere to a subset of expectations and codes that govern their own subcultures. In fact, these groups tend to abide by compulsory and minute codes of conduct that, in their minuteness and forcefulness, resemble those of institutions such as monasteries, corporations, or the military. This is similar to members of highly individualistic cultures—that is to say, cultures that encourage individuals to see themselves as unique, independent, self-reliant, and self-directed, cultures that value individual determination and perseverance. We also tend to conform to social requirements. The mainstream American culture, for example, is arguably the most individualistic in the world (Suh et al., 1998), and yet Americans also tend to conform and to adapt to the requirements of the social system. Bear in mind, first, that economic growth in the United States has historically hinged on consumption (among other factors), which means that, as suggested, the personal desires and motives of consumers have to reflect, at least minimally, the needs of the market itself and the ideas and values engineered by it.

But, second, and more importantly, Americans undergo, much as members of any other society, a process of *socialization* whereby the person, from birth on, learns the social and cultural codes, how to display them, and what to expect if he or she violates them. Which teaches him or her how to fit in, which allows him or her to partake from the social order and to become part of a larger and stronger (social) organism, a family, a church, a country, a nation, etc. Hence, like any member of any other society, Americans also undergo, and typically comply with, various mechanisms of *social control* and *behavior modification*: precisely, the social mechanisms that enforce collectively relevant beliefs, norms, and values, mechanisms that not only reward conformity but also punish those who overstep these social norms. If you go to a wedding wearing the normative, expected attire and display the normative behavior, you will be welcomed and thus rewarded. On the other hand, if you go wearing a T-shirt, for example, and thus infringe upon the codes, you will likely receive raised eyebrows, cold shoulders, be subjected to gossip, etc., which are, of course, punishments and, more generally, mechanisms of social control that keep people from going against the norm. (The law is a mechanism of social control organized and enforced by the government itself.)

Perhaps, as some researchers have argued, Americans, much as the members of other individualistic cultures, conform less if compared to members of collectivistic cultures—cultures that encourage individuals to see themselves *not* as unique but as active members of a larger social order, cultures that value group accomplishment over individualistic perseverance, cultures that underscore the notion that fate is, above all, a collective accomplishment. Nevertheless, the point to keep in mind is that all human beings, regardless of their culture, *must* conform to at least a minimum of social demands and must *accept* social norms and values. And our conformity, for this reason, legitimizes these norms and values, and helps society to sustain, enforce, and maintain a certain civic order, certain societal rules, a tradition. Conformity thus facilitates social interconnection, cohesiveness, stability, and continuity. And in this particular sense, conformity—and attendant mechanisms of behavior modification and social control—are not only helpful but also necessary for any society. In fact, no society can survive without them. But on the other hand, these same mechanisms also have the potential to harm and defeat individuals and groups, as we discuss next.

The Risks of Noncompliance

Again, just as some people conform more readily than others, others resist social injunctions and demands more readily and frequently than others. But anyone who resists is likely to face retaliation from society itself. At a minimal level, these involve raised eyebrows and cold shoulders, as noted, but retaliation may also involve degrees of ostracism that can be injurious, psychologically, physically, socially, economically, and legally.

Here is a telling example: In 2017, a Saudi woman named Manal al-Sharif was imprisoned and endlessly harassed by Saudi authorities *and* by fellow citizens merely because she dared to drive a car, which meant going against the social rules in that country. As she noted, "[T]he secret police took me from my home in Saudi Arabia in the middle of the night, while my 5-year-old son was sleeping. I might have disappeared without a trace—if it wasn't for one brave witness [...] who took the risk of live-tweeting the details of the incident" (2018). Her son was bullied and bruised at school on account of the "unfeminine" behavior of his mother. Her brother was detained twice for giving her the keys to his car and was subsequently harassed to the point of having to quit his professional job and having to leave the country with his wife and children. Her father had to endure sermons from the local imam, who equated women who drive with prostitutes. (Another woman, Loujain al-Jatoul, who also campaigned for the right to drive, had to flee to the Emirates where she was reportedly kidnapped by Saudi agents, taken back to Saudi Arabia, imprisoned, "held in solitary confinement, beaten, waterboarded, given electric shocks, sexually harassed and threatened with rape and murder," as recounted by the *New York Times* [Kristof, 2019].) And yet, despite these risks, Manal al-Sharif insisted on defending her elemental right to drive a car. And, for this reason, concerned Saudi citizens further retaliated and used social media to demand, among other things, that she be flogged in public.

As this courageous woman said, *fighting against oppressive societal norms is often harder than fighting against openly oppressive and tyrannical laws* (paraphrasing).

This idea is important. Explicitly oppressive laws, precisely because they are explicit and thus visible, can be easily identified and therefore resisted. Oppressive social *norms*, on the other hand, pass themselves off as, precisely, *normal*. They are often seen as simple common sense. And hence they tend to be invisible—*as mere norms*: People generally do not see them as the arbitrary societal rules that they are but, again, as mere, commonsensical standards of normality. These kinds of rules of conduct seem commonsensical *not* because they, in fact, make sense, but because the people who see them as such grew up with them and were socialized to think of them as okay, as something expected. As Thomas Paine, the 18th-century English-American revolutionary, argued, sometimes the will to follow "common sense" does not stem from the power of "commonsensical" ideas themselves, or from their intrinsic goodness, but simply from the fact that people tend to get used to inherited ideas, often unthinkingly and mechanically abiding by the imaginations and by the rules of the dead generations. The Saudi folks who demanded that their neighbor be flogged in public—because she wanted to drive a car—had a life-long mental training that simply marked their hearts and minds with the preposterous notion that it is not normal, and that it is indeed immoral, for women to drive a car.

Note as well that, for this reason, social norms may also pass themselves off as morally correct—even when they are morally repellent. So when citizens such as Manal al-Sharif defend a basic and simple right, and thus go against these preposterous manifestations of "common sense" and "morality," their actions are naturally resisted. And these actions are resisted not by dictatorial institutions that uphold dictatorial laws but also by citizens who see themselves as reasonable and virtuous—citizens who see the actions of these "traitors," as Manal al-Sharif was often labeled, as threats to reason and virtue themselves. The larger idea is that, throughout history, oppression and evil have often stemmed from collectively relevant (and warped) standards of normality, from malevolent nonsense that passes itself off as virtue and reason, and from people who mechanically conform to such standards.

The foregoing example is perhaps too obvious in any context outside Saudi Arabia. Less obviously and closer to home, let us consider persons who transgress the codes of gender that apply not only in Saudi Arabia but also in the United States. Persons who, for example, choose *not* to deploy the gestures, the sign language, the dress codes that American men and women are expected to deploy so that others can identify them as men and women "proper." These transgressors are also likely to endure more than just disapproving looks. Hate crimes against gay men and lesbians—indeed the murdering of members of these communities—tragically illustrate this idea. And, more generally, those who transgress the codes of gender may suffer a disproportionate burden of mental health problems, such as stress and depression, as data pertaining to the health status of gay men and women clearly show (Meyer, 2003).

To be sure, sometimes noncompliers become cultural heroes, as the example of Manal al-Sharif suggests, or as the civil rights movement or the feminist movement illustrate. But more often than not, people who transgress dominant norms, rather than becoming cultural heroes, tend to become handicapped: socially, they are often ostracized or scorned rather than celebrated; politically, they may become disenfranchised; economically, they may carry disproportionate burdens; psychologically, they may experience extra fear, anxiety, and depression. Transsexual men and women, for example, have a much harder time finding adequate employment, adequate housing, adequate education, and adequate health care, regardless of their skills and of their character. Even the noncompliers who eventually emerge as cultural heroes also tend to first pay the price of noncompliance. Some of the artists who opened entire new fields of aesthetic expression and experience—from the painter Vincent van Gogh to the poet Charles Baudelaire—also experienced the sort of little daily miseries that often punctuate the existence of *true* outsiders (who are not merely fashionable eccentrics). Many of such artistic pioneers in fact died forsaken, even despised. The case of Nelson Mandela, who spent 27 years in prison, also illustrates this idea in the most sobering manner. Or consider Nobel Laureate Malala Yousafzai, who, as noted, was shot in the head when she was 12 years old for the crime of wanting to attend school.

Compliance with Absurd or Belittling Social Norms

The everyday existence of noncompliers is likely to be burdened, *even if the social codes that noncompliers violate are arbitrary and absurd, and even if these codes aim to dehumanize them or other citizens in general.* The example of Manal al-Sharif suggests that most Saudi women, save daring exceptions, had internalized the bizarre notion that driving was somehow unfeminine, immoral, and embarrassing, and they were thus ready to comply with it. This idea, the idea that people often comply with absurd or dehumanizing norms or with norms that damage their own existence, counterintuitive as it might be, warrants a full theoretical explanation, which I will provide subsequently. But for now, let us consider a couple of additional examples closer to home and closer, perhaps, to your own immediate world.

Let us go back to the 1950s. American girls and women of this generation were socialized, in general and save exceptions, to believe that they would find fulfillment primarily, or even exclusively, in their God-given role as nurturers (Friedan, 2001). This particular belief system, which Betty Friedan, the leader of the second wave of feminism, termed the "feminine mystique," postulated that women's natures had been intended for nurturing. Men and women often thought that women could, therefore, fulfill their biological fate primarily in the domestic sphere, nurturing the family, the children, the garden, the pets, taking care of the meals, the cleaning, etc. Naturally, in principle, there is nothing wrong with these activities, which can enhance the life of a family. But what is indeed problematic is the idea that women, as the mainstream culture maintained, may not find fulfillment through other means, through any other life paths. This belief system postulated that women should exclude themselves from the public sphere and from any life path that would drive them away from their role as nurturers. Hence, from a young age, women were discouraged from pursuing careers, businesses, and occupations with higher levels of responsibility, as these were seen as not feminine and indeed as unfeminine. And, hence, women were discouraged from being financially, intellectually, and socially independent. Noncompliers (i.e., "nonfeminine" women who strove to attain education and positions of power) often faced daily petty retaliation from both men and women, from strangers and from kin. These outsiders brooked much ill-treatment precisely because they went against the *arbitrary, absurdly limiting and belittling* social codes that governed femininity.

More contemporarily, the work of Michael Kimmel, an American sociologist who has devoted most of his career to studying masculinity in the United States, can help us understand how gender codes might have, perhaps, marked the life of some of our friends and kin. If Friedan showed that gender norms had diminished the lives of women, Kimmel has similarly shown that gender codes are damaging the lives of millions of young American men today. Men who often find themselves, much as their grandmothers in the '50s, unable to go against the codes of their gender, *however absurd and belittling these codes of masculinity might be.* Let us consider initially an obvious example: "bro codes" about drinking. Kimmel (2008) describes the following scene pertaining to drinking rituals:

> Nick starts his night by ingesting some vile concoction invented solely for the enjoyment of the onlookers. Tonight the drink of choice is a 'Three Wise Men,' a shot composed of equal parts Jim Beam, Jack Daniels, and Johnnie Walker. Other variations include the more ethnically diverse (substitute Jose Cuervo for the Johnnie Walker), or the truly vomit-inducing (add a little half-and-half and just a splash of Tabasco). The next drink comes at him fast, a Mind Eraser, another classic of the power hour [the time that Nick and buddies reserve for fun]. It's like a Long Island Iced Tea except more potent, and it is drunk through a straw as quickly as possible. Shot after shot after shot is taken, the guys become all the more loud and obnoxious, and the bar manager brings a trashcan over to Nick's side, just in case. [...] Not surprisingly, the trashcan comes in handy. Nick's body finally relents as closing time approaches. He spews out a stream of vomit and the other guys know it's time to go. Fun was had, memories were made, but most importantly … he puked. His friends can rest easy: a job well done. (Kimmel, 2008, pp. 95–96)

For many of the Nicks who inhabit Guyland, getting sick in such a manner is clearly preferable to breaking the norms that govern their world. As Kimmel reports, doing fraternity pledges that involve, for example, cleaning vomit, walking around grabbing the penises of other pledges while being mocked and insulted, or, in fact, risking being killed in hazing rituals is also seen as preferable to breaking these norms. Every year, Kimmel notes, about 1,400 college students aged 18 to 24, almost four students per day, are in fact "killed as a result of drinking [and] nearly half a million suffer some sort of injury" (Kimmel, 2008, p. 106). Andrew Coffey was a student at Florida State University. He died after drinking an entire bottle of bourbon, simply because his peers asked him to do so to join their fraternity. Coffey could have said, "No, I don't want to drink an entire bottle of hard alcohol." But it was seemingly easier for him to drink it and to thus fatally poison himself. Or consider another case (not a fatal one this time): "Nicholas Mauricio arrived at Tallahassee's Memorial Hospital on April 9, the 20-year-old Florida State University student was going in and out of consciousness. Blood from a cracked tooth tricked out of his mouth. There was a lump the size of a golf ball on the back of his head. Doctors quickly discovered that his skull had been fractured and he was suffering from multiple brain bleeds," as reported by the *Washington Post* (Farzan, 2018). Mauricio, the *Post* notes, had been named Scumbag of the Week by the "brothers" he wanted to join, had accepted this nomination, and had also *accepted to be beaten by them*, which caused the massive brain injuries, which resulted in a sequel of problems, including impaired cognitive function, paranoia, and panic attacks. He could have said "no" as well. One would think that it would be very easy for anyone to say, "No, I don't want to be beaten." Yet it was seemingly preferable for him to be treated the way he was treated, in accordance to the given normative order, the symbolic universe within which folks can very well accept the job of Scumbag of the Week.

The tragic deaths mentioned in the foregoing are deaths by conformity. They help us see that sometimes it is good, when not literally vital, to go against certain social codes (in this case against "bro codes"). They also help us see that supine obedience to norms, codes, and traditions can be bad when not literally fatal.

Note also that, much as their grandmothers, the guys in the foregoing examples did not invent these norms—the rules that often guide their behavior. They merely inherited them without thinking too much, it would seem, about whether they made sense or whether, all things considered, they were good or bad for them. Had they closely considered these norms, they would have seen that they were not that great. Beyond the humiliation and harm described earlier, a pile of data shows that young American men, particularly the Nicks described by Kimmel, are failing in unprecedented ways in virtually every area of achievement that is important at their age. This includes succeeding in school, moving away from the parental house, becoming financially independent, and finishing school when they are supposed to. In comparison with women of their age, young American men are nearly twice as likely to live with their parents. In comparison to the previous generation, they are more likely to depend on parental money. The list is long. Chances are that you can look around and see for yourself. Philip Zimbardo, one of the most prominent contemporary social psychologists, has in fact described this scenario as the "demise of guys." Guys who are, in this sense, the victims of a form of oppression that they do not see as oppressive at all. And why do we call it "oppression"? From the Latin *premere,* the same origin of the words *press* and *depression, oppression* refers to the action of keeping something down—for example, keeping these guys from reaching their potential. The idea is not that Guyland is governed by a dictatorial bro regime and its oppressive laws, of course. But that it is largely governed by *norms* that are hindering, when not handicapping, these guys; norms that are sometimes literally killing them. And bear in mind that norms, as Manal al-Sharif noted, can be far more effectively oppressive than dictatorial laws. Norms can be far more effective than laws when it comes to preventing individuals or groups or generations from reaching their potential.

Of course, many young men are succeeding, and some of them come from Guyland. But many of those who are failing are the blind victims of a particular, and particularly damaging, narrative about masculinity. This is a story that no longer emphasizes, as it did for previous generations, the idea that "real men" are, above all, providers. And that, therefore, "real men" have to assume the responsibilities inherent to being providers—namely, having a steady job, being financially independent, and so on. Instead, the new narrative that governs Guyland emphasizes other widespread ideas and values, such as "real men drink real beer." Relatedly, this narrative also provides justification for young men to further extend their adolescence, as Kimmel has shown, so, save all the exceptions, the transition between childhood and adulthood is today no longer a transition. Instead, it is often a separate phase of development, which some psychologists have termed "kidulthood": a cross between being nominally an adult, while still clinging to a kid-like worldview. A worldview that, as noted, tends to reject responsibility and to embrace "fun" instead (and let us clarify: fun is, of course, good, by definition, but when it actually means *failing in areas of achievement that are developmentally appropriate, this* kind of "fun" is oppressive, when not fatal sometimes). If you look around, you will likely find guys who, for example, still cling to digital versions of toys, say, to combat games that, closely examined, are digital versions of old GI Joe. These digital games, which the industry designs for "kidults," the main target audience, fulfill similar child-like fantasies: karate chopping, killing bad guys, shooting enemies.

The current narrative about masculinity, in any case, combined with structural economic factors beyond their control, such as an economic shift toward service industries that cater to stereotypically feminine jobs, is making the lives of many young men more difficult than they have to be. This narrative is decreasing their focus; it is making them poorer and more dependent, not to mention less reflective and less introspective. And yet, as noted, many of these men see it as normal and even as desirable. Which is why this story about masculinity is binding them to behaviors that are negatively affecting their lives.

"The Life Others Expected of Me"

Sociologist Talcott Parsons has shown (1968) that social codes tend to be enforced not only by groups or organizations with the authority to enforce them but also, more generally, by social actors themselves. As suggested, if people grow up with certain social norms and see that certain behaviors are simply expected in certain social groups or situations, they will likely internalize the norms in question and will hence see and judge the world and others from that vantage point—the vantage point of the only normative order that they know. When this happens, such persons will also become the enforcers of these norms. And, indeed, they will likely tell themselves that they should abide by the norms in question. They may very well become their own censors or critics, often judging their own actions, behaviors, ideas, clothes, hair, body, choices in life, not by standards invented by them but by the ready-made standards given to them by society or by a certain group: a fraternity, a church, a group of peers, etc. Let's return to George Herbert Mead (1934). He helped us understand that we, in fact, often *see ourselves through the eyes of others* and that we, therefore, conduct ourselves according to their standards. There are legitimate reasons for, and advantages associated with, adhering to collectively relevant norms, to traditions, to the views of others, as we will discuss soon; however, as noted, there are also important risks. Beyond those risks previously discussed, let us consider the following story.

Bronnie Ware, an Australian nurse who spent several years attending terminally ill patients, has reported that the number one regret of those facing death is not having had the "courage to live a life true to myself" and living, instead, "the life others expected of me" (2012, p. 37). The risk of unreflectively complying with social norms, and thus *capitulating to the words and the gaze of others*, is living, like some of Ware's patients, guided only by inherited standards, by a given and unchosen list of ideas, and thus experiencing life as the absence of a life. Ware narrates the moving story of Grace, a woman in her 80s, tormented not only by a painful and humiliating terminal condition but also by the regret of having lived a life under the gaze of a tyrannical husband. "Why didn't I just do what I wanted? Why did I let him rule me?" These were Grace's final regrets. But she also reflected, in a sociological key, about the fact that this was not merely her own personal failure. Grace saw that this was the failure of many women of her generation. Her predicament was not simply an *individual* failure but, above all, a *societal* failure. Society itself had to be reformed and repaired. Important aspects of her troubled existence were done to her and to women of her generation. And yet, of course, she was also an accomplice in this process. Grace ruefully realized that such a life had been chosen for her, not by her, while also seeing that it had been her own individual choice.

Conformity, to be sure, does not mean that we merely succumb to external pressures against our will, or against our better judgment. It means that we often *choose* to abide by such social codes and thus come to live the lives we do—the sort of lives that may, perhaps, elicit regret when we see them in a retrospective fashion, or when we come to face our final hour. And, as also follows from the example of Saudi Arabia earlier, conformity means that people may become spokespersons for the social narrative—regardless, it is important to insist, of whether it makes sense or not. Grace picked up absurd and indeed belittling ideas *from other women* who were undergoing a similar predicament—women who had, nevertheless, became enlisted and deputized by these ideas, by the narrative that befell their generation.

"Imagine Saying This to Our Children"

The earlier examples illustrate the idea that men and women often fall prey to their own instincts, natural and useful as they sometimes are, to follow the will of a larger (social) organism (e.g., groups of peers), even when doing so does not make rational sense. This aspect of human nature is important for the life of a social species, but it also accounts for many of our troubles, much of our suffering, and many of our delusions and humiliations. And it is, therefore, important for democratic societies to understand and to intervene in this aspect of social life. Doris Lessing has argued the following:

> Imagine saying to our children: "in the last fifty or so years, the human race has become aware of a great deal of information about its mechanisms [information provided particularly by sociologists and social psychologists]; how it behaves, how it must behave under certain circumstances. If this is to be useful, you must learn to contemplate these [social] rules calmly, dispassionately, disinterestedly, without emotion. It is information that will set people free from blind loyalties, obedience to slogans, rhetoric, leaders, group emotions." (1987, p. 61)

Although Lessing imagines a society where schoolchildren are encouraged to learn this sort of lesson, she also realizes that no government and no political party will actually design curricula to teach children "to become individuals able to resist group pressure" (1987, p. 62). Why? Because such institutions and organizations often depend on group members who follow group thinking. Thus, she suggests, it is up to us. It is up to parents, teachers, and friends. It is up to the civil society to nurse these ideas, to encourage *not* fashionable eccentricity or potentially dangerous deviance but an ongoing process of psychological decolonization.

Why Do People Go to Extremes Merely to Conform?

As noted, human beings are an exquisitely social species and therefore the feeling that we belong in a social environment, or to a clan, tribe, fraternity, church, etc., is very important for us. This is why we have, in various ways and degrees, a tendency to follow norms—a tendency that helps us become part of the groups that abide by the norms in question. Let us now add the perhaps strange idea that this sense of belonging, the feeling that we partake from a group and that we follow its norms, can be literally vital, as we will see in this second part of the chapter.

Let us start this discussion by going back to Emile Durkheim (2007), who showed that people are more likely to commit suicide when they fail to find, and conform to, social norms. He called these "anomic suicides." ("Anomic" means "normless": Anomic societies revolve around rules and norms that are either very weak or that have ceased to elicit compliance from citizens. These societies are thus poorly organized, poorly integrated, and rather anarchical.) Durkheim, that is to say, has shown that people who do not have enough norms to follow, or people who face social norms that have become irrelevant or unimportant, *are more likely to kill themselves*. He has shown that a minimum necessary of adherence to, and respect for, norms can be literally vital (an important issue that we will discuss subsequently).

On the other hand, he also shows that people who have to follow too many and too strict norms are also more likely to find their existence unbearable. Hence, Durkheim also speaks of "altruistic suicides," the opposite of anomic suicides. Altruistic suicides involve oppressive and ultimately crushing morals, crushing social rules and norms: Suicide bombers provide examples of "altruistic" suicides, not because their ideals are in fact altruistic but because terrorists often feel that their actions, murderous such as they are, are actually guided by higher moral principles—principles that, in their minds, are in fact so superlative and so morally correct as to justify the sacrifice of human lives, including the lives of those who abide by these supposed values.

But why would weak or inexistent norms lead to suicide? Why is it that not being able to follow norms can be psychologically damaging and even physically damaging? Let us further elucidate these questions by first considering death spells.

Death Spells

Imagine the following scenario: A member of a tribal community breaks a social taboo and is therefore judged and found guilty. To be sentenced and punished, the infractor will be brought before a sorcerer who will invoke the spirits, recite an incantation, perhaps point a dirty bone toward the accused person, and, having thus secured powers over life and death, will finally cast a death spell against this person. Now that the absurd ceremony is over,

> a consensus is reached among all concerned that the end [of the infractor] is near, and the victim's friends and family retreat as from the smell of death. They return, but only to wail and chant over the body of a person whom they consider already dead. Physically the victim still lives; psychologically he or she is dying; socially he or she is already dead (Wade, 1988, p. 206).

Death spells, primitive and scientifically inept as they are, are often effective, nonetheless. Researchers are not sure exactly what physiological mechanisms precipitate these demises, but there are strong indications that they are "psychogenic," anteceded by psychological disturbances, such as depression, as well as "sociogenic," having their origins in social factors. As I have suggested elsewhere, the victim of death spells must remain within the community, but he "is existentially removed from it; divested of his social roles, status, removed from normal contact with others" (Narváez, 2012). Socially, he or she is dead, which "often gives way to supralethal psychological disturbances [e.g., depression] that can antecede physical death" (Narváez, 2012). Researchers working on the absorbing, truly fascinating field of death spells have shown that the breakdown of the social ties that connect the individual to the world can be literally fatal for intensely social creatures like human beings. Hence, returning to Durkheim, the breakdown of social norms that sustain these social interactions and social ties may lead to the feeling of isolation, depression, and, thus, higher rates of suicide. For some individuals, the breakdown of social norms can work like a death spell.

Isolation Experienced as the Collapse of Reality

Relatedly, let us consider phenomena pertaining to physical isolation to further illustrate how vital it is for us to partake in a social environment and, for this reason, how eager we can be to comply with social requirements, which allows us to fit in and to partake from a group.

Years ago, a colleague and I took students to a penitentiary in West Texas. For my part, I was interested in showing these students the solitary confinement cell, in particular, so as to impress upon them precisely the importance that social interaction has for human beings. The cell was a small, padded, entirely white room with no furniture at all (even light switches were on the outside). This eerie box, which closely resembled the cells of psychiatric wards, had a hole in the middle, "the bathroom," the sheriff explained. The cell was padded to prevent inmates from injuring themselves. The sheriff also noted that sometimes, after removing the inmate, guards had to enter the room armed with high-pressure hoses, as some prisoners, presumably experiencing symptoms of psychosis, besmirched the walls and themselves with their own feces. (Modern solitary confinement cells, a criminal justice professor has told me, are already equipped with internal hosing mechanisms that serve this purpose.)

Some people withstand solitary confinement more stoically than others. But typically, "the experience is disorienting, unsettling, and no less acute than the hunger and the thirst that come from a prolonged fast" (Alter, 2013, p. 82). Psychiatrist Stuart Grassian (2006) has reported that inmates in solitary confinement often experience hallucinations, perceptual distortion, loss of "perceptual constancy" (e.g., some objects may be perceived as changing sizes, same noises may become softer and then louder); memory loss; impulsive self-mutilation; difficulty with thinking, which may lead to acute psychotic states; fearfulness; agitation; paranoia; and hypersensitivity to sensory stimuli (e.g., some inmates may scream in response to noises from water pipes). Grassian's research, as well as many other studies (e.g., Liederman, 1962), have helped us see that isolation often leads, in fact, to a specific kind of disease characterized by a breakdown of the person's sense of reality. Charles Dickens visited a Philadelphia prison and described the sight of a sailor in solitary confinement in the following way: "Why does he stare at his hands and pick the flesh open, upon the fingers, and raise his eyes for an instant [...] to those bare walls?" (in Grassian, 2006).

Beyond helping us understand the importance of social interaction, this kind of research has also allowed us to understand that the reality that human beings experience is largely socially constructed, the product precisely of social interaction, and that it cannot be a purely individual construction. We shower, get dressed in the morning, choose certain clothes to put on, etc., not *only* because these things make sense in our heads but also because they *make sense in the presence of others* within a social context. These activities make sense, above all, as social norms. So in isolation, a situation where social norms do not exist, these everyday behaviors will eventually cease to be fully meaningful or meaningful at all. Isolation progressively diminishes meaning; it can, in fact, erase the meaning that everyday life has for us; and this progressive absence of meaning can lead to psychological breakdown. In this particular sense, isolation can work like a death spell as well.

Other people thus help us confirm that some things "make sense" and others do not. The presence of others, the gaze of others, the viewpoints of others, largely sustain our meanings. Meaning is, in this sense, largely othered, collectively sustained (and collectively constructed, as we will soon see). The experience of reality is likewise othered, sustained by a social context. And, therefore, the absence of others is often experienced as the absence of reality, a strange predicament that closely resembles madness. It is not a coincidence that the experience of solitary confinement—"no-touch torture," as human rights activists have named it—is often characterized by the same symptoms that characterize psychosis.

José Mujica, former president of Uruguay, was imprisoned in his youth for political reasons and spent two years confined to the bottom of a well. Some of his comrades who were also imprisoned lost their reason to similar conditions of existence, and it appears that the goal of their jailers was, in fact, to fracture the prisoners' very sense of self, their grasp of reality. But Mujica managed to retain his sanity, in part by "befriending" a frog and some rats, that, in such circumstances, provided the illusion of a social link. Michel Siffre was a French explorer who volunteered to participate in a research study about solitary confinement, spending six months in a cave in Texas. By day 79, he descended into a severe bout of depression and considered suicide. Much as Mujica, however, Siffre also clung to a newfound "friend": a mouse that helped him regain his will to live. When he accidentally killed the mouse, he sunk again into depression, which became, as he later wrote, "overwhelming."

Such is the need for social contact among human beings. Some speculative theologians have defined Hell not as a place of eternal flames, but as a state of complete and eternal isolation, accompanied by deafening silence and total darkness—a state of "nonbeing."

Hospitalism

Let us discuss a final example that also bespeaks the vital importance that human contact has for us. During the Second World War, England was virtually devastated. Children were orphaned in disproportionate numbers, and nurses were overworked, attending to soldiers near battlefields as well as wounded civilians in the cities. Orphanages were, therefore, severely overcrowded and severely understaffed. But the English managed to secure the basic necessities for the survival of the children: food, warm rooms, clean diapers, safe cribs, medicine. Yet these infants and children eventually began to show noticeable deficits: Many of them were not developing normal cognitive abilities and indeed their physical growth was sometimes stunted. Some of them in fact died. How was this possible given that they had their necessities covered? Rene Spitz, a now famous English pediatrician, studied the problem and discovered a stunning and truly sobering fact about human development. These children failed to develop normally *not* because they lacked food, or warmth, or medicine but because they lacked human contact. The overworked nurses did not have time to hold them, to caress them, to return their gaze. The children's brains were not developing properly because of this tragic fact. Their brains needed social contact. Stunningly, their bones were not properly growing either—*not because they lacked milk and calcium but because the children lacked the company of other human beings.* Such symptoms were originally characterized under the label "hospitalism," a pediatric failure to thrive that has origins in *social*, not originally physiological, deficits.

To summarize, because we are social animals incapable of initially surviving and growing without the presence of others, we may easily feel that social groups and networks around us are like shelters of sorts. And for this reason, we can also easily sense that the norms that govern the lives of these networks are like keys to these shelters, links that allow us to partake from the lives of these groups. Bear in mind that noncompliance with these norms will automatically make us outsiders. And precisely because a social context is so important for us, societies, groups of peers, tribes, clans, fraternities, churches, monasteries, military institutions, etc., often elicit a genuine desire, an almost instinctive readiness to follow social norms that, in the end, can affect or indeed determine our biography, our life, and, as the example of Grace suggests, even how we die.

CHAPTER VII

"Social Animals"

Norms and Normality

Let us provide a formal definition of social norms. Norms, for us, are unwritten codes of conduct that provide standards of, precisely, *norm*ality for members of societies, organizations, or social groups such as churches, fraternities, or other such ingroups. Norms are collectively relevant standards of behavior that members of social groups tend to follow *regardless of whether the standards in question are good or not, logical or not, valuable or not*. Inasmuch as we follow them, these social rules or codes tie us not only to the groups and communities where these codes apply but also to certain ideas, values, and behaviors. Over time, they tie us to certain habits: habits of thought, habits of the heart, habits of conduct, so that these social codes can indeed shape our biography. Ideally, societies, as well as social groups, should aspire to have a maximal number of norms that are good, logical, ethical, and valuable. This is perhaps the best definition of an advanced society and of a forward-thinking group. But in reality, even the most advanced societies and groups are at least minimally governed by norms that fall short of these ideals. And it is easy to see why. Human beings can be very smart, but we are also fallible creatures. We often have prejudices. We easily embrace errors. Social norms do not fall from heaven already formed; we constantly produce them and produce them anew, and they may therefore be, like ourselves, imperfect, when not entirely erroneous. The same is true for broader social narratives in general: The whole cultural apparatus that surrounds our lives and that encourages a certain way of thinking and acting in citizens—can be sustained by errors as well.

An obvious example of an unambiguously good and logical social norm is, say, stopping at a red light (which is also a law, a particular type of norm governed by the state, rather than enforced by society itself). If we fail to follow this norm, we may kill ourselves or someone else. An example of a bad social norm is, as we saw, rejecting a career simply because, according to a given social narrative, the career in question is "unfeminine" (e.g., being a scientist, a politician, a member of the military, a boss). As we also saw, women who followed these kinds of norms found their lives, paychecks, and intellectual abilities diminished.

For us, having the advantage of hindsight, as well as an external and hence more objective viewpoint, it is easy to see that these kinds of norms have been bad. But it is usually difficult, when not impossible, for people to ascertain which of the norms *they* follow are good and which ones are bad. This is so because norms, the cultural air they breathe, establish standards of normality, and things that are accepted as normal are generally accepted as valid as well. Although it is easy for an external observer to see, for instance, that there is nothing abnormal about a woman driving a car, for many Saudi women, this was just wrong ("flog her!"). People, in general and save exceptions, tend to accept their cultural norms more or less wholesale without taking first an objective distance from them to figure out whether these seemingly normal codes of conduct are actually normal or beneficial. This is the sort of objective distance that might allow us to dispassionately and objectively examine the ideas and values of a previous generation, or those of a different culture. And just as an external vantage point makes it easy for us to see if the norms of other cultures are good, or absurd, or harmful, an external observer may likewise be able to see the norms operant in our own culture more objectively. This person may therefore see the, perhaps, absurd or harmful nature of some of *our* standards of normality.

Because it is difficult for people to see which of their own norms are good or bad, people can easily end up embracing bad ones. And when this happens, people may end up embracing undesirable views and behaviors, as well, because norms promote attendant views and behaviors (for example, the odd idea that women must not drive promoted behaviors alternative to driving; and the worldviews of the people who embraced this norm were tinted or filtered by it). At a broader level, societies themselves may also embrace undesirable norms, as suggested. After all, societies are formed by individuals, and individuals can make these sorts of mistakes. Institutions, countries, and entire generations may therefore establish normal practices and conventions that may hinder their own development. Of course, other factors can affect the advancement of a group or of a country, including the availability of natural resources, geography, etc. But cultural norms tend to play a critical role as well. Norms may strengthen or harm a society, as well as specific groups within society, including, for instance, American women of the 1950s generation, women who could not drive a car in Saudi Arabia, or the Nicks that Kimmel describes.

For these reasons, *it is imperative for citizens to be able to be in dialogue not only with morality and the law, as we noted, but also with normality itself.* Citizens have to try to determine, judiciously and deliberatively, whether their *normal* social lives are in fact beneficial, rational, well informed, and in this sense actually normal. Let us consider some examples that illustrate this idea—the idea that *it is important to develop a sense of literacy about normality itself.*

The Way We Dress

Let us begin with "sartorial norms," which govern how we dress and why. Few American parents would dress their girls in blue and fewer still would dress their boys in pink because we tend to think that these colors are masculine and feminine. But, of course, colors in themselves are neither. We have simply made them gender specific, and they could have been constructed, and have been constructed, differently, following different gender associations. Even up to the first quarter of the 20th century, blue was generally considered girlish and pink boyish. In 1914, the Sunday Sentinel noted, "If you like the colour note on the little one's garment, use pink for the boy and blue for the girl, if you are follower of convention." In 1918, the trade publication of Earnshaw's infant department noted, "The generally accepted rule is pink for the boys and blue for the girls. The reason is that pink, being a more decided and stronger color, is more suitable for the boy, while blue, which is more delicate and dainty, is prettier for the girl" (also cited in the *Ladies Home Journal* of that year) (in Paoleti, 2012). The point here is *not* that we are either right or wrong to dress our boys and girls with color-coded garments (that, in any case, is for you to decide). Instead, the idea is that norms can be entirely arbitrary, even when we strongly feel that there is a natural reason for their existence—for example, a natural reason for boys not to wear pink. Here are other examples of this: Most American parents would also feel strongly against dressing their boys in skirts. And yet, by the end of the 19th century, dressing boys up to 6 or 7 years of age in skirts (the time also of their first haircut) was normative in the United States. Many Americans also feel that it is not normal or natural for men to wear skirts, high heels, wigs, and/or makeup. Yet at different times in history, it was normative for (heterosexual) men to wear these things. Leather skirts were part of the military uniform of Roman soldiers, for example. During the kingdom of Louis XIV, in the 17th and 18th centuries, high heels, wigs, and makeup were marks of power among noble men, and in this sense, these accoutrements increased their masculinity score.

The Way We Eat

Culinary norms, which govern what we eat and how, can provide perhaps the clearest examples of, precisely, how norms that are arbitrary can nevertheless elicit a visceral commitment to them.

Few things would seem more revolting to average Americans than eating a cockroach. Yet in Madagascar, various parts of China, Thailand, and South Africa, cockroaches are commonly eaten (Fischler, 1990). What this means is that *if* our culture trained us from day one to eat cockroaches, as is the case in these other places, we would happily enjoy these things, perhaps with friends and dates, and during family dinners and celebrations. And what *this* means, in turn, is that the seemingly *natural* and visceral revulsion we feel about the idea of eating a cockroach is not natural. It is cultural. It is a question of having grown up with some culinary norms instead of others. Unsurprisingly, our norms and injunctions against eating this kind of revolting insect will seem the right ones. But, perhaps surprisingly, there is no natural or objective reason for *not* eating this or any other kind of edible insect.

There are natural reasons for not eating, say, poisonous plants, but no such natural argument can be made against eating edible insects. If there were natural injunctions against doing so, no one would eat them, but they are eaten, often as delicacies, around the world. Edible insects include, for example, a type of cricket and butterfly larvae in Mexico; ants and certain worms in Peru and Thailand; snails and cheese worms in France; spiders in Papua New Guinea; wasps and bees in China, Burma, and Malaysia; certain varieties of butterflies and moths or their larvae in Indonesia, Japan, China, Madagascar, and Zimbabwe (Fischler, 1990); tarantulas in some areas in Thailand and Cambodia; and certain caterpillars and locusts in China. We could go on. To be precise, we could list 1,400 species of edible insects. But the point, for now, is that our revulsion against eating insects is neither natural nor shared universally, and that, more importantly, this revulsion might even be nonsensical as well. Bear in mind that protein from insects is healthier than the protein from the meat most Americans enjoy. Protein is often more concentrated in insects so that whereas 100 grams of hamburger provide about 21 grams of protein, 100 grams of African termites, for example, provide 38 grams of protein (Fischler, 1990). Insects are also far cheaper and easier to farm, and these farming practices are far more sustainable than ours.

Still, you could argue that, regardless of these seeming benefits, insects are, nevertheless, revolting creatures and that eating them would therefore be just bad. But the point is that, because this sense of revulsion is culturally driven, it can be changed, like all things cultural. To be sure, groups of citizens as well as governments the world over are trying do just that. They are trying to modify existing culinary norms in their own countries and to make it desirable to eat insects, precisely because of the benefits of these kinds of proteins and farming practices. Perhaps, then, your grandchildren will find it odd that folks of your generation were so hesitant about eating the insects of the land while, at the same time, enjoying the insects of the sea, shrimp, periwinkles, and so on. Such as it is, chances are that you are already eating and enjoying insects regularly. Cochineal bugs, for instance, are commonly pulped and used as natural food colorants in the United States in foods such as yogurt, sushi, some pastries, canned foods, and many others. The Food and Drug Administration legally allows for various amounts of insects in a wide range of staple foods sold in the United States. Peanut butter, for example, may contain an "average of 30 or more insect fragments per 100 grams"; canned or frozen spinach may contain an "average of 50 or more aphids, thrips, and/or mites per 100 grams"; citrus fruit juices may have an "average of 5 or more Drosophilia [common fly] and other fly eggs per 250 ml or 1 or more maggots per 250 ml," etc. (U.S. Food and Drug Administration, 2018).

Perhaps, then, the taste of insects is not that revolting after all. Perhaps the sense of disgust you likely feel is not on your palate, but in your head only, the inheritance of a certain cultural tradition assigned to you at birth. Perhaps, then, we should change this tradition, accept this kind of protein more openly and forthrightly, and thus enjoy, as well, the various farming and environmental benefits listed earlier (not to mention the new flavors and textures that this might, perhaps, add to our cuisine).

Consider other types of food available in this wide world of ours: dogs and cats in parts of China; horses in France, Belgium, Spain, Germany, and Japan; frogs in France, parts of Asia and Peru; rats in 42 cultures (Fischler, 1990); guinea pigs in most of the Andean Region; dormice in Ancient Rome; donkeys in parts of Spain. (Not to mention odd food fads, such as eating human placenta, a practice observable particularly in Central and Northern Europe, as well as in the United States and Canada. In Canada, this practice is common enough so as to prompt the Ministry of Health and Social Services to issue an official warning against its possible ill effects.) Here is an ancient recipe for dormice, a type of mouse of the Mediterranean region: Stuff them "with a forcemeat of pork and small pieces of dormouse meat trimmings, all pounded with pepper, nuts, laser [an aromatic herb] and broth. Put the dormouse thus stuffed in an earthen casserole, roast it in the oven, or boil it in the stock pot" (in Starr, 1977). To prepare *balut*, a dish from the Philippines, you simply boil a fertilized egg incubated for 14 to 21 days, depending on preference; and then you eat the half-formed chick or duckling directly from the shell. In France, a Mecca for foodies, people "regularly feast on all sorts of foods that elicit disgust in other cultures (although less and less, it is true): snails, frogs, live oysters, intestines of various animals, head of calf, marrow, lamb brain, calf kidney, pork liver, the feet, ears, or tails of pigs" (Fischler, 1990, pp. 27–28, my translation).

Importantly, this idea applies, beyond France, to any other country: Peoples the world over, likewise, "regularly feast on all sorts of foods that may elicit disgust" in others. Being served a bucket of modified chicken and a bucket-size serving of soda in a car might elicit disgust in cultures outside the United States, for example.

The fact that the foods that some cherish will revolt others begs the question, who is right? Sociologists, of course, are not trained to determine which country has the better cuisine (this is a discussion for gastronomists). But, nevertheless, we may try to help folks see that,

a. their likes and dislikes, however visceral the feelings, are mostly the result of socialization, of a certain kind of cultural training;

b. that these likes and dislikes, and therefore the culinary tradition itself, can be changed, and that it, in fact, often changes. For example, when first introduced in Europe, potatoes were typically disdained, often regarded as a devilish aphrodisiac and therefore as an indecent type of food, and yet they eventually became a literally vital staple for Europeans; and

c. that such changes in the tradition may result in advantages for the society as a whole, including, for example, improved health, improved sustainability, cheaper and better calories and proteins, lower rates of animal suffering, and benefits for the environment.

Dirt, Excreta, and the History of Repugnance

Lastly, consider norms that regulate the ways we deal with dirt, bodily odors, and excreta (urine and feces). Even a quick glance into the history of disgust will show that today, we place more emphasis on hygiene than ever. Historian Katherine Ashenburg (2007) has wryly noted that current social norms dictate that persons, particularly in frontstage situations, should ideally smell "like an exotic fruit (mango, papaya, passion fruit) or a cookie (vanilla, coconut, ginger)." In our epoch, for a human being to smell like a human being has become a "social misdemeanor," Ashenburg adds (2007). Bodily odor, as Irving Goffman has also argued, has become a "territorial violation" that is instantaneously perceived and generally disapproved, when not resented so that the infractor is typically shunned, avoided, or socially punished, say, by disapproving looks, by gossip, etc. This norm about bodily odors makes our sense of repugnance about this kind of smell, precisely, "normal" and, for this reason, seemingly universal. It would be hard for many of us to imagine that for most of human history, this has not been the standard social expectation at all. And it would be even harder to imagine that, not unusually, some people also considered quite normal—in fact, *preferred*—the company of men who smelled "of the army, of farm work, and of manliness!" to quote the Roman philosopher, Seneca (in Ashenburg, 2007). Furthermore, bodily smell was not only accepted as normal but was also often eroticized (and still is in some cultures, such as the Hazda in Tanzania). From the battlefield, Napoleon writes a note to his wife, Josephine: "I will return to Paris tomorrow evening. Don't wash" (in Ashenburg, 2007).

If we were to imagine, say, a meeting of the "Founding Fathers," or a Shakespearean play with men and women of the Elizabethan period, or an assembly of the 12 apostles, or a well-attended opera premiered by Mozart, or a Roman Legion, we would likely imagine these scenes from our perspective. And to the extent to which we do imagine these people according to our olfactory standards, they would either be free of bodily odors or would be dispensing a polite and "fresh" scent, "like an exotic fruit [...] or a cookie." But this perspective would be erroneous. "The scent of another's bodies," as Ashenburg reports, was "the ocean our ancestors swam in, and they were used to the everyday odor of dried sweat. It was part of the world, along with the smells of cooking, roses, garbage, pine forests and manure" (2007, p. 2).

This was also the case with excreta. In many, perhaps in most, ancient societies, feces and urine were regarded as resources. "In India, ancient Sanskrit texts outlined the medicinal use of urine through *shivambu* (auto-urine therapy)" (Bracken et al., 2007, p. 220). Greeks, Romans, and Celts used human urine to launder fabrics and even to dye their hair. In many European, Arab, Asian, and pre-Columbian societies, feces were considered an agricultural resource, a notion that, in Europe, "clearly continued [...] into the middle of the 19th century" (in Bracken et al., 2007), and that in Japan extended to the 20th century. In this country, 23,950,285 tons of excreta were reportedly used as fertilizer in 1908 alone (Bracken et al., 2007). But beginning with modernity, we began to develop a phobic concern with excreta, particularly motivated by advances in medicine (hygiene), as well as by the marketing strategies of a growing odorizing and deodorizing industry (which also coincide with the modern olfactory norms noted earlier). These cultural changes have resulted in vast networks of "waste" disposal the world over, which has been one of the most important advancements in global public health, tantamount to the discovery of penicillin and the invention of the syringe. Modern waste disposal, to be sure, has saved millions of lives. But these disposal systems have also created unnecessary environmental pressures and an unnecessary waste of money and effort.

In 2009, certain areas in Brazil faced severe droughts and attendant economic loss. Their many-fronts response included a countrywide campaign under the banner "*Xixi no banho!*" (roughly: "pee in the shower!"). This was a public awareness media strategy, full of humor, cartoons, and charm that encouraged, precisely, this new cultural norm, the adoption of which could have saved up to 1,500 liters of water per second in the city of Sao Paulo alone, thus ameliorating drought conditions while producing no public health risks. Should these kinds of well-studied and practicable new norms be adopted in the world—*which would involve changing our cultures and our normal concerns with excreta*—the world could likewise save money and environmental resources, while creating no additional public health concerns. The not-for-profit organization Recode has been at the forefront of just such consciousness raising, norm-altering efforts in the United States (while also working on the kinds of technologies and legislations that could allow for a cultural, legal, and technological transition to this kind of new and improved normal). Recode director Molly Winter has waggishly noted, "Thinking about where it all goes is the first step in activating what are actually superpowers in our poo and pee [...] And if we use them well, we can live healthier and more beautifully" (2016). The Bill and Melinda Gates Foundation, in turn, has recently invented a toilet that, requiring neither water nor connection to a sewage system, takes human feces and urine and converts them, as Bill Gates has noted, "into products with potential commercial value, like clean water, electricity, and fertilizer" (Gates, 2018). The use of this invention could save water, energy, money, and effort globally. And for this to happen, the primary remaining obstacle is to change our, for now, *normal* concerns with excreta, the cultural norms that govern this aspect of everyday life in most of the world.

These examples show, in summary, that norms can be very powerful determinants of our likes and dislikes, of our habits of the mind, habits of the heart, and habits of the palate, as well as the way we normally relate to the world. In their ability to affect these things, norms can powerfully determine how we live our lives and confer advantages and disadvantages upon us as individuals and as societies. And it is entirely up to us to figure out which seemingly normal ideas, behaviors, products, predilections give us trouble, which ones make us less free, which ones help us, which ones involve the unnecessary waste of money and other resources, and which ones make our communities stronger.

To reiterate the broader point, sociology may help us see that we have to be able to be *in constant dialogue with norms themselves*, rather than mechanically accepting the normality of a world where we have been thrown in by chance.

The habit of questioning normality may also bring innovation and creativity, as well as enormous business opportunities for those who can read through this aspect of the world. Bill Gates has noted that his new invention, the waterless toilet, is currently difficult to accept, as it goes against the accepted standards of normality. Yet, he adds, it can eventually create a hitherto unseen and global market, "*a multi-billion business opportunity*," "an opportunity to meet the needs of 4.5 billion people around the world" (2018, my italics). What other business opportunities are hidden by the seeming obviousness of our current standards of normality? What other opportunities for creative thought are likewise hidden by the same norms? Dissecting these standards, seeing through these norms, that is to say, can create previously unseen opportunities in areas so diverse as cuisine, farming, and the environment, as well as technology and commerce. (At the very least, the ability to dissect the given norms allows us as individuals or as a society, to insist on another central idea, to avoid conforming to norms that may well be absurd, belittling, or damaging.)

Deviance as Positive

Some norms can be very beneficial, as also suggested, and history provides many examples of them. But even the briefest glance at history will also let us see many examples of social narratives, norms, and values that, as we see them today, are arbitrary, stupid, cruel, demeaning, dehumanizing, and damaging to individuals, to the environment, and to legitimate groups in society. Beyond the examples provided earlier, let us consider this important historical perspective.

At various points in history, for instance, it has been normal to burn cats alive for public entertainment. The spectacle took place on a stage. A cat was tied to a rope, the animal was hoisted above a bonfire, and it was slowly lowered in the direction of the fire for the public to jeer, cheer, and laugh as the cat howled in pain and terror. Cruelty in general has been, and to an extent is today, a normal form of entertainment. Infanticide (killing infants) has also been normal for much of history. Members of the feudal nobility sometimes waged war against their peers by massacring their enemies' *peasants*. Slavery has been a constant for most of history (and, historically speaking, it was very recently that we discovered the brutality of this form of "common sense," as it was seen in previous epochs). Indeed, it was normal for captains of slave ships transporting human cargo to throw captives to the sea if the captain deemed that they were too sick to make it to their port of destination. (Sharks in the Caribbean, the sea used by these vessels to reach American shores, had learned to follow those vile ships.) In the American South, it was not uncommon for a farmer to father his own slaves while also thinking of slavery as a God-designed system. Thomas Jefferson himself fathered at least one, if not seven, of his slaves (Foster et al., 1998). In the American South, *up to the 20th century*, many African American men and women were tortured and/or killed for such crimes as not addressing a police officer as "mister," or for voting, or for testifying against a white man accused of raping a black woman. For most of history, many poor people have been executed, in the most tortuous and cruel manner, and for the most frivolous and trivial reasons, such as criticizing the royal garden. An estimated 80,000 European women were burned alive in public squares because they were suspected of being witches, and such suspicions sometimes hinged on also breathtakingly frivolous reasons, including thinking that the woman in question, usually a peasant, was too beautiful or too ugly, or "suspiciously attuned to nature" (e.g., knowing about medicinal plants), or a "free thinker." Some of these women were judged according to the also normal and commonsensical standards of the time, which included, for example, removing the witch's clothes, throwing her on the floor, and then poking her naked body with a long needle so as to find "the soft spot" that the devil had left after penetrating her body. Other tests, which were also regarded as commonsensical, consisted of throwing the captive woman into a pond or lake and deeming her guilty if she *floated* (many medieval women, particularly if old, suffered from osteoporosis on account of typically poor nutrition and thus floated). Yet another kind of "commonsensical" trial involved reading a passage from the Bible to the accused woman, written in Latin—a language she did not understand—and deeming her guilty if she did not shed tears in response to the biblical drama.

Such examples of "commonsensical" errors and cruelties abound in history. It is indeed breathtaking to see the full extent to which "common sense" has harbored errors, including bizarre and utterly brutal errors, as exemplified in the foregoing. Hence, it is not difficult to see that many deviant persons—that is to say, persons who go against the accepted common sense, from Nelson Mandela, to painter Paul Gaugin, to Martin Luther King Jr.—have sponsored positive social renewal and creativity. Precisely because they went against lesser or even damaging and yet "commonsensical" norms, values, or practices, they were able to help, or to beautify, or to redeem their communities and epochs. Let's return to Emile Durkheim. He also showed that acts of deviance—that is, acts that go against mainstream social norms and codes—are indeed necessary for societies. Consider Grace again, for example. Had she decided to go against the rules that governed gender relations, she would have died, most likely, without regrets. And had her generation spoken against these impoverishing social rules, society as a whole would have become enriched, as it eventually did, particularly through feminist movements, movements that, for the most part, exemplified (positive) deviance.

Deviance, let us insist, is often beneficial for the individual and for the community. If we were to imagine a society without any form of deviance, such a society would be not only dreadfully predictable and monotonous but also without hope for those who, like Grace or Manal al-Sharif, endure oppressive conditions. Such a society would be stagnant. And let us remember that stagnant waters foster poison and stench, and that only lower forms of life (bacteria, viruses) are attracted to them. Again, a degree of conformity is vital for any society. But deviants can also contribute to the health and to the creativity of a society, as the examples of Mandela, Gauguin, Manal al-Sharif, and many others suggest. A healthy society, going back to Mead, is one that provides clear codes of conduct for individuals—while also allowing for forms of deviance. Such a society thus allows for social stability but also for social change. It aims to have a balance between tradition, which grounds individuals in a shared past, and innovation, which allows individuals to face the future and change normal standards and thus innovate for it.

Now, of course, violent criminals are also deviants, and they do not contribute to social renewal. But *positive* deviance helps us think through and beyond the social code, which is the only way we could sort out the aspects of our culture and collective life that are bad. Likewise, some deviant subcultures, called "countercultures," can also become sources of social renewal, creativity, and hope. Countercultures are often important for democratic systems, as they sponsor new ways of thinking and new experiences, while also fostering new norms, traditions, or laws, or new aesthetic forms, (e.g., new music, new cuisines) and new lifestyles. (And it is critical not to confuse countercultures with "deviant subgroups," such as cults or gangs, which are driven by dogmatism, ignorance, and animosity, and contribute not to renewal but to suffering.) Let us, in fact, speak of "positive crimes," which are sometimes associated with countercultures. These involve the breaking of absurd, tyrannical, or dehumanizing laws, such as the laws that prevented women from voting, from driving, from owning property and the laws that defended slavery. These crimes—that is to say, breaking these sorts of laws—can also create higher forms of social life. Abolitionist movements, which, of course, existed at the margins of the law, provide examples that illustrate this idea.

Crime as Positive

Indeed, let us emphasize the idea that good citizens disobey bad laws, a concept known as "civil disobedience," associated particularly with the work of American philosopher Henry David Thoreau (1817–1862). Thoreau argued that an honest person cannot recognize "for an instant" an unjust form of government as his or her own. Doing so would be tantamount to complicity. When a person breaks despotic laws, he or she is engaging in a form of violence against the social order, but when he or she *obeys* despotic laws, the person is not only engaging in violence, that of the regime, but also legitimizing and perpetuating such violence. In this sense, obeying the law can be worse than breaking it, as Thoreau also maintains.

And thus a criminal defined in this particular sense can be more helpful for his or her country than a law-abiding citizen. This is an idea that largely made the United States the country that it is today. This idea also became an American gift to the world in general, inspiring other important civil rights movements elsewhere, including, for example, the India Independence Movement, led by Mahatma Gandhi and others. In the United States, one of the most iconic images depicting the civil rights movement is that of Rosa Parks holding her booking number *after being arrested for having broken the law*. Indeed, consider the civil rights movement as a whole and recognize that, often operating on the margins of the law, it was heavily influenced by Thoreau's ideas about civil disobedience. To be sure, many of the great liberation movements in the United States and around the world were led by men and women who saw, with Thoreau, that "under a government which imprisons any unjustly, the true place for a just [person] is also a prison" (Thoreau 2012). Under an unjust government, the truest actions of such a just person are criminal in nature—a form of crime that provides hope for oppressed groups and that, particularly if it inspires a social movement, can redeem the nation itself.

We have seen that, according to the criminal code extant in North Korea, listening to "decadent music" constitutes a crime. Under the Taliban, it was a crime for a girl to attend school. Up until 2017, trading, bartering, buying, or selling an infant was only a misdemeanor, not a felony, in Pennsylvania. In Virginia, in 2018, having sex outside marriage was a Class 4 misdemeanor punishable with a fine. Laws do not fall from heaven. They are made by men and women who are more or less intelligent, more or less decent, and more or less dogmatic. Ideally, all legislators are good, and ideally, all laws are good, of course, but *not* because they are legislators or laws and therefore must be inherently good. What laws, in your view, are or have been absurd? What laws have been cruel, demeaning, dehumanizing, and damaging to individuals, to the life system, or damaging to legitimate groups in society? What laws are bound to change? Which ones have changed from your parents' generation to today and why? Was it because people finally recognized that these laws were irrational or demeaning? Or was it because these laws were correct, just, and logical, and yet they were eventually deemed incorrect? What forms of "common sense" and what aspects of "normality" are likewise stupid, cruel, dehumanizing, and damaging to individuals, to the environment, and to legitimate groups in your society?

Max Weber

Thus norms and laws contribute to shaping the life course of the individual and the historical course of a society. Let us add that the *ideas* that a culture produces also play a critical role in this regard. Collectively relevant ideas can indeed decisively shape the array of social institutions and human experiences, and penetrate and mold the most intimate and enduring aspects of individual and national life. To consider this enormously important perspective, we now turn to one of the giants in the human sciences, German sociologist Max Weber.

Weber's most important work, *The Protestant Ethic and the Spirit of Capitalism* (1958), is an analysis of the economic development of Western countries, where he shows that, on trend, Protestant countries developed faster than Catholic ones. (Indeed, even today predominantly and historically Protestant countries, such as Germany and the United States, are still industrial and financial engines in the world, and, on the other hand, countries such Spain and Ireland, for all their splendors and accomplishments, have had a significantly slower course of economic development. To be sure, parts of Spain and Ireland were arguably part of the European third world up until the first quarter of the 20th century.)

When Weber zooms in and traces the development of *regions* within countries, he observes the same pattern: Generally, predominantly Protestant regions, cities, provinces have also been the richest and Catholic regions have been the poorest. And then when he zooms in all the way to the microlevel of factories, he finds the same pattern yet again: Protestant workers have generally fared better than their Catholic counterparts. Likewise, lastly, with people within the general population: Protestants have tended to own more capital than Catholics.

Weber's (broadly accepted) data, of course, beg the question, why is this so? Why has, historically, Protestantism been the route to economic development and not Catholicism? In short, Weber's famous answer is that these religions have provided collectively relevant and culturally entrenched ideas that have either facilitated or, in contrast, slowed down economic development. Let us consider some of these ideas, their historical progression, and their economic consequences.

Protestantism is an umbrella term that encompasses religious denominations whose roots can be traced to the ideas of Martin Luther, the German Catholic monk who, precisely, *protested* against his own church, and who denounced it as a fraudulent institution—an institution that, Luther argued, had betrayed the faith, the scriptures, and the original teachings of Christ himself. Luther's protest—indeed his rage against his own church and his superiors all the way to the pope—was spurred particularly by one event that, in Luther's eyes, epitomized what he saw as the moral bankruptcy of Catholicism—namely, the "selling of indulgences." This was a well-entrenched fundraising tradition within Catholicism, the selling of divine favors to anyone able to buy them, for the customer to either reduce the penuries of a particular soul in purgatory (a friend, business partner, a concubine) or, as many worshipers believed, to buy a spot in heaven itself, regardless of whether the customer in question had led a life of true righteousness.

Luther was possibly obsessive and even neurotic, constantly wracking his mind and soul and body, even as a child, in search of possible hints of sin that may imperil his salvation. And for this obsessive champion of righteousness, the selling of celestial favors was nothing less than a fraud, itself sinful, and, worse, it also robbed the faithful of the true path of salvation. For Luther, this path could *not* be given by an institution such as the church but by God Himself. For the believer, Luther argued, it was, in fact, a question of bypassing the institution itself to establish a *personal* relation with God, a *personal* understanding of the scriptures, a path of salvation that had to be carved by the individual himself or herself. It is thus commonly maintained that, for this reason, Luther's most important invention was individuality itself. This means that he deemphasized the role that the institution formerly had in terms of salvation and emphasized, instead, the role, precisely, of the individual. This was an individual who had to learn the message of Christ by himself or herself, according to his or her own devices, establishing a direct and intimate, rather than a mediated, relationship with God. To facilitate this personalized relationship with God, Luther, for example, translated the Bible, which was formerly available only in "the sacred language," Latin, a dead and ancient language whose splendorous ghost lived only in books and in the minds of the specialists able to decipher them. No regular believer spoke it. And yet every regular believer was asked to be guided by the teachings of this holy book, in Latin, and to recite some of the prayers in a language that had no meaning for him or her outside of the meaning given by a priest, by the institution, externally. Against the wishes of this institution, Luther "desecrated" the scriptures by translating them into the "vulgar" but nevertheless common language of the worshipers themselves. And he thus encouraged, again, a think-for-yourself-about-salvation attitude and approach.

Expectedly, officialdom asked him to recant, to deny his own views and to apologize for them. But in his turn, arrogating the role of defender of the true faith, Luther instead declared a sort of religious war against the church and against his superior, the pope himself. The church, of course, excommunicated him, which in essence condemned him to the eternal fire. But some clerics, and some principalities, and, eventually, some countries sided with him and his position. And yet other countries sided with his now mortal enemy, the pope, and the institutions of the Catholic Church. This fateful split, or "schism," in the Christian world led to a bitter, protracted and unusually violent and bloody war, the Thirty Years' War, that day after day, siege after siege, famine after famine, encouraging raping and torturing, devastated a large portion of Europe, leading to a final and bitter peace agreement. This treatise left a finally pacified, but broken, rancorous, and still divided Europe, divided, precisely, between Protestant and Catholic countries.

Let's return to Weber. He began his main analysis at this point, tracing the subsequent differential economic development of Western countries, as noted earlier.

Unintended Consequences of Religious Beliefs

Lutheranism and its various branches, such as Calvinism, have provided many ideas, of course; ideas that, their theological complexity notwithstanding, can nevertheless be reduced to three roots that are important for our analysis:

a. The concept of *predestination*: the notion that persons are born *already marked* for either heaven of for hell

b. *Asceticism*: the notion that the righteous life is *not* one of indulgence but of sacrifice and constant training for self-mastery—the mastery, above all, of one's appetites, especially of sexual appetites; and

c. The idea that believers have been appointed by God to fulfill a mission on earth, their "*calling*," which involves their trade, occupation, or profession.

Let us begin with the calling. What this meant was that, for the believers, performing their duty in their chosen fields—say, as a housewife, as a carpenter, as an academic—was a way of following God's plan. Heeding their calling was seen, indeed, as a form of worship that many saw as more real and effective than ritualized forms worship, such as attending services or reciting prayers. Say a carpenter who was brought up on this notion, would be likely to believe that, in making his chairs, he was also following some sort of divine plan. And hence he would also think that his duties as a tradesperson—sawing, sanding, nailing—were not really commanded by a boss, or by a client, but by God Himself. For someone who believed in the notion of the calling, these duties had to be performed well and attentively, even joyously, precisely as if these mundane activities were a special form of worship. These folks often worked as if making chairs, or making anything else associated with their calling, was an effective way of communicating with God. ("Shakers," for example, who are rightly famous for their outstanding skills in carpentry, reportedly made their chairs not for this or that customer, but for any angel that may choose to sit in them.)

It is not difficult to see how and why *the calling* provided ideological support not only for a culture where work ethic became normative but also for a certain kind of economic model, a productive one at that. It is easy to see that, in these communities, producing such goods as chairs, or cars, or providing services was facilitated by these kinds of internalized ideas and by the culturally relevant norms and values that these ideas promoted. It is easy to see, in other words, that, save all the exceptions, these were hard-working, and hence economically productive, communities. It is not a coincidence that the pilgrims who settled in New England, who came to America to, above all, establish a society fundamentally based on the teachings of John Calvin, were especially productive and that indeed they prospered rapidly so that even today, New England is one of the regions in the United States with comparatively high standards of living.

But how is it that the notions of predestination and asceticism contributed to economic development? For these believers, the question of whether they were predestined or not was, of course, important. In fact, it was a central preoccupation, when not a source of obsessive anxiety. For, after all, the stakes were high. Predestination meant that you were already destined to either partake from the everlasting bliss of heaven or to suffer unspeakable and eternal tortures in an infernal underworld. Hence, these men and women naturally tried to figure out whether they were marked for heaven or for hell. But the theology told them that they could *not* possibly know God's infinite mind, nor his plans for mere individuals such as themselves. Yet, they were also told, these worried believers, that they could gather some hints about God's plan from life itself. Are you fulfilling your calling? Are you, say, getting good grades? Yes? Then this is, perhaps, a sign that God is holding your hand. Are you doing well as a carpenter, or as a banker, or as a doctor, or as a student? If so, you might well be one of the chosen ones. And if, in contrast, you are doing poorly, if you are obtaining bad marks as a student, if no one buys your chairs, it might be a sign to the contrary, which, of course, very much added to a culture that emphasized hard work, as described earlier.

There were other hints as well. Are you able to master your appetites? Are you able to jump-start your day when the alarm clock rings at five in the morning? Or, in contrast, do you groggily press snooze and go back to sleep? Are you indulgent, or lazy, or worse, a debauched being? If so, perhaps the eternal flames are waiting around the corner. Which in turn, quickly added to a culture that valued a sense of asceticism and frugality. Thus these communities and cultures encouraged not only hard work but also frugality and therefore a sense of financial restraint, and the idea that saving money, rather than spending it on sumptuary and frivolous things, was important. This facilitated investment, and, in summary, it encouraged a cycle of hard work, frugality, and investment, which, going back to Weber, in the end facilitated the economic development of these individuals as well as of the communities and countries.

Weber shows, in summary, that these three ideas—which count among the pillars of Protestantism broadly conceived to include Calvinism—informed not only the strictly religious life of the worshiper. For these ideas eventually trickled down to inform, and indeed to shape, much of the everyday life in Protestant communities. In fact, these ideas eventually underpinned not only the beliefs of worshipers but also the very culture of Protestant communities and countries. So that in these communities, it became easy to find workers who—not necessarily believing that their work had been assigned by God Himself—assumed that, as culture dictated, they had to be attentive to, mindful of, and glad for their duties. These kinds of folks needed minimal supervision and delivered maximal work. Work in these communities thus became an aspect of ethics in general; hence, the notion of "work ethic," a secular version of "the calling," became a cultural given—the atmosphere that many Protestants simply breathed as they grew up.

Catholics, on the other hand—their various and wonderous accomplishments in fields such as the arts notwithstanding—grew up with a very different cultural atmosphere. Every day, they breathed very different ideas. For the sake of brevity, let us consider only one of the ideas that were, and still are, easy to find in the Catholic families, communities, and countries that Weber studied. Consider the notion that poverty gets the worshiper closer to the message of Christ. A Christ who, after all, did say that "it is easier for a camel to go through the eye of a needle than for a rich man to enter the kingdom of Heaven" (Matthew 19:23). This idea, representative of a larger constellation of beliefs and norms and values, does not particularly encourage productivity and hard work. If an individual comes to believe that wealth makes it harder for him or her to enter into the kingdom of heaven, this person will not be especially motivated to accumulate wealth. Likewise, with a culture or a society that holds this or similar beliefs. It will be difficult for this society, for this kind of country, or even for this kind of continent, to marshal the motivations that drove many of the anxious, frugal, and yet productive Protestants (save all the exceptions).

Weber does not imply that Catholicism is somehow poorer theologically than Protestantism. He is not making theological comparisons of any kind (in any case, should you wish to do so, it is up to you to decide which of these religions is closer to the scriptures, or whether both are removed from them, or to make any other well deliberated assertion about them). Weber is only noting that these systems of religious belief, Catholicism and Protestantism, facilitated differential forms of economic development. More generally, he is helping us see that *the ideas a society embraces do indeed matter*.

The Life of Ideas

The larger and more important Weberian perspective is not limited to the role that religion has had on economic development. More broadly, he wants us to see that ideas not only matter but also that they are like living entities—living in, with, and through us, and through our communities. He wants us to consider the notion that, as living social forces, ideas often demand that individuals, and even nations, follow a certain pathway, biographical or historical—a pathway that can be either beneficial or damaging, or even entirely defeating.

Weber also helps us see that ideas, so to speak, don't care about our welfare, or about the welfare of our country. It is as though ideas, as psychologist Susan Blackmore has noted after Weber, care about their own survival only. It is as though ideas are, in this sense, a bit like genes in that genes "care" about the survival of the species only to the extent to which this guarantees the gene's own survival, regardless of whether the surviving species becomes, by virtue of these genes, more *or* less noble, more *or* less beautiful, more or less intelligent, better or worse. The case is similar with ideas. They are powerful factors of the evolution of a society. And, like genes, ideas are, so to speak, keen on surviving, keen on climbing into the brains of individuals to be passed on to the next generation. And yet ideas are not necessarily keen on making the individual or the community nobler, or making life in this community freer, or more beautiful. Some ideas, of course, do that. For example, the idea that disease is not the work of a demon but caused by germs so that washing one's hands is good—has saved billions of lives and has made communities stronger. But sometimes the very opposite is the case so that some ideas can be both widely accepted and widely impoverishing. It is as though these sorts of bad ideas struggle to survive and do succeed in going on generation after generation, while at the same time debilitating a community and robbing life itself of beauty and freedom.

Ideas, as Durkheim also maintains, are, in any case, "realities – forces" (1995, p. 230), adding that "collective representations are forces even more dynamic and powerful than individual representations" [1995].)

In summary, Weber showed that belief systems, in general, often modify—empirically and durably— the historical horizon through which they emerge and life as lived every day, including, in all likelihood, your own biography. It follows, then, that social struggles for the control of meaning are, and historically have been, crucially important. These struggles have not been about mere meanings separated from life and consigned to books and libraries but have been about the character of life itself. As the title of this chapter states, we are "social animals." This does not mean that we tend to form societies. On the contrary, the point is that societies largely form us. Societies lend their nature to us. The ideas that they produce often become part and parcel of ourselves. What this means is that the meanings that provide the glue for a society can form or deform our spirit; and that these social struggles for the control of meaning are not only about ideas and theories but ultimately about key aspects of the human spirit itself, and its historical evolution or development.

Let us finally add that, historically, these social struggles for the control of socially relevant meanings have involved, sometimes, zealots or fanatics who have defended dogmatic narratives, as we have been arguing in the foregoing. But these struggles for meaning can also involve, and have historically involved, literate and aware citizens who try to anchor their country and the collective imagination in truth, as also noted. This Weberian perspective is particularly relevant today, at a time when late capitalism is transforming our era's stock of meaning. In an era when post-truths have become culturally and politically important, Weber's polemic prompts us to wonder whether it is still possible for us, as a civil society, to play a significant role in shaping our stock of meaning and own collective consciousness, the belief systems that sustain and in various ways guide our own human experience. If we were to outsource this task primarily to the market, or to experts, or to "engineers of souls," or to the political classes, what consequences may follow?

CHAPTER VIII

Situationism

Brown Eyes and Blue Eyes

As shown in the preceding chapters, deviating from norms and/or collectively relevant ideas can be good for individuals and for societies, and certain forms of deviance indeed bring forth prosperity, creativity, justice, and hope. But even such positive forms of deviance present risks for the deviants involved; and, as I have suggested elsewhere, "even the great deviants, from Mandela to Van Gogh, pay the price of non-compliance" (Narváez, 2012). For this reason, "it is in general easier for social actors to internalize, to mirror, and to vivify [to bring to life, to enact] aspects of the social order than to attempt to change them" (Narváez, 2012). In this chapter, we extend this discussion and branch off to an important area of studies called "situationism" to discuss the ways in which the immediate and momentary environment can elicit compliance from us, even to the point of altering fundamental aspects of our personalities, our beliefs, or even such things as perception and memory—which are often seen as strictly biological and not affected by environmental conditions.

On April 5, 1968, the day after Dr. Martin Luther King Jr. was assassinated, a teacher at a school in Riceville, a tiny town in Iowa, faced expectedly difficult and saddening questions from her third graders. Who was this king? And why was he killed? The teacher, Jane Elliott, who would eventually become an internationally known lecturer, provided at first some of the standard answers. The king, she explained, was actually a man named Martin Luther King Jr., and he was killed because he was fighting to end discrimination and prejudices against "negroes." The very young, all-white, and still confused students were only vaguely capturing the idea. Concepts such as discrimination and prejudice were difficult for them, not only on account of their age (8-year-olds, mostly) but particularly because these children had never actually experienced any form of discrimination. How could you possibly understand pain, for example, without having experienced it? How would you understand redness without having ever seen the color red? Elliott asked the children, "Do you think you know how it would feel to be judged by the color of your skin?" A vague and uncommitted "yeah" is heard in the video that records the exchange. The teacher replies, "No, I don't think you know how that would feel unless you had been through it, would you?"

She decided to conduct an exercise to help the children understand racism, not by reading the dictionary definition but by experiencing it (see Peters, 1971). She also hoped that such an exercise might contribute to help us, as a culture, to understand racial discrimination and indeed any other form of discrimination. She divided the classroom in two, with blue-eyed children on one side and brown-eyed children on the other. The first day, she began by explaining that blue-eyed children were, of course, better than brown-eyed children. The video registers the initial resistance, astonishment even, and certain sadness among the newly labeled "brownies" (kids with brown eyes). Some of them dispute the claim. But Elliott deploys effective pseudologic and eventually convinces not only the resistors but also the classroom that blue-eyed children might be actually better than the "lazy," "clumsy," and "not-so-smart" brownies. Moreover, she explains, because brown-eyed people are inferior, they have to receive a different kind of treatment than the hard-working and smarter blue-eyed kids. It is only fair. Hence, brownies, for example, cannot directly drink from water fountains (a reference to the "white only" water fountains that were standard under the Jim Crow laws that were superseded only in 1964). Blue-eyed children do not want to risk drinking from fountains contaminated by the darned brownies, and so brownies had to drink from a paper cup. To be sure that blue- and brown-eyed children would be easily identified, she asked brownies to wear a band around their necks (perhaps a reference to the manner in which Jewish people were marked with the Star of David by the Nazis).

Thus the day went on. Some of the minor and normal and expected little failures of the brown-eyed children, such as writing their cursives "sloppily" on the blackboard, were attributed to their inferior nature. And, likewise, the minor and normal and expected little successes of the blue-eyed children were attributed to their superior nature. The results of this experiment shocked Elliott herself, and they would eventually shock the academic world. "Marvelous, cooperative, wonderful, thoughtful" children, as the teacher calls them, began to change. In only *one single day* of being thus labeled, blue-eyed children turned into "nasty, vicious, discriminating little third graders." Imagine their recess. The formerly wonderful blue-eyed kids are now bullying the brownies and name-calling, even though the previous day no one had noticed anyone's eye color, naturally. Some of the brownies, in turn, became submissive but also belligerent. On the verge of tears, a brown-eyed boy confesses to the teacher that he had punched a blue eye "on the gut," because the blue eye had called him names.

Remarkably, the very cognitive performance of brown-eyed children was also compromised. Brownies were simply not using, and perhaps were unable to use, their brain potential. Their young brains had extra tasks to handle: coping with their "inferior" social status and with the labels now being hurled at them, the cognitive noise that inevitably lowered their performance. Blue-eyed children performed better than brownies. The next day, the roles were reversed, with blue-eyed children now assuming the inferior position and brown-eyed children being superior. As the roles were reversed, so were their behaviors and performances, with some blue-eye children now engaging in cowed behaviors and performing at a lower level and brown-eyed children outperforming them, discriminating against them, labeling them, etc.

This experiment changed the children's understanding of discrimination dramatically. Years later, the participants were interviewed, as adults, and many reported that those two days in Ms. Elliott's classroom had changed their view of the world. Importantly, this experiment, along with many others, also contributed to changing how we view, *as a culture*, the role that discrimination, social labeling, and social positioning (e.g., being positioned as brownies in contraposition to "blue eyes") can have on those labeled. Indeed, this exercise was important because it opened a window, not only into the behaviors of these third graders but also into broader social dynamics. Eventually, we came to see that what took place in this classroom in Riceville, Iowa, can also happen, broadly speaking, at the level of social groups, of generations, of countries, as we will presently discuss.

But first, let us also note that Elliott's experiment was controversial. Some parents and concerned citizens in the little town of Riceville recriminated the teacher for putting their children in stressful situations and plausibly argued that she had infringed upon ethical standards. Eventually, she was invited to discuss her views on TV, and a viewer called the station to recriminate Elliott, arguing that black children were "used" to being discriminated against and were, therefore, better able to handle such situations. In contrast, white children, the caller's odd argument went, were not used to discrimination, were thus more vulnerable to it, and, therefore, could more easily become scarred by such situations. Elliott responded with characteristic wit and not without causticity. She asked why "we" (whites) are quick to become concerned when white children suffer one day of discrimination while also being quick to ignore the fact that black children suffer *a lifetime of discrimination*. (Note that Lyndon Johnson had signed the Civil Rights Act in 1964, desegregating the country only four years before Elliott's experiment took place and that, as Elliott argued, black children born in the '50s had, in fact, spent most of their lives in a legally segregated and officially racist country, routinely experiencing the sort of discrimination that Elliott's students had experienced for one day.) As suggested, Elliott's response turned out to be very important from the point of view of sociological research. If the children's behavior and performance were transformed in only one single day, what happens, then, when people experience a lifetime of discrimination? Furthermore, what happens when people experience a lifetime of negative or, in contrast, *positive* labeling? In which ways do such variables as social class, gender, race, sexual identities—which are often labeled with positive and negative valences—affect us and our life course?

Golem and Pygmalion

Golems are magical creatures that populate Jewish folklore, often depicted as lumpy, brownish, robotic beings made of clay. They are sometimes made to be protectors of the people, and they are good at first, but according to some tales, the people eventually begin to see them with suspicion. Can such odd-looking, and somehow ensouled creatures be trusted? As people begin to grow weary of the Golem, the creature, in turn, grows defensive, expectedly, and a bit mean in response. And thus people grow wearier, and the Golem grows meaner, and so on in an ensuing vicious spiral to the point that the Golem, although designed to be a protector, becomes a menace that has to be destroyed. An initial lesson from such tales is that prophesies about wrongdoing sometimes become self-fulfilled. If the people expect wrongdoing from the creature, they are more likely to get wrongdoing from it. But perhaps there is a larger and tacit lesson here: Stereotyped labels placed on people can become enacted by the person thus labeled so that if a society labels these brownish, lumpy creatures a *menace*, such creatures are likely to become a menace. When Elliot said that blue-eyed kids are the worse ones, those kids in their mini-society in fact performed accordingly. If we *as a society* label all blue-eyed children "not so smart," they will be more likely to perform poorly, as it happened in Elliot's classroom. Social psychologists call this "the Golem effect."

The opposite of it is the "Pygmalion effect," the idea that positive expectations can influence those addressed such that they will eventually act in a manner that fulfills these expectations. "Pygmalion," incidentally, is the title of a play by the Irish playwright George Bernard Shaw in which Eliza, a poor, poorly spoken young woman from a tough area in London is trained by a professor of phonetics to pass herself off as a duchess at a party. Expecting a duchess, the wealthy and snobbish partiers overlook Eliza's "mistakes," her social blunders, and focus, instead, on the signs of "nobility" that she appears to give off. The partiers thus fall for the trick. (And they also reveal, these snobby partiers, that their negative judgments about the purported lower nature of the working classes are superficial and conceited.) Thus Eliza, a bedraggled peddler of flowers, *becomes* ladylike. People expect ladylike behavior from her and, thus having a green light, she delivers.

Shortly after Elliott's experiment took place, a principal at an elementary school near San Francisco, contacted a Harvard psychologist named Robert Rosenthal, who had researched aspects of the Golem and Pygmalion effects. Rosenthal had shown that handlers of rats who are led to believe that their rats have been "bred for superior learning ability *obtain performance superior to that obtained by [people] led to believe that their rat had been bred for inferior learning ability*" (Rosenthal & Fode, 1963, my emphasis). The school principal on the other side of the phone, Lenore Jacobson, was interested in these ideas. Would these theories, she asked Rosenthal, perhaps apply to children who are sometimes preemptively labeled "likely achievers" as well as to those preemptively labeled "likely underachievers"? Are such labels likely to become self-fulfilled prophesies? Do such labels work, so to speak, like magic spells that societies cast upon people, thus creating, as if by magic, aspects of their minds and aspects of their lives?

Eventually, the educator and the psychologists teamed up to conduct a formal study to determine the possible effects that labeling schoolchildren could have (Rosenthal & Jacobson, 1963). They approached an unidentified elementary school in California and asked permission to conduct a series of cognitive tests among students. Then, after assessing the abilities of the children, they gave the teachers a list of "academic bloomers," which tacitly labeled the other kids as "nonbloomers." To put it bluntly, the school was divided between the smart and not-so-smart kids. Eight months later, the research team went back to the school. They retested the students and discovered that, sure enough, bloomers had now scored, on average, *10 to 15 IQ points more than their non-blooming peers*. This was really a very important gain in intelligence. Four of every five bloomers had experienced at least 10 points of improvement in their intelligence tests, and, in contrast, only half of nonbloomers experienced 10 points of improvement or more. As the researchers had predicted, bloomers had indeed bloomed.

What is stunning about this study is that the research team had divided bloomers from nonbloomers *randomly, regardless of their intelligence*. That is to say, "bloomers" were at first *no different from "non-bloomers" except for the fact that they had been so labeled*. Like Elliott's students, bloomers were only regular kids who were simply expected to perform in accordance with labels they had been assigned, and so they did. In fact, they literally *became* smarter. What explains this stunning gain in IQ? The teachers attributed the bloomers' small, normal, and otherwise nonsurprising little achievements to their superior nature. They were less frustrated by their mistakes, which were also attributed to the natural little hurdles of the blooming process. Thus eager teachers spent more time, patience, and mental energy ensuring that the blooming process was unfolding smoothly. And in doing so, they were instrumental in fulfilling the researchers' initial "prophecy," which said, again, that bloomers would eventually outperform their peers.

This study begged many sociological questions. What happens, then, when a society as a whole preemptively labels some children "likely achievers" on account of positive stereotypes associated, for example, with their race, and/or class, and/or gender? Are these persons more likely to bloom as well? And what happens when a society, on account of negative stereotypes, labels other children as potential underachievers, or potential troublemakers, or even as likely deviants or potential thugs? What portion of academic success and failure among children and adults stems not from the innate potential of the students but from the ways in which the social environment addresses them? What portion of your own successes and failures might be attributable to your own innate abilities or, on the other hand, to how society perceives you?

We don't have clear answers to these specific questions, but we do know that the way society labels you can affect your life in general. For example, from the very moment proud parents say, "It's a boy!" or "It's a girl!" these parents—and their culture—expect certain behaviors, manners, attitudes, worldviews, sartorial standards, even professions or occupations that are deemed appropriate to the gender of the baby; a baby that, as he or she grows up, is likely to fulfill at least some, if not all, of these societal expectations. Because this baby is likely to be thus molded or fashioned, to an extent, the phrase "It's a boy!" is not merely a description of the gender of the child in question. It is also a label in the sense expressed earlier. And as such it can very well work like a magical spell that, cast on the child, transforms the person, or indeed determines aspects of his existence, even central aspects of his identity and worldview. This is similar to other labels related, for example, to race, class, caste, and religious affiliation, as well as the various divisions and attendant labels that tradition bequeaths to a society and to the people in it. When a society says to a young boy "you are white," "you are black," "you are a Brahman," "you are Catalonian," that society is not merely describing the pigmentation or the caste or ethnic affiliation of the child. These labels can also have transformative effects and affect, perhaps even determine, the mind and life trajectory of an individual.

Little Hanna

Note also that stereotypes associated with gender, race, and class actually do bias people's perceptions pertaining to the potential success or failure of children. Consider now the following study conducted by Princeton University researchers John Darley and Paget Gross (Darley & Gross, 1983), who asked Princeton undergraduates to assess the potential success of a child, fictitiously named Hanna. Once again, students were divided into two groups. The first group watched a video of Hanna playing in stereotypically working-class settings, and the second group watched her playing in seemingly wealthy surroundings. The first group studied Hanna's "biographical information" (concocted by the researchers), which confirmed her supposedly working-class background. The second group read information that confirmed Hanna's supposed upper-class upbringing. Both groups then watched another part of the video that showed Hanna at work in certain school-related tasks. This portion of the video was designed so that it could neither confirm nor disconfirm Hanna's academic ability. Sometimes Hanna was shown doing very well, and at other times, she was shown doing very poorly, with no clear trend that could actually allow viewers to objectively assess her academic potential.

Then the students evaluated how she had performed in those school-related tasks. Students who were primed to see Hanna as wealthy were more likely to see her as performing above her fourth-grade level. They saw her as a potential bloomer. And those who were primed to see her as poor generally judged her to perform below her fourth-grade level. They tacitly saw her as a potentially difficult student, indeed as a potential failure. Elliott, Rosenthal, and Jacobson allowed us to see that labels placed on children (e.g., "bloomers," "blue eyes") are likely to result in differential levels of achievement in the children thus labeled. Darley and Gross helped us see that, in general, people easily label others, children included, and that societies are likely to label people *not* on account of the actual potential of those being labeled but often on account of preconceived ideas, images, and biases. To insist on the key questions, to what extent do these sorts of preconceived ideas and biases and related labels mark the lives of individuals in society? To what extent do positive or negative social biases determine the differential rates of achievement we see in society? To what extent has prejudice determined aspects of your life course?

On the surface, the studies outlined earlier helped us see that achievement does not always stem from innate abilities. Of course, innate abilities do exist and sometimes become the determining factor of success. But achievement can also be contextual and contingent on external circumstances. More profoundly, these studies also helped us see that human beings are very malleable and indeed largely constructed by contextual and contingent circumstances often beyond our control. One day under the brown-eye label was enough to momentarily construct aspects of the brownies' identities and aspects of their social and academic performances. Only six months after having received a positive label, children improved in terms of their intelligence, as measured by IQ testing. So, to insist on the central question, what would one expect from "brownies," or from "bloomers," or from Brahmans, or from the Hannas of the world if they spent a *lifetime* addressed by such labels? How would such societal perceptions affect not only their life trajectory, as noted, but also who they become as human beings?[1]

Can Social Situations Transform Your Moral Judgment?

Enter now Philip Zimbardo, a social psychologist from Stanford University. It is 1971. We are now in Palo Alto, California, a wealthy suburb about 45 minutes south of San Francisco. In one of the beautiful campus buildings, Dr. Zimbardo is concocting an experiment funded by the U.S. Navy and the Marine Corps. He has gotten money to recruit a group of psychologically healthy Stanford students and divide them, much as Jane Elliot did with her students, into two groups and ask them to perform two kinds of roles. All these Stanford students will be first screened, by means of a battery of psychological tests, to ensure that only those who are sound of mind will take part in the experiment. After the screening process, some of them will become guards at a mock prison, and some will become prisoners. They will spend two weeks in elaborately constructed holding facilities in the basement of the psychology department. Prisoners will be arrested at their dorms. They will be handcuffed and transported in actual police vehicles. They will be booked. They will be given a degrading prison uniform. They will be taken into custody and placed in a cell. Guards will also be in uniform. They will be given batons, keys, and reflecting pilot sunglasses so that the prisoners cannot make direct eye contact with them, and, of course, they will be given power as well. How will these psychologically healthy and smart Stanford students respond? Elliott's children, as all children, were more malleable than adults, more easily affected by the labels placed on them (brownies and blue eyes). But how about Zimbardo's students? Will the labels—"guard" and "prisoner"—also change these high-achieving adults? If so, in what ways? Will their new social positioning as guards and prisoners affect how they actually see themselves? Or will they remain their old, normal selves? Will their upbringing allow them to behave morally in their new roles? Or, in contrast, will this new environment override their moral education?

Elliott's "blue eyes" became "vicious," as the teacher said. Zimbardo's guards became brutal. The at first normal, decent Stanford students began to, in accordance with their new roles as guards, implement scenarios specifically designed to demean, humiliate, and fracture the prisoners' will. In their turn, prisoners became submissive, at times pathetically so. One of them became a resistor, assuming a stoic and apathetic role. And all students, in any case, began to confuse their new roles with their own selves. Their newly assigned roles began to displace key aspects of their personalities. The students began to incarnate

---

1   American sociologist Howard Becker further noted that labeling often constructs deviant behavior, deviant identities, and, indeed, crime. Imagine a young kid growing up in a poor inner-city area. More likely than not, he will dress like his peers and imitate their behaviors and speech patterns. As such displays are stereotypically seen as threatening, outsiders will likely see him a potential threat—regardless, initially, of his character. A Golem effect may now unfold. But this time, the child is likely to grow up internalizing the notion that he is, in fact, a potential threat and thus behave in a manner befitting his acquired identity. Becker also helped us to see that mainstream groups often label certain *things*, not just people—clothes, music, use of certain substances, speech patterns, etc.—as deviant, regardless of whether they are objectively harmful or noxious. As noted, he argued, for example, that the use of marijuana is deviant not on account of the act itself but because some cultures simply see it as bad (while other cultures see is as normal). Hence people who engage in certain behaviors, dress in a certain manner, listen to certain kinds of music, etc., are likely to conjure up a Golem effect of sorts—a label, and its effects in life, regardless, again, of the objective nature of their behaviors.

their roles, to bring them to life, forsaking, in the process, central aspects of their normal selves. So much so that the experiment had to be aborted by the sixth day, as the make-believe situations rapidly changed core aspects of the participants' demeanors and characters (Zimbardo, 1971).

In the end, this experiment showed that social roles, when accepted as legitimate by an institution or by society, can quickly elicit behaviors concordant with the assigned roles (e.g., guards or prisoners). But more importantly, it also showed that such socially legitimized roles can also elicit *a desire to adapt* to the role *and a will to forsake* core aspects of the self, and even the core values and ideals that formerly provided guidance for the person in question. These can be abandoned as well. They can be stolen, we might say, by the new social circumstances. We have noted that human beings, unlike other social animals, are largely constructed by social circumstances. Let us add that, save exceptions, we can easily be constructed anew, formed or deformed by a given context. Hence the lesson that arises from this and similar research studies is that a society has to be mindful of the institutions and, in this sense, the contexts that it creates; for, in doing so, a society may well be creating aspects of the very spirit of the citizen, socially relevant dispositions, and behaviors that can cause good or evil.

Can Normal Citizens Act Like Nazi Soldiers?

Let us now look at another classic study in the area of social psychology. Stanley Milgram, a professor at Yale University, and a friend of Zimbardo, actually, similarly upset the very foundations of his field of study with another experiment worth describing in some detail (Milgram, 1975). Zimbardo describes his friend's experiment thusly:

> [Y]ou have responded to an advertisement in the New Haven newspaper seeking subjects for a study of memory. A researcher whose serious demeanor and laboratory coat convey scientific importance greets you and another applicant at your arrival at a Yale laboratory [...]. The task is straightforward: one of you will be the "teacher" who gives the "learner" a set of word pairings to memorize. During the test, the teacher will give each key word, and the learner must respond with the correct association. When the learner is right, the teacher gives a verbal reward, such as "Good" or "That's right." When the learner is wrong, the teacher is to press a lever on an impressive-looking apparatus that delivers an immediate [electrical] shock to punish the error [...]. The shock generator has 30 switches, starting from a low level of 15 volts and increasing by 15 volts to each higher level. The experimenter tells you that every time the learner makes a mistake, you have to press the next switch. The control panel shows both the voltage of each switch and a description. The tenth level (150 volts) is "Strong Shock"; the 17th level (255 volts) is "Intense Shock"; the 25th level (375 volts) is "Danger, Severe Shock." At the 29th and 30th levels (435 and 450 volts) the control panel is marked simply with an ominous XXX: the pornography of ultimate pain and power. (Zimbardo, 2007)

You also meet another volunteer who, just like you, is there for the study. He is a middle-aged man, bespectacled, clean, mild mannered. He is wearing a suit. The scientist, courteous and yet a bit severe, tells you that you and the other volunteer will be randomly assigned to one of two roles, either that of a learner or that of a teacher. He flips a coin and tells you that you will be the teacher and then tells the other volunteer that he will be the learner. Both of you are ready, and he escorts you to the lab where he shows you the shock generator, explains the procedure, and takes Mild Mannered

Learner to the next room, where he is strapped so as to receive the electrical shocks that you are required to administer when he provides wrong answers. You will then take your position in a room where you can hear the reactions of the learner when you shock him with electricity: protestations, cries, screams, and pleadings, depending on the voltage. Just so that you know exactly what you are doing to the learner, the doctor gives you a sample of a shock, 45 volts, which hurts and makes you recoil. And then he asks you to imagine the shocks that you will be increasingly administering to the learner. You now realize that you will be asked to increasingly hurt a mild-mannered and seemingly pleasant man you just met.

Milgram's colleagues, particularly those in the field of psychiatry, predicted that only about one-tenth of 1% of participants would actually administer shocks up to 450 volts. Such a percentage, they reasoned, represents the portion of the population afflicted by the sort of psychopathologies that could make it likely for them to torture the learner simply because a man in a lab coat asks them to do so. Normal people, the experts also reasoned, simply know better. Normal people are not torturers. Would you yourself torture a random learner in such a cruel and even contemptible manner merely to comply with the situation presented to you? Stunningly, about 61% of the "teachers" did shock the learner past the point of "danger, severe shock," all the way to the 450 volts. As with Zimbardo's students, the normal, regular citizens of New Haven, a sort of quintessential suburb in Connecticut dominated by Yale University, also forsook core aspects of their moral systems merely to comply with the situation at hand.

The learner, as you might have guessed, was a confederate, an actor working for the researcher. He was not being shocked but was merely playing the part. The teachers had been tricked into thinking that they were administering electrical shocks to other participants, the unlucky "learners."

Most participants in this study thus behaved like the Nazi soldiers tried at Nuremberg, who attempted to defend their murderous actions by arguing that they were only following orders. One of the most important moral philosophers of the 20th century, Hannah Arendt, has argued that what is truly disturbing about these war criminals is not really their apparent monstrosity. Rather, it is the fact that, upon close inspection, they often turn out to be "terribly, terrifyingly normal," Arendt said (1977), much like the "teachers" that Milgram recruited. Indeed, it is absurd to think that Germans, including the Nazi soldiers themselves, somehow had a natural predisposition toward monstrosity or sadism. Of course, they did not. No nation has a "natural" predisposition of this kind. What is horrific about Nazism is that it illustrates, in the most sobering manner, the *transformative* power of ideologies and of the situations that ideologies can create. This period in history helps us see that the meanings and social scenarios that we create—or fail to create—can lead to profound changes in the human spirit. Some such scenarios may result in episodes, or entire historical periods, marked by devastation and depravity.

"Herd Instinct"

Along with Zimbardo and Milgram, Arendt also helped us see that much of the evil that has scarred the world is produced by social conditions that elicit a "herd instinct," as philosopher Friedrich Nietzsche called it. This is a will to comply. It is a human susceptibility to follow the norms of a group, mechanically, *while ignoring the consequences* of these actions, even if these consequences are horrible and obvious. Indeed, Zimbardo and other social psychologists have produced a sort of recipe, a list of variables, step-by-step instructions on how to fracture the moral system of most regular people so as to make us compliant even with cruel goals (and, of course, the purpose of this is to avoid creating such circumstances).[2] Zimbardo has shown that social scenarios where the "right" variables come to align largely explain the actions not only of Nazi soldiers but also of al-Qaeda members, American soldiers who committed atrocities against inmates at the Abu Ghraib prison in Iraq, and, possibly, most such atrocities perpetrated in the world.

Milgram's study has been replicated in various settings and various countries in Asia, Europe, and Africa, and the results have always been the same: Roughly 62% of participants in these countries simply go with the "scientist's" demands all the way to 450 volts. This research, it is worth noting, generated a slew of follow-up studies intended to amplify its findings and to answer some of the questions it generated. In one such study, college students were generally willing to shock a defenseless, whimpering puppy, merely because a guy in a lab coat asked them to do so. In another, 21 of 22 nurses administered an excessive dose of a medication (actually an innocuous placebo) merely because an unknown "doctor" asked them to do so, etc.

These sorts of studies, to be sure, have generated not only important theoretical questions but also important ethical questions. How can anyone, in the name of science, be allowed to inflict these kinds of psychological wounds on study participants? Bear in mind that participants in these studies are likely to leave the research setting with an ego injury, having been rudely awakened to thus-far concealed aspects of their selves and having encountered an alien dimension right underneath their otherwise familiar sense of self. To be sure, the near consensus in the research community today is that jeopardizing study participants in such a manner constitutes a violation of ethical rules, and research institutions therefore mandate that their researchers include explicit and sufficient provisions to minimize psychological harm (as well as physical and legal harm). Hence the sort of research conducted by Milgram, for example, would be banned from most official research settings today, particularly in the United States.

Yet one cannot help but underscore that these studies also generated critically important theoretical questions. Are most human beings—more than 60% of us according to Milgram's results—potential torturers whose moral behavior hinges not only on their capacity to think and make decisions but also, and perhaps primarily, on the random scenarios we find ourselves in? Does the evil that we see in the world, as Zimbardo would later ask, stem primarily from individuals or from *social situations*? Are evildoers, in general and save psychopathological cases, instruments of external forces that operate behind their backs? If so, can societies, governments, or citizens curb these social forces, thus curbing what we might call the *rate of evil* in them? Finally, and perhaps more importantly, who are the resistors? What in them allows them to withstand social pressures and to act concordantly with their own moral systems? The single nurse in the study mentioned earlier who decided to disobey the obviously dangerous instructions from the unknown doctor is clearly a moral hero. Can we as a society sponsor and nurse such moral strength in

---

2   Variables that in combination may dehumanize normal people include an institution or a group that supports the perpetrator's actions (so that the perpetrator may justify these actions as mere adherence to larger institutional practices or as solidarity with a group), a figure of authority (e.g., a scientist or a commander who issues unambiguous orders), and anonymity of the victim (e.g., concentration camp prisoners who are not seen as individuals but as dehumanized masses identified by numbers). When combined, these variables can (A) encourage groupthink (avoidance or repression of ideas that go against the group); (B) diffuse responsibility so that responsibility for wrongdoing does not seem to fall on the perpetrator and blame can be placed on the institution, group, or authorities who issue orders, a process that lessens moral emotions such as remorse; and (C) these variables can also deindividuate the perpetrator so that his personal judgments and standards are suspended. These factors, A, B, and C, encourage the individual to submit to a larger entity—for example, to an institution or organization (e.g., an army, a political party), to a professedly greater cause (e.g., scientific knowledge, the will of God), or to a group of peers (e.g., a gang). In the end, this process can cause an otherwise normal person to behave unscrupulously and cruelly.

people? What sort of interventions might be effective in this regard? Perhaps, as Doris Lessing notes, we should teach our schoolchildren the following: "If you are in this or that type of situation, you will find yourself, if you are not careful, behaving like a brute and a savage if you are ordered to do it. Watch out for these situations. You must be on your guard against your own most primitive reactions and instincts" (Lessing, 1987, p. 58). This is one of the key lessons from sociology and social psychology.

It is also worth noting a curious fact at this juncture. It appears that the resistors, those few beautiful souls, are oftentimes folks who know how to laugh. Naturally, the ability to easily laugh is not a necessary and sufficient factor of resistance, but it seems that it does help. Lessing reminds us that "the researchers of brain washing and indoctrination discovered that people who knew how to laugh resisted best [...] Fanatics don't laugh at themselves [...]. Bigots can't laugh [unless cruelly]. Only the civilized, the liberated, the free person can laugh at himself, herself" (Lessing, 1987, p. 45). The idea is that fanatics and bigots are generally unable to take an ironic distance from ideology, from the serious preaching that has addressed them, or from inherited ideas and traditions, which they take all-too earnestly and seriously. Not knowing how to laugh at ideology, at the given dogmas, and thus not knowing how to distance themselves from them, they are easily engulfed. Hence we have another important lesson from social psychology: The ability to take an ironic distance from the most solemn aspects of the inherited belief system is often the mark of the civilized and of the free. An ironic attitude can be, in this sense, an individual as well as a social asset.

The Power of the Situation

In the field of social psychology, a near consensus has been reached about some of the central aspects of human nature: Save important exceptions, human beings generally tend to adapt to new social environments, often quite rapidly, and in doing so, we sometimes forsake core aspects of our selves, the standards and behaviors that make us *us*. But just what aspects of the self can be modified by the social situation? As I have noted elsewhere,

> subjects wearing purportedly fake sunglasses cheated at higher rates than subjects wearing authentic glasses, as though the fakeness of the glasses were rapidly absorbed by the participants in this study (Gino et al. 2010). Subjects solving word puzzles with words stereotypically associated with elderly people walked more slowly from the researcher's office to the elevator than subjects whose puzzles involved neutral words (Bargh et al. 1996). Subjects asked to imagine characteristics of a professor scored higher in trivia pursuit questions than subjects asked to think about soccer hooligans (Dijksterhuis 2005). Study participants squeezing a soft ball were more likely to perceive gender-neutral faces as female, and those squeezing a hard ball were more like to perceive these faces as male (Slepian et al 2011). Participants holding warm cups of coffee were more likely to judge peers as friendly than those holding cold cups (Williams and Bargh 2008). Participants holding heavier clipboards were more likely to judge the opinions of leaders as more important when compared to participants holding lighter clipboards (Jostmann 2009), etc. (Narváez, 2012).

Similarly, office workers at a university in England contributed more money to the office coffee coffers when a drawing of two eyes was placed above the box where they were supposed to pay for their coffee anonymously. Workers contributed less money when the eyes were replaced with flowers (in Alter, 2013). Groups of people who are subtly primed to recall negative stereotypes about their gender or race performed worse when engaged in cognitive tasks if compared to groups of people not primed to recall these stereotypes. English boys, ages 7 to 8, for example, were primed with the stereotype that boys do worse at school than girls, an idea that the researcher casually slipped before administering a battery of tests to the boys. And, sure enough, those kids performed worse on reading, writing, and math tests (Hartley & Sutton, 2013). There are over 300 scientific articles describing the very many ways in which "stereotype threats," as these situations are called, can affect the performance of a variety of groups in a variety of situations. The opposite, "stereotype lift"—that is, priming people with "positive" stereotypes about themselves or negative stereotypes about others—can positively affect their performance.

Indeed, it is important to see that some situational variables can produce positive and desirable effects. Social psychologists Amy Cuddy asked a group of research participants to assume a "power pose" for two minutes (i.e., to expand their bodily posture, a signal of domination in the animal world), and she asked a second group to assume a submissive pose, also for two minutes (these participants had to make themselves smaller, a signal of submission among animals). She tested the blood of all subjects before and after creating this situation and found that the blood of people in the "power" condition had changed, registering, (a) increases in testosterone, the hormone associated with feelings of dominance, and (b) decreases in cortisol, the hormone associated with feelings of defeat and stress. Participants in the submissive condition, in contrast, experienced increases in cortisol and decreases in testosterone. (Hence Cuddy's implied advice: If you monitor your body so as to avoid "speaking" a subordinate bodily language, you might be able to decrease feelings of defeat and even increase feelings of being in control.) Mandy Len Catron, professor of English at the University of British Columbia, devised an experiment designed to test the idea that two strangers exposed to certain situational variables could fall in love. Summarized in her book *How to Fall in Love with Anyone* (2017), which already gives you a big hint about the outcome of the study, the experiment did suggest that situational variables could lead to falling in love with a stranger. The situation, in this case, involved exposure to "escalating levels of intimacy." Participating subjects met a stranger and asked him or her questions that were increasingly intimate. They began with something like, "What is your name?," for example, and then eventually progressed to something like, "When was the last time you cried and why?" (Catron herself ended up establishing a romantic relationship with an experimental subject who helped her test this intimacy scale.)

A large number of scientific studies have shown the extent to which human beings are affected by the immediate environment (as well as by the long-term environments that accompany our lives, as we will see next), so much so that this constitutes an area of study in its own right, known as "situationism." These researchers have shown that situations can affect a broad constellation of experiences, affects, and dispositions, for better or for worse. Ap Dijksterhuis, a researcher from the Netherlands who specializes in unconscious behavior, has said that imitation and priming (that is to say, the context or the immediate situation) "can make us slow, fast, smart, stupid, good at math, bad at math, helpful, rude, polite, long-winded, hostile, aggressive, cooperative, competitive, conforming, nonconforming, conservative, forgetful, careful, careless, neat, and sloppy" (in Iacoboni, 2009, p. 201). Priming and the power of situational variables can, in fact, affect aspects of the human experience that otherwise seem to be entirely biological. This includes the way we experience pain (as we will subsequently discuss), and even visual acuity, as demonstrated by Harvard researcher Ellen Langer and her colleagues: "[M]ind-set manipulation," these investigators report, can indeed "counteract physiological limits imposed on vision" (Langer et al., 2010).

New York journalist Eyal Press (2012) has noted that the mystery about human nature is not why *some* people comply or why some people are affected by the situation at hand, but *why some people are immune to the power of the situation,* why *some people manage to go against the flow.*

E.E. Cummings, one of the revered American poets of the 20th century, argued that, "To be nobody-but-yourself—in a world which is doing its best, night and day, to make you everybody else—means to fight the hardest battle which any human being can fight; and never stop fighting" (1958, 13). Let us consider a person who did manage to be nobody-but-himself: the 13-year-old, river-loving, pipe-smoking, constantly-on-the-run, not-above-lying, quintessentially American hero, Huckleberry Finn, Mark Twain's famous character. From day one, Huck's friends, his church, his tutors, his entire world tells him that black people are mere property. The cultural air that he has always breathed is saturated with the idea that aiding a slave to run away, helping him or her to be free from the chamber of horrors of slavery, is a crime, like stealing—an offense punished by God with the unspeakable tortures of hell. But already an outcast and thus an outsider, already able to see his world from a distance and from above, Huck eventually begins to see the profound immorality of this supposed moral rule, the plain injustice of these laws, the flat idiocy inherent to this aspect of common sense. And in the end, he simply decides to help his friend Jim, a slave, to run away. "All right, then," Huck says, "I'll go to hell!" Clearly, not everyone can be Huck. Clearly, not everyone can fight and never stop fighting the battle that Cummings has in mind. But the few resistors who can, those who are able to stand their own moral ground, are very much needed by any society, as they provide examples of moral strength as well as hope for those oppressed. They are, in fact, urgently needed in dark times (Press, 2012), times that tend to spur the dangerous manifestations of the herd instinct in human beings: times of war, of ethnic and religious conflict, of terror. "Such people," Doris Lessing adds, "such individuals, will be a most productive yeast and ferment, and lucky the society who has plenty of them" (1987, 76).

Can the Environment Alter Your Memories?

Elizabeth Loftus, distinguished professor at the University of California, Irvine, tells us the following story:

> In 1986 [Jane] Cool, a nurse's aide [...], sought therapy from a psychiatrist to help her cope with her reaction to a traumatic event experienced by her daughter. During therapy, the psychiatrist used hypnosis and other suggestive techniques to dig out buried memories of abuse that Cool herself had allegedly experienced. In the process, Cool became convinced that she had repressed memories of having been in a satanic cult, of eating babies, of being raped, of having sex with animals and of being forced to watch the murder of her eight-year-old friend. She came to believe that she had more than 120 personalities—children, adults, angels and even a duck—all because, Cool was told, she had experienced severe childhood sexual and physical abuse. The psychiatrist also performed exorcisms on her, one of which lasted for five hours and included the sprinkling of holy water and screams for Satan to leave Cool's body. (Loftus, 1997, p. 70)

Subsequently, the patient filed a lawsuit against the psychiatrist. These horrific memories, she told the court, had been implanted in her through questionable psychiatric practices. Eventually, the case was settled out of court and the plaintiff was awarded 2.4 million dollars in compensation for the psychological damage inflicted by the practitioner (Loftus, 1997, pp. 70–75).

This and other similar court cases pertaining to implanted memories are at best anecdotal. They do not count as scientific evidence to support the idea that memories can be inserted into someone's brain or that memorial processes can be manipulated by other persons or by external circumstances in general. But they do beg these important questions: What if memory itself—the very core of the self—were, in fact, manipulable, controllable, implantable? If so, is it possible that someone may have a degree of control over your own memories? And if so, with what consequences, good or bad, for you?

Consider the following experiment conducted by Elizabeth Loftus, who pioneered this area of study. She recruited a group of adults and gave them a plausible but entirely invented story that at age 5 they had been lost in a shopping mall and had been eventually rescued by an elderly person (Loftus, 1997). These subjects were told that the researchers had gotten this (fake) episode of their lives from close relatives (e.g., a parent) and that the purpose of the study was to see how various relatives remember the same life events. Typically, study participants were initially skeptical ("I never got lost in a mall," etc.); but, eventually, about one in four subjects came to "remember" the fictitious story, sometimes adding detail and vividness to the (non)event. Startlingly, some of them developed memories so intensely real that they continued to believe that they had been lost in a mall, even after the researcher debriefed them and told them that this was only an invented story. Loftus has conducted other studies, and she has managed to implant a range of memories in subjects, pertaining to a threat to their lives as children, about witnessing demonic possession as children, seeing wounded animals as part of a bombing, and so on. As Loftus and others have shown, it is, in fact, possible to alter aspects of a person's recollection of the past, precisely to the extent that we can speak of "memory implantation" (Loftus, 1997; Braun, Rhiannon, & Loftus, 2002).

These studies have also raised important questions: Can memories be implanted outside the laboratory? Can memories be implanted as we go about our daily lives?

Before answering these questions, it is important to discuss the nature of memory to provide the needed background knowledge. Memory very seldom involves total recall—a complete and veridical rendition of the past. And total recall is not necessarily desirable, as we typically experience many irrelevant things that are not only unnecessary to remember, but that, if recalled in their entirety, would be experienced as cognitive noise. They would have the effect of clogging the reconstruction of the past with superfluous details. Our memories are, of course, generally and roughly reliable, but, in various ways and degrees, they usually involve reconstructed elements as well. As psychoanalyst Donald Spence has argued, it is important to distinguish between "historical truth," what actually happened, and "narrative truth," what we recollect. The latter, Spence notes, is inexact and can be logically inconsistent or indeed contradictory, while nevertheless being honestly regarded as accurate. Although we usually believe that we have a pretty precise recollection of past events, it is ,in fact, normal for us to alter our recollections, suppressing elements, embellishing, inflating them (although not necessarily to the point of total distortion, of course). The human brain, in any case, doesn't have a reliable mechanism for sorting out all false events, or for accessing the historical truth of our experiences directly and consistently. And, hence, memories can be distorted or even directly implanted. (Which is why, for example, it is problematic to use eye witness testimony, as it often happens in courts of law, as the main or even as the sole evidence to condemn someone, even to condemn him or her to death.)

Importantly, reconstructive mnemonic processes, as Loftus shows, do not occur randomly. They are often influenced by specific external circumstances that can modify or indeed create aspects of our reminiscences, without our knowledge or control. If, for example, we grow up being told that a certain group in our community is bad, we will be more likely to remember events involving members of this group in ways that confirm our beliefs or prejudices about them. And the idea is *not* that in having these memories, we are expressing a conscious or explicit bias. These memories can very well be, so to speak, entirely honest, even if they express unconscious stereotypes of prejudices.

Beyond these impersonal cultural processes that may affect our memories, can our memories also be altered by interested operators? This is a question that cannot be fully answered at present. But there are indications that this may be the case. Memories, we know, can be affected by the power of the situation and, it would seem, such situations can be designed and controlled by interested parties. Katherine Braun, a researcher from Harvard Business School, has shown that marketing, for example, can reshape aspects of memorial recollection. Commercial advertisements, as Braun and colleagues (2002) report, can "alter how consumers remember their own past." Naturally, marketers *cannot* just implant a cache of memories in consumers. But, nevertheless, "advertising can make events (even impossible ones) seem more likely to have happened to consumers as children" without consumers being "aware [that] they have been influenced" (Braun et al., 2002).

Memory itself, in summary, can be modified, even constructed or reconstructed, in different ways and degrees, by external situations, including interested mechanisms, such as those studied and deployed by marketers.

Summary and Conclusion

The human mind—our memories, meanings, values, attitudes, dispositions—often adapt, for better or for worse, to the appeals and charms, the nudging, the pressures, the threats of the social world around us. Again, the self "always co-arises with the other" (Narváez, 2012) and cannot arise by itself alone. Those of us who are members of individualistic cultures tend to believe that each of us is a separate, first-person *singular,* as we learn in grammar classes. But we grow up, we develop our mind, we come into being through internal, as well as *external,* or social input. Thus we can never be entirely singular and can never merely invent ourselves independently of our social and historical horizons. The situations we encounter, the ideas of others, their emotions, their attention, their gaze do help us become who we are. This truly makes us part of a larger (social) organism, which, if we are lucky, can strengthen our spirit. But it can also weaken us. It can make us vulnerable to the collective beliefs, to the will of our social world, a will we often assume as our own. It can make us vulnerable, in particular, to what Nobel Laureate in literature Mario Vargas Llosa has termed "the call of the tribe": the call of stereotyped group thinking that often appeals to an all-too human herd instinct. This is also why it is important to try to see through collective beliefs, to read the world, rather than taking it for granted.

CHAPTER IX

The Sociology of Cognition

T HE SOCIAL WORLD can shape our ideas, memories, and attitudes, including our moral attitudes, as we saw. Let us now see the extent to which our environment, our surroundings, affect our cognitive development as well. The development of your cognitive abilities —that is to say, the strategies that, as you grow up, your brain develops to make sense of the world—initially tends to follow a biologically determined pathway. It normally follows preprogrammed patterns that are broadly applicable to all normal human beings regardless of their environment or culture. But beyond this broad and universally applicable pattern, cognitive development is also affected, either subtly or massively, by environmental and cultural factors, as we will discuss next.

From Egocentrism to Sociocentrism

Swiss psychologist Jean Piaget (1977) was arguably the first to discover the basic patterns of cognitive development and the extent to which biology, as opposed to culture, affects the broader curve of development. Perhaps Piaget's biggest discovery was that this curve, from babyhood to adulthood, involves a progressive transition from "egocentrism" to "sociocentrism," two important terms that we will develop in the pages that follow. For now, let us first say that at the beginning of your life, your mind was mostly inwardly directed; that when you were a baby you were primarily preoccupied with your own sensations, feelings, thoughts, and needs, egocentrically; and that you were generally unable to see the world from the perspective of others. Yet as you began to grow up, you came to slowly realize that other people actually have their own needs, private thoughts, feelings, and sensations—their own perspectives, their own individual minds, which can be very different from yours. You, that is to say, as all other babies, transitioned from having an egocentric view of the world to having a sociocentric one. So in the latter phase of your life, you were able to see not only that others had a perspective and worldview of their own but also see the world through their eyes. You were influenced by these external worldviews, which indeed came to inform not only your own way of seeing the world but also the way you saw, and presently see, yourself.

According to Piaget, by age 7, children can, so to speak, effortlessly climb into other people's brains to see the world from these perspectives. And he implied that, as the child subsequently moves from childhood to adolescence, she, in fact, incorporates the points of view of others into her own so that she comes to see the world and herself partly through the eyes of others. For example, she may judge herself, her clothes, appearance, body, and her behaviors according to other people's standards, and, more broadly speaking, according to the standards of her society and culture. Cognitive maturation, as Piaget showed, thus involves social maturation: increased social awareness, a sense of being more and more attuned to the thoughts and perspectives of others.

In 1956, Piaget conducted a simple experiment that initially allowed him to outline his theory of the transition from egocentrism to sociocentrism. It was famously called the Three Mountains Study (aka the Three Mountains Task). Children were asked to face one side of a biggish toy mountain that had a few features visible *only* to the child and not to the researcher, who was sitting at the opposite side of the table, and then the researcher asked the kid to describe what he, *Piaget,* was seeing on his side of the mountain. Interestingly, children before age 7 typically told Piaget, incorrectly, that he was seeing what *they* were seeing. Only after age 7 were kids able to get the answer right. When dealing with the same task, kids 7 and up generally answered that the researcher could *not* see the features that were visible only to them. Only these older children appeared to understand that other people (e.g., the researcher) had a point of view entirely of their own, entirely independent from the child's point of view. In contrast, younger children seemed to sense that others see the world as though through the child's own eyes (Piaget, 1977). These kids tended to generalize and universalize their own perspectives.

To be sure, some psychologists have criticized this particular research study, and it might be more correct to assume that children overcome egocentrism earlier, as early as 3 and a half, as some researchers have suggested. Alison Gopnik, an investigator of childhood cognition at the University of California, Berkeley, has argued that even 18-month old children can understand the idea that other people have different feelings and tastes. In one study, Gopnik showed that at this age, kids could remember that other people seemed to like broccoli over crackers, *independently of what they, the kids,* like best (crackers, presumably), so when these kids were asked to feed these other people (the researchers), they correctly gave them broccoli, rather than crackers (Gopnik, 2000). Gopnik and colleagues, therefore, suggest that these young children were already able climb into the mind of the researcher and understand her point of view (her individual taste) and how it differs from their own. Young children, these researchers have argued, can have at least some sense of other people's perspectives. Perhaps they are not fully egocentric, as Piaget believed.

But regardless of its possible flaws, Piaget's theory did open a field that, perfected by a variety of such follow-up studies, helped us better understand the general stages and patterns of cognitive development. And at present, the general agreement among researchers is that human beings typically go, as Piaget originally thought, from a rather self-centered view of the world to a view that progressively incorporates the points of view of others and indeed aspects of their worldviews.

We also know that, in varying degrees, we, in fact, adopt socially constructed ways of thinking as we internalize collective standards and related judgments—an idea that has had profound implications for our understanding of human nature. W.E.B. Du Bois, one of the most important African American intellectuals of the 20th century, noted, for example, that as a child of age 5, he was already unable to see his skin color merely as a color. (He was born only 3 years after the Civil War, in 1868, and died in 1963, one year before Lyndon Johnson signed the Civil Rights Act into law, and he, therefore, lived only in an officially racist and segregated country.) Instead, he saw it from the point of view of the dominant ideas about race and about blackness in particular. As a "little thing [...] in the hills of New England," he says, he saw his skin through other people's eyes (2011): He saw not only himself in the mirror but also the collective memory about race as though it were embedded in him and, indeed, as though it were masking his truest self. In the racist context of his day, he thus saw himself as though he were filtered, indeed concealed by these narratives and diminished by them. What this example illustrates is precisely the idea that, as suggested, when we look in the mirror, it is also difficult to see just a pure image entirely isolated from social meanings. A baby, often by month six, can recognize her image in the mirror as her own, and this image is mostly free from societal contents. For example, the baby typically will not see herself as "white," or "black," or "Hispanic," or even as "girl," with all the cultural implications embedded in these terms (and hence embedded in the person's self-perception). In contrast, when we, as adults, see our image reflected in the mirror, we can easily see these cultural contents—contents that may, in fact, mask our truest self. We generally see our reflected images as attached to social categories and related evaluations: "black," "white," "man," "woman," "straight," "gay," "doctor," "mother," with all the positive and/or negative cultural implications associated with them.

Of course, some of us might be much more preoccupied with the points of view of others and much more influenced by socially constructed meanings. And others might be much less preoccupied with these external ideas and, therefore, freer from them. Du Bois, for example, was eventually able to lift the veil that his culture had placed before his eyes and hence see himself and the world without racial filters. Of course, he saw his skin color, but he saw it disassociated from the dominant racial ideology. He now saw himself simply as a young man with a dark complexion and not, as the racist context dictated, as a "negro." He thus discovered his "better and truer self," he says (Du Bois, 2011). And he thus discovered his potential—a prerequisite for eventually becoming a key intellectual and political figure in the 20th century.

Again, it is possible to see ourselves without *biased* or prejudiced cultural filters but, in general, it is easy to grow up seeing ourselves as our society sees us. Indeed, from the foregoing discussion about Golem and Pygmalion effects, it follows that our very own self-regard can be affected by the labels, positive or negative, that society places on us. Self-regard is othered, as George Herbert Mead argued (1934). Our identity develops within a social context. And, in this sense, it develops *as a social phenomenon*—as an artifact of a culture, of a time and of a place. As noted, this can be good, because this process inserts us in a larger social organism and can also strengthen our spirit, but it can also be bad: This is suggested by Du Bois's story, but one can also consider the feminine mystique and how women who developed a related "feminine" identity found their potential, and thus their fate, curtailed.

The Sensorimotor Stage

Piaget identified four phases or stages of cognitive development, whereby the baby, and then the growing child, and, finally, the adolescent, make sense of the world. Let us outline this process.

Piaget called the first of these phases the "sensorimotor stage," which, he argued, occurs from birth to about 2 years of age. "Sensorimotor," because children in this age bracket make sense of the world mostly through *direct contact with it*: through their senses and motor mechanisms. As the child grabs things, puts things in her mouth, crawls, toddles, and falls, she develops not only mechanisms of sensory perception and her muscles but also her mind. You don't need to see and touch the table in your house to understand its properties (hardness, smoothness, and so on). But a baby initially has to touch the table, has to see it, perhaps has to bump against it to thereby comprehend, initially without words, that this object is hard, smooth, etc. You don't need to experience distance to understand the concept. For a baby, in contrast, distance is, above all, an experience—for example, related to crawling from point A to point B. And, in this sense, crawling is not merely a physical activity for this child. It is also a biological prototype for a future idea, a biological archetype for the abstract concept of distance, and, hence, the beginning of the child's understanding of geometry, and in this sense of some mathematical concepts.

The following poem by, Fernando Pessoa, one of the most important Portuguese poets, may further clarify this idea:

I am a shepherd
My thoughts are my flock
And my thoughts are sensations
I think with eyes and ears
With hands and feet
And with nose and mouth.
To think of a flower is to see it and to smell it.
And eating a fruit is tasting its meaning. (Pessoa, 2010, my translation)

This is similar to the sensorimotor baby, who is also a shepherd of thoughts that are, above all, fugitive sensations, someone who thinks with ears and hands, for whom the meaning of *fruit* and *flower* is given by her mouth and nose.

Unlike this sensorimotor baby, you have a complex grid of words and symbols in your head that helps you classify, as though from a distance, most things and events in your immediate world. These symbols, as they *re*present things—as they bring things back to your mind and back to the *present* moment—allow you to understand and manipulate objects without directly touching them or seeing them. In general, you do not need to have direct contact with things themselves to understand what they are, or their characteristics and properties. In contrast, the sensorimotor baby has initially no words and no symbolic categories that would allow her to *re*present objects encountered in the environment. And, therefore, she cannot recognize or manipulate things indirectly, abstractly, or symbolically. Indeed, at birth, she is thrown into a world *devoid of distinct objects*, as she cannot clearly identify, for example, a table or a chair as something distinct and separate from the context. You and I see a table as obviously different from a chair. But from this baby's perspective, these things are indistinctly situated in the midst of a fluid and, so to speak, oceanic context. From this baby's perspective, the table doesn't have a presence of its own, as a separate thing unto itself. And, in general, she is not able to bring separate and distinct things to her mind the way we do. At birth, indeed, a baby cannot quite make sense of her own body. She does not experience, for example, her flailing arms as clearly identified bodily parts under her control, and she may, for instance, scratch her face without realizing that her own arms are the causes of her pain.

To reiterate the important idea, this baby can only bring things to her mind initially through direct contact, not through indirect symbolic representation, of course. Her experience of the world is thus radically different from yours, a different "trip," a visit to an unknown planet, such that it would be very difficult for you to see, or even imagine, the world from that strange sensorimotor perspective.

Note also that the symbols in your head help you organize the vast array of things and events in the world and help you divide them into categories. For instance, you categorize people as separate from animals, from plants, from things, etc. And you subcategorize people as men and women, for example, or animals as dogs, lions, and so on. In contrast, the sensorimotor child has yet to develop such categories ("people," "animals"). Naturally, she will eventually grasp them, but initially in a very rough manner. Initially, she will not understand that "people," which has now emerged in her mind as a category about things in the world, can be subdivided, for instance, into men and women. (Indeed, she may be very surprised to learn that not all people have vaginas, for example.) Similarly, when the sensorimotor child learns the word "dog," it will not be obvious to her that "dog" is something separate from cats, wolves, etc., and she may, therefore, assume, quite naturally, that "dog" stands for all furry, four-legged things, including cats, stuffed animals, or any such thing coming into her purview. Again, eventually this child's world will become populated by *distinct* and specific categories of objects, objects that exist both in the external physical world and in her internal world, in the emerging world of her mind, which in this sense emerges as an increasingly accurate model of the external world.

As Piaget noted, it is fair to say that the infant who initially begins to suck all objects within reach has probably two main, and initially wordless, categories: "things to be sucked," including the maternal breast, the rattle, her hand, etc., versus "other things." The idea is that this form of direct contact with the world—sucking objects—initially allows her to develop mental categories. This also allows her to make sense of the things that she senses as, precisely, objects that belong to some categories and not to others. Thus she begins to make sense of the world, and to categorize the objects out there, initially in a direct and sensorial manner.

As noted, when this baby begins to crawl, she begins to grasp, primarily with her body, the idea of distance, but also concepts such as separation and the notion of space itself. Thus these early *bodily references*, sensorial and motoric, eventually help her develop *abstract categories and concepts that have to be first learned by the body.* Then and only then can things in the world become consigned to the mind as abstractions. (Although, as we saw in Chapter 2, concepts constructed by sensorial information are limited, because sensorial information is relatively poor and limited itself. As Plato may agree, although the senses tell the child, and tell us, that a table is "hard" and "solid," the concepts of "hardness" and "solidity" provide only a superficial understanding of reality. Like Plato, Piaget also helps us see that, as the human mind develops upon a particular sensorimotor structure, and its development is thus appropriate to our particular biological form, the human mind is initially limited by the capacities and limitations of our *particular life-form.* This limitation, returning now to Plato, may be overcome by the development of knowledge, the sixth sense, as we called it, that can pierce through this limited bubble constructed by the five senses.)

Another characteristic of the sensorimotor stage is that objects, for the baby, are initially "*impermanent,*" as Piaget noted. A friend leaves your line of sight, and you do not think that he has vanished. The sensorimotor infant is not quite sure what happens to a person or to an object when they leave her line of sight—for example, when dad exits the room. For this baby, objects are not invested by the quality of permanence that we ascribe to them as a matter of course. For her, objects seem to appear from nowhere to then vanish when she can no longer perceive them, as though objects were in constant flight from themselves. Objects enter the purview of her senses, become present, real, and then vanish in a rather mysterious manner. Things are, in this sense, constantly falling in and out of the reality that this baby is able to perceive. And it is for this reason that she has a lot of fun playing peekaboo, because in her mind, she is, in fact, bringing the other person into being (when she sees the person) to then magically conjure the person away (when she ceases to see the person. Imagine how interesting it would be for you to actually bring a person into being, to then conjure such person away at will).

For the reasons provided earlier, this child is not at all a smaller version of yourself. Her world, once again, is not only different from ours, but is indeed very hard for us to fathom.

The Preoperational Stage

The second stage of cognitive development proposed by Piaget is called "preoperational." It begins, in Piaget's account, more or less at age 2, when the child begins to speak with some fluency and thus begins to see the world *through symbols,* replacing concrete objects with abstract representations. This stage lasts more or less until age 7, according to Piaget's model. As the child develops a symbolic register—that is, as she develops increasingly complex categories of representation for the objects in the world—she no longer needs to make sense of objects directly through her hands, eyes, mouth, etc. She is no longer a shepherd of thoughts that are, above all, sensations. She can now make sense of things indirectly, precisely through words, through symbols. She develops an increasingly *abstract* understanding of reality. She is a shepherd of thoughts that are, above all, thoughts.

But, of course, this does not mean that this child is correct about everything. Her thinking is, for example, profoundly influenced by fantasy. She often senses that objects, such as a table, are invested with almost personal qualities, which the child projects onto the object in question. In her eyes, the table may appear to be invested with a character on occasion, and in this sense with something of a spirit. Hence she may think that the table has been "mean" when she bumps her head against it. In fact, this child may retaliate by turning back and hitting the table with her hand or yelling at it. Indeed, there is a sense in which the child lives in an *animistic* world—a world where things have their own "animus," Latin for spirit, soul, or character. In this sense, the child's world has some commonalities with the world of our remote ancestors, the primitive world where people assumed that such things as volcanoes, rivers, mountains, trees were invested with a spirit and with characteristics such as meanness or goodness. This was a world where men and women tried to appease natural forces by means of prayer, of sacrifices, of the intermediation of priests, and so on. (This is the world of Agamemnon, for example, the Greek king of the *Odyssey*, who sails to Troy to avenge his honor, the man who has to sacrifice his daughter, Iphigenia, to the Wind, for the Wind to push his ships to Troy.) The preoperational child is, in this sense, a little closer to this primitive world where things are, so to speak, ensouled. This is a world where a person may communicate with objects and where reality itself is thus invested with a sense of agency that can be friendly or not, that can be appeased or propitiated.

The poetry of Pablo Neruda, one of the most important poets of the 20th century, may help us better understand how a preoperational child sees the world. In one of his most endearing books, *The Book of Questions* (2018), Neruda asks, "What irritates the volcanoes that spit fire, coldness and fury?" "Does the smoke chat with the clouds"? "Why don't the immense airplanes fly around with their children?" "Why do leaves commit suicide when they feel yellow?" "Why do clouds cry so much to thus become happier and happier?" "So, do tears not yet cried have to wait in little ponds? Or do they come from invisible rivers that run toward sadness"? (2018, translations are mine). The preoperational child, similarly, lives in a world of vaguely ensouled objects that have qualities and indeed "behaviors"—that cause the series of events that comprise reality, the reality that the child experiences.

For some psychologists, the idea that the preoperational child lives in a world that has animistic characteristics cannot be empirically ascertained because these children cannot articulate this concept at all. This is true, of course. A 3-year-old will not be able to tell mom, "Yes, mother, though objects seem inanimate, they are nevertheless invested with something akin to a soul or spirit." But animism in this child is not a concept. It is above all a feeling. You can get a very brief glimpse of it when you yourself, let us say, curse at your phone when it dies on you, or at a car that doesn't start. The idea is that, in the case of the child, this feeling is simply more vivid, not so fleeting, more real, extended to many things, and far more constant.

Because this child does live in a rather animistic world, she often ascribes the wrong *cause* to the events she encounters. Again, let us imagine that she bumps her head against the table and thus suffers pain. She may feel that the cause of her pain is the table's meanness. She may vaguely think, perhaps poetically, that the cause of a volcanic eruption is the volcano's irritation, its feelings of vengeance, etc. The preoperational child, therefore, easily falls under the spell of fairy tales and other such fantastic worlds, as these worlds bespeak how her mind actually works, how she herself makes sense of the world. Fairy-tale worlds are invested, as the child senses them, with a strong presence, with a distinctive force and an aura that escape the adult mind (save, perhaps, the mind of a poet). Importantly, this preoperational world is, in the mind of this child, artificially created by someone or something. When a kid in this stage of cognitive development tells you, for instance, that "the wind is blowing," she may literally mean that an entity, maybe a Mr. Wind of sorts, is producing the gentle movement of trees outside. The clouds, she may also vaguely sense, are white perhaps because someone has made them white.

The world of the preoperational child, in summary, behaves in ways that are logically inadequate (although perhaps poetically noteworthy), which parallels the child's initial lack of logical competency.

Let us illustrate how the mind of this child works by referring to one of the first and most famous experiments conducted by Piaget. One at a time, preoperational children were shown two glasses of identical size, each containing the same amount of water. A third glass, skinnier and taller, was placed beside the shorter glasses. The children correctly understood that the two identical glasses had the same amount of water. But when the researcher poured the contents of one of these identical glasses into the skinny and tall glass, the children typically thought that the tall glass now had *more* water than the shorter glass. Children at this age have not mastered logical operations. For you, if glass A = glass B, and B is poured into C, it logically follows that A = C. But this simple operation is not so simple for these children. They typically rely not on logic but on the information provided by the senses, which can override logical information. The skinny glass *looks* taller, so it follows, as the children sense, that it must have more water. This perceptual operation—it *looks* taller—overrides the *conceptual* and logical operation. This experiment, called the "Conservation Task," helped Piaget understand that preoperational children typically trust the information provided by their eyes, by their senses, in general, more than the information provided by any fledgling logic growing in their minds.

Concrete Operational Stage

The third stage in Piaget's theory is the "concrete operational stage." From about age 7 to about age 11, the child already has symbolic categories in her mind that allow her to organize and abstractly categorize things in her world. Now she fully knows, as well, that there is a clear difference between her perspective and that of others. And she has begun to understand and use basic logical operations, including mathematical operations, such as addition and subtraction. This child can now solve the Conservation Task correctly. She now realizes that both glasses—the short-squat and the skinny-tall glasses—end up having the same amount of water. Concrete operational children are beginning to trust not only the information provided by their eyes but also the logical input provided by their maturing brains (and, yes, brains continue to develop until about age 25). Their view of the world is more attuned to the way you see the world, although not identical to your perception. This child's world is similar to, but not quite like, yours. Not yet.

Imagine that you ask these children the following question: If A is more than B and B is more than C, then is A more than C, or is C more than A, or are they the same? Interestingly, these children will generally have trouble answering that, as it logically follows, A is more than C. Again, they can think logically but may not have all logical operations down quite yet. Here is another experiment: The concrete operational child and the researcher began to run exactly at the same time, and they stopped running at the same time as well. Both, therefore, ran for the same amount of time. The researcher, however, sometimes pretended that the child was faster and that she, therefore, ran farther. When this happened, the child typically thought that she had run for a longer period of *time* because, as her simple explanation usually went, she had run for a longer *distance*. These children often conflate the concepts of time and space, particularly children in the younger side of this stage. For them, such things as temporality and spatiality are not entirely clear yet.

Concrete operational children have begun to incorporate *inductive* reasoning in their thinking. That is to say, they have begun to make generalizations based on particular observations. For instance, they have observed that, time and again, things fall to the ground, and, based on these observations, they can understand that something in the ground, which grown-ups call "gravity," pulls all things down. Inductively, they may thus understand the basic ideas pertaining to Newton's theory of gravity, and, indeed, they may be able to understand the larger and more abstract Newtonian premise: that big things tend to pull little things toward them, gravitationally. But as Piaget shows, these children typically have trouble with *deductive* reasoning. They have trouble *deducing* what sorts of outcomes must necessarily follow from a general premise. Imagine, for example, that you give them a broad, general premise such as follows: "All bears who live the North Pole are white," and then you ask them, "If Bobo is a bear who lives in the North Pole, what is Bobo's color?" These children will likely hesitate and provide an answer that does not necessarily follow from the given premise. They may say, for instance, "Let's ask mom; she will know." Although beginning to think logically, this child is not ready to understand scientific reasoning in a fully meaningful manner yet. Her potential for reading the world is limited and she can be easily manipulated into believing irrational or illogical notions. A grown-up who remains in this stage of cognitive development, not an unusual occurrence, may likewise be manipulated into believing these sorts of views and will be vulnerable to propaganda, fake news, odd conspiracy theories, the ideologies of fringe religious sects, and so on.

Formal Operational Stage

The fourth and final stage in Piaget's theory is called *the formal operational stage*, which involves refinement of abstract thinking and progressive mastering of logical operations. From about 11 to about 15 years of age (although this stage of cognitive development may continue into adulthood), the child and then the adolescent begin to master both inductive and deductive reasoning. Also, the person developing formal operational abilities will be able not only to think abstractly but also to think *about* her thinking process. She can more easily have thoughts about her thoughts, a process known as "metacognition," and she can, therefore, monitor her thinking, judge it, assess it, and correct it. Whereas younger children tend to think dogmatically—without pausing to question received ideas—adolescents in the formal operational stage can more easily question received ideas or dogmas, including those that they have inherited from their culture. And they can also engage in abstract trial-and-error operations to solve problems or to find answers to complex questions.

Younger children can engage in trial-and-error operations, needed, for example, to turn an electric toy on, pushing buttons until discovering the right button, or trying differently shaped pegs until discovering the right hole for the right peg. But *formal operations* involve more complex trial-error manipulations, including manipulations that are entirely abstract, carried out entirely in the person's head, after considering hypothetical scenarios that have no concrete referent in the real world.

You talk to a child who has *not* yet acquired the ability to perform formal operations and ask her the following question: "How would the world be if people didn't have hands?" This child is likely to provide a simple and concrete answer. She may say, for example, "People would not be able to shake hands" or "people would not need mittens during winter," which, more than actual answers, are reiterations of the original premise. In contrast, an adolescent who has begun to conduct *formal operations* is more likely to manipulate this premise in her head to thus assess various possible outcomes. Therefore, she might provide answers that are less concrete, less obvious, and more abstract. She might answer, for instance, that if people didn't have hands, human civilization would have taken a different course to accommodate this scenario. She might provide details that illustrate her answer and that logically follow from the original premise. Or, going deeper still, she might consider the evolutionary implications of this scenario and suggest that even the history of our species would have been radically different, as the human brain has largely evolved to make and use tools, etc. A person further down this formal operational road may even add, for example, that, having such a different path of evolutionary development, our sense of reality itself would have been different. The capacity for formal operations, in other words, makes the person readier to approach reality as a scientist, readier to read the world, and readier to consult the world itself. (On the other hand, this person would also be less likely to be manipulated or swayed by dogmas, or by illogical or irrational ideas or narratives.)

Formal operations involve more advanced, less concrete mental output, usually achieved by means of cognitive training, self-training, and advanced schooling. As these operations largely depend on environmental input, not all people reach this stage.

Let me finally clarify that the attainment of even the most basic cognitive skills occurs partly via environmental input. So when the sensorimotor baby initially touches a table, for instance, or when she first bumps her head against it and thus begins to grasp notions such as hardness, she is already receiving environmental input, of course, which is needed to develop her cognitive abilities. Again, basic patterns of cognitive development, the first three phases, occur more or less automatically, as expected outcomes of normal biological development, but this *assumes* normal environmental contribution. This assumes that the baby and child are able to explore the physical space; that they have people to talk to, to imitate, to play with, to hold hands with; that they have toys, and so on. Hence, as discussed, children who do not experience a normal environment—for instance, children who don't have normal social contact—are likely to develop significant, even profound, mental and even physical deficits.

Society and the Human Brain

Particularly during the last stage of cognitive development, the environment contributes to the variety of ways in which your brain becomes wired. "Environment," here, includes not only the external physical space but also uterine, social, cultural, technological, economic, and historical factors that, as we will presently see, also contribute to the development of the brain itself.

The brain, let us say the obvious, is not merely the three pounds of mass housed in the skull. More properly, it is a network of brain cell *connections*, sometimes called "neuronal pathways," which grow with, or are constructed by, our experiences in the world. The brain's biological structures are present at birth, regardless, of course, of the culture of the person. Every normal human being has a visual cortex, a frontal lobe, a hippocampus, etc., and in this sense, all humans share a cerebral template. Yet each human brain is unique as well, precisely to the extent to which it is constructed by our unique experiences in the world. The hippocampus, for example, which is partly responsible for spatial navigation, may physically change when a person's routine involves constantly navigating a complex spatial domain such as a city (e.g., cab drivers before GPS), or when a person ceases to use navigational abilities (e.g., as a result of the invention of GPS). These two scenarios may, respectively, strengthen or weaken hippocampus, generating plainly visible physical changes. A person exposed to music from an early age will have a more complex sound processing system in her brain, etc.

Biological factors of course contribute to establishing neuronal connections, sometimes prevailing over environmental, cultural, and/or socioeconomic factors. For example, aspects of intelligence may be inherited from the parents, and this may become the decisive ingredient that overrules the contribution of the environment. Genetic or chromosomal factors associated with mental retardation can also have a determining influence. Yet the environment can have powerful effects and can become the determinant variable. Note, as well, that people can freely choose activities that can help brain development, activities that could overrule the input of the environment. Freely chosen behaviors can become mapped in the brain, and people may *freely decide* what to consign to their brains and thus how to construct them (thereby freely create aspects of what they become).

To What Extent Is Your Brain Externally Constructed?

Michael Merzenich, emeritus professor at the University of California, San Francisco, and a foremost neuroscientists in the area of "brain plasticity" (brain adaptability) has helped us better understand how the human brain is "constructed" precisely by the constellation of experiences that befall us. He has helped us see that experiences can shape, and even determine at times, the kinds of persons that we become. Because the environment can play a decisive role in the construction of the brain, Merzenich explained, the details of our brains today are "vastly different" from those of the average person who lived a hundred years ago, for example. Today, for instance, the average IQ is 100—30 *points higher than the average IQ 100 years ago* (Flynn, 2012a). If regarded by today's average, the average IQ a hundred years ago would be bordering mental retardation, and if the average person today travels back in time, he or she would be one of the super smart ones, if judged according to the IQ metric. How did this happen? Today, to provide a partial answer for now, the environment demands more abstract thinking and thus powerfully contributes to gains in IQ because such tests measure, in part, the ability to think abstractly. By the same token, we might also argue that the details of our brains are bound to be vastly different, as well, from those of persons who experience vastly different cultures and social circumstances (an idea also supported by Rosenthal's theory of the Pygmalion and Golem effects discussed in the foregoing).

The human brain, in any case, is the most plastic organ. It is built for adaptability and change. It adapts and changes, physically, in response to environmental pressures, including those related to cultural or technological changes. (And this is why a discussion of these processes does belong in a book like this, which pertains to the ways in which the social world affects our way of being.)

The well-established fact about gains in intelligence over time is called the Flynn effect, as it was studied by James Flynn, professor of political studies at the University of Otago, New Zealand. Let us go back to the factors account for this astounding gain in intelligence, as measured by IQ testing. A century ago, people expected to attain lower levels of schooling. The education system did not emphasize abstract logical thinking the way we do today; it emphasized practical and concrete thinking. Today, we have much wider access to education, including higher education, not to mention more advanced educational techniques and technologies. We demand much more logical thinking from our children. In contrast, life was much more rural a hundred years ago (today it is centered in cities) and for this reason, people were typically confronted with more hands-on, practical demands: farming, herding, etc. Farming itself was much less mechanized, less systematized, less "scientific" and thus encouraged more concrete thinking. Our great-grandparents were generally in the habit of learning to *use* things in the world, and in contrast, we are in the habit of *understanding* them. Jobs today are more cognitively demanding. Our everyday experiences, if compared to those of our great-grandparents, tend to remove us from the concrete, objective world. Our world is much more mediated—by mass media, by digital media, by devices that, removing us from the direct and concrete reality, encourage us to think more abstractly. Our world today is much more digital. Theirs was much more analogical.

Flynn said, in summary, that today, "we've put on scientific spectacles, and they had on utilitarian spectacles" (Flynn, 2012b). Hence, partly because of the circumstances that tend to befall the average person today, IQ scores have gone up.

Flynn's research provides support to Merzenich's idea that the brain of the average person a hundred years ago was indeed constructed differently. More generally and more importantly, it supports the broader idea that the environment, including its cultural and technological aspects, can contribute powerfully to brain wiring and development. Hence the environment contributes to central aspects of personhood and to the overall development of the human experience and spirit.

Environmental Threats to the Brain

It is important to note, as well, that although our environment demands more abstract thinking, it demands *less* from other brain functions and systems. For example, although it is likely that "the analytic portions of your brain are enlarged compared to your ancestors'," as Flynn himself said, it is also likely that "the rote memory portions are not" (2012). In fact, it is likely that the Digital Age has diminished certain brain functions, as we will see next, beyond our capacity to recall (Carr, 2011). As Flynn noted, it is, in any case, best to think that our brains are simply more modern, rather than better built. They are more adapted to the demands of our particular, modern environments, for better and for worse.

Let us also say that the human brain can change not only over time (e.g., from generation to generation) but also with culture and even with social class. Mark Kishiyama, a researcher of cognitive neurophysiology at the University of California, Berkeley, has shown that socioeconomic status (SES) itself can also have profound implications for brain development (Kishiyama et al., 2009). Kishiyama and colleagues studied the brains of 26 children, 13 of whom were categorized as being of low SES and 13 as high SES. Their results were sobering indeed. They showed that low SES can negatively affect brain systems related, particularly, to executive function: the ability to pay attention, to retrieve things from memory, to plan, to organize, and to use effective time management strategies.[1] Furthermore, the low SES children also had problems with working memory, the capacity to hold various pieces of information in one's mind (for instance, keeping in mind complicated step-by-step instructions, or the ability to narrate a complex story or event fluently). This makes people better at taking standardized tests, at writing, and at reasoning in general. These children also had problems with "semantic fluency," the ability to process language and to communicate fluently. And, finally, they had trouble with "cognitive flexibility," which is related to the ability to consider two or more concepts simultaneously—for instance, processing interconnected concepts, the sort of conceptual grid that you find when studying complex material. Some of these low SES children performed at a level similar to that of people who had suffered a stroke. Indeed, we also know that that SES may have a significant effect on gray matter itself (Hanson & Hair 2012). By means of neuroimaging analyses of a cohort of respondents aged 4 to 22, researchers Hanson and Hair have shown that gray matter was diminished in children who came from poor families, about 3 to 4 percental points below the developmental norm (2012).

---

1   Children with executive function deficits might have difficulties, for instance, if asked to read and then retell a story in an organized, coherent, detailed, and sequential manner.

Of course, poverty in itself is *not* related to brain deficits. Some of the great geniuses have come from impoverished backgrounds, and many of them have contributed to the world precisely because they experienced poverty firsthand, which gave them an unsheltered vision of the world. Literary giant Albert Camus comes to mind, for example. The son of an illiterate charwoman and a poor farmer, Camus grew up in Algiers with no electricity, no toilet, no books, no money, and yet rose to become one of the most important philosophers and novelists of the 20th century, winning the Nobel Prize for literature in 1957. In physics, Joseph von Fraunhofer, who grew up as child servant working in conditions of semislavery, rose to become one of the most notable geniuses in the field of applied optics. We already mentioned the work of Menchu, another Nobel Laureate. Examples like these abound. Neither Kishiyama nor Hair and colleagues have shown that lack of money is in itself related to brain functioning or brain wiring. Instead, their research suggests that, inasmuch as poverty involves impoverished environments and repeated scenarios where children cannot deploy their brain potential, it may affect the development, the wiring, and the construction of the human brain. Although people can freely choose activities that can contribute to brain development, many people encounter a *limited and limiting set of possible experiences to choose from*. For example, one out of every four children in the world experience the kind of poverty that makes it difficult, when not impossible, to freely choose to expose their brains to enriched cognitive environments: good books, libraries, etc. Such worlds can limit not only choices but also aspects of brain development and hence cognitive output.

Your Brain on Media: Positive and Negative Effects

Poverty is *only one* of the many environmental or social factors that can negatively affect brain development. Let us consider others that are closer to the experience of most college students.

Carnegie Melon University professor Luis von Ahn has reported that by age 21, an average American male has spent about 10,000 hours playing computer games (2013). This is almost exactly the number of hours that American students need to go from fifth grade to graduating from high school, so gaming, in this sense, provides a parallel track for brain development. Importantly, 10,000 hours are also the average hours of training that a person needs in order to achieve virtuosic performances—for example, in music. Ten thousand hours of musical practice will physically affect the brain of the musician, precisely so as to make him or her virtuosic. Von Ahn has also reported that, "Over 200 million hours are spent playing computer and video games *every day* in the United States" (2008, my italics). According to the media research firm A.C. Nielsen, the average American spends about nine years of his or her life *only watching TV*, thus reaching the age of 65 after having watched *about two million TV commercials*. Indeed, according to the 2007 U.S. Census Bureau's Statistical Abstract of the United States, American adults and teens spend almost *five months per year* (3,518 hours) using the Internet, listening to personal music devices, watching TV, and reading newspapers. Such levels of exposure to media environments begin early. For example, "About two-thirds of children in nursery school and 80 percent of kindergartners use computers" (DeBell & Chapman, 2006).

Again, the human brain is thus exposed to a very different environment today, if compared to any other era. This new environment is not only more abstract but also more fractional: constantly popping up with bits of information that vie for our attention, as any Internet user can easily recognize. And in this sense, our brain's world is also less linear, linearity involving constant attention to a certain task, the sort of thing that you do when reading a book, for instance, *if you read it for a long while without interruptions*. As noted, a possible outcome of these levels of exposure to digital environments is increased abstract thinking, but there are other possible consequences as well. Philip Zimbardo says,

"Boys' brains *are being digitally rewired in a totally new way* for change, novelty, excitement, and constant arousal" (2011, my emphasis); and let us underscore that this kind of novelty, excitement, and constant arousal is generally provided not by educators or artists, but by industries interested in making money above all. This type of "digitally rewiring," Zimbardo adds, is the reason why "they are totally out of sync in traditional classes." Not surprisingly, this kind of rewiring—suited for playing computer games, including those that are toys in disguise, killing bad guys, etc.—doesn't help when studying. A brain wired to look for constant change, constant novelty, constant adrenaline-driven arousal—will also be constantly distracted when, for example, reading a book in preparation for an exam. This partly accounts for the generational problems, the achievement deficits incurred by many young men today, as discussed earlier.[2] On the other hand, this might be contributing also to the increases of attention deficit disorder symptoms experienced by this generation. As researcher Ra Chaelin and colleagues from the University of Southern California have noted, "More frequent use of digital media may be associated with development of ADHD symptoms" (2018), problems that are more prevalent in males, which is consistent with the fact that males are exposed to these kinds of games more often than females.

It is, of course, easy to recognize the almost miraculous positive potential of these new media. For example, we can retrieve specialized information in a manner of seconds, which for previous generations was a comparatively lengthy process, and this is a huge advantage to students such as yourself. But it is not a good idea to mechanically accept the rhetoric and the propaganda which argue that only good things will come from these media. To be sure, the new digital environments we typically experience in our everyday lives may negatively affect the very shape of brain cells, called neurons, particularly in digital natives, precisely as a result of prolonged exposure to digital environments (Carr, 2011). Beyond problems or attention and concentration, consider memory again. The Internet, and by extension the smartphone in your pocket, have become extensions of your brain and of your memory, in particular, a prosthetic memory of sorts. So, unlike people from any other era, you don't need to remember too many facts, simply because you can outsource the job of remembering to these machines. But what happens when members of a species decrease the use of some capacities and some organs? Such organs, we know from biology, tend to become "vestigial." That is to say, if an organ loses its value because in a new environment it is no longer needed, it will therefore lose related functions and capacities, like a muscle that is not exercised.[3] Of course, this does *not* mean that our memory will just disappear, because human beings will always need to exercise memorial functions regardless of technologies such as the Internet. But this does mean that outsourcing memorial functions to machines will likely result in losing some memorial capacities. Betsy Sparrow, a professor of psychology at Columbia University, has shown that when people face complex questions today, they often expect to have the help of devices and that, as a result of relying on machines and thus not forcing memorial capacities into action, people in fact ending up with "lower rates of recall," on trend (2011).

Carr also notes that reflective capacities can be compromised as a result of overexposure to media. These capacities involve the ability to stop and think about what is occurring at present, a conscious awareness of what one is doing and thinking and why. Bear in mind that media such as video games

---

2   Another likely consequence of such exposure is that this generation of digital natives is more at home in the immediacy of the present and much less acquainted with the past, with tradition and history. Accordingly, this generation may be less likely to apply the lessons from the collective past so as to improve the collective future.

3   The Kiwi birds of New Zealand, for instance, didn't have to use their wings, as their predators disappeared, and their food was easily found on the ground. Thus their wings became vestigial and eventually disappeared altogether.

discourage reflection. If a player stops to think about what he is doing and why, he will most likely lose, be killed by the bad guy, etc. And to be sure, these kinds of media encourage the player to act *not reflectively* but *reflexively,* with *reflexivity* involving automatic, less conscious, less intentional, and more unthinking actions. And these kinds of declines in reflective ability are really very important because this ability—precisely because it allows us to take an objective distance and observe our thinking process and behavior—allows us to have better control over what we think and do, which can help us correct our behavior and course of action when needed. These abilities also help us to observe, assess, and judge the events around us, including the media messages, news, information, and propaganda that we encounter. In a paper curiously entitled "On the Reception and Detection of Pseudo-Profound Bullshit," researchers from the University of Waterloo, Canada, reported that reflective abilities help the person detect claims to truth and profundity that are "actually vacuous" (Pennycook et al., 2015). Folks who are not very good at *reflectivity* are far more likely to *reflexively* accept these kinds of vacuous or "bullshit" statements. The weakening of our reflective capacities may make us more vulnerable to such things as commercial or political charlatanism, propaganda, post-truths, and fake news, all of which can damage not only our worldviews, even our health and finances, but also the democratic process in general; for, as discussed, democracy needs aware, awake, and knowledgeable citizens.

To summarize, areas of cognition that might become affected by the new media environments include memory, the ability to concentrate, the ability to engage in extended linear thinking, for example, reading a long book, as well as the ability to contemplate and the capacity for solitary and self-reflective thought (Carr, 2011).

"Dopamine Feedback Loops"

In this context, it is critical to discuss the role that new media have in society, whether they are affecting the brain itself, and the impact they may have on the democratic process. Let us focus on Facebook, in particular, as this is arguably the platform that has had the biggest impact on social life. And let us first say that, although we don't have enough data to reach a conclusion about the role that these kinds of social media play with respect to the brain, their sheer scale calls for a deliberative discussion about their possible consequences.

The first thing to note is that, ubiquitous such as they are, these media have effectively provided new environments for the human brain. As noted, neurological adaptations to digital environments may have very positive effects.[4] But, as Carr has argued, the brain adapts regardless of the consequences of such adaptive processes. It adapts without thinking about the consequences of rewiring itself so as to fit into new environments, and it can, therefore, change in a way that, although functional with respect to the new environment, may, nevertheless, involve decreased capacities. One may safely bet that the one person in the world who knows the most about how Facebook works to recruit and retain customers is Chamath Palihapitiya. He was one of the founders of this venture (and now a billionaire) and the person in charge of expanding the customer base, which he did pretty well, recruiting, in fact, a big portion of the world population, including, perhaps, you yourself. He thus played a crucial role in this global phenomenon, Facebook, this multibillion-dollar corporation that

---

4   Indeed, some researchers, such as Jane McGonigal, a designer of games herself, have suggested that exposure to some games can lead to exceedingly positive outcomes for the world in general, as gaming, purportedly, can make players feel empowered, confident, etc.

has changed aspects of politics, marketing, and everyday life the world over. Let us see how he feels about these accomplishments:

> I feel tremendous guilt. I think we all knew in the back of our minds, even though we feigned this whole line of, like, there probably aren't any really bad unintended consequences—I think that in the back, deep, deep recesses of our mind we kind of knew something bad could happen, but I think that the way we defined it was not like this. *It literally is at a point now where I think have created tools that are ripping apart the social fabric of how society works, that is truly where we are.* And I would encourage all of you to really internalize how important this is. If you feed the beast that beast will destroy you. If you push back on it, we have a chance to control it and rein it in. And it is a point in time where people need a hard break from some of these tools and the things you rely on. *The short-term dopamine-driven feedback loops that we have created are destroying how society works:* no civil discourse, no cooperation, misinformation, mistruth [...] it is eroding the core foundations of how people behave by and between each other [...] *You are being programmed* (2018, my emphasis).

"Destroying how society works"? "*You are being programmed*"? Clearly, we need to examine Palihapitiya's line of thinking. Facebook is free. How is it that a free product generates multibillion-dollar profits? Facebook is a well-oiled machine of data collection, your data and the data of 2.3 billion people around the world, data that this platform sells. In this particular sense, the very profitable product that this company commercializes is *you*. The genius of Facebook founders is having discovered that your preferences, likes and dislikes, what you write, what you post, even what you write and then delete (Tufekci, 2017) are precisely a product and indeed a source of vast profit, which they have amassed.

More profit for them equals being able to generate more data: denser psychometric profiles of more and more customers. And to get more data, it is critical for them that users spend more and more time on their platform, because the more customers click, and type, and update, the thicker their data become and the more money the company makes. How to achieve this desirable goal? By creating for the costumer "short-term dopamine driven feedback loops," as the father of the idea, Palihapitiya himself, said. Sean Parker, also one of the creators of Facebook, puts it this way: "The thought process that went into building [Facebook] was all about, 'How do we consume as much time and conscious attention as possible.' And that means that we need to sort of give you a little dopamine hit every once in a while" (in Allen, 2017).

This idea is the master key to how this platform works and what it may be doing not only to the habits and the routines of users, psychologically, but also to the brain, neuropsychologically. But this concept, "short-term dopamine driven feedback loops," is not easy to understand, and it would be useful to examine it, beginning with the key term, dopamine.

Dopamine is a little molecule that we all have in our brains, a neurotransmitter, responsible, among other things, for our feelings of well-being, satisfaction, and pleasure in higher quantities. You eat a pizza with friends and experience the perhaps familiar sensation of feeling good about the event, the sensation that puts a smile on your face and that puts you in a good mood. You get an A on an exam, and there it is again, this kindly little mood that comes to brighten your morning. The reason why you are able to feel these affects can be reduced to *dopamine*, the levels of which have increased in your brain, moderately, by the experience of being with friends, by the pizza itself, by the good news of having obtained a good mark on your exam. If you have a compromised neural system, so that your brain is not able to produce this little surplus of dopamine, you might not feel those positive effects. You would be prone to indifference, perhaps to sadness and depression, and, depending on other factors, a doctor might have to give you a medication to help your brain release dopamine at adequate levels, while also inhibiting its reabsorption or reuptake. If this medication works, it might rekindle your interest in the little pleasures of life, simply because you would now be able to experience these dopamine-driven pleasures. So now, doing such things as going out for pizza with friends, or doing well on an exam, would be more rewarding and would therefore make more sense.

But back to Palihapitiya. What does it mean for Facebook to be based on "short-term dopamine driven feedback loops"? It means that this application is explicitly designed to give the consumer little "hits" of dopamine, as Parker says, that should be short-lived but ideally constant. So customers would derive a sense of satisfaction and meaning from the application while they are on it—a feeling that would encourage them to keep on clicking, to keep on adding data, and to keep on coming again and again for more. How do you deliver these little "hits" to the customer? For example, by adding a "like" button for your friends to give you props and likes, which increases, momentarily and modestly, the levels of feel-good dopamine in your brain such that over time you would associate Facebook (or any other such platform) with the feeling of liking being on it. The model here is that of the Russian psychologist Ivan Pavlov. And you recall Pavlov's dogs, which were exposed to the sound of a bell every time they had food so that eventually they associated food with the sound of the bell and were therefore excited by the sound itself, to the point indeed of salivation. Facebook likewise strives to create a positive association for the user by rewarding him or her with "little hits" of feel-good dopamine for doing the things that generate profit for the company: posting, typing, and, thus, adding to his or her psychographic profile, which is the company's product. This "positive association" is simply the feeling of wanting to be on this platform. It is the feeling that, perhaps, already ebbs from time to time throughout your day, constantly nudging you to open your page (or any other such platform also based on the same dopamine-loop model).

This platform, in summary, is a machine that, to collect your data, gently inserts you into a feel-good feedback loop, with "feel-good" and "loop" being the key words here. But why would this seemingly innocuous little pleasure be so bad, as Palihapitiya, the man who designed this thing, so passionately said? (Again, we "have created tools that are ripping apart the social fabric of how society works," and indeed, *"you are being programmed."*)

"You Are Being Programmed"

The full answer to the previous question is beyond our focus, but here is the partial answer that concerns us. The data that Facebook collects can easily allow a client to profile users by preferences—for example, political or religious preferences; preferences pertaining to fashion, to food, pets, traveling, brand names; preferences for the occult; sexual preferences; preferences for healthy food or for fast food; preferences for conspiracy theories, and so on. Such a client could, therefore, accurately guess which Facebook users are susceptible to what message, a dream come true for marketers and for political operators. Facebook captures this kind of information; information pertaining to what images, ideas, or pitches cater to users' fears, hopes, prejudices, and beliefs—information that, of course, can allow this company's clients to push the users' buttons and motivate their behavior.

This platform, in other words, captures not only *demographic data*, such as likely marital status, place of residence, pet ownership status, gender, etc. Far more importantly for them, they also capture *psychographic data*, which show, once again, what can make you tick and come back for more. Whereas demographic data may describe a set of customers as, for example, young, white, and college educated, *psychographic* data may sort out these costumers in terms of, say, higher or lower than normal levels of anxiety or gullibility, or high or low IQ, or neurotic tendencies, or a sense of fairmindedness, or membership in a certain church, in Alcoholic Anonymous, etc. Facebook, for example, could in principle determine if some users have manic characteristics, which could help, say, a client from the gambling industry to microtarget these persons with the industry's products (Tufekci, 2017). Bear in mind that folks who have manic tendencies have a hard time controlling their impulses and are hence easy targets for this kind of industry. Facebook could also determine if a customer is a religious extrovert, or neurotic, or wholesome, or fair-minded, or credulous. And, together with his or her demographic profile, these data could allow yet other kinds of industries to target him or her with certain products, services, or, importantly, political agendas or ideologies.

Despite various investigations on how this platform commercializes and shares its data, it is not clear just where this information ends up at the end of the commercial cycle. We don't know, for example, the full extent to which political parties or foreign states use it for propagandistic or strategic purposes. But what is clear is that, in general, anyone able to buy these data, *the* source of profit for this company, will have at least some control over the "motivic structure" of targeted populations. As the *New York Times* has noted, "Facebook capitalizes on personal information to influence the behavior of its users, and then sells that influence to advertisers for a profit. It is an ecosystem ripe for manipulation" (NYT Editorial Board, 2018). Dan Gillmor, director of the Knight Center at Arizona State University, has likewise noted, "It's reasonable to believe that sooner or later, we're going to see widespread manipulation of people's decision-making, including in elections, in ways that are more widespread and granular, but even less detectable" (in Wesby, 2018). This is why Palihapitiya himself said, with absolute candor and clarity, "*You are being programmed.*" And this is why his own solution is, "I don't use these tools anymore," and "I don't let my kids use this shit."

In summary, simply to collect and sell data, social media platforms, in general, are thus developing powerful "deep surveillance" tools that are allowing economic and political entities to have a higher degree of control over the behavior of populations, for example, their voting behaviors. Interestingly, these tools have individual as well as global implications: They can target specific individuals but also populations on a national or even a global scale. This is, of course, great for the businesses and the politicians that benefit from deep surveillance. But it is not so great for democracy, because this kind of *behavior control* is not compatible with the idea of "a land of the free," with the Lincolnian ideal of a government "by the people." (Not to mention that this is not that great either for those who, as Palihapitiya says, "are being programmed.")

The Important Questions

We have to be reflective about these media, even if they are likely compromising our capacity for reflection, as noted earlier. Indeed, as a society, we have to know what these things might be doing to the brain itself. Zimbardo, Carr, and many others have already argued that the new media is digitally rewiring the brain of users (e.g., "for novelty [...] and constant arousal," as Zimbardo noted). We also know that only four weeks of Facebook *deactivation* "increased subjective well-being" in a large cohort of study participants, as Stanford and New York University researchers have reported (Allcott et al., 2019). We know that classic symptoms of depression can develop among preteens who spend time on Facebook, a phenomenon clinically known, in fact, as "Facebook depression." And we know that Facebook use may lead to sleep problems (Kaimal, Sajja, & Sasangohar, 2017) as well as (behavioral) addiction, a phenomenon characterized as "Facebook Addiction Disorder" (Brailovskaia & Margraf, 2019). Hence, we can legitimately ask what is in fact happening to the brain of users of social media, such as Facebook, 2.3 billion of them? Does "programing" the person mean programing the brain itself over time? If so, what would be the consequences of this for the individual, for society as a whole, for the idea of "a government of the people"? How is Facebook affecting your own brain and your views and behaviors, including, again, your voting behaviors?

As noted, we don't know the answers to these concerns. Sean Parker has said, "God only knows what [Facebook] is doing to our children's brains" (in Allen, 2017). But, to insist, we do know that in this area we have to develop a sense of public literacy, "social media literacy" (as an individual, you yourself probably want to know whether the social media you use, for about 50 minutes per day, if you are the average user, may be affecting your behavior, sleep response, aspects of well-being, and, indeed, your brain.) As a society, we cannot afford to passively *assume* that these powerful and pervasive tools will not have negative unintended consequences. We cannot afford to allow technicians, like the makers of Facebook, who appear to have very little social literacy, to "feign [...] this whole line of, like, there probably aren't any really bad unintended consequences," as Palihapitiya so candidly said.

More generally and importantly, we have to be able to understand that the human brain—*and thus what we are as human beings—is partly an effect of the environments that we have created, those that we have failed to create, and those that we strive to create in the future*. We have to understand, as Carr implies, what sort of environment could make us not only more abstract thinkers but also better thinkers. How will the human brain, and thus the human spirit, evolve in the future? What role will the globally expanding market, marketers, media technicians, and corporations play in this process? How is your own brain responding to these processes? What role are you yourself playing in terms of the wiring of your brain and the development of your cognitive capacities? These are difficult questions, of course, but they are also vital for your generation.

Your Brain Has Also Evolved to Mirror Other People

One last consideration about how your brain is constructed by the environment: Your brain has been designed not only to mirror aspects of your environment but also to mirror the operations in other people's brains (Iacoboni, 2009).

We begin mimicking only minutes after being born (Meltzoff & Moore, 1977), and we mimic throughout our lives, generally without being aware that we are doing so. Social psychologists call this the "chameleon effect," the notion that we do not simply set out to mimic others, consciously, but, much as chameleons, we mimic without intending or even knowing that we are doing so. Mimicry is important for social animals in general, and it is particularly important for such an intensely social species as human beings. As mimicry researchers Tanya Chartrand and Rick van Baaren have noted, "Mimicry is everywhere—we all do it, and do it frequently. Even a casual glance at people interacting at an office, restaurant, bar, park, or at home will reveal many manifestations of our proclivity to mimic others [...] We aren't trying to imitate the other person, and we aren't aware of mimicking them," yet we do (2009). Unconscious mimicry helps us pick up accents, emotional styles, and even a culturally relevant repertoire of gestures, bodily rhythms, and bodily techniques, as we will discuss in a subsequent chapter. Why do we mimic? Because unconscious mimicry can be very good for us. It helps us learn from others; it is related to acquisition of language and motors skills; it fosters empathy; it enhances the likelihood of being liked by, and liking, others. And it also is good for society, incidentally, as mimicry, for the reasons noted earlier, provides a sense of group cohesiveness and social integration.

Giacomo Rizzolatti, one of the first neuroscientists who identified and mapped the mirroring abilities of our brains, has shown that an entire cluster of neurons, appropriately called "mirror neurons," developed in the human brain *precisely to model the actions, the emotions, the gestures, the movements of others* (Rizzolatti & Craighero, 2004). Our brain, as neuroscientist Marco Iacoboni has reported, is "built for mirroring" (2009). "Brains," Iacoboni said, are "capable of mirroring the deepest aspects of the minds of others, even at the fine-grained level of a single cell [a single neuron]" (2009, 34). But why are our brains so intent on synchronizing with other brains in range and, so to speak, dialing into them? Because "we are exquisitely social creatures," Rizzolatti said, and because "[o]ur survival depends on understanding the actions, intentions, and emotions of others. We simulate these automatically, without logic, thinking, analyzing" (in Blakeslee & Blakeslee, 2008, p. 166). As Sandra and Mathew Blakeslee explained, "[W]hen you watch someone else perform an action—say using a broom—you automatically simulate the action in your own brain" (2008, p. 166). When you see someone using a broom, your brain's motor neurons, which control your own movements, are firing in a similar manner as the motor neurons of the person using the broom. Thus, although you don't have a broom in your hands, your brain is, so to speak, using a broom, nonetheless. (Although, of course, you don't begin to move your arms in a sweeping motion, because your brain is also telling you that these motor functions are happening to someone else, thus inhibiting you from actually replicating the motor actions of others.) "When you see me doing something, you understand because you have a copy of the action in your brain. It's so strange. You become me. When I see you grasping an object, it is as if I, Giacomo, were grasping it" (Rizzolatti quoted in Blakeslee & Blakeslee, 2008, p. 166).

Consider this extraordinary fact, discovered by Polish-American psychologist Robert Zajonc: Precisely because we tend to mirror others, the very faces of couples living happily together have "higher facial similarity (they look more like each other) after a quarter century of married life than at the time of marriage" (in Iacoboni, 2009, p. 115). There are various possible reasons for this sense of "facial convergence" among couples, diet, for example: Couples may eat the same foods and may thus alter their facial fat deposits in a similar manner. But in a large measure, facial convergence is related to mirroring mechanisms, particularly mediated by empathy between the partners such that the face of each one of the partners, as it is constantly mirroring the other, therefore develops its facial muscles in a similar manner. Hence their faces become invested by the face of the other partner.

Indeed, we tend to mirror not only movements and gestures, such as yawning, but also affects and sensations, such as "pain, laughter, smiling, affection, embarrassment, discomfort, disgust, stuttering, reaching with effort, and the like, in a broad range of situations" (Hatfield, Cacioppo, & Rapson, 1993, p. 22). As you know, if you are observing a stranger yawn, you will often yawn (and the effect is stronger if the yawner is your friend). Video games are effective because the gamer's brain models the make-believe virtual experiences so that, as far as the brain is concerned, you are in the midst of danger, violence, and excitement (hence hormones such as adrenaline are being released). Those seeing someone being hit by a ball at a game often grimace, or duck, or groan, even if minimally and even if without realizing that they are doing these things. Those talking on their cellular phones tend to synchronize their steps. Those in the midst of a crowd often mirror the stormy spirit of the crowd, engage in "crowd behavior," lose a measure of impulse control, lose a sense of individual responsibility, and are, therefore, less capable of experiencing such emotions as guilt and shame.

These neuroscientific findings may seem counterintuitive, possibly because "Western culture," as Marco Iacoboni said, "has made us blind to the intersubjective nature of our brains" such that we generally prefer to think that our brains, just as our selves, are somehow self-created. But the human brain—although it receives internal, personal input—is profoundly affected by external conditions as well as by other people. Your brain is othered, and thus you are othered. In the next couple of chapters, we will expand this idea and see the extent to which the social world can also alter such things as perception: for example, how you see color and form, how you hear sounds, and how you experience sensations, even pain, disgust, or embarrassment. We will see the extent to which the social world can indeed affect the very way in which you experience your body. Society, we will also discuss, is strongly tied to your mind but also to your body, and history is present in both.

CHAPTER X

Society and the Human Body

WESTERN CULTURE, WE saw, has encouraged the idea that the human mind is an individual construct, while also discouraging the idea that the mind, and indeed the brain itself, is necessarily *inter*personal, always embedded in social processes that are indispensable for its development. Let us now add that Western culture has also made us blind to the intersubjective nature of our bodies, to the ways in which our world affects the very ways in which we experience our bodies. In this chapter, we will examine and correct this blind spot in Western culture. To do so, we will begin by examining two ideas that Westerners have historically assumed as a matter of course: the millennial notion that the body is distinct and separate from the mind and the likewise age-old notion that the experience of being in the body is exempt from the influences of culture.

Western Biases About Human Nature

One of the two main branches of the Western tradition began on the Ionian coast, in what is Turkey today, in the 6th century BC, launched by Greek poets and philosophers who lived on the eastern geographical fringes of the Greek world. (The second branch takes us back to the Hebrew tradition and its main treatise, the Bible.) Early on, the Greeks posited the idea that human nature involves a body and a soul, two distinct and separate entities that comprise what we are.[1] Recall that Plato was the first to produce a fully fledged "dualistic" theory about human nature—"dualistic" in that it postulated, as noted in Chapter 3, that human nature encompasses two separate and distinct entities, *the body and the soul*, the material versus the spiritual portions of the human experience. This idea, we also saw, eventually spread not only throughout the Greek world but also throughout the West, particularly as it influenced the ever-expanding Christian tradition; a tradition that, via Augustine's theology, which was influenced by Plato, taught that the body is separate from the soul, much as the earth is separated from heaven. So if we fast-forward to our own era, modernity, our period indeed

---

1   It was arguably an Ionian poet-philosopher named Xenophanes (570–475 BC) who first set in motion this idea as he began to think about the differences between mortals and immortals (the gods) and how our nature is marked by the finitude of our bodies.

emerged simply assuming this age-old Platonic and Christian doctrine. Arguably, the person who launched this period, modernity, was René Descartes, perhaps the most influential 17th-century philosopher and a champion of modern Platonism. Among other things, Descartes convinced us, moderns, that while the human body is like a machine, the soul is like a "ghost in the machine." Indeed, for him, the body is like a "corpse" that is driven by this ghost, precisely, the soul (1988). Descartes decisively influenced not only academia (theology and philosophy, in particular) but also Western culture, our collective imagination, and indeed how we think and see ourselves. Perhaps you assume, after a Cartesian-platonic fashion, a separation between body and mind, body and soul, or body and spirit.

Hence, since ancient times, Westerners have typically learned and assumed that the ideas in their heads (in their minds, in their souls) develop independently of what their bodies experience, precisely because the mind is supposedly separated from, and independent of, the body. We have historically assumed, to be sure, that our capacity to reason, which distinguishes human beings from all other animals, is entirely unrelated to the body and to things such as movement and perception. But these age-old assumptions—although entrenched in our culture, in our traditions, in our philosophy, in our theology, in our oldest belief systems, and, perhaps, in our own minds—are wrong. And, in fact, they have distorted our conception of human nature, and have to be discarded in favor of new ideas that provide a better view into the human experience.

The Mind Is Rooted in the Body

Many research studies have shown that your mind cannot possibly develop without the input of your body (e.g., Damasio, 2005 and 2006). Recall that the crawling baby who first touches a table and bumps her head on it is already fashioning concepts such as solidity and hardness—concepts that must be initially understood *by her body* before being eventually consigned to her mind. Scholars George Lakoff and Mark Johnson (1999) have shown (1999) that a constellation of other mental categories (e.g., "support," "balance," "contact," "pushing," "pulling," "propelling," "motion," "nearness," "distance," "dynamism," "stasis") must also be understood initially by the body before being eventually consigned to the mind as concepts. Imagine that a baby grows up and as an adult thinks, say, that "math is *hard*," or that "dictatorships aim to have a *grip* on citizens," or that "Americans are *warm*," or that "such and such movie *stinks*," or that "so and so is *weighed down* by responsibilities," etc. Abstract ideas such as these, of course, stem initially from sensorimotor input ("hard," "grip," "warm," etc.). They originate in bodily experiences that, as also noted in the foregoing, provide organic prototypes for these metaphors that help us make sense of the world.

Even the most basic and elemental mental categories, such as "causality," for example, begin when the baby uses her fingers, limbs, and muscles to cause events to occur. When she bumps her head against the table, she not only begins to grasp "hardness" but also causality, the cause of pain. The idea of *causality* also begins when she eats or drinks and causes satiation, or when she is cuddled by a loving parent and thus experiences a sense of well-being, trust, comfort, etc. Other basic mental categories, such as "space" likewise begin with motor mechanisms and in this sense with the body itself. Crawling, again, helps the baby experience distance and thus helps her understand space (in fact, spatial intelligence develops with bodily input). Indeed, we can also think of moral categories, such as good and evil. They did not fall out of the blue, or appear with time itself, ready-made. They stem, ancestrally and originally, from our physical capacity to experience pain and pleasure: "[W]ere it not for the possibility of sensing body states that are inherently ordained to be painful or pleasurable there would be no suffering or bliss, no longing or mercy, no tragedy or glory in the human condition," as noted by Antonio Damasio, one of the foremost neuroscientists today (2005). As I have argued elsewhere,

> in a child, notions of good and evil (as well as the feelings of love and hate) are first understood bodily and pre-reflectively, particularly in terms of pleasure and unpleasure. "Good" begins to emerge as the baby's needs (e.g., hunger) meet positive environmental responses (e.g., the mother breastfeeds him); and in this initial sense, "good" means "good for survival." It is a (pre-social, pre-reflective) verdict of the species. Similarly, "evil" is originally nursed by negative environmental reinforcement [e.g., the baby is hungry, and her hunger is not readily appeased]. Good and evil, that is to say, begin to emerge through an initial economy of internal [bodily] claims and external responses. Of course, in the adult these normative parameters are not primarily physiological [or] bodily [...]. But such parameters, which largely organize consciousness [...], have to be understood initially by the body; and bodily claims have to provide organic prototypes for them. Good and evil, that is to say, are not substances in themselves, as the Manicheans believed. And the civilizing process neither creates them *ab ovo* [from thin air], nor extracts them from a Platonic heaven of moral principles to then install them into consciousness. Instead, these moral parameters begin with the amoral claims of biology in interaction with our culture, which assigns meanings and values to these bodily sensations or needs. (Narváez, 2012, p. 62)

Hence, the body is an essential supplier of raw ingredients for the mind. This includes cognitive and even moral categories and metaphors that structure not only how we think but also what we *can* possibly think. Descartes's error, which became a basic and central Western error that has endured until our own day and age, was to believe that mind and body are somehow causally independent of one another. (Even though he says that body and soul "commingle" with one another for us to have the illusion that both body and soul are part of us, part of "one.") And this error, as we will presently discuss, has had profound and long-lasting consequences for Western culture and perhaps even for your own understanding of human nature, your own nature included.

Evolution of Mental Categories

The body has provided these mind ingredients throughout the evolution of our species, and it is worth providing a brief evolutionary perspective to better see how much the human body has lent its nature to our mind.

Each object in the world cannot have a separate and distinct place and label in your mind because you would need a nearly infinite and thus ungraspable vocabulary to designate each separate thing. If you were to see, say, each single tree as a distinct and individual entity, you would need a word, a separate mental label for each tree. This is not possible, and therefore we have to lump all trees into one category and assign only one label to it, precisely: trees. Jorge Luis Borges, one of the greatest 20th-century writers, wrote a story about a man who couldn't forget: Ireneo Funes, "not only remembered each leaf of each tree on each hill, but also each one of the times that he had perceived it or imagined it." Whereas for us "a circle in a blackboard, and right triangle [...] are forms that we can fully intuit," Ireneo could fully and automatically intuit "the stormy mane of a colt [...], the changing fire, the endless ashes" (2012, translations are mine). But far from this being an advantage, it was a great misfortune for him. Ireneo was cursed by memory itself, condemned to live in a "vertiginous" world where no broad categories existed, deprived of the elemental ability to use conventional symbols to make the world mentally manageable and understandable. A working mind, in contrast, is unlike this vertiginous and anarchic stream of images, ideas, and sensations. It involves the ability to reduce the vastness of reality to a manageable number of discrete and commonly shared categories.

The lesson in Borges's story is that the ability to forget, to ignore, to erase, *and thus to reduce the reality to symbols* is what makes the world intelligible, what gives us meaning, and what gives us a (limited) human mind.

Indeed, all animal species have, *and have to have*, some capacity to categorize and to thus reduce reality. Even an amoeba must have categories, such as self and other; otherwise, it would end up eating its own body. Yet the categories that animals must have do not emerge randomly. Instead, they emerge to fulfill the needs of the specific species. For example, animals that are food for predators must reduce the animal kingdom to predators versus nonpredators; otherwise, they would not escape at the sight of a predator and would not survive. Similarly, a tiger, let us say, is also born with a specialized mode of categorizing. For over two million years (primitive tigers emerged during the Pleistocene), the minds of tigers evolved to fulfill the needs of their particular bodies, as a functional supplement of their bodies. Tigers have to see other animals as easy prey versus not, fast versus slow, aggressive versus not, edible versus not, etc.; otherwise, their chances of eating and surviving would be reduced. In this sense, their claws, jaws, teeth, frontal vision—shape their (predatory) minds, minds that evolved to cater to the needs of their bodily forms. *An animal's body, hence, helps shape the categories in the animal's mind.* The body of an animal lends its nature to what some ancient cultures called the "animal's spirit."

This is similar to humans: Our mental categories often stem from our own, human life-form and bespeak the needs of our own bodily characteristics. Of course, unlike other animals, we can deliberatively and consciously create mental categories that have nothing to do with evolution and nothing to do with our bodies. For instance, we might decide to categorize people according to their sense of fashion. But central mental categories—such as hardness, softness, edible, inedible, time, space, causality, and so on—bespeak the characteristics of our life-form and the capacities and limitations of our bodies. Antonio Damasio has noted,

> [T]he mind arises from activity in neural circuits, to be sure, but many of those circuits were shaped in evolution by functional requisites of the organism, and ... a normal mind will happen only if those circuits contain basic representations of the organism, and if they continue monitoring the states of the organism in action. In brief, neural circuits represent the organism continuously, as it is perturbed by stimuli from the physical and sociocultural environments, and as it acts on those environments. If the basic topic of those representations were not an organism anchored in the body, we might have some form of mind, but I doubt that it would be the mind we do have ... I am not saying that the mind is the body. I am saying that the body contributes more than life support and modulatory effects to the brain. It contributes a content that is part and parcel of the workings of the normal mind. (2005, p. 226)

The human body thus contributes to the brain itself, which can neither evolve nor develop as disembodied. It can do so only through brain-body interactions. Implied by Damasio's argument is the idea that by having a radically different body with a radically different sensorium, we would also have a radically different mind. Let's go back to Richard Dawkins. If we were the size of a neutrino, even elemental assumptions about the solidity of matter, as we saw, would not have arisen in our imagination at all. And, hence, such a fundamentally different body would be catered to by a fundamentally different mind. The body, in any case, is not merely a support system for an independent mind, for the Cartesian ghost that independently drives the body machine made up of flesh and bones. For all his wondrous accomplishments, Descartes was wrong to suggest that the "soul" (or mind) and the body have radically different natures. Instead, because the body has been the essential supplier of mind ingredients, *the human spirit is a sort of appendage of evolutionary biology*. Recall as well that human thought develops by means of sensorimotor input so that a healthy baby who cannot explore the world with her body—with her senses and through movement—will experience severe cognitive deficits, even if initially her brain is without defects. Without the normal input of the body, the mind of this child will not be normal. If we can imagine a child who grows up not being allowed to crawl, this child will not have a clear sense of elemental mental categories such as causality or even spatiality. As Lakoff and Johnson have noted,

> Reason is not disembodied, as the tradition has largely held, but arises from the nature of our brains, bodies, and bodily experience. This is not just the innocuous and obvious claim that we need a body to reason; rather, it is the striking claim that the very structure of reason itself comes from the details of our embodiment ... Thus, to understand reason we must understand the details of our visual system, our motor system, and the general mechanism of neural binding (1999, p. 4). The mind is inherently embodied. (1999, p. 4).

Another Important Western Bias

Lakoff and Johnson have also stated that the millennial idea about the mind–body separation is simply over, and we have to move on (1999, p. 3). Let us turn to a second and likewise millennial and important Western bias. Westerners not only tend to think that bodily experiences are unrelated to the mind but also that these experiences are unrelated to the world, to our time and place. This is also a mistake.

Consider a particularly illustrative example, the experience of pain, to initially see the extent to which the world, indeed our culture, lends its nature to bodily experiences. Typically, we, heirs of the Western tradition, think that pain is like a bodily gauge that indicates the level of tissue damage, machine-like, much like a thermostat indicates temperature. And we tend to think that every normal human body has the same normal pain thermostat so that all human beings would experience the same painful stimulus in the same manner, regardless of their ideas and regardless of the related cultural traditions, meanings, or values that influence these ideas. Furthermore, when we feel the sting of pain ourselves, we typically do not experience this sensation as a bodily *as well as a* mental event that, in its mental dimension, is affected by inherited ideas that we have internalized. Yet this view is erroneous as well. We do not experience pain like machines, in a Cartesian fashion. We experience pain, and in this sense our bodies, as encultured creatures, as bearers of mental contents that connect us to our world. Save very extreme physical suffering, which we will discuss soon, pain is *not* determined merely by physiology. It is inextricably invested by the ideas and beliefs of the sufferer, which can "subtly or massively recast our experience of pain" (Morris, 1993). Culture can, in fact, "dictate the level of pain perception" (Chang, 2009). Indeed, to understand "the unique pain we feel today," as historian David Morris has argued, we have to understand the culture that has marked these bodily experiences (1993, p. 5), the systems of cultural meaning through which physical suffering is expressed.

The Cultural Dimensions of Pain

Harvard researchers, Kurt Gray and Dan Wegner (2008), conducted the following experiment: They recruited two groups of students and administered mild electrical shocks to each participant. Subjects in Group 1 were told that the shocks were administered *intentionally* by someone off stage and Group 2 was told that the shocks were administered unintentionally. As these researchers predicted, participants in Group 1 experienced more pain than those in Group 2, as self-reported and as measured by biological markers, such as skin conductance (amount of sweat in the palms of the hands). These students' beliefs, the ideas in their heads, made the difference. "[T]he experience of pain," the researchers report, "*changes depending upon the psychological context in which people are harmed*" (Gray & Wegner, 2008, p. 1261, my emphasis). Relatedly, we can also consider the hundreds of studies pertaining to placebo and nocebo effects, an idea universally accepted in the medical field. A placebo is a make-believe medication that may, nevertheless, effectively remove pain, if—and only if—the sufferer truly believes in its effectiveness (which explains "miracles" involving pain alleviation or the removal of pain by incantations and magic). A nocebo, in contrast, is a make-believe medication that can increase pain, but only if the sufferer believes in its effectiveness as well (which may explain some magical curses: instilling pain by means of incantations). The lessons of these and similar studies are as follows:

   a. Experimentally, you can change the sensation of pain itself, depending on how you prime your subjects. You can divide them in two or more groups and prime them differently to create various mental conditions so that each group experiences the same noxious stimulus differently (although not radically differently).

   b. Pain is not just a standardized thermostat, a machine-like gauge. Again, it is a sensation invested by meanings and can therefore be subjective, to an extent. Pain is often like an opinion of the body and the mind combined.

   c. Because pain can vary depending on the meanings that mediate the sufferer's experience, it can be affected by cultural meanings. Cultural meanings can mediate painful experiences.

   d. Cultural meanings, at least in this sense, mediate the experience of the body in general.

Note that different cultures and different social groups may regard pain differently. Men and women are often socialized to regard pain differently. Culture often trains men to think of pain as a test of masculinity; women are not socialized to think of pain as a test of femininity. Some groups believe that pain can bring the sufferer closer to the divine, and others see it as bringing us closer to the netherworld, the natural habitat of wickedness. Some branches of the Christian tradition have exalted the experience of pain; they have lavished pain with salvific, atoning, and redemptive properties.[2] Other groups have seen pain as a source of wisdom, even as *the* source of human wisdom. The Norse, for instance, thought that pain was not only a source of insight but also a window into the human condition. Yet other groups think of pain as something that, above all, must be avoided. In the United States today, we typically see pain as something merely pathological and our only approach is to prevent it and to remove it. The idea that pain may be, instead, mined for insight will seem preposterous to most Americans (who, in this

---

2   Some Christian groups have regarded pain as a gift, "the "gift of tears," the "gift of a laceration," which "tenderly wounded" Saint John of the Cross. "None of my sufferings," Saint Margaret-Mary Alacoque said, "has been equal to that of not having suffered enough" (Cioran, 2004).

sense, suffer twice: the physical sensation itself compounded by the psychological discomfort, the stress, the anxiety, the sense of wrongness, that are often added to the sensation.)

What follows from the lessons listed earlier is that people whose beliefs fall into each of these different parameters *are likely to experience physical suffering differently*, which is further suggested by experimental and anthropological research. Of course, there is *no* direct correspondence between the ideas in the head of the sufferer and his or her perceived level of pain. But *some* degree of correspondence is expected. Madelon Peters, an expert on pain management, reported, "Processes at an organic (spinal sensitization, cortical reorganization), individual psychological (pain cognition and beliefs, hypervigilance), and social level (learned behavior) may contribute to pain perception and pain behavior and ultimately to maintenance of pain" (in Lautenbacher & Fillingim, 2004, p. 71; see also Melzack & Casey, 1968). Indeed, Patrick Wall has said that cultural factors not only contribute to the experience of pain but also exert a stronger influence than genetic factors (2002). Wall and his colleague, Ronald Melzack, have also provided examples that starkly illustrate how pain can be perceived very differently in different cultures and with very different outcomes:

> One of the most striking examples of the impact of cultural values on pain is the hook swinging ritual in practice in part of India [Kosambi, 1967]. The ceremony derives from an ancient practice in which a member of a social group is chosen to represent the power of the gods. The role of the chosen man (or "celebrant") is to bless ... children and crops ... What is remarkable about the ritual is that the steel hooks ... are shoved under his skin and muscles on both sides of the back. ... [A]t the climax of the ceremony ... he swings free, hanging only from those hooks embedded in his back, to bless the children and crops. Astonishingly, there is no evidence that the man is in pain during the ritual; rather, he appears to be in a "state of exaltation." (Melzack and Wall 1996, pp. 16–17)

The authors add that,

> There are many examples of comparable procedures in other cultures. In East Africa, men and women undergo an operation entirely without anesthetics or pain reliving drugs—called "trepanation," in which the scalp and underlying muscles are cut in order to expose a large area of the skull. The skull is then scraped by the doktari as the man or woman sits calmly, without flinching or grimacing, holding a pan under their chin to catch the dripping blood. Films of this procedure are extraordinary to watch because of the discomfort they induce in the observers, which is in striking contrast to the apparent lack of discomfort in the people undergoing the operation. There is no reason to believe that these people are physiologically different in any way. Rather, the operation is accepted by their culture as a procedure that brings relief of chronic pain. (Melzack and Wall 1996, p. 17)

Naturally, past a certain level of tissue damage, pain may acquire an animalistic and universal quality. Extreme pain overrides cultural meanings and thus becomes a fundamentally physiological event. Groans of very intense pain speak the universal language of agony and are released independently of the will of the sufferer, as though uttered by someone else who, taking possession of one's body, voices this animalistic form of communication. But beyond these extreme experiences, the idea that pain is *strictly a bodily experience* that has nothing to do with either the mind or with culture is a residue of old Western biases—biases that, as noted, have encouraged the idea that the body is separated from the mind and from the cultural meanings hosted by the mind.

Embodied Collective Memory

Not only pain but the entire constellation of bodily experiences—seeing, hearing, tasting, smelling, bodily rhythms, gestures, parameters of disgust and repulsion, standards of hygiene, etc.—are also affected by culture. Consider perception—hearing in particular. Of course, the human ear is the same across cultures and, in this sense, hearing is a universal experience that is unrelated to the culture of the percipient. On the other hand, some sounds can change people's affects and neurochemistry, also regardless of the person's culture (Goodman, 2010).[3] Yet hearing also involves learned and culturally relevant dimensions. Alfred Tomatis, an ear, nose, and throat physician from France, has shown that ears often become attuned to culturally significant sound frequencies, particularly those related to the percipients' native language. The German ear, Tomatis shows, more easily recognizes frequencies between 100 and 3,000 Hz; the French ear more easily recognizes sounds between 1,000 and 2,000; the English between 2,000 and 12,000, and so on (1991).

Of course, percipients from each of these countries are *not* deaf to frequencies outside these ranges. They are simply more conscious of familiar sound nuances that, as speakers of a certain language, they have been hearing from the time they were in the womb (from the 16th week on)—a process that trains their brains to detect and to exaggerate these sound nuances. (And let us clarify that we ultimately hear with the brain. A person may hear voices that are not there, for example, which does not mean that this person *imagines* these voices but that he or she actually hears them, just as you hear the voice of your friends.) People, therefore, unconsciously emphasize sounds related to their language, while also *tuning out* other, foreign sounds. For this reason, if you learn a second language as an adult, it will be initially difficult to actually hear the sonic shades of foreign words, and hence it will also be difficult to reproduce them, to pronounce these words how native speakers pronounce them, and you will have a foreign accent, partly rooted in an inability to *hear* like natives (Tomatis, 1991). We can also consider tonal languages. In China and Vietnam, there is a higher proportion of people with either perfect pitch or the ability to identify musical notes correctly, if compared, for example, with Americans. Why? Mandarin and Vietnamese are tonal languages; the meaning of words in these languages can vary depending precisely on the intonation of words. And hence speakers grow up with an ear keenly attuned to tone and are more likely to develop a sound-processing system in their brains that highlights and exaggerates tonality, which explains their generally higher abilities in this area of perception.

For these reasons, there is a sense in which ears are "ethnic ears," Tomatis says. Ears typically become "conscious" of, attuned to, culturally relevant sounds. And hearing is thus not exclusively a biological phenomenon, limited to detecting vibrations through the acoustic systems of the ear and the brain; hearing, like pain, is also attached to meanings and invested by them.

Save the voice of their mothers, which they hear in the womb, newborns hear *just sounds*—sounds entirely devoid of any meaning. Unlike you, they cannot hear the "creaking door," "the airplane," "the

---

3   Joachim Ernst-Berendt, an expert on sound and its effects on human beings, explains that loud noises were our original alarms (from *all'arme*, a call to arms, in Italian). Loud noises have been important for survival, and our bodies have, therefore, evolved to respond to them more or less automatically. Hence, "As soon as the volume exceeds 80db, blood pressure rises," Ernst-Berendt explained. "The stomach and intestine operate more slowly, the pupils become larger, and the skin gets paler—no matter it the noise is found pleasant, or disruptive, or is not even consciously perceived [...] Unconsciously, we always react to noise like Stone Age beings. At that time a loud noise almost always signified danger" (in Goodman, 2010, p. 65). Note, indeed, that sounds have been used as weapons of war [Goodman, 2010, p. 65], precisely because they can induce these sorts of physiological responses; for example, they were used to torture prisoners at Abu Ghraib.

rustling of leaves," for example, and they hear, instead, a stream of acoustic events that have not yet been touched by their culture. You, on the other hand, *cannot help but* hear "the airplane," "the rustling of leaves," etc. You cannot help but hear sounds inherently invested by meanings, meanings typically connected to your culture. Adults, in other words, typically hear sounds that are mediated by culture, and culture is thus present in our hearing as well. Walter Benjamin, an important social critic, has said, "During long periods of history, the mode of human sense perception *changes with humanity's entire mode of existence*. The manner in which human sense perception is organized, the medium in which it is accomplished is determined not only by nature but by historical circumstances as well" (Benjamin, 1968, p. 222, my emphasis). Researchers Marshall Segall, Donald Campbell, and Melville Herskovits have reported, "To a substantial extent we learn to perceive." (1966). To be sure, hearing is sometimes a form of culturally based interpreting and indeed a form of creating so that "some sounds may seem 'elegiac,' 'sad,' 'prurient' to some percipients and not to others, particularly when they have different ethnic ears" (Narváez, 2012).

The Sociology of Perception

Like our ears, our eyes also seem to provide a direct representation of the world, a depiction that is entirely unaffected by our culture. Yet just as it affects hearing, culture also affects vision. Just as an infant may hear pure sounds entirely devoid of meanings, he may also see pure visual elements devoid of meaning. But for you it is often difficult to separate meaning from vision, mind from eye, and to see a mere throng of images and colors detached from a mental subtext. Instead, you generally project meaning onto the thing perceived, automatically and mostly unconsciously. Just as you don't hear pure noise but, say, "a car," you don't see a stream of visual sensations but also "a car," "fall colors," etc., and even such things as a "feminine" shade of pink or the "masculinity" of blue. Your optical input typically co-arises with mental input. Seeing involves *optics*—the retinal, physiological event—as well as *vision*, the manner in which the physiological event becomes invested with meanings. And vision, as it is connected to meanings, is also connected to culture, to changing and fluid historical and even socioeconomic factors.

Consider, for example, the paintings of 17th-century Flemish painter Peter Paul Rubens, one of the great masters who, in the popular imagination, painted plump nudes and seminudes. Today, we generally do not see these "Rubenesque" models as icons of beauty, the way the painter and the average 17th-century man saw them. Why? Because standards of beauty have changed such that it is generally difficult for contemporary persons to see beauty in those ample female bodies. But if we were to climb into the brain of the average 17th-century person and see these nudes through his eyes, we would be more likely to see these ample feminine bodies as icons of beauty. This is so, in part, because these bodies belonged to the leisure classes; they did not signal hard labor; they were not the bodies of peasants; they were seen, to use contemporary vernacular, as "classy." Of course, there are always exceptions to the manner in which people perceive beauty, but the fact that 17th-century eyes were more likely to see these figures as beautiful is demonstrated by the vast success and popularity of Rubens's and similar paintings. In contrast, we see these images with 21st-century eyes. John Berger, one of the most important British cultural theorists, notes that we see paintings from another era "as nobody saw them before" (1990). Indeed, the perception of beauty may vary not only over a period of time but even with social class as well. French sociologist Pierre Bourdieu has shown that members of the upper classes in France, for example, are a little more likely to see the picture of a sunset as uninteresting or even as ugly than members of the middle classes, who are more likely to see it as beautiful (Bourdieu, 1987).

These examples show that, in general, eyes see through the filter of the culture where the percipient has been reared.

But beyond the perception of beauty, vision, broadly speaking, partly depends on social narratives and conventions, and it can therefore change with time and place. Asians reared in collectivistic cultures, for example, often gather more contextual visual cues than Westerners, who focus on visual cues pertaining to individualized, central figures. People steeped in philosophical traditions that deemphasize the value of individuality (e.g., Asians) tend to visually deemphasize central, individualized figures and thus miss visual cues related to them (Nisbett & Masuda, 2003). In contrast, Westerners reared in cultures that emphasize individuality tend to collect more visual cues pertaining to central figures. Or consider perception of form: Westerners, who also grow up surrounded by geometrical, architectural patterns, learn to perceive aspects of form differently than people who grow up surrounded by the more anarchical geometry of the forest. Here is the eponymously named *Müller-Lyer optical illusion; try to compare the length of these two lines:*

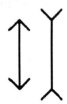

Although these lines are identical in length, people typically see them as a having different extensions—a fact that, Franz Müller-Lyer thought, illustrated the transcultural, universal nature of perception. Yet, as we know today, members of some cultures—those unaccustomed to the geometrical and architectural patterns that Westerners see every day of their lives—do not fall for this optical trick. They simply *do not see this aspect of form like we do* (in Alter, 2013). Or consider the perception of color: Members of some cultures can identify some color nuances more readily than others (Berlin & Kay, 1969). And it is not that some cultures are color-blind if compared to others, of course, but human eyes, to borrow the image from Tomatis again, may well be more "conscious of" some color nuances and thus more easily recognize some colors than others, often depending on whether their language has a word for a particular hue. Bear in mind that hues in nature are on a spectrum, rather than given as discrete categories, and that because a spectrum has no discrete demarcations, and hues gradually change and fade into other hues, there is an infinite variety of colors. (The rainbow does not have seven colors, as we generally assume. This is only one way of lumping this spectrum into discrete categories.) Different cultures may categorize or label these hues differently, and the language of color may thus vary from culture to culture as well as over time. Because labels related to colors help us to be more conscious of certain colors, the way we perceive color may therefore change across languages, cultures, as well as from one historical period to the next.

Consider some examples: The Dani of Papua New Guinea, for example, have only two words for color, "*mola*" and "*mili*," usually translated as "cool" and "warm." For the ancient Romans, the color *caeruleus,* often translated as "blue," actually encompassed shades of yellow, green, indigo, and violet. The color vocabulary of ancient Greeks was also very different if compared to ours (we still don't know why the *Iliad* and the *Odyssey* described the color of the Aegean Sea as "wine-dark," for example). In Greek, "colour terms denoted more than simply (in our terms) 'colour'"; they also denoted "luminosity, saturation, texture, smell and even things that had nothing to do with colour such as 'agitation' and 'liquidity'" (Bradley, 2009). In Greek, a table would not be "brown" but "cedar," or "pine," or any other such wood hue, *and* these words could denote properties such as texture and smell, which for the Greeks were intrinsic to the hue in question. For them, indeed, color encompassed not only different categories but also different phenomena—phenomena that are so different as to be hard for us to bring to mind.

Many more such examples could be provided. The point, in summary, is that the language of color and, therefore, the perception of color can vary. And, hence, language and culture are present in the way we see the various hues and in the way we see in general.

Technology Also Affects How and What We Perceive

In comparison to previous historical periods, today we are exposed to a bigger, more constant, and louder stream of sounds, and for the first time in history, noise pollution has become a public health concern (World Health Organization, 2009). (Noise pollution has, in fact, changed patterns in nature. European robins, for example, are vocalizing at night, as the daytime sound blocks their ability to communicate [Fuller, Warren, & Gaston, 2007].) But on the other hand, we hear much more music than persons of any other epoch. Before we began to record music (Edison patented the phonograph in 1878), the average person listened to music on such occasions as carnivals, masses—and social rituals, in general. And today, the average American adolescent listens to 2.31 hours of music per day without counting fragments from media such as YouTube, which adolescents use for about 7.38 hours a day (Rideout et al., 2010). The world is different, and the world of sound is different as well. And if we follow the logic of Tomatis's research, we should expect that aspects of hearing could have also changed to reflect these technological changes so that if Tomatis speaks of "ethnic ears," we may also speak of "historical ears" that are more conscious of their own soundscape—ears that, in our case, have modern aural habits, rather than, say, medieval or Roman ones.

Similarly, technologies of visual representation affect vision. You are not surprised or confused when you see an image that has been foreshortened, for example. But about 2,500 years ago, when the foreshortening technique was first invented in ancient Greece, people were amazed. For thousands of years, human beings had not seen tridimensionality on bidimensional surfaces and were stupefied and probably confused when they did. This was a visual revolution, as art historian Ernest Gombrich has noted (2002).[4] Similarly, *all technologies of visual representation* have influenced vision so that the history of these technologies bespeaks, indeed, a history of vison (although not of optics, recall the difference between optics and vision). The brothers Auguste and Louis Lumiere invented the filming camera in France at the end of the 19th century, and when in 1895, they first showed a "moving picture" of a train advancing toward the camera, the stunned audience reportedly felt "fear, terror, even panic," as the German magazine *Der Spiegel* reported. Optically, your eye conveys the same information as that conveyed by the eyes of this audience. But visually, your eye tells you a different story such that you are not frightened or confused when you see a "living photograph" of a train moving toward you. Susan Sontag, an American cultural critic, has said,

> Through photographs, the world becomes a series of unrelated, free-standing particles; and history, past and present, a set of anecdotes and *faits divers* [diverse, brief, and rather disconnected facts]. The camera makes reality atomic, manageable and opaque. It is a view of the world which denies interconnectedness, continuity, but which confers on each moment the character of a mystery.

(Sontag, 2001)

---

4   The discovery of this technique, "the greatest discovery of all [was] a tremendous moment in the history of art when ... artists dared for the first time in all history to paint a foot as seen from in front" (Gombrich 2002, 81).

French photographer Henri Cartier-Bresson has similarly argued that the prephotographic reality was typically experienced as continuous flux, movement, growth, and decay, and that this mode of perception changed with the invention of photography. The camera's ability to freeze the flux of events in the world—its ability to reveal instants, moments, "stills" formerly not available to the prephotographic eye—helped us see entirely new aspects of the world. It educated our eyes in radically different ways:

> Because photography plunges its flashing hand into the flux of time to dig something discrete out, our mode of relating to the world has been altered. Our relationship with processes was altered. Altered was in fact our relationship to time itself. Today we can preserve moments in time; we can save the past, shot by shot, as a series of "stills." These stills invoke absences, perhaps familial absences filled with a sense of domestic or melancholic sweetness, which, though ordinary for us, become precisely "moments," fixed aspects of our past, parts of who we are. By contrast, such mode of self-perception hardly existed in the days when the past was linked primarily to storytelling. Such "moments," such ocular proofs of our past, hardly existed when our personal histories were verbal and not visual. (Narváez, 2012, p. 167)

Let us also consider "the age of mechanical reproduction," when for the first time in human history images are massively reproduced. In previous epochs, when human-made images were rare, images were invested with a strong sense of singularity, with an identity of their own so that beholding a painting, for example, was a different event. Such images often had central religious and ritualistic functions; they often exacted deference and wonder—qualities that become diluted in our age, when formerly iconic images, housed in sacred spaces such as churches or palaces, may easily become mass-distributed posters or refrigerator magnets, for instance. The way we see images has been thus altered, as these perceptual events are no longer accompanied by the affects and meanings that formerly characterized them. In "the age of mechanical reproduction," images have thus lost their "aura," as Walter Benjamin has argued (1968).

Consider, lastly, olfactory perception. As discussed, Katherine Ashenburg argued that in our day and age, it is normative to smell "like a cookie," or a fruit, or a flower when in public, a modern development that derives neither from nature nor strictly from medical theory pertaining to hygiene, but also from *olfactory habits* encouraged by an enormous deodorizing and odorizing industry (Narváez, 2012, p. 27). The sense of repugnance often associated with bodily smells today may be experienced as an automatic verdict of nature, but, although natural to an extent, it also involves a certain cultural narrative, habits of thought that over time become attached to the perceptual experience. "Much as the ear, the nose is also 'adaptable and teachable,'" Ashenburg has noted (Narváez, 2012, p. 27). And, hence, as noted in Chapter 7, other cultures with other traditions developed very different and also very "normal" and "natural" meanings related to human scents. For example, some Andean and Amazonian cultures ascribed to, and still ascribe to, benefic and magical powers to such things as flatulence and excreta (Narváez, 2003).

The Sociology of the Body

Beyond the senses, the entire constellation of embodied experiences reflects, in different ways and degrees, culturally relevant meanings, aspects of history, the technologies that irrupt to change social life. "[M]odes of weeping, humor and laughter, modes of experiencing pleasure [...], desires and libidinal investments, taste, the taste of the gullet and of the mind, our motivic structures, our visions of self and other, the way we see our own bodies [...] are all tied to the world" (Narváez, 2012, p. 27; see also Narváez, 2006).

The brain itself, we saw, is constructed so that aspects of brain function—memory (Loftus, 1997), intelligence (Flynn, 2012), executive function (Kishiyama, Boyce, Jimenez, Perry, & Knight, 2009), and spatiotemporal ability (Fausto-Sterling, 1992)—are affected by environmental input. Even the most trivial aspects of embodiment can also be affected by the social world (Narváez, 2012, p. 27). Hair, for example, often expresses social narratives, conventions, and structures. It often signals masculinity or femininity, conservative or nonconservative politics, class position, religious affiliation, etc. Culture, politics, and history can be found, in this sense, in people's hair. Indeed, because hair carries a good deal of social signification, hairstyles have been legislated by many states and religions. When the Manchu conquered China in the 17th-century, for example, the conquerors ordered Chinese men to shave their heads and grow a long braid characteristic of Manchu warriors, and the penalty for those who refused was death. Peter the Great, in Russia, passed laws to regulate the use of beards and taxed them in an effort to modernize his country. The Old Testament admonishes, "Ye shall not round the corners of thy heads neither shalt thou mar the corners of thy beard" (Leviticus 19:27).

Animal Nature Versus Human Nature

Let us recapitulate. At birth, nature gives us a body but not a predetermined and universally valid set of future bodily experiences. Much as the human mind, the human body is also learned, othered, and, indeed, achieved to an extent. Of course, all bodily experiences have biological roots and, in this sense, are experienced in a similar manner across all cultures and historical periods. But aspects of the bodily experience are also learned in cultural contexts. Contexts that, inasmuch as they mold mind and body, also mold human nature itself. The fundamental difference between animals and human beings is that whereas animals adapt to environmental determinants generally beyond their control, human beings create environments that, in turn, create key aspects of what we become. Consider the following example, provided by John Berger, pertaining to peasants,

> Because of the very varied hard physical work they do [they have a certain physique and a certain] physical rhythm ... directly related to the energy demanded by the amount of work which has to be done in a day [which] is reflected in typical physical movements and stance. It is an extended sweeping rhythm. Not necessarily slow. The traditional acts of scything or sawing may exemplify it [...] In addition, peasants possess a special physical dignity: this is determined by a kind of functionalism, a way of being fully *at home in effort*. (1980, p. 37, original emphasis)

Physical and cultural environments created by peasants typically shape the manner in which peasants use, experience, and display their bodies. But peasants are not unique in this regard. All persons from all cultures encounter physical spaces and cultural meanings and traditions that contribute to the progressive acquisition of bodily habits and related bodily automatisms. The given environment encourages a "second nature" in each of us, a way of experiencing and expressing the body that, although invested by culture, seems entirely natural. And, indeed, sometimes the process whereby people acquire a bodily memory is so sweeping and formative, as Berger's example suggests, that observers may see the resulting habits and bodily automatisms, not as a record of circumstances but as the person's fundamental, God-given nature. Such observers confuse "second nature" with nature itself and may assume, for example, that the peasants described by Berger are simply born to be at home in coarse effort. These observers may assume that the nature of these peasants is simply different than their own. And, indeed, peasants have been seen historically through this kind of an *essentialist* lens, a lens that reveals the supposed "essence" of people, their supposed truest nature. Medieval lords, for instance, often saw peasants as possessors of an animalistic nature, as beings that were essentially different from members of the dominant classes. And indeed, up to the 19th century, peasants were often seen as the incarnation of original sin: "The peasant is just that, sin, original sin, still persistent and visible in all its naïve brutality," a French priest noted; a view that, as historian Eugen Weber has argued, reflects a "consensus [in France] that runs through the first three quarters of the [19th] century" (Weber, 1976).

The broader point here is that, throughout history, human beings have often seen members of other cultures, ethnic groups, and socioeconomic classes as possessors of a different nature. Historically, we have been *unable* to see that culture affects the seeming "nature" of its members, that culture can shape not only the collective memory of a group but also their *embodied collective memory*. And in this sense, we have historically confused the culture of people with their nature, an age-old confusion that has had profound consequences: racism, colonialism, and attendant violence, physical, psychological, economic, environmental have been to an extent caused by these kinds of errors.

Summary and Conclusion

Culture and social circumstances, affecting bodily experiences such as perception, can affect how people experience such things as beauty, ugliness, repugnance, or pain. Society can affect how we experience the body. And, particularly as it affects perception, society can thus affect how we perceive and experience reality itself. Importantly, these social circumstances, which affect mental and bodily experiences, do not always emerge spontaneously in history. Although such pressures are typically systemic—not controlled by anyone in particular—they can also fall under the control of institutions, such as those of the market, of religion, and of the state. Think of fundamentalist societies, for example. Here you have an institutional system whose aim is, first, to penetrate the consciousness of citizens (with dogmatic ideas and values) but also, second, to encourage certain types of embodied memories that bring these meaning and values to life. These societies demand that women, for instance, not only internalize traditional ideas and values *but also that women embody the tradition*. So the clothing standards of these women, their hairstyles, bodily rhythms, gestures, speech patterns, management of emotions and desires often reflect the inherited ideas and values of (supposed) femininity. And, hence, these bodies enact and bring to life the given culture, the given tradition, and the given dogmas of the past. This is an example of an embodied collective memory that develops largely as a result of a concerted institutional effort, an effort that is in turn guided by traditions, by ideology, and by the guardians of this ideology. Ideology, in this sense, can be translated into "nature" through a process of naturalization.

Let us finally clarify that all societies, traditionalist or not, democratic or dictatorial, modern or not, rich or poor, tend to employ the mind as well as the body to replicate customary values, meanings, traditions—to thus foster social cohesion and social control.[5] In all societies, these processes

---

5   Yet the body is also a channel for social change: If the bodies of women in fundamentalist societies, for example, no longer reflect the traditional values, those values begin to lose the organic grip that they formerly had in everyday life, and these societies would, therefore, be more likely to shed these traditional values. They would be more likely to give way to new lifestyles, to new traditions, and to new aspects of social life.

can fall under the purview of institutions that, while contributing to the creation of the dominant embodied collective memory, contribute to the creation of the "nature" of the group in question. Understanding these ideas today is critical, perhaps more important than ever before. In our era, human nature, mind and body, is influenced by the dominant economic system, post-industrial capitalism, which, much as the traditionalist cultures mentioned earlier, is very good at creating embodied collective memories. We do not know how this process will unfold in the future, or what advantages or disadvantages it may produce, but it is worth wondering whether this system, which is expanding globally, will be able to regulate post-industrial bodies to meet its own systemic needs. What would be the consequences of this?

CHAPTER XI

The Emergence of Race

I N THIS AND the subsequent chapter, we move on to a different and important topic area, race (a topic that is, nevertheless, connected to the previous discussion pertaining to the sociology of the body, as we will soon see). Let us right away note that it is not possible to understand the concept of race without a minimum necessary evolutionary and genetic perspective. For, after all, this concept—namely, the idea that there are human subspecies or races—already assumes that subspecies or races did evolve, carving overlapping but ultimately separate genetic niches, precisely: "races." Let us, therefore, begin this discussion by providing the minimum necessary background knowledge pertaining to both, evolution and genetics.

Evolution by Natural Selection

In many areas in West Central Texas, cats are generally not spayed or neutered, and it is easy to find hordes of feral and semiferal cats roaming the streets. Let us imagine that these cats are pushed out of the cities and into a prairie. This would not be good news for the squirrels in this prairie, because they will have a new predator, a new "environmental pressure," in the biological lingo. Naturally, these cats will start eating those squirrels that are easier to catch, the slower ones (assuming that these predators are hunting by speed, not by ambush). And these slower rodents will be the ones with certain characteristics that make them slower; perhaps, they will have shorter legs, let us say, or will be tubbier and heavier. For squirrels, of course, vary from individual to individual. Just like us, some of them are heavier, or bonier, or slower, or faster than others. And, again, the cats will begin killing, and continue to systematically kill, those squirrels whose physical characteristics make them easier prey. If this process continues, after a couple of decades, the squirrels in this prairie will look a little different than their cousins in nearby areas. After all, squirrels with certain physical traits are being systematically eliminated, and these kinds of animals are less likely to pass on their particular physical traits to the subsequent generations. The squirrels that, after a couple of decades, you would be able to see in this prairie will look, perhaps, leaner and meaner and faster. But although they would be a little different than their cousins in other nearby areas, at this point, these animals would still be, as you would expect, squirrels.

Yet if this process continues—not for another couple of decades but for, say, a couple of million years—then these rodents would change in a far more noticeable way. They would likely change to the point that, although still looking somewhat like their cousins in nearby territories, they would be different enough to be categorized as a different species of squirrel. In biological terms, this hypothetical scenario would result in these rodents' "speciation" from a parent species, from the original, and by this time ancestral, species of prairie squirrel. And what about the cats? Assuming that their main source of food is squirrels, they would also be changing and evolving along with these rodents. As these rodents evolve into a leaner and meaner and faster subspecies, the cats that are slower, say, tubbier and short legged, would have a harder time catching the faster squirrels. And, hence, these types of cats would have a harder time eating and surviving, and would be systematically eliminated as well. And they would be less likely to pass on their "slower" and tubbier traits to their offspring. In such a long period of time, two million years, we would see a different subspecies of cat emerging in the prairie, most likely one that looks bigger and faster, like a lynx or a bobcat, for example. These cats would have thus "coevolved" with the squirrels whose own process of evolution would have created an environmental pressure for the cats themselves. This is more or less what happened, to provide an example from real life, with cheetahs and African wildebeests. The bodies of these species coevolved, creating especially fast subspecies of cats (cheetahs) and also very fast antelopes (wildebeests).

This easy to understand scenario pertaining to cats and squirrels summarizes one of the three main concepts that underpin the theory of evolution, one of the most important scientific theories of the modern era. This is the concept of "evolution by natural selection," famously propounded by rockstar naturalist, Charles Darwin. Evolution by natural selection means that the environment itself, so to speak, "chooses" this or that trait from the various species in it. In our example, it is as though—one hunting event at a time, one generation at a time—the prairie itself chose certain lean, mean, and fast traits in both squirrels and cats. It is as though this environment thus shaped these species, little by little, to the point of transforming them into ultimately separate subspecies, with their own genetic niche (a niche that would, of course, overlap with that of the parent species to the extent to which the speciated rodents retain some of the ancestral traits).

Mutation and Evolution by Artificial Selection

The environment is not the only vector, or force, or mechanism that can shape a species to the point of speciation. Another mechanism is "evolution by artificial selection"—namely, farming, breeding, gardening. All these activities involve someone, a farmer, a breeder, a gardener, who (artificially) chooses certain traits from animals or plants. Traits that, as constantly favored by these persons, will pass on to the next generations. A breeder of dogs, for example, may like fluffy and long ears, as well as very short legs in his or her animals. Nature itself would *not* choose these traits, in all likelihood, as they would make it harder for the animal to run, and thus to hunt, and thus to eat, and thus to pass on these cute but cumbersome traits to subsequent generation. But if the breeder in our example does like and does breed these kinds of traits, and if this kind of selection continues for a long enough time, this process will eventually result in dogs with these characteristics. This sort of artificial selection of traits, in plants and animals, may also lead to speciation, the eventual crossing of plant and animal species into a different, so to speak, genetic "splinter group."

Here is a third possible mechanism of speciation: genetic mutation. The word mutation doesn't have the best connotation in our culture, and it is often used to denote monstrosity. But mutation—that is to say, errors in the transmission of the genetic code of one animal to its offspring—could result in desirable traits, even in traits that we, human beings, may see as beautiful. Blue eyes, for example, are the result of mutation in a gene, known as OCA2, which is in part responsible for eye pigmentation. Once upon a time, no human beings had blue eyes, until this mutation occurred. Once upon a time, there were no white bears either (polar bears), and a mutation also occurred that changed the genetic material responsible for the color of the (originally brown) bear's fur. Hence, a white bear was born. And in the midst of the ice age, when this mutation occurred—in the midst of a world full of snow—this white fur conferred an advantage upon this bear, namely, camouflage. This animal was able to more easily hunt, eat, survive, and pass on these "white fur genes," which, given the advantage of camouflage, were likely to prosper among the offspring that inherited them. Eventually, a new kind of bear, which we call "polar bear," speciated from a parental species of ancestral brown bears.[1]

Human Evolution

The appearance and evolution of human beings also involved natural selection. If we kept on unraveling our lineage beyond the hominid order, we would eventually find genetic links that connect us to such things as fish, amoebas, and fungi. But our human origins proper go back to a first hominine, which means "ancestrally related to the genus homo, human," called *Sahelanthropus tchadensis*. "Toumai," as this hominine is also known ("hope of life" in the local language) lived about seven million years ago, around Chad, in West Central Africa. We are not certain, but Toumai is likely to have been a member of a subspecies that, diverging from apes, began to develop human features. It lived during a time period when ancestral apes, under various environmental pressures, began to evolve so that some humanlike traits began to emerge.

Sahelanthropus had unmistakably apelike features, such as fur and a brain the size of a chimp's brain; but as noted, it also had some vague humanlike features, such as an upright position for walking. If you were to see it, it would not strike you as human at all, but as a strange and oddly humanized upright chimp. Perhaps you might view it as a missing link of sorts. And, indeed, although it has been difficult to trace how its line eventually evolved, many scientists believe that Toumai's descendants evolved into the genus *Homo*, "human," within which our particular subspecies, *Homo sapiens*, eventually emerged about 200,000 years ago, also in West Central Africa.[2] (And let us clarify that distinguishably human subspecies—the genus *Homo*, proper, as opposed to *anthropus*, "primate"—had already emerged about 2.4 million years ago, roughly 4.6 million years after the appearance of Toumai.)

The genus *Homo* included various subspecies, for example, *Homo naledi, Homo erectus, Homo abilis, Homo rudolfensis, Homo heilderbergensis, Homo neanderthalensis, Homo denisovan,* and *Homo floresiensis*. These speciated into the genus *Homo* from about 2.4 million (*erectus*, the oldest of the *Homo* lineage) to about 100,000 years ago (*floresiensis*, likely the human subspecies to speciate last, although not enough data exist to affirm this hypothesis conclusively). Some of them coexisted along with us, *Homo sapiens*, but not necessarily in contact with us, save *Homo neanderthalensis*, who did share territories with us. They were all, let me insist, distinctly human while nevertheless different from one another, biologically and genetically. And, hence, although paleoanthropologists do not speak of these as "human races" but as "parallel species," it is nevertheless fair to describe them as "human races," if only to underscore the

---

1   A wonderful discussion of this is provided in the magnificent TV series *Cosmos*.

2   Or, as the competing but, among scientists, less popular view suggests, perhaps we evolved from *Australopithecus afarensis*, a hominid who lived between 3.9 and 2.9 million years ago, in Eastern Africa, in the Afar region of Ethiopia.

fact that, although they were all properly human, they also had their own distinct biological and genetic markers or particularities.

To illustrate these various particularities, let us compare *us*, *Homo sapiens*, with *Homo floresiensis*, for example, so-called because it inhabited the Indonesian Island of Flores, north of Australia. *Floresiensis* was tiny, about 3.5 feet tall, roughly the size of a 3- or 4-year-old modern human child. It is known as "the hobbit" on account of its size. This comparatively small human, although a toolmaker and mostly likely a skilled hunter, also possessed a considerably smaller brain, the size of a chimp's. The hobbit had no chin, long feet, rather different bone structures, and other distinctive anatomic and genetic characteristics. Yet if you were to see *him*, he would immediately and definitely strike you as a human, definitely not as an ape. But you would also immediately see that this tiny "hobbit" was a very different kind of human, an impression that would be confirmed by biological and genetic analysis. Although having genetic and biological commonalities with us, floresiensis was a member of its own genetic splinter group. It was a separate human race.

As noted, *floresiensis* lived at the same time as *sapiens* (although there is no indication that these subspecies ever encountered one another). But the traces of this hobbit disappeared about 17,000 years ago, the time when they presumably became extinct, probably as a result of volcanic activity in the region.

Hence, a time traveler going from Europe to the Island of Flores about 20,000 years ago would have seen two different human races: *sapiens*, his or her own race, and *floresiensis*. The same time traveler visiting parts of Europe and the Middle East 40,000 years ago would also be able to see that his or her fellow *sapiens* shared the same living areas with yet another human race, *Homo neanderthalensis* (or *Homo sapiens neanderthalensis* in the competing classification). Like *floresiensis*, *neanderthalensis* also shared more biological similarities with members of its own subspecies than with us. *Homo neanderthalensis* encompassed an overlapping but also ultimately distinct genetic niche; it was another genetic splinter group. If *floresiensis* would perhaps strike our time traveler as a hobbit, *neanderthalensis*, in keeping with Tolkien's world, might strike our traveler as a dwarf. *Neanderthalensis* was shorter if compared to us. Males were about 65–66 inches tall and females were about 60–61 inches, but they had a comparatively robust musculoskeletal frame with longer arms and were far stronger than us. Their teeth were bigger. They had bigger brow ridges and a sloping forehead. Whereas they were, in all likelihood, sprinters, we were long-distance runners. They seem to have had a bigger brain as well. Indeed, given their greater brain/body size ratio, it is possible that they could have had stronger cognitive abilities, although this is not supported by the archeological record. Our cultural products were far more complex than theirs. While they were making rudimentary spears, for example, we are already making flutes. They had a shorter life span as well as a shorter reproductive life. In contrast, we have a longer life span. We also have a high rounded skull, facial retraction, a light and gracile, as opposed to a heavy and robust, skeleton, a smaller head and brain. Similarities included a gene associated with language, which was present in both *sapiens* and *neanderthalensis*, as well as the ability to vocalize.

Once again, *neanderthalensis* was a distinctly *human* subspecies, and yet it was significantly different from other human subspecies, including us. Our time traveler would have thus come to see three human races, properly: *sapiens* (his or her own race), *floresiensis*, and *neanderthalensis*.

But *Homo neanderthalensis* also disappeared about 30,000 years ago. (How would the census categories be today if these subspecies had managed to survive? How would the world be today if they had survived?) Other human subspecies, such as *Homo denisovan*, likewise died off. And yet others, such as *Homo erectus*, emigrated out of their original habitat, Central Africa, and eventually adapted to different environments and evolved into, precisely, *neanderthalensis* and most likely into *floresiensis as well*. We are not sure why these other races that existed side by side with us became extinct. Perhaps we outcompeted them, perhaps the rise of *Homo sapiens* contributed to their demise, as the "replacement hypothesis" suggests. We are, after all, a predatorial subspecies, responsible for the disappearance of many other animal species. But whatever the case, *all other human races died off*, for better or for worse. And thus we, *Homo sapiens*, were the only human subspecies or race that managed to survive. We were also on the verge of extinction. Our own population was largely destroyed, particularly by severe droughts in Central Africa, our ancestral territory, and was indeed reduced to about 2,000 to 10,000 members only. But in the end, we were the only human race that managed to survive and eventually multiplied, migrated, conquered, and populated the entire world.

George Church, a pioneer in the field of synthetic biology, has noted that today, we have all the necessary technology to recreate *Homo neanderthalensis*, a process known as "de-extinction," the recreation of extinct species (Church & Regis, 2012). And scientists envision the possible creation of a Neanderthal cohort that perhaps would have a cultural identity, and even political clout. Here is another interesting perspective: In China, in 2018, a geneticist named He Jiankui claimed to have created the first genetically modified human embryo, which presumably resulted in a genetically edited baby. There is controversy about this claim, but if it is the case that we can now "edit" newborns to specification, this could also lead to the appearance of a new species by means of accelerated artificial selection. You ponder about the cultural, ethical, political implications that these editing procedures or a Neanderthal de-extinction would have. Let me only say, for my part, that until either *neanderthalensis* or *floresiensis* or *denisovan* become *de*-extinct, or until a new species is edited out of the human genome, we are stuck with only one human race, us, all of us, all of us regardless of our appearance, all of us *Homo sapiens*.

People of Color: The Original Peoples of Europe

Again, we originally evolved in Africa, but pushed by climatic changes, including severe droughts occurring as a result of the last ice age, we migrated.[3] As we moved north, and progressively settled farther and farther away from the equator, the sun lessened in intensity, and it became colder so that we began to cover more of our bodies for longer periods of time. These new conditions created new environmental pressures for us, and we adapted. In particular, our skin became lighter and lighter to absorb enough vitamin D, which synthesizes as the sun strikes the skin (Jablonski, 2004). This was important, particularly because lack of vitamin D is related to bone deformity, including pelvic deformity, which would have had reproductive consequences for our species, *Homo sapiens*. Naturally, those who remained in equatorial areas, with more sun and more ultraviolet radiation, retained a darker skin, a natural sun blocker that, while allowing them to synthesize vitamin D, also helped them prevent problems such as skin cancer and damage to sweat glands (Sturm, Teasdale, & Box, 2001).

Now, the skin is, of course, the most visible organ, and skin color, for this reason, may seem genetically important. But to date, only 11 of the 21,000 or so genes in the human genome (the entire collection of human genes) have been identified as involved in skin color (Quillen & Shriver, 2011).[4] Hence,

---

3   This was a second migration. The earlier ancestor of the modern human lineage, *Homo erectus*, appears to have emigrated out of Africa about 1.9 million years ago, shortly after evolving from *Homo habilis*. *Erectus* probably reached Asia 1.8 million years ago or so. Its descendants seem to have been replaced, killed off, in the wake of the second immigration, by the more advanced *Homo sapiens, us*.

4   Let us clarify that this number, 21,000, is the number of genes that, as it were, actively code for different kinds of proteins and therefore generate, for example, your nails, hair, skin, and other tissues. In addition, however, there is an as of yet undetermined number of genes that are noncoding. There are many thousands of these, and therefore the total number of genes, coding and noncoding, is much greater than 21,000.

genetically, these latitude-related variations of skin color, the main marker of "race," involve only a tiny fraction of what we are as a species. These genetic changes pertaining to skin color were not big enough for speciation to occur. These changes were not big enough to separate us, *Homo sapiens*, into various, speciated, latitude-based, color-coded subspecies or races.

Note also that this process whereby *sapiens* coming from Africa developed lighter pigmentations in higher latitudes was slow and gradual, of course, like all evolutionary processes. And that, for this reason, the first Europeans (*sapiens*), the original peoples of Europe, were dark skinned. Many ancestral Europeans, in fact, retained dark skin as late as the end of the Mesolithic, about 10,000 years ago. "Cheddar Man" was a Mesolithic skeleton found precisely in Cheddar Gorge, England. As revealed by genetic analyses, this man had the kind of skin color that we find in sub-Saharan Africa. Cheddar Man—this original and primeval Briton from whom many Englanders descend—was black, although he also had blue eyes, the result of a mutation discussed earlier, which had recently occurred. Thomas Booth, one of the bioarcheologists from the Natural History Museum in London who worked on the DNA analyses that led to this discovery, noted that Cheddar Man "is just one person, but also indicative of the population of Europe at the time. They had dark skin and most of them had pale colored eyes, either blue or green, and dark brown hair" (in Lotzof, 2018).

Beyond skin color, other changes also occurred as a result of the Out of Africa migration. As I have noted elsewhere (2012),

> [B]odies also responded to other geographical pressures. The differential height of "races," for instance, resulted, in part, from such pressures as those related to heat intensity. Longer and slender bodies (e.g., sub-Saharan) are optimal for heat reduction, and shorter bodies (which one may associate with Eskimos, for example) are optimal for heat retention. Other geographical factors, such as availability of specific nutrients, humidity, and altitude, also contributed to other "racial" features. High altitudes, for instance, anthropologically defined as 10,000 feet and above, tended to mold shorter and stockier bodies, an adaptive trait that is partly explained by the typical cold weather in these regions, as well as by the lower availability of breathable oxygen, which results in larger lungs and hearts and thus in larger thoraxes (hence, the typical "racial" features of Andean "Indians," for example).

In addition to geography, which created some of the central racial physical differences that we see today, other differences resulted from genetic mutation, from errors of copying the genetic information from one generation to the next. Again, blue eyes resulted from mutation occurring about 10,000 years ago (University of Copenhagen, 2008). But neither these adaptive traits nor these changes by mutation modified our genome to the point of speciation. Again, our species is too recent in origin for speciation to have occurred. Our species was only "pseudo-speciated," pseudo-speciation being the artificial designation, the simple naming of purported subspecies or human "races." As we will discuss next, this process of naming the different human "races"—because it is not grounded in genes and simply obeys changing cultural narratives—has resulted in likewise changing lists of "racial groups," which have varied from culture to culture, even from state to state and indeed from province to province, as well as over time.

Race and Genes

If *Homo sapiens* had become speciated into the various "races" listed in the U.S. census, we would expect that each of these "races" would comprise various genetic splinter groups. But, for better or for worse, no such splinter groups have been found among human beings. In fact, what we have found is that human beings are genetically very homogenous, very similar to one another, 99.9%, to be precise.

The percentage of genetic variation among human beings is thus very small. If you look around, you will see a great diversity of bone structures, body mass indexes, hair and skin colors, head circumferences, not to mention differences in innate or genetically determined abilities, musical, intellectual, etc. But if you were to see the genes of these sundry and diverse people, their seemingly enormous variations would be reduced to a tiny fraction of their genes: 0.1%. And, more importantly, most of this genetic variation occurs *within*, rather than *across,* "races." To better understand this crucial fact, imagine a large group of people divided into two "racial" groups, say, Asians and Whites. We would expect

- a. that all people in these two groups, even if they look different, would be genetically similar, their genetic differences being, as noted, of the order of about 0.1% only; and
- b. that if you were to randomly pick an Asian person from this group, he or she would likely share *more genetic commonalities* with another randomly chosen *white* person than with a randomly chosen Asian person. Vice versa, a randomly chosen white person would likely share *more genetic commonalities with an Asian person* than with another white person.

Here is another way of saying this: A friend of yours who identifies as white is likely to share *fewer genetic commonalities* with another one of your white friends than with one of your Asian friends. The same pattern would apply to persons in all other "racial" categories. Again, most genetic variation occurs *within* "races," it turns out. Of course, this is *not* always the case; it is only the trend that population geneticists would expect. And two random persons from *one* "racial" group may very well share *more* genetic commonalities than two persons from two different racial groups.

Note also that the amount of genetic variation across or within "races" depends on how you define "races," how you delimit racial boundaries. But in general, population geneticists have found *more,* rather than *less,* genetic variation *within* "racial categories." Richard Lewontin (1993), an evolutionary geneticist from Harvard University and one of the leading human population geneticists, has shown that about 85% of all identified human genetic variation occurs,

> between any two individuals from the same ethnic group [say, Irish]. Another 8% of all the variation is between ethnic groups within a race—say, Spaniards, Irish, Italians, and Britons—and only 7 percent of all human genetic variation lies on the average between major human races like those of Africa, Asia, Europe, and Oceania (1993, p. 38).

Yet another way of expressing genetic variation is by continents: "5–15% of genetic variation occurs between large groups living on different continents," as the Human Genome Research Institute (HGRI) noted, "with the remaining majority of the variation occurring *within* such groups" (National Human Genome Research Institute, 2005, pp. 519–532, my emphasis). But no matter what racial definitions you use, "the vast majority of genetic variation exists *within* racial groups and not between them. Race is an ideology and, for this reason, many scientists believe that race should be more accurately described as a social construct and not a biological one," as the HGRI, the most authoritative research institution in genetics, also noted (National Institutes of Health, 2014, my emphasis; see also Lewontin, 1993, p. 36; Marks, 2002; Goodman, 2012; Gould, 2002).

Conventional racial boundaries (white, black, etc.), therefore, do not encompass distinct or specific genetic splinter groups. Such boundaries exist in the public imagination, but they do not exist in reality.

The idea that there are human races, for this reason, is untenable, not demonstrable scientifically. As a recent PBS series noted, race is merely "an illusion" (Pounder et al., 2003).

Genetic Clustering Among Human Groups

It is, of course, possible to find some genetic commonalities among groups of human beings. Some groups, for instance, promote endogamous marriages, so since members of the group cannot marry outside the clan, the tribe, the religion, you do find more commonalities *within* these groups. But these commonalities do not amount to races or human subspecies. One of the most influential royal houses of Europe, the Hapsburgs, for example, abided by these sorts of strict, almost incestuous, endogamous rules (it was common for these noble men and women, who ruled between 1438 and 1740, to marry cousins and uncles). But this, and other such groups, although having internal genetic commonalities—do not encompass separate human subspecies, of course. Indeed, nature does not favor these kinds of genetic in-group commonalities and their existence tends to be short-lived. On account of many generations of inbreeding, the Hapsburgs eventually produced heirs with inherited genetic defects so that this powerful royal line declined and disappeared altogether. (Historians Will and Ariel Durant have described the last Hapsburg King, Charles II of Spain, as "short, lame, epileptic, senile and completely bald before 35, always on the verge of death but repeatedly baffling Christendom by continuing to live" [2011]. He was known as *"El Hechizado,"* the Bewitched, on account of his persistent epileptic seizures.)

Before the Industrial Revolution of the late 18th and early 19th centuries transformed transportation systems the world over, most men and women also married within their own typically small town or village, or at the most within their own country. Thus prior to the 18th century, it was possible to find relatively atomized groups with internal genetic commonalities. But these commonalities, yet again, did not separate these groups into human subspecies or races either, and they did not encompass our modern racial categories, white, black, etc. Such groups, in any case, have all but disappeared with modernity, a period that exponentially increased not only routes of communication but also routes of genetic exchange, "gene flow": the dispersal of genes from relatively small areas to increasingly larger and larger areas. Genetic analysis of Hitler's surviving relatives, for example, revealed that he had Moroccan and Sephardic (i.e., Jewish) ancestry, and hence the most rabid advocate of "racial purity" was also a node in a web of gene flow that expanded well beyond Germany. In our era, gene flow is a process so extensive that it could be described as a process of genetic globalization.

Finally, it is also possible to separate human beings into various groups according to line of descent from various ancestral clans, going back to thousands of years in time. And precisely because these populations share deep ancestral roots, they may share some genetic commonalities as well. But such "haplogroups" do not comprise human subspecies or races either. The hundreds of existing haplogroups involve hundreds of ancestral lines of descent that, however, eventually converge into an older one, into a single human clan, an African group of *Homo sapiens*, as discussed, from which all human beings on earth descend, regardless of their haplogroup. Let us imagine, for example, that your haplogroup, as determined by your dad's ancestry, goes back to an ancestral East Russian clan. This would make you a member of Haplogroup C, which encompasses the original peoples of Mongolia, Far East Russia, Polynesia, Australia, Korea, and India. And let us imagine that you, therefore, see yourself as ancestrally Russian and hence as white. But this ancient Russian clan will, in turn, have its older roots in Africa. That is to say, if you keep unraveling your line of descent, you will find that, although your ancestral grandfather was East Russian, your deeply ancestral grandparents were Africans. This idea might be hard to fathom, but regardless of your skin color, you are, as any other human being on earth is, originally and ancestrally African. To be sure, "the genetic variation outside Africa," as stated by the HGRI, "is generally a subset of the variation within Africa" (2005).

Race as a Colonial Ideology

If there are no actual human subspecies or races, how, then, did racial ideologies, racial categories, and racial identities come into being?

Ancient cultures typically cared very little about race. Clan, caste, trade affiliation, gender, class, and even the language of people, were generally much more important for these cultures than skin color. These aspects of life were far more important in the ancient world than any incipient notions pertaining to race. But nonetheless, the idea that there are various human races is ancient, and indeed, racism can be also found, sporadically, in ancient times. Biological anthropologist Barbara King (2002) has noted that ancient Egyptians, for example, had some color-coded racial categories that included the "red people" (themselves) and the white and black peoples.[5] And in Egypt, priestly groups regarded Semites (Jewish people) as racially inferior. Indeed, anti-Semitism arguably started in Alexandria, the capital of Egypt (Gager, 1983).

But our contemporary racial categories, our current understandings of race, the ways we see skin colors, are actually very recent, as is our keen and widely spread interest in race and in all things racial.

Although the concept of race is ancient, our own modern racial categories have their main roots in a medieval myth about a divinely ordained hierarchy of all things, known as the "Great Chain of Being." This notion, which was extended in Europe, posited that animals, plants, metals, people (e.g., the king, the nobles, the merchants, the peasants), and even celestial beings (e.g., angels, archangels) were created to be more or less important in the eyes of God. According to this and related medieval myths, each being occupied a higher or lower position. On top of this Chain of Being was the Supreme Being, God. And in society, each person and each social group likewise possessed a nature that befitted their social position so that the king was higher in the social order simply because he was a higher being (the form of address, "Your Highness," used even today, is related to this old idea). The king simply possessed "more spirit," they thought, and was therefore closer in spirit to the highest being, God. In contrast, the peasant was a lesser creature according to these ideologies and scales, and hence had a correspondingly low social standing that befitted his or her own supposedly lower nature. In some versions of this myth, the peasant was lower than the "noble" dog. In others, gold, shiny and incorruptible, was closer to God than iron.

When the European colonial forces encountered the "New World," these ideas about a Chain of Being came in handy as a way of justifying the purportedly natural, God-ordained differences between the European colonizers and the peoples they encountered. These exotic lands were "heathendom." And their peoples were "heathens": men, women, and children who, because they were so removed from the Supreme Being, automatically came to occupy a lower position in the Chain of Being.

Some of these "heathens" had only elemental forms of social organization and relatively inferior, indeed primitive, technology, not to mention barbaric practices, including human sacrifice. But others, such as the Aztecs, Mayas, and Incas were advanced, even by European standards, in areas such as civil

---

5   Note also that the history of the people of Ancient Egypt spans about 3,000 years and that their racial thinking changed with changing historical and cultural factors. Hence, for some Egyptians, the costumes, speech, occupations, or physical location of other groups were more important than their skin color (McKoskey, 2004).

engineering, architecture, astronomy, systems of government and administration, agriculture, metallurgy, and art. Their cities were sometimes bigger and better administered. Tenochtitlan, for example, the capital of the Aztec Empire by 1325, boasted monumental architecture and had a population of about 200,000 people. In contrast, Seville in Spain, one of the European jewels even today, had only about 60,000 inhabitants. One of the first Spaniards to see Tenochtitlan, Bernal Diaz del Castillo, noted that upon seeing this magnificent city, the Spaniards "were amazed, and said it was like the enchantment, on account of the great towers and buildings" (in Caistor, 2000). The Inca citadel of Machu Pichu, in Peru, is seen even today as one of the wonders of the world. The Incas knew no famine, one of the chronic and especially ghastly problems in Europe. But all of these hundreds of cultures—developed and not—lumped as heathens, ethnics, or natives, were eventually seen as only *one* race, an inferior one at that. All of them became "Indians," simply because the Europeans who discovered the New World thought that they had reached India, rather than an unknown continent. (Some of them speculated that they had reached China, instead of India, and, for this reason, American "Indians" could well have been called "Chinese.")

The colonial order, including the old American colonies that provided the foundations for modern America, produced the first modern "theories" about race—not because colonist had had any data pertaining to population genetics or biology, of course, but primarily because these theories justified the colonial rule. These racial theories had political, economic, and religious functions, not scientific ones. They allowed colonists to justify an economic order that necessitated the enslavement of human groups, groups designated as separate and inferior and thus as deserving of enslavement, including, natives, but also Africans, Chinese, the Irish, and others. It is worth quoting at length from the American Anthropological Association's official statement on race:

> Today scholars in many fields argue that "race" as it is understood in the United States of America was a social mechanism invented during the 18th century to refer to those populations brought together in colonial America: the English and other European settlers, the conquered Indian peoples, and those peoples of Africa brought in to provide slave labor [...]. From its inception, this modern concept of "race" was modeled after an ancient theorem of the Great Chain of Being [...] Thus "race" was a mode of classification linked specifically to peoples in the colonial situation. It subsumed a growing ideology of inequality devised to rationalize European attitudes and treatment of the conquered and enslaved peoples. Proponents of slavery in particular during the 19th century used "race" to justify the retention of slavery. The ideology magnified the differences among Europeans, Africans, and Indians, established a rigid hierarchy of socially exclusive categories underscored and bolstered unequal rank and status differences, and provided the rationalization that the inequality was natural or God-given. The different physical traits of African-Americans and Indians became markers or symbols of their status differences [...] As they were constructing US society, leaders among European-Americans fabricated the cultural/behavioral characteristics associated with each "race," linking superior traits with Europeans and negative and inferior ones to Blacks and Indians. Numerous arbitrary and fictitious beliefs about the different peoples were institutionalized and deeply embedded in American thought. Early in the 19th century the growing fields of science began to reflect the public consciousness about human differences. Differences among the "racial" categories were projected to their greatest extreme when the argument was posed that Africans, Indians, and Europeans were separate species, with Africans the least human and closer taxonomically to apes. (American Anthropological Association, 1998).

Race as a Modern Ideology

These mythical narratives about race were modernized by the work of an important 18th-century Swedish botanist named Carl von Linné, Linnaeus, in the Latin version of his name. He was the first to provide a supposedly scientific classification of human "races," assigning a proper Latin nomenclature to them (his student, Johann Blumenbach [1752–1840], was also instrumental in building this modern racial taxonomy).

Like the vast majority of men and woman of his age, our pioneering botanist was unquestioningly racist. This was so simply because racism, which not only justified the colonial expansion but also the enrichment, and in this sense, the advancement of most of Europe—was seen as a "proper" and even a "respectable" attitude during his time. Indeed, the most respected thinkers of the epoch—actually important, otherwise brilliant and helpful philosophers, such as Voltaire in France, Immanuel Kant in Germany, John Locke in England, David Hume in Scotland, and politicians such as Thomas Jefferson in the United States, made public racist proclamations. And they did so with confident ease, fearing no repercussions of any kind. Indeed, at least up to the 17th century, slave trading itself was *not* seen as an immoral or even as a vulgar business. Engaged in the British slave trade, for instance, were "dukes, earls, lords, countesses, knights—and kings," as historian Milton Meltzer reports (1993, p. 45). "The slaves of the Royal African Company were branded with initials D.Y. for the Duke of York," the king of England and Ireland (Meltzer, 1993, p. 45).

Hence, Linnaeus was simply thrown, at birth, into a racist world and cradled and nursed by unscientific but naturalized and nearly universally accepted habits of thought about the "human races."

And it was not surprising, therefore, that this otherwise brilliant taxonomist, the "prince of botanists," as he was known, provided the first "scientific" racial catalogue that was candidly, and we might say "honestly," racist. The first to pioneer a modern and useful taxonomy for the natural order, this botanist quickly succumbed to racial ideology when it came to cataloging the human "races," and he simply arranged them according to the scales of his time. Hence, *Homo europaeus*, Latin for "European human," automatically climbed to the top of the scale. And this scale also relegated such races as "the monstrous" and other purported inferior "human subspecies" to the bottom. All these races, he thought, were endowed with innate traits, different morals, and, indeed, different characters and temperaments so that Europeans were "sanguine" (confident, optimistic, able to face difficult situations with ease) and Africans were "phlegmatic" (calm, unemotional), for example. Among "the monstrous," let us note in passing, were folks like the Fuegians, from Tierra del Fuego, south of Chile and Argentina, a people who would be eventually hunted down almost to extinction in the 19th century, particularly by British militia and mercenaries who got paid one-pound sterling for each man, woman, or child they murdered. Why were the Fuegians—and not people like these monstrous mercenaries—"monstrous"? Because Linnaeus, as many of his contemporaries, still believed that in faraway lands, in deep "heathendom," one could find truly bestial, animalized, and inherently degraded subspecies of human beings, not only the "monstrous" but also the "flatheads" or the "troglodytes," for example. And like most people, he also assumed that such colonial genocides were part and parcel of the advancement of civilization.

This was the perspective that informed his early and purportedly scientific racial catalogue—the catalogue that provided the first "scientific" basis for the modern theories of race.

Biology as Ideology

As Richard Lewontin has shown (1993), historically, biology has often been indistinguishable from ideology, as the foregoing examples illustrate. Indeed biology, Lewontin notes, has served to cast a "scientific" and respectable aura on all kinds of ideologized and otherwise unrespectable, or even cruel and inhuman habits of thought. This includes race but also gender, sexuality, class, and other aspects of human life that have often been distorted by biologists who used their discipline primarily to express their moral opinions and prejudices. To be sure, historically, bias has not only been "biology" but also policy, policy informed by "biology."

But perhaps race, in particular, has been the area of inquiry that has been more blatantly distorted by influential and well-regarded scientists in this field, at times ridiculously, at times horrifically. Recall that the most revolting aspects of the Second World War were sponsored and legitimized by race theorists who saw themselves as objective biologists. It is worth fetching an image from the Second World War in this context: Nazi soldiers forced "racially inferior" Jews to process the corpses of fellow prisoners killed in the gas chambers of the concentration camps. A main task of these Sonderkommandos, as they were called, was to search for, and to pull out, gold teeth from corpses often piled outside these gas chambers—gold that was eventually used by Nazi dentists to fill the cavities of high-ranking Nazi officers. These and such vile events were supported by biologists and by "scientifically" legitimized racial ideologies. They were justified by then respected scientists, such as Alfred Ploetz, the propounder of a theory of "racial hygiene," the basic concept in the Nazi's ideological arsenal.

Linnaeus's work was arguably the first clear example of the ideological uses of biology. To his credit, he was probably never fully conscious of the moral implications of his racist theories. For, in the mind of many of his contemporaries, being racist was not only tantamount to being reasonable, as noted, but also, you guessed it, "scientific," "advanced," and "progressive." Indeed, when writing his racial catalogue, Linnaeus was likely moved by the most "noble" scientific ideals of his time, particularly the ideal of progress. And to his credit as well, he did not assume forever fixed racial categories, but categories that could be, perhaps, malleable and hence presumably bettered (although this is not explicit in his theory). But racist biology continued to prosper up to the 20th century, influencing even the generation of baby boomers—a time when the world had already been revolted by the criminal and politically self-serving uses of biology wielded by the Nazis and others.

Two hundred years after Linnaeus, the American physical anthropologist Carleton Coon developed a similarly influential, and then also "authoritative," classification of the human races, one that also reflected the dominant ideology of the time. Coon published his main work, *The Origins of Races*, in 1962, a time when the United States, much as the Sweden of Linnaeus, was under the firm grip of ideological and self-serving interpretations of race. The United States was then an officially racist country, as it was desegregated only in 1964, when President Lyndon Johnson signed the Civil Rights Act into law. This modern American scientist, much as his Swedish predecessor, also argued that the "Caucasoid" race, the equivalent of Linnaeus's *Homo europaeus*, was higher in the evolutionary scale. And he also noted that the "Negroid" race was "primitive" and indeed less evolved. Arguably, Coon's theory contributed the most to the 20th-century ideology of racism and to the racist ideas that still linger, in various ways and degrees, in the public imagination even today. And it is worth insisting: unlike Linnaeus, Coon was fully conscious of the moral implications of his theories. He knew very well that these kinds of ideas were at the root of Nazism and hence at the root one of the largest genocides seen in human history.

There were also important differences between Linnaeus's and Coon's taxonomies, in addition to the fantastic "races" that Linnaeus invented (e.g., the flatheads), which were, of course, rejected by Coon. For Linnaeus, the hierarchy of human races was divinely ordained, and for Coon it was the effect of differential evolution. Coon argued that there were five races: Caucasoid, Negroid, Mongoloid (Asians and Native Americans), Capoid (Khoisians from southern Cape of Africa), and Australoid (Australian natives). And he said that each of these races had evolved separately. For more than a million years, he thought, each one of these groups had evolved in separate ecological niches and had thus speciated, and developed genetic specificities that separated them into distinct human races. Unfortunately for Coon, *Homo sapiens*, the subspecies from which all modern human beings descend, originally emerged and evolved in Africa about 200,000 years ago and—only about 80,000 years ago—migrated out of Africa, as we noted, to various other geographical locations in the world. This modern dating, pertaining to *Homo sapiens's* appearance in, and emigration from, Africa, results from advanced scientific methods that were not available to Coon. And it is very important. Although 80,000 years might seem to be a long time, it is evolutionarily a very brief period. It is not enough time for speciation to have occurred. Coon's ideas about separate evolutionary paths, and, therefore, his theories about "races" were thus superseded by modern science. Modern scientific advances, in fact, simply demolished the all-too-common scientific reports about separate evolutionary pathways for each of the "human races." (Although Coon was the most prominent scientist in the business of racial classification, it is easy to find a slew of coetaneous reports insisting on the idea of separate evolutionary paths for each of the "races.")

Let us finally note that Coon's racial taxonomy, scientifically invalid such as it is, is still influential today.[6] Consider the fact that average people usually take the biological validity of races for granted and the idea that there are, in fact, human races, each possessing their own set of natural and observable characteristics, including mental or even moral traits. Indeed, it would be fair to suppose that most people in the world assume that their own racial identity is grounded in nature, in biology, in a specific and separate genetic splinter group, also associated with certain innate characteristics or traits. Why have erroneous racial categories endured even up to today when the near consensus among scientist is that our ideas about race involve untenable habits of thought attached to skin colors? Is it because, social animals that we are, we are wired to like the idea that we are part of a group, including a race, and have a related tendency to think in terms of "us and them"? Is it because, as also noted, human beings often prefer belief over knowledge? Whatever the case, a narrative about the various supposed races is still encysted in the collective imagination. Should this narrative decrease along with increases in public literacy pertaining to population genetics, this form of literacy would transform our ideas, our identities, the way we regard ourselves and others. Such a form of public literacy, such a new way of reading the world, would fundamentally change the world as we know it today. As noted in Chapter 1, when entire population begins to read the world, the world is, in various ways and degrees, transformed.

---

6   Consider current U.S. census categories, for example: White, Black or African American, American Indian or Alaska Native, Asian, and Native Hawaiian or Other Pacific Islander. They are similar to Coon's. This does not mean that the Bureau is a channel for the sort of racism explicit in Coon's theories. On the contrary, it has significantly aided the cause of racial equality by, for example, tracing patterns of differential income and employment among the "races," which has provided support for affirmative action programs. Furthermore, the Bureau recognizes that "The racial categories included in the census questionnaire generally reflect a social definition of race recognized in this country and not an attempt to define race biologically, anthropologically, or genetically." Yet, the census' categories had direct roots in Coon's categories.

CHAPTER XII

The Social Construction of Race

L ET US FOCUS on one racial category, white, to better understand the idea that our racial classifications are, above all, habits of thought, rather than actual representations of human subspecies or branches of human evolution. As noted, the ancient Egyptians already had color-coded racial categories, but the contemporary notion that there is a white race that encompasses descent from any of "the original peoples of Europe, the Middle East, or North Africa," as the U.S. Census Bureau defines it, is very recent. In this chapter, we will trace the origin and historical development of this definition, which captures mainstream beliefs about whiteness, to answer the following questions:

a. When did this narrative about whiteness come into being?
b. How and why was this narrative constructed?
c. How did this changing narrative affect the experiences, identities, and lives of people and peoples?

Ancient, Medieval, and Renaissance Ideas About Whiteness

As suggested, the idea that there are races is ancient and some forms of racism could be found in the ancient world (e.g., anti-Semitism in Egypt). Let us add that for some of the ancients race was indeed important. Julius Caesar, for example, thought of himself as a descendant from the goddess Aphrodite and thus "of the race of the Gods," a strong marker of his identity, as one would expect. But in general, clan, trade, gender, language, and social status (e.g., slave vs. citizen) were far more significant for the ancient peoples when it was a question of determining the supposed nature of a person (except the few who came from mythical stock, like Caesar). These affiliations, clan, trade, etc., were more important markers of "nature" than skin color or phenotype. The ancient Europeans, in any case, did not have the notion that there was *a* race that encompassed nothing less than *all* "the original peoples of Europe," say, Caesar and his mortal enemies, the despised and "inferior" barbarians. A race that, in addition to including all the peoples of Europe, also encompassed *all* the peoples of "the Middle East, or North Africa." This idea—our contemporary, pan-European definition of whiteness—indeed could not have arisen among these various, sundry, and perpetually warring ethnic groups; groups that generally saw their neighbors as possessors of a different character, morality, and spirit; groups that often saw different natural traits in members of the various trades, tribes, clans, etc.

The original peoples of Europe—the Romans, Greeks, Gauls, Franks, Saxons, Celts, Goths, Alani, Vandals, Vascones, etc.—simply did not think of themselves as "'White,' as sharing the same racial boat by virtue of being 'Europeans'" (Narváez, 2012).

How about the time period that followed the ancient Classical Age?[1] The subsequent Middle Ages—the period that spanned from the fall of Rome to the barbarians in the 5th century AD, to the 15th century—also produced some racial narratives and categories (Heng, 2011). These medieval categories of race included, for example, "Jew," "white," and "black." But this period did not produce the contemporary narrative about a pan-European white race either. Bear in mind that medieval notions of whiteness were not intended to place all "white people" in the same category or scale. The whiteness of a peasant, for instance, did not place him in the same category as the lord, who was endowed with a supposedly superior nature on account of his "superior blood," regardless of their shared skin color. In the medieval world, social status was also an essential determinant of a person's supposed nature or essence. Recall that medieval lords often saw peasants as not too different from animals and that even up to the 19th century, peasants were sometimes seen as the incarnation of sin itself. Similarly, the whiteness of the lord did not put him in the same category as the king, who was endowed, as also noted, with "more spirit" and therefore with a different and far superior nature or essence.

This strange absence of whiteness, as we know it today, is starkly and bluntly illustrated by the Elizabethan Era, the era that closed the door of the Middle Ages while opening the door to the English Renaissance. This is the time period that witnessed the ascent of a Golden Age in English history, the proliferation of exquisite and timeless poetry, music, literature, and theater, including, of course, Shakespearean theater. Importantly, this professedly genteel age also witnessed the economic development of Britain, partly as a result of commercial and territorial expansion that included the exploration and eventual annexation ("stealing" is a more accurate term) of newfound lands in North America, India, and Ireland. (Large-scale takeover of land began after the death of Queen Elizabeth I, after whom this period was named.) With respect to race, and whiteness, in particular, let us first say that the colonial annexation of these territories was justified partly through racial narratives that depicted the native populations as inferior and therefore as deserving to be ruled by the professedly superior English civilization or race. And, second, let us also underscore that this prospering English empire deployed this colonial strategy not only to justify the subjugation of the "inferior" peoples of North America and India. They created a narrative about the "inferior" *Irish* as well; a narrative that portrayed the English as bearers of a very different nature than that of the "beastly" Irish.

This historical circumstance is important for our understanding of the history of race in the West. And so, before continuing to trace the evolution of our modern concept of whiteness, it is worth pausing at this point to see how the English constructed this racial theory to justify the colonization of Ireland. A theory that, accounting for the supposedly innate traits of the "barbarous" Irish, eventually served as a template for the English depiction of Native Americans, and, to an extent, for future English-derived narratives about race, in general.

---

1   The Classical Age was the historical period that saw the unparalleled development of Greek culture, the conquests of Julius Cesar, and the expansion of Rome, all of which occurred alongside the relatively modest accomplishments of the "barbarians," as the Greeks called such peoples as the Gauls, Franks, Saxons, Celts, and Goths.

The Social Construction of Irishness

Humphrey Gilbert and his half-brother Walter Raleigh were two famous English soldiers, explorers, and adventurers chosen by the English Crown to undertake the process of private colonization in Ireland—a process that, beyond having economic aims, also had strategic military motivations, as the English saw (Catholic) Ireland as a possible beachhead for Catholic invaders from Spain. Gilbert and Raleigh, these devout Protestants, saw the Irish according to the prevailing English view, as historian Ronald Takaki notes (2008). The Irish, Gilbert believed, were savages and nomadic herders who were tribally organized and impossible to civilize. (And you can already see the similarities between these views and the subsequent English depiction of Native Americans as tribally organized savages who also had to be forcefully subjugated.) In the eyes of English colonists, in general, the Irish were innately predisposed to "idleness" and "sloth"; they were "loose, barbarous and most wicked"; "so blindly and brutishly informed for the most part as that you would rather think them atheists or infidels." They lived "like beasts" (in Takaki, 2008, p. 29). And thus, "every Irishman shall be forbidden to wear English apparel or weapons upon pain of death. That no Irishman, born of Irish *race* and brought up Irish, shall purchase land, bear office, be chosen of any jury or admitted witness in any real or personal action," as the colonial law dictated (Takaki, 2008, p. 29, my italics).

As noted, colonial forces fabricated racial narratives and "theories" and ascribed "racial" characteristics to native populations—partly to justify colonial expansion. Let us add that colonists also created these racial narratives out of honest ignorance. For, of course, they simply were unable to measure their views against scientific evidence, as modern sciences such as genetics did not exist. But this combination of colonial greed and honest ignorance whereby "races" were constructed by colonial powers served to justify not only a rapid process of colonial expansion but also colonial genocides, in the Americas, Africa, *as well as in Europe*, as the case of Ireland unambiguously illustrates.

Indeed, the English constructed a racial theory of "Irishness" precisely to justify their colonial expansion in Ireland and the brutal and murderous treatment of "Irish aboriginals." Only under the lens of these colonists did the Irish become "bestial" and have to be treated accordingly. Only then could the Irish be "legitimately" deprived of rights and of their land, no matter the means used to achieve this, and no matter their suffering. William Fitzwilliam, an English lord deputy and lord justice in Ireland, noted, "Nothing but fear and force can teach [the Irish] duty and obedience" (in Lyons, 2004). And, indeed, to teach this "barbarous" race proper duty and obedience, the English deployed not only force but also truly barbarous savagery of their own. The young Gilbert "slaughtered wholesale," as historians Don Jordan and Michael Walsh have noted. He took pride in "putting man, woman and child to the sword," as he himself wrote. Indeed, he,

> pursued a campaign of terror: he ordered "the heads of all those … killed in the day, should be cut off from their bodies and brought to the place where they encamped at night, and should there be laid on the ground by each side of the way leading into his own tent so that none could come into his tent for any cause but commonly he must pass through a lane of heads … [It brought] great terror to the people when they saw the heads of their dead fathers, brothers, children, kinsfolk, and friends." (Gilbert quoted in Takaki, 2008; ellipses in Takaki's text)

In the end, the English established a firm two-tier social system in Ireland (colonist vs. colonized; top vs. bottom), which, also in the usual colonial fashion, allowed the invaders to steal land and labor methodically and effectively from the "wicked" and "inferior" "Irish aboriginals."

Gilbert, incidentally, was knighted in recompense for his actions. And thus his notorious brand of dash and racist savagery was legitimized and sanctioned in his eyes and in the eyes of his compatriots, by the Queen and by God Himself. (This is also another characteristically colonial move, whereby murderers such as Gilbert often emerge, in the final historical account, as civilizing heroes and thus as members of the "superior race." And the heirs of the conquered, the colonized population, sometimes grow up learning, through the educational system implanted by the invading forces, about the civilizing exploits of these heroes thus tacitly learning, as well, about their own "uncivilized" past and their own "uncivilized" race," a race that, being barbarous, had to pay the toll, in collective suffering, of civilization—civilization appearing here as a sort of treat provided by the superior race.) After such success, Gilbert embarked on an American adventure, seeking this time the fabulous riches supposedly owned by the American "savages," but he met his fate in the sea, aboard a storm-tossed brig called the Squirrel. For the sake of providing a full account, let us note that this murderer, who "slaughtered wholesale," faced his death stoically, even courageously. Before the storm that sank his ship fully developed, he had a chance to transfer to a safer ship called the Golden Hind, but he chose not to desert his men. And he reportedly died with the book *Utopia* in his hands, the fiction by Thomas More about a nowhere republic that had achieved perfect social harmony, a pagan paradise where reason had managed to vanquish Greed and Egotism.

The English racial and racist savagery, however, did not end with Gilbert's death. Under Oliver Cromwell, who was eventually named lord protector of England, Scotland, and Ireland, a campaign of Irish ethnic cleansing was conducted. Under this "protector"—another "civilizing hero" who also saw the Irish as inferior and "barbarous wretches"—an undetermined number of men, women, and children, including young children, were forcefully transported to the American colonies and Barbados, primarily, where they were often sold as slaves and as indentured servants (who often died before the indenture period was over). These were "political prisoners," often men who resisted the English invasion, Catholic priests, peasants whose farms were stolen by the colonizers, unemployed people, people "who could not give account of themselves" as the law dictated, and abducted children (Akamatsu, 2010). Peter Stubber, the governor of Galway, a city captured during the Cromwelian invasion, noted that the "usual practice [was] to take people out of their beds at night and sell them for slaves to the Indies" [Akamatsu, 2010]. Barbadian historian Hilary McDonald Beckles has traced the story of an Irish woman who, priced at sixpence per pound, was bartered at a market for a pig (Akamatsu, 2010). Cromwell's son, Henry, the major general of the English forces in Ireland, was asked to send "1000 Irish Wenches" to the Indies. Although "we must use force in taking them up," as he replied, the request could be easily fulfilled, and in fact, he also offered to send, in addition, "1,500 to 2,000 boys aged 12 to 14" (in Akamatsu, 2010).

This process, termed "the Irish slave trade" by some historians, "did not end with Cromwell; for at least a hundred years, forced transportation continued as a fact of life in Ireland," as historians Jordan and Walsh report (2007). And slave trading of Europeans during this period also involved Scots and even English men, women and children, the so-called surplus people, the destitute, people convicted of crimes, and orphaned children—all of whom were also marketed like chattel in the American colonies and sold sometimes for a determined period of time, usually seven years, as "indentured servants," and sometimes for life (Jordan & Walsh, 2007).

Irish Immigration to the United States

Hence, the English saw the Irish, in the typical colonial fashion, as racially different and racially inferior. The idea of a broadly European "white race" evidently did not apply in this context either. Furthermore, the notion that the Irish comprised a separate race did not end with the English-Irish colonial occupation. When large-scale Irish immigration to the United States occurred in the 19th century, the newcomers were often seen not only as culturally but also as morally and indeed *physically* different from the already established English and northern European groups. As Yale historian Mathew Jacobson (1998) has reported,

> In racial matters above all else, the eye that sees is "a means of perception conditioned by the tradition in which its possessor has been reared." The American eye sees a certain person as black, for instance, whom Haitian or Brazilian eyes might see as white. Similarly, an earlier generation of Americans *saw* Celtic, Hebrew, Anglo-Saxon, or Mediterranean physiognomies where today we see only subtly varying shades of a mostly undifferentiated whiteness. (Jacobson, 1998, p. 10, original italics).

And let us be explicit: Anglo-Saxon and northern European groups in the United States often saw the Irish not only as a physically different but also as an inferior race (Chase, 1980; Steinberg, 1989; Takaki, 2008). This was, after all, the old tradition in which their ancestors had been reared. As one American pundit commented, the Irish had more characteristics in common with the "Minnesota savages" than with Anglo-Saxons (in Jacobson, 1998, p. 19). To be sure, in the 19th century, the "antagonism between the English and the Irish [...] was at the time a *racial* conflict between Anglo-Saxons and Celts" (Jacobson, 1998 my emphasis).

Even by the beginning of the 20th century, Protestant Anglo Americans often did not see the Irish in the United States as fully white. They saw them as European ethnics with inborn and generally undesirable characteristics of their own. Only eventually did Protestant Anglo Americans see the Irish as simply and unambiguously white. And, of course, the Irish themselves eventually adopted this racial denomination and identity (Ignatiev, 2008). Indeed, they eventually became "Caucasians" in everyone's eyes—a term that, incidentally, is at least geographically questionable, if not downright absurd; for neither the Irish nor any other European group west of the Caucasus is of Caucasian origin. The Irish do not have their origins in the Caucasus Mountains located in Eurasia, an area that encompasses cultures, languages, and ethnicities (e.g., in Azerbaijan, Armenia, Chechnya) that are removed from Ireland and from mainstream Western Europe. The fact that many people came to regard the Irish as "Caucasians" further highlights how the concepts of race, in general, and "Caucasianess," in particular, have been constructed with little attention to science, or even to basic cultural geography. And this also shows that racial nomenclatures, even if easily disputable, often become widely accepted and taken for granted nevertheless.

The Many European "Races"

Although Linnaeus had already coined the concept of *Homo europaeus,* and thus suggested the existence of a pan-European race, even the briefest glance at the 20th-century history of Europe shows that Europeans generally did not give much credit to a pan-European narrative about whiteness. Let us recall the Nazi discourse on race. They did not fight for any sort of "white" race, but for what they called the "Arian race," specifically, which in their view was different and superior to other European "races," such as the Alpine race, the Iberic, Hittite, Slav, and others.

Indeed, if we were to focus in on specific European countries, it would be easy to find *regional* racial rivalries. Let us consider Spain, for example. Some Spanish race theorists, such as 19th-century Galician medical anthropologist, Varela de Montes, emphasized the idea of a *human race* rather than races in plural (in Pereira-González, 2001). And others, such as Galician historian Ramón López de Vicuña, emphasized, like Linnaeus, the idea of a superior European race (Pereira-González, 2001). But other eminent scientists underscored the "superiority" of local and indeed *provincial races*. In March 15, 1898, Dr. Bartomeu Robert, eminent Catalonian clinician, gave a conference to inaugurate his mandate as mayor of Barcelona, entitled *La raça catalana*, The Catalonian Race. In this lecture, he set out to demonstrate the superiority of this supposed race by comparing the "cephalic index" of the Catalan cranium to that of other peninsular races. (Incidentally, the cephalic index, rather than skin color, was often seen as the key marker of race, particularly of these European "races," a marker no longer seen as valid, another indication that race is a narrative that changes overtime.) Bartomeu Robert "demonstrated" that whereas Valencians had a rather oval cranium, Asturians and Galicians had a rounder and thus more "primitive" one, which was similar to that of "primitive" North Africans. In contrast, the amazing Catalonian cranium was neither. In the scale of cephalic indexes, it occupied a sort of Goldilocks zone, which explained, in Robert's view, the greater mental acumen of the superior Catalonian race (in Ansede, 2017). In turn, Galician historian Manuel Murguía, also by the end of the 19th century, "demonstrated" the physical, mental, and moral superiority of the Galician race (which he called "Celtic Galician"). This proud race was so strong indeed that when members of other Spanish races married into it, the "fruits of that union" generally inherited Galician traits, including a good disposition for the liberal arts as well as a rather rare "gift for intelligence" (in Pereira-González, 2001, my translations).

Returning to the United States, the mainstream view was also that the new European immigrants, the Irish as well as other "darker European races," comprised a cauldron of mostly undesirable races. William Cook, an early 20th-century lawyer, for instance, provided an instructive catalogue in this regard. In his American Institutions and Their Preservation, published in 1929, Cook observes that Russians, because they are only as good as "hewers of wood and drawers of water," comprise a race that cannot enter into the American institutional system either. Jews are also a "strange race." They have "little physical courage" and will, therefore, "never really enter American life." Polish people, yet another "inferior" European race, are not capable of rising to "intellectual heights." They are not ethical. They "require a strong hand." In 1922, Kenneth Roberts, an American journalist and author of popular pulp novels, said,

> The American nation was founded and developed by the Nordic race, but if
> a few more million members of the Alpine, Mediterranean, and Semitic races
> are poured among us, the result must inevitably be a hybrid race of people as
> worthless and futile as the good-for-nothing mongrels of Central America and
> Southeastern Europe [e.g., Greeks, Bulgarians, Albanians]. (in Perea, 1996)

Around this time, the *New York Times* submitted that the Jews who had settled in the Lower East Side in New York simply "cannot be lifted up to a higher plane because they do not want to be" (in Brodkin, 1998, p. 29). The Harvard president Lawrence Lowell was "open about his opposition to Jews at Harvard" and to the "Jewish invasion" (Brodkin, 2002, p. 30). Robert Yerkes, president of the American Psychological Association in 1917, warned the public about the "feeblemindedness" of the southeastern European or "Mediterranean races" (Brodkin, 2002, p. 30). William Cook was also concerned with the increasing presence of members of these Mediterranean races in the United States. Italians, in particular, have undesirable innate characteristics that make them, precisely, Italian, as Cook argued. They are members of a "fiery" race. They are unscrupulous and "quick to take offence."

They are a "hopeless mass." Other pundits indeed urged their ghettoization. By the beginning of the 20th century, some Italians were objects of racially motivated mob lynching. (Meanwhile, many Italian pundits were extolling the virtues of the *Razza Italiana*, the supposed Italian race, which they saw as the true civilizing force in the West.)

Indeed, let us focus on Italian immigrants to the United States for a moment and turn to a court case that illustrates how this immigrant group was perceived up to the first quarter of the 20th century. In 1922, a "Negro" from Alabama, named Jim Rollins, was taken to a local court accused of the crime of miscegenation, having had sex with a consenting white woman named Edith Labue. Normally, such cases were hopeless for the defendant, especially in places like Alabama, where they frequently ended up in the lynching of the suspect, his public torturing and execution. But in this case, Rollins managed to end up in court. And, indeed, the defense deployed an argument that proved immediately effective: The woman in question, Rollins's lawyer pointed out, was Italian, a key piece of information that prompted the judge to swiftly dismiss the case. The judge reasoned that the fact that she was Sicilian "can in no sense be taken as conclusive that she was therefore a White woman" (Jacobson, 1998, pp. 4 and 62). Here is what the judge decided:

> At that time there was no evidence whatever to sustain the material allegation that Edith Labue, the codefendant, was a white woman [...] This fact was essential to a conviction in this case, and, like any other material ingredient of the offense must be proven by the evidence beyond a reasonable doubt and to a moral certainty. The mere fact that the testimony showed this woman came from Sicily can in no sense be taken as conclusive that she was therefore a white woman, or that she was not a negro or a descendant of a negro. (Rollins v. State, No. 6 Div. 927. Court of Appeals of Alabama 18 Ala. App. 354; 92 So. 35; 1922 Ala. App. January 17, 1922, Decided.)

Thus the case was "reversed and remanded."[2] A whole library of similar examples could be provided, examples that illustrate American views about the various supposedly inferior European races. Far from being isolated or peripheral, the examples provided were part and parcel of the American mainstream imagination. They illustrate the idea, postulated earlier, that even up to the first quarter of the 20th century, our narrative about whiteness ("descent from any of the original peoples of Europe") was not part of the mainstream U.S. culture. These examples illustrate that, instead, the dominant narrative simply assumed the existence of many European races—races that occupied different positions in a hierarchical order, from superior to inferior. Who decided who was superior? Generally, the members of the race in question: Germans often favored their Aryan race, Catalonians the Catalonian race, Galicians the Galician race, Italians the Italian race, and so on. (Although, as noted, some race theorists did favor the notion of a superior European race, and others the idea of a human race.)

---

2   Let us note also that this court "did not find that a Sicilian was *necessarily* nonwhite," Jacobson says (1998, my emphasis). But the point is that "its finding that a Sicilian was *inconclusively* white does speak volumes about whiteness in 1920s Alabama" (Jacobson, 1998, my emphasis). Of course, some Americans during the first quarter of the 20th century might have seen Italians as white. But those who saw Italians as white generally regarded them as inconclusively white, indeed as lesser whites who, for example, may not be protected by the law, including racial laws, such as those pertaining to miscegenation (Jacobson, 1998).

The Contemporary Narrative About Whiteness Emerges

The Founding Fathers and early legislators already used broad and vague descriptions of whiteness and "free white persons," and some early Americans did equate whiteness with Europeanness.[3] Early America, in any case, did not witness widespread racism against the "inferior" European groups mentioned in the foregoing, save the Irish and Jews, arguably. Early America was an extension of England, and the English and a few northern European groups comprised the vast majority of European immigrants so that, because the country was not the European melting pot that it eventually became, early Americans did not have a particular reason for developing racial antagonisms against other European groups. Any other groups simply went unnoticed, demographically and culturally. The kinds of racial prejudices expressed by Americans like William Cook began to clearly emerge only in the 19th century, precisely as the country began to see increasingly massive waves of European immigrants who were neither English nor northern European and who were largely Catholic and poor, when not illiterate as well.

Paradoxically, these prejudices also appeared with the newly emerging "sciences of race"; sciences that, as it often happens, were deputized by the also emerging racial prejudices and the resulting racial ideologies. Among these new sciences (discredited today), eugenics, the science of breeding the best persons and thus adding the best genes to the genetic pool, had a central place; this was a science, incidentally, that, although born in the United States, directly influenced the Nazi's ideas about "racial hygiene." Only with such sciences, as Mathew Jacobson noted, did "the language of racism proper" develop. Only then did "the language of 'genus,' 'species,' 'types,' 'poly-' and 'monogenesis,' 'craniometrics,' 'phenotypes,' and 'genotypes' frame discussions of human groups, their capacities, and their proper relationship to one another" (Jacobson, 1998, p. 32).[4] And the emerging racial language, developed by these emerging sciences, was further expanded, at the cultural and political levels, to frame the meanings and implications of these immigration processes, occurring in the late 19th and early 20th centuries.

In this context—where keen interest in racial science is coupled with keen concerns over migration of different European groups—"whiteness" emerges as not quite applicable to the new and "darker" European immigrants. As we saw, pundits often warned the public about the risks associated with the supposed congenital traits and natural defects of these new groups. Groups that were sure to increase, as some pundits warned, not only the levels of "feeblemindedness" but also rates of insanity, assaults, rapes, kidnappings, and many other social ills (Haney Lopez, 2006). It is at this point in U.S. history that the notion that there are many European "races"—as opposed to a single pan-European "white race"—more clearly and distinctly emerges within the public imagination, which begins to sort these groups into various and hierarchically ordered racial slots.

---

3   Early Americans often saw themselves as the heirs of the English and in this sense as racially Anglo-Saxons and thus different from other Europeans. Thomas Jefferson, for instance, believed that the English were "our ancestors" and the creators of the Magna Carta our "Saxon ancestors." On the other hand, he also believed that Saxons were naturally predisposed toward freedom and were different than Germans, as Germans possessed a nature actually given to relinquishing freedom (Goodman, 2012). He appears to have believed that Saxons and Germans were, we might say, different species within the genus whiteness. Note as well that Jefferson, as other contemporaries, was not particularly prejudiced against the Irish. Once he referred to them as the "wild Irish," but it would be erroneous to argue that he held the Irish in racial contempt.

4   Genus is the broader taxonomical classification that includes various species. The genus "*canis*," for example, includes, the species *Canis lupus*, gray wolves, and *Canis latrans*, coyotes. Poly- and mono-genesis refer to whether one or more races appeared originally. "Craniometrics" is the discipline of skull measuring. "Phenotypes" are the outward and visible expression of different types of genes, called "genotypes." Some genotypes may result of phenotypic expressions such as skin color in humans, for example.

The idea that generic European ancestry endows a person with a race, a white race, began to take hold, progressively at first, only by the end of the 1920s (Jacobson, 1998) and became fully accepted, and eventually simply taken for granted, only by the middle of the 20th century. At this point in history, Americans, including the descendants of the "darker Europeans," are merely born into the idea that there is a pan-European white race. This was "a time when the children and grandchildren of European immigrants to the U.S. melted into a common culture, in a common 'pot,' and eventually into a common 'White race'" (Narváez, 2012; see also Haney Lopez, 2006; Jacobson, 1998). When in 1961 John F. Kennedy was elected president of the United States, for example, no one saw him as a Celt anymore. No one saw him as a savage who is impossible to civilize, as a possessor of inborn qualities that befit the "barbarous" and "beastly" Irish race. Instead, Kennedy was merely and naturally seen as white. And in this sense, he was now seen as biologically equal to native Englanders, Italians, Jews, Russians, Poles, etc., who were now seen as white as well. And, of course, members of all these groups also began to see themselves as white, through the lenses of this new racial metric. Note also that these folks *did not see this new metric as new*, as the result of recent historical and cultural developments. They did not see their whiteness as a newly emerging cultural narrative. They simply saw it as a biological fact, as "race," as a genetic bracket—one that, as a mere aspect of nature, had always existed. At this point in history, this sort of identity, this sort of self-perception, begins to take hold of the mental habits of the new generations in a natural and automatic manner.

The Melting Pot

Whiteness, in other words, emerges at this point in time as something *encompassing* (pan-European) but also *singular* (one race) and *homogenous* (there are no inferior and superior European races, only "white people"). But let us again state the obvious: This pan-European notion of whiteness is "falsely homogenizing," as legal historian Ian Haney Lopez explained: "'White' is capitalized to indicate its reference to a specific social group," he said. "But this group is recognized to possess fluid borders and heterogeneous members [...]. 'White' does not denote a rigidly defined, congeneric grouping of indistinguishable individuals. It refers to an unstable category which gains its meaning only through social relations and that encompasses a profoundly diverse set of persons" (Haney Lopez, 2006, xxi–xxii). White is "not a monolithic or homogenous experience, either in terms of race, other social identities, space, or time. Instead, whiteness is contingent, changeable, partial, inconstant, and ultimately social" (Haney Lopez, 2006, xxi–xxii). (This is also true of the other "races": The term Asian, which includes a very broad array of peoples, from India to Japan to China and others, is falsely homogenizing; the term "black," which refers to the largest genetic repository in the world—namely, Africa—is also falsely homogenizing, etc.)

The American melting pot—the "melting" of these various European races that erases the distinctions between "inferior" and "superior" Europeans—produced a new racial ideology for our own day and age. So, prompted by these newly naturalized habits of thought, even today, we think of the "white race" as something homogenous, singular (one race), and biologically demarcated (encompassing its own genetic splinter group). This notion, which is as ideological as the older idea about the various "darker" European races, has created the new racial identities that we simply assume and take for granted today.[5]

---

5   And, of course, when this new definition of race is assimilated and taken for granted, all other Europeans, regardless of whether they are natives to Europe or natives to the United States, are, likewise, seen as white. This process had parallels beyond U.S. borders.

Another obvious fact: it is not that the "darker" European groups made a biological or genetic transition into a different, and now truly white, race. Rather, these groups merely left the old customs, traditions, names, attires, languages, and dialects behind, and thus melted into the American mainstream. African Americans, Asians, and other darker "races" could not melt, not on account of their perceived "nature"—their temper, tempestuousness, intellect, ethics, etc.—but on account of their comparatively more salient and surface physical traits. Although groups such as Poles, Irish, Italians, Alpines, and Jews were often perceived as possessing different moral *as well as different physical* characteristics—it was nevertheless easier for them to eventually melt, as these physical characteristics were not as salient. (And, of course, their supposed innate "moral" traits were mere habits of the heart, cultural artifacts that could change as these groups became assimilated into the American mainstream.) The subsequent generations melted into the mainstream as they adopted new ideas, new norms, new values, new lifestyles—a new collective memory. When this happened, the darker Mediterraneans and the lighter Alpines, the "passive" Hebrews and the "fiery" Celts, etc., emerged as *one*, as a single (white) "race." A "race" that, now seen as a human subspecies, is also seen as something eternal, as something that had always existed.

These European ethnics, in summary, experienced the following trajectory:

a. initial racialization and, in various ways and degrees, demonization;
b. progressive acculturation accompanied by acceptance into the mainstream;
c. melting; and
d. internalization of a white and pan-European racial identity.

White by Law

It is also worth noting that just as some of these new European immigrant groups, Mediterraneans, Celts, etc., became white, other immigrant groups transitioned from being officially white to being something else. Up until 1952, any immigrant had to be considered white, by law, to become an American citizen. The rationale for this law was that whiteness involved a certain inborn character, an innate capacity for self-government that other "races" lacked, and therefore only white persons could reasonably exercise the duties inherent of citizenship. For this reason, many immigrant groups, East Indians, Arabs, and others, went to court to defend their purported whiteness to attain the legal status of a citizen.

Interestingly, although some European immigrants were initially *not* seen as white in the United States, as *Rollins v. Alabama* (1922) suggests, the U.S. courts granted some non-European immigrants a white status. U.S. courts ruled, for example, that East Indians, Arabs, and Syrians were white (Haney Lopez, 2006). In 1897, the courts also determined that Mexicans were, likewise, white (Haney Lopez, 2006). These American courts initially decreed the whiteness of these non-European groups (e.g., East Indians) based on expert testimony or "scientific evidence." But in the end, the judges decided to revise their rulings based on "common knowledge" (Haney Lopez, 2006). And common knowledge now dictated that these groups were actually not white and the decisions were overturned. These examples also illustrate the idea that race, as defined by the U.S. courts in this case, is, precisely, "common knowledge": an ingrained and collectively relevant habit of thought and in this sense a folkish set of beliefs. They also suggest that neither skin color nor phenotype in themselves have a meaning beyond the meaning assigned by dominant cultural narrative (although these cultural meanings can be real *in their effects*, as we will soon see).

It is precisely because "race" is a cultural artifact that it tends to change with time and place. Bear in mind that culture is always changing. Laws, norms, values, dress codes, fashions, traditions, and language change again and again. This also happens with "race": "Irish" and "Caucasian" have become exchangeable labels, while yesteryear they were charged with opposite connotations. East Indians were non-white and then became legally Caucasians, then ethnoracially Indians, and now they are Asians according to the census. The "Negro race" was differentially defined from state to state in the United States. In Florida "Negroes" were people who had one-eighth African ancestry; in Virginia, the ratio was one-sixteenth; in Alabama, blackness was defined having any "African blood." Hence a person could change his or her race simply by moving from one state to the next. In Alabama, a person could be black regardless of his or her skin or hair color. A black person in Alabama could well be white in Virginia, according to the law. Then and today, social constructs pertaining to race involved *fluid* definitions, and context-steered self-perceptions and identities.

"Race" as Embodied Collective Memory

Importantly, let us finally add that these kinds of fluid racial ideologies affect not only the *minds* of people who hold racial identities. They also affect how we experience and express our bodies. Consider what Cornel West, one of the most important African American intellectuals today, has to say about blackness:

> White-supremacist assaults on black intelligence, ability, beauty and character required persistent black efforts to hold self-doubt, self-contempt and even self-hatred at bay. Selective appropriations, incorporation and rearticulation of European ideologies, cultures and institutions alongside an African heritage—a heritage more or less confined to linguistic innovation in rhetorical practices, stylizations of the body in forms of occupying an alien social space (hairstyles, ways of walking, standing, hand expressions, talking) and means of constituting and sustaining camaraderie and community (e.g., antiphonal, call-and-response styles, rhythmic repetition, risk-ridden syncopation in spectacular modes in musical and rhetorical expressions)—were some of the strategies employed [by African Americans]. (West, 1999, p. 129)

Though blackness, West notes, involves innovation and rearticulation, it also involves the enactment and even the literal *embodiment* of ideologies; ideologies that are expressed by ("racial") gestural patterns, bodily rhythms, and ways of occupying space, for example.

But the broader idea to keep in mind is *not* that blackness alone involves aspects of ideology that are experienced and expressed at the level of the body. Rather, this applies to "race," in general. And to further illustrate this important but difficult idea it would be useful to consider a contrasting example: Let us focus on the first colonies settled by English puritans in America.

As noted, these groups came to New England primarily to establish a new society according to the norms and rules of their religion, which they could not do in England. And indeed, they successfully established new and rapidly prospering communities; communities that generally abided by a version of Calvinism, a radical version of Protestantism propounded by French theologian John Calvin. Calvinism was a starkly proscriptive and prescriptive religious ideology, and, not surprisingly, the first laws and norms in these societies were stark and proscriptive as well. For example, these laws punished the worship of other gods with death. And their social norms, in general, regulated the very details of everyday life in a similarly rigid and micromanagerial manner, including the proper attitudes of women, proper clothing styles, emotional control, sobriety, etc. (Tocqueville, 2000). An association of concerned New Englanders emerged to regulate the proper length of hair, for example. Hair, they said, could be longish but not too long, as this was a mark of "foppishness," and it involved a sinful degree of concern with one's appearance. Alexis de Tocqueville—the legal scholar and sociologist who visited early America in 1831 from France—described these pervasive social regulations as a form of "petty, intrusive, and mild despotism" (Tocqueville, 2000), which was the very cultural air that these men and women breathed from day one.

Let us add that this religious ideology, petty and mildly despotic such as it was, was nevertheless advantageous in some ways. Again, puritans were supposed to be able to control their appetites (sexual appetites above all). They were expected to have control over their impulses; for example, the impulse to buy superfluous appurtenances, to spend too much time taking care of one's appearance, etc. They were expected be in charge of themselves and *not* to be ruled by their own instincts and passions. Hence, although mildly despotic, this ideology encouraged a sense of self-governance in citizens. This version of Calvinism also encouraged a work ethic (recall that, for Calvinists, hard work signaled that the person was marked for heaven), as well as thriftiness, and the notion that economic prosperity was a sign that the individual was guided by the hand of God. This was the religious narrative that served as an engine for the rapid economic development and expansion of these communities (Weber, 1958).

Let's go back now to our discussion on race. Cornel West implied that blackness involves an embodied collective memory: a system of meanings experienced and expressed by the body itself (through "stylizations of the body ... hairstyles, ways of walking, standing, hand expressions, talking," etc. [West, 1999, p. 129]). So too with these English settlers and their descendants. One day at a time, they internalized *and also embodied* this microregulatory but efficacious symbolic order: this set of ideas and values, of abundant prescriptions and proscriptions. Their sexuality, for example, was generally puritanical, primarily reproductive and, as much as possible, devoid of "immodest" thoughts and emotions. The gestures, the gait, the bodily rhythm of these early puritans likewise tended to express modesty. Their emotional styles were, also as prescribed, restrained, controlled, temperate. Their hairstyles similarly reflected the dominant ideas and values. And these processes whereby puritan ideologies and social rules and norms became literally embodied—also contributed to how "whiteness" was experienced, perceived, and expressed in early America. Again, although "race" involves a cultural narrative, this narrative results in certain cultural practices, in related experiences and habits, in the acquisition of certain emotional styles, as well as certain gestures, "stylizations of the body"—in a constellation of embodied practices, and related automatisms and habits.

"Race" involves, in summary, *a cultural training that can mold aspects of the mind and of the body*—a training that can thus mold certain traits in the population; traits that have historically been perceived as markers of race, as the natural or "racial" characteristics of the various ethnic groups. In the case of these English-American settlers, being white involved a strict cultural training that resulted in certain habits and in certain dispositions that became naturalized among these men and women, who regarded these "natural" characteristics as markers of their race.

Let us go back to the idea that, up until 1952, whiteness had to be a prerequisite of citizenship in the United States, because being white purportedly conferred an *innate, natural, racial* capacity for self-governance. What follows from the foregoing discussion is that any sense of self-mastery attained by these puritan citizens and their descendants—was derived neither from nature, nor from "race," nor from whiteness. It was derived primarily from a religious ideology, puritanism, which, in different ways and degrees, became naturalized, the second nature of many citizens. And yet, these *acquired* dispositions and capacities for self-government, as noted, were eventually seen as an inborn, natural, and defining characteristic of the "white race." Other "races"—for example, Italians, Irish,

Semites—had embodied very different cultural narratives. Their embodied memories reflected aspects of Catholic and Jewish doctrines and meanings. And, hence, these new European immigrants were seen, in the late 19th and early 20th centuries, as possessors of a different "nature," and were therefore discriminated against. They were heirs of different traditions, had therefore experienced a very different process of naturalization, and expressed a different embodied collective memory that came to be seen, in a stereotyped form, as an "innate" set of traits, as a mark of *their* "race": of the "fiery" Mediterranean race; of the "passive" Hebrew race, etc. Race, to insist on the main idea, is not a mere cultural narrative. It also involves an embodied collective memory, which people, even in our day and age, tend to perceive, precisely, as "race."

CHAPTER XIII

The Sociology of Domination

An Effective Mechanism of Domination

As follows from the previous chapter, ideologies perdure *particularly as they become lived and organically enmeshed within everyday life, thus functioning as a more or less automatic, unconscious, and seemingly natural aspect of social life.* As noted, fundamentalist societies, for example, not only tend to penetrate the minds of citizens but also create embodied memories that bring the traditional belief systems to life. Recall that, for example, women in these societies are expected to internalize *and to embody* the given ideas and values so that their gestures, speech patterns, clothing standards, hairstyles, etc., often reflect the traditional belief system. Such ideologies, we also noted, perdure not only because folks accept them, psychologically or cognitively, but particularly because these ideologies become incarnated in these folks, literally embodied, and thus *real*ized, expressed, constantly enacted through everyday life. Ideologies in this sense can become part and parcel of life as *lived* every day.

Ideologies pertaining to race often work in a similar manner. Aspects of these ideologies and narratives can become embodied and organically woven into the social fabric; and as such, as embodied collective memory, these ideologies help sustain and reproduce the social order. Race theorists Hazel Markus and Paula Moya (2010) have said that race is something constantly "done." Let us go back to the example of fundamentalist societies to illustrate this idea: Some women in these societies conduct themselves—act, perform, behave—according to the given standards of femininity. They, in this sense, "do" gender. Inasmuch as they do, they come to occupy their "proper" place in their society. If and when this occurs, they not only enact but also reproduce the narrative about gender, and the attendant gender hierarchy. Their gender identities, and the way they perform these identities, serve to support the given ideology and the given social system. This is similar to race: People often "do" race. People often half consciously enact an inherited narrative associated with race, to their advantage or disadvantage, and thus recreate and reproduce the inherited social arrangement. Racial identities, in this sense, have helped maintain and reproduce not only the given racial narrative or ideology but also the given social system. Let us go back to the colonial system, which provides very stark but easy to understand examples pertaining to these ideas.

The colonial order in the United States, as it depended on the enslavement of people, needed slaves who would not rebel, who would not disturb the given economic system. Their submission was accomplished, first, by sheer terror: The punishments that insubordinate slaves had to suffer were breathtakingly brutal. But much more cunningly and insidiously, this system exacted submission by instilling "proper Negro" identities, particularly in members of the second, third, and subsequent generations of slaves. Of course, many of these men and women rebelled, and many did so in a heroic and exemplary manner, as we will see soon. But others—who breathed only a polluted racist atmosphere from birth—adopted the "proper" identities, which Malcom X associated particularly with house servants. These men and women could not but see their dehumanizing condition as *normal*. And these normalized racial identities helped sustain the colonial order not only because they allowed the masters to easily exact resources from these slaves but also because these identities seemed to confirm the prevailing racist ideology. This ideology said that slaves' proper and normal station in life was to serve a master. The very identities of these slaves, who saw their condition as normal, served to legitimize this ideology: In the eyes of the average person, these slaves seemed to embody servitude, seemed to possess a nature that bespoke the truthfulness of this mendacious and cruel ideology.

For these reasons, racial ideology can be an effective mechanism of social control. But these ideologies also hold the potential for resistance and, therefore, for hope, renewal, and creativity. If "race" is done, as Marcus and Moya say, it is also often undone. Although people often live, articulate, and go about the world "quoting" racial ideologies, people also can, and do, rearticulate these ideologies, reenact them, and enact them anew. When this happens, people extrude this kind of ideology from the fabric of everyday life. As race theorist Harry Elam has argued, social actors often "[reconfigure] established gestures, behaviors, linguistic patterns, cultural attitudes, and social expectations associated with race" (2010). Indeed, as Cornel West also noted, race can be, and has historically been, part of "a very rich culture of resistance" (West, 1999). Yet, as we will presently discuss, this path is not without pitfalls and barriers.

Internalized Barriers

When a society broadcasts the idea that a particular group has *natural*, genetic, and, therefore, *unchangeable* deficits, it thereby makes life difficult for the group in question. Groups that are seen as "inferior," for instance, the Dalit (or "untouchables") in India, typically become excluded from normal opportunities, or legally deprived of them, or exploited, or enslaved, or exterminated. On the other hand, why would such a society "waste" resources on people whose lower social and economic status are not seen as resulting from limited access to opportunities but from their inferior and incorrigible traits? Racial ideologies, to state the obvious, create external obstacles for targeted groups.

But less obviously, these ideologies can also instill *internal* obstacles in targeted individuals: self-negating beliefs, attitudes, and behaviors.

We saw that dogmas and errors are often accepted as truths. Let us add that these dogmas and errors sometimes become self-fulfilled prophecies and that, in this sense, are often regarded as *objectively* true. Recall Jane Elliot, who divided her classroom in groups of blue- and brown-eyed children and recall that when the kids believed that brown-eyed children were superior, the brown-eyed kids outperformed their blue-eyed peers. It is not true, of course, that brown-eyed children are superior. But this idea, when accepted as true, became self-fulfilled and, in this sense, seemed to be objectively true to these kids. It is not true either that people with brown eyes perform at a low level, but "brownies," nevertheless, were actually performing at a lower level when placed in the inferior condition. Remember, more generally, our discussion on labeling and, particularly, the Golem and Pygmalion effects, and the idea that negative or positive labels are sometimes enacted by those labeled. Recall also that negative or positive labels elicited inferior or superior performance, even from rats whose handlers were tricked into believing that their rats were bred for either inferior or superior performance. We saw that indeed similar results were obtained from elementary schoolchildren who were labeled "academic bloomers," which tacitly labeled their peers nonbloomers. Recall, finally, that "bloomers," in only a few months of being thus labeled, gained an astounding 10–15 IQ points more than their peers, even though at baseline, bloomers and nonbloomers were no different in terms of academic potential.

These ideas can provide an important perspective pertaining to the history of racial ideologies. One of the most tragic consequences of these ideologies is that *sometimes,* rather than generating a rich culture of resistance, as West has correctly noted, they generate Golem and Pygmalion effects. And, to the extent to which they do, these ideologies become self-fulfilled prophecies so that as this process unfolds, more people regard them as "objectively" true.

Racial Ideologies as Tools of Domination

Consider the following fragments from U.S. history. The generations before the "Black Is Beautiful" movement of the 1960s had whiteness as the single standard of beauty. White features were typically seen as "objectively" more beautiful, an idea reinforced by the majority of social institutions, from school textbooks, to movies, to billboards, to pulp fiction, to TV, to the toy industry, to the beauty industry. Indeed, these sometimes emphasized the supposed ugliness of black features so that black children, for example, often preferred dolls with white features, and they indeed ascribed more positive characteristics to them. One of such experiments, conducted in 1939, showed that 59% of the black children recruited to participate in the study thought that black dolls simply "looked bad" (Clark & Clark 1939). Similarly, many black men and women, internalizing the purportedly objective standards of beauty, sought to change key physical characteristics at least up to the 1960s (though the argument could be made that such things as skin whiteners are lucrative industries even today). This included hair color, hair type, and skin tone, in a myopic attempt to achieve a measure of beauty. (And sometimes because "whitening" conferred practical advantages socially and economically.) Indeed, the first black millionaire was reportedly Madame C. J. Walker, whose cosmetics company manufactured these sorts of whitening products. To be sure, emblematic supporters of the Black Is Beautiful movement had to overcome, first and foremost, their own internalized, self-directed racism before fighting against it. Malcolm X himself "was among the millions of Negroes," as he says, "who were insane enough to feel that it was some kind of status symbol to be light-complexioned—that one was fortunate to be born thus" (1987, p. 3).

Let us consider one of the quintessentially American novels titled *The Bluest Eye*, by Nobel Laureate in literature Toni Morrison (1997). The narrative is set against the backdrop of the Great Depression, the period that saw the collapse of the American economy, particularly during the 1930s, when about 60% of Americans plunged into poverty. The novel revolves around Pecola, a young black girl who develops a progressive obsession with having blue eyes, a tenacious idea that eventually evolves into madness. Having blue eyes, little Pecola feels, would alleviate some of her daily miseries, almost magically. And it would also make her pretty, the increasingly obsessive wish of a girl who had been told throughout her life that, on account of her darker features, she was ugly, even embarrassingly so. About Pecola's family, the narrator said,

> You looked at them and wondered why they were so ugly. Then you realized that it came from
> *conviction, their conviction.* It was as though some mysterious, all-knowing master had given each

one a cloak of ugliness to wear, and they had each accepted it without question. The master had said, "You are ugly people." They had looked about themselves and saw nothing to contradict the statement; saw, in fact, support for it leaning at them from every billboard, every movie, every glance. "Yes," they had said. "You are right." And they took the ugliness in their hands, threw it as a mantle over them, and went about the world with it. (1997, p. 39, my italics)

Black feminist bell hooks (spelled without capitals) has noted that, historically, for some black families, it has not been the gender of the newborn that has mattered most but rather the newborn's (lighter) skin tone (1996). She, in fact, describes a sort of caste system within some Black communities, where lighter skinned African Americans sometimes discriminated against their darker skin peers (hooks, 1996). Thus, in the 1950s, so-called "paper bag parties," for example, were social events where darker skinned individuals were not admitted, as admission was limited to those with "paper bag" color. Indeed, as hooks has noted, it was not uncommon then for African Americans to prefer lighter skinned peers for spouses, friends, and even coworkers, thus enacting, reproducing, and, indeed, reinforcing the dominant racial ideology and the official Jim Crow segregation against African Americans in general.

Racist ideologies can break the psychological defenses of targeted individuals, install self-defeating beliefs, judgments, and attitudes; and thus become self-fulfilled. Naturally, there are many exceptions, often heroic cases, from Rigoberta Menchú, to Frederick Douglass, to Rosa Parks, to the myriad anonymous resisters in all epochs and places. But as we will presently see, internalized obstacles are also real. Indeed, they are sometimes the most insidious and the hardest to overcome. Importantly, beyond race, this also applies to other groups that on account of gender, sexual identity, caste, or class, for example, are negatively labeled by a society.

Gender Ideologies as Tools of Domination

Let us extend this idea by turning to gender ideologies, going back in time again, also to the 1950s. Many American women during this time period thought that their gender identity—indeed, femininity itself—was incompatible with feelings of power (Friedan, 2001). Such feelings were purportedly "unfeminine." And so many women, particularly white middle-class women, saw their gender, and thus their very being, as incompatible with, for example, higher level professions, medicine, law, politics, business, etc. These sorts of careers—which require professionals who feel at home in power, who can take charge, who can tell others what to do—were not only deemed "masculine" but also unfeminine. Of course, not all women internalized this idea, and there were many career women during this this time period, but on trend, women's lives centered on chores, husbands, and children. Such a life, according to the dominant common sense, was supposedly encoded in a woman's nature; as nature itself had designed women to nurture so that women were professedly designed to remain in the domestic sphere, nurturing the family, taking care of the meals, the laundry, the garden, the pets, the dishes. This was seen as the natural, logical way of fulfilling one's own biological fate. That was the counsel that peers, family members, churches, schools, movies and TV shows, and commercial advertisements often gave to the average young girl and woman.

Hence many women—who had grown up breathing only this sort of ideological atmosphere—made appropriately "feminine" life choices that restricted their own intellectual, economic, and political potential. Absorbing the ideas provided by the feminine mystique, many women gender-typed themselves and actively and desirously embraced "feminine" lifestyles, "feminine" attitudes—a "feminine" and, not surprisingly, largely disadvantageous worldview. They made choices that normalized, legitimized, and reproduced a cultural narrative designed to undermine them. This ideology, for example, said that, on account of their gender, women are weak of character (and therefore deserve masculine protection). Women who internalized and embodied this idea, and thus made life choices that portrayed them as weak of character, thereby confirmed the purported truthfulness of the ideology. They rendered it legitimate. And, indeed, they thus served as channels whereby these ideas and judgments spread and reproduced within society.

The Concept of Hegemony

As with race, gender ideologies can also become *hegemonic*; "hegemony" being a social process whereby dominated or oppressed groups adopt the ideas and judgments of the dominant groups, even if these are the very ideas and judgments that put the dominated groups at a disadvantage. For example, during the 1950s, women typically adopted the worldviews of men. The Black Is Beautiful movement was battling hegemonic notions about beauty. The story of Pecola poignantly illustrates the idea that persons targeted by racial ideologies may come to see their supposed ugliness, or to feel that their own potential is, as a matter of fact, limited.

A concept that we owe to the Italian Marxist sociologist Antonio Gramsci, hegemony involves collectively relevant narratives, a socio-logic that saturates everyday life to the point that these narratives are no longer seen as the narratives of a particular culture but as mere common sense. This is a socio-logic that thus delimits the very scope of common sense. In the examples provided earlier, it was simply "commonsensical" for many women to think of themselves as not good for academia, or for business, or for politics, or for anything else outside the domestic sphere. Pecola cannot see that her culture, rather than she herself, is the one with the ugly (racist) features. Little Pecola sees herself through the eyes of a racist ideology that distorts her perspective. And the general idea is that hegemony distorts your own private perspective; that it preemptively eliminates thoughts that are truly your own; that it makes you see the world and yourself through the dogmatic perspective of a cultural narrative. To borrow an image from Ralph Waldo Emerson, hegemony suppresses "your private heart," your most authentic form of self-expression, which, for Emerson, was the necessary source of truth and creativity.

And for this reason, as with race, hegemonic gender ideologies can also produce strong Golem effects. For if a society as a whole says that women are not fit for such professions as medicine, this society is likely to produce young girls who, seeing themselves from this perspective, do not dream of becoming doctors and who, therefore, do not develop their potential in this particular area. In the 1950s, the period addressed by the second wave of feminism, over a quarter of parents interviewed by Gallup surveyors said that they would recommend the career of medicine to a young man, and only *2%* said that they would recommend it to a young woman (Boulis & Jacobs, 2008). In 1965, the percentage of women who graduated from a medical school was only 6.9% (of all medical school graduates) so that 93.1% of recently graduated doctors were males.[1]

Note, as well, that if a society says that members of a particular "race" are not very good at something, like writing, or music, or science, it may likewise produce kids, in this particular "racial" group, who will not dream of becoming writers, musicians, physicists, doctors, and professors, regardless of

---

[1] In contrast, today (when the second wave of feminism has largely defeated this way of thinking), 47.8% of recently graduated doctors are female and *more* parents were willing to advise the career of medicine to a young *female* than to a young male (Boulis & Jacobs, 2008). Since the 1950s, the statistical "curve" of women in medicine has increasingly gone up, from about 7% of women doctors in the 1950s to 17% in the 1990, to 22% in the 2000.

their actual potential. And these kids, neither developing the interest nor the skill in this area, are also more likely to become adults who are not well suited for these sorts of careers. Bear in mind that identity is not only about how one sees oneself but also about how one *judges* one's own abilities and deficits. Identities often encourage people to think that there are things they can and *cannot* do, thus either fostering or inhibiting their potential. When they inhibit the potential of a group, ideologized identities can become "weapons of mass destruction," as media researcher Shuddhabrata Sengupta has argued (Grzanka, 2014, p. 86).

Self-Monitoring, Self-Consciousness

Let us uncover another possible internal obstacle associated with racial ideology. Jean-Paul Sartre, one of the most important French philosophers of the 20th century, suggested that stereotypes against Jews often had the effect of instilling a special kind of anxiety in some of them (Sartre, 1948). This was a social anxiety related to avoiding "acting like a Jew." It was the fear of acting in a manner that would confirm the stereotype. Sartre says that some Jewish people were thus "poisoned by the stereotype others had of them." They acted as though they were under constant observation, as though they were not free to act according to simple, spontaneous volition, precisely because their actions were anteceded by the question, "Am I acting like a Jew?"

Racial stereotypes—racial ideologies in general—can also instill this particular kind of self-consciousness, the sense of constantly seeing oneself in the act of acting, in the act of speaking, in the act of interacting with others. As W.E.B Du Bois noted in the foregoing, "race" sometimes means seeing oneself through the eyes of others. Of course, self-monitoring and self-consciousness can be good, because if you cannot monitor yourself, you cannot improve, and, indeed, the capacity for self-monitoring is the prerequisite of moral action (and it is what makes us human: No animal has this capacity, no animal can judge itself as we do). But the sort of self-monitoring that Sartre is describing does not have self-improvement as its aim. It aims to portray the self as "normal," and it therefore assumes that the self will likely be seen as abnormal. This recurrent form of *status anxiety* is thus similar to anxieties rooted in social stigma—for example, stigma attached to homosexuality, which may also elicit the need to "pass," to seem "normal." Indeed, it is similar to anxieties attached to such stigmatized conditions as having a visible blemish or a conspicuous psychological peculiarity, which may also result in self-monitoring patterns and recurring social anxieties.

Let us note that stigmatization of "racial" features has often been similar to the stigmatization of disability, even of "monstrosity." Let's go back to Pecola. She is constantly gripped, sometimes devastated, by such status anxieties. She is a constant source of shame even to her family, and she herself is constantly spellbound by self-judging shame. Her story illustrates the power that racial stigma can have upon a person, and the kinds of self-judgments it can produce. And importantly, note also that her shame is unlike other forms of shame. It is viscerally real and yet it is also inexplicable, as she cannot pinpoint its origin, the broader social, historical reality that is its source. She feels ashamed even though she has not done anything wrong. And thus this negative emotion seems to have no origin; it simply and mysteriously ebbs as she goes about the world. As she cannot trace it, she cannot process her shame, or contradict it, or resolve it. This emotion is thus outside her control. It, instead, controls her. Indeed, as the novel goes on, it will progressively obsess her and steer her toward the mental illness that inexorably awaits her in the future.

Self-consciousness derived from racial ideologies (or other stereotyped narratives about our group) is not the kind of self-reflective attitude that humanizes us. It is a way of thinking and living that can be dehumanizing. In extreme cases, this sort of self-consciousness can be "dirtying," to use a term from another one of Toni Morrison's novels, *Beloved* (1987). One of the main characters in this novel, Sethe, a runaway slave, fears that "anybody white could take your whole self for anything that came to mind. Not just work, kill, or maim you, but dirty you. Dirty you so bad you couldn't like yourself anymore. Dirty you so bad you forgot who you were and couldn't think it up" (Morrison, 1987, p. 293). Such a form of self-consciousness involves an ego injury deep to the point of eventually resulting in the ego injuring itself. This is why the Black Is Beautiful movement regarded self-love as "a radical political agenda," as bell hooks says (1996, p. 122), an issue that was "central to black liberation struggle" (hooks, 1996, p. 123), a central aspect of the process of mental decolonization.

Invisibility

Relatedly, racial ideologies can create another kind of psychological deficit, not the sense of being under constant observation but rather the sense of being invisible. Pecola's case is also illustrative of this. The entire world—TV ads, billboards, peers—return her gaze in a way that underscores her purported ugliness. But precisely because she is "ugly" in the eyes of this society, she is also invisible: This collective eye cannot see her as she actually is: a normal child. Her normality is filtered out and hidden by this ideology. Her truest self thus becomes invisible, even to herself. Let us turn to W.E.B Du Bois again: "the Negro," he said, "is born with a veil." He is not seen for what he is but through the veil of the stereotype, through the filter of a racial ideology (2011). Indeed, anyone whose person is anteceded by a stereotype about his or her race, gender, sexuality, nationality, caste, class, etc., is invisible in this sense, not because he or she is a "spook like those who hunted Edgar Allan Poe," as American novelist Ralph Ellison said. Instead, "I am invisible, understand, simply because people refuse to see me [...] When they approach me they see only my surroundings, themselves, or figments of their imagination—indeed, everything except me" (1980, p. 3). Cornel West was once trying to hail a cab in New York City to go to a photo shoot for one of his books. Ten empty cabs passed by and not one stopped for him. Cabbies presumably saw a random black male, with all the ideological implication that this image can have. Thus the Princeton professor, the world-renowned intellectual—the true Cornel West—became invisible.

This sort of veil, this cloak of invisibility, as Du Bois said, "yields no true self-consciousness" either, because it "only lets him see himself through the revelation of the other world" (2011). Again, there are exceptions, of course. West, for instance, is able to assess his potential correctly and thus see his true self, as one may safely guess. But this "other world," the world that stereotypes the person, constantly nudges the targeted person to feel that, in the eyes of others, he or she is a blemished being. And this social insistence, if constantly reinforced, can break ego defenses and instill a similarly negative self-perception in the person so that the person's truest self may become invisible *to him- or herself*. Again, Du Bois also described the sense of always "measuring one's soul by the tape of a world that looks on in amused contempt and pity" (2011). Pecola, in this sense, is an example not only of false self-perception but also of false self-consciousness.

The perspective of gender applies here as well. Friedan said, "The feminine mystique permits, even encourages, women to ignore the question of their identity [and so] it makes [women] unable to *see* themselves" (2001, p. 72, my italics). A young woman is watching TV, let us say, and there it is, the latest commercial depicting another skinny model, far thinner than the norm. If this woman who is watching TV then feels that her normal body is below a standard, her body has thus become invisible to herself. If this woman, to consider an extreme circumstance, also gets the idea that women in general must cultivate and care for their bodies, above all else, and that, therefore, the mind of a woman is of secondary value, she might also become blind to her own intellectual potential. True self-consciousness, in contrast, involves seeing oneself without such cultural filters, with one's own eyes, not through the eyes of others, not through the eyes of a narrative about one's race, or gender, or any other such thing.

Consider anorexia nervosa. Although it can be primarily a neurological or neuropsychological disorder—entirely unrelated to either culture or ideology—anorexia is sometimes "sociogenic," a problem rooted, at least in part, in culture. If sociogenic, anorexia often tells the story of women who, like Pecola, cannot see their true selves. Anorexics are thin, but they typically cannot see themselves as thin, sometimes literally so. Clinicians who ask these patients to guess the diameter of their arms, for example, typically find that these patients overestimate this diameter, which suggests, precisely, that they can literally not see the emaciated proportions of their arms. Hence, sometimes anorexia involves the inability to see oneself except through the eyes of ideology, of a certain narrative about femininity that says that a normal body is abnormal—a narrative that more or less equates feminine beauty with weakness, weakness that is accentuated and exaggerated in the emaciated body of the anorexic.

Similarly with "bigorexia," which is a pathological striving, associated with men, to become bigger and more and more muscular. If anorexia is sometimes a pathological version of losing weight (which otherwise can be healthy and desirable), bigorexia can be a pathological version of bulking up (which otherwise can be healthy and desirable as well). Much as anorexia, bigorexia also results in a range of possible health problems, particularly associated with abuse of anabolic steroids and other "health supplements."[2] Bigorexia is also a disease that passes itself off as an aspiration, as a value. Like anorexia, bigorexia also often tells the story of individuals who sacrifice their sense of self at the altar of ideology—an ideology that, in this case, says that masculinity grows not in proportion to one's sense of responsibility, of honor, etc., but in proportion to one's muscles (e.g., Fussell, 1991). Like anorexia, bigorexia also bespeaks an inability to see oneself except through the lens of ideology.

The Cunning of Ideology

It goes without saying that many people rise above racial or gender ideologies. Even the most patriarchal societies have produced women who have left profound marks in history. And even the most dehumanizing racist societies have also produced men and women who manage to reach the upper stages of the human condition, eventually serving as civilizing heroes who help democratize and humanize their own societies. Few epochs have been more sexist than the European Middle Ages. Yet Joan of Arc, for example, was a (15th-century) illiterate teenager who managed to convince the uncrowned king, Charles VII, that she had been appointed by God to lead the French troops against the English invaders, and, having not an inkling of military strategy, she led very successfully military campaigns, driving the enemy away from key posts. (Her end, however, was tragic: Betrayed by her country and church, she was condemned, under the charge of

2   These health deficits might include thyroid problems, kidney malfunction, liver-related problems including hepatitis, possible gallstones, increased possibility of cancer, isolation, diminished social bonds, nervous anger, premature baldness, bouts of diarrhea, acute acne, possible chronic rectal bleeding sometimes necessitating the wearing of diapers, lower sperm count, increased body hair, "impoverishment of the span and intensity of relations with the other gender" (Fussell, 1991, p. 167), "crater-like trenches of scar tissue [which competitive bodybuilders] dig in their behinds through repeated injections, which can create knots the size of a pomegranate that have to be removed by surgery every so often" (Fussell, 1991, p. 167).

heresy, to be burned alive. She was 19 years of age. Centuries later, she was canonized, in 1920, and became one the patron saints of France and one of the most revered military leaders in the world.)[3]

Similarly, with regards to race, it would be difficult to find a society that has produced a more deeply oppressive system of slavery than the American South. Yet Frederick Douglass, for example, was an illiterate slave who rose to become a key advocate for abolitionism, becoming the adviser of none other than Abraham Lincoln, who referred to him as "my friend." Douglass's autobiography indeed reads like a Tolstoy-grade novel about a young man trapped from birth in a venomous and well-greased system designed to dehumanize him so as to extract free labor from him; a man who, learning to read and write on his own, eventually escapes and, initially marooned in the most absolute isolation, nevertheless conceives an effective plan to erode and eventually abolish this seemingly invincible social machinery; a man who thus helps redeem the very country that had tried to destroy him. More recently, Rigoberta Menchú also epitomizes such epic and strategically effective struggle against a most ingrained and viciously racist system. Menchú's life also bespeaks a struggle against overwhelming odds, not only against triumph but against sheer survival. Much as Douglass, she also grew up in a country, Guatemala, that was a chamber of racist horrors for members of her "race," Indians who had for centuries been subjected to systematic humiliation, exploitation, and ethnic cleansing. Yet Menchú, who initially operated in absolute isolation, as well, managed to eventually become the symbol of indigenous resistance, winning the Nobel Peace Prize in 1992 "in recognition of her work for social justice and ethno-cultural reconciliation based on respect for the rights of indigenous peoples," the Nobel Committee noted. In the end, her testimony also helped reform this foul system, bringing key members of the Guatemalan military to trial—including two former presidents—and exposing them as the murderers that they were. Much as Douglass's, her work also helped redeem the very country that had tried to destroy her.

Yet it usually takes a great deal of effort to overcome not only the external but also, particularly, the internal obstacles that ideologies sometimes install within the very spirit of targeted individuals. Racial and gender ideologies—ideologies in general—are cunning. They are often good at constructing the self-defeating identities that they purport to explain. The ideologies of gender have succeeded at exacting legitimacy from women, the very persons who need to discredit them. Inasmuch as targeted persons internalize the ideology and thus perform at the level expected by it, such ideologies "verify" themselves, as argued, so that the ideological beliefs and judgments become "truer" and therefore more effective, more seductive, more belittling, and thus truer still. Because ingrained ideologies are often good at becoming self-fulfilled prophecies, they are also good at generating their own fuel, the energy that allows them to grow. For these reasons, ideologies have been, historically, very powerful tools for oppressing some groups, for limiting their life options. And thus ideologies have also been, historically, very important areas of struggle among social forces: for example, feminists versus defenders of traditional femininity, abolitionist versus defenders of slavery, civil right activists versus defenders of the traditional order of things. Indeed, history has often been a struggle between ideologues (defenders of ideologies) and *awareness specialists*—namely, people who strive to show the ideological nature of certain beliefs, laws, and "commonsensical" ideas.

---

3   Or consider Eleanor of Aquitaine (born circa 1122 and died in 1204). She was one of the wealthiest, most powerful, and most enlightened European rulers during the High Middle Ages, a time when women were generally despised as lesser beings. Hildegard von Bingen (1098–1179) was one of the most important German composers, a philosopher, a polymath, and a nun who also rose to prominence during a similarly misogynistic era.

Ideology Versus Awareness Specialists

Second wave feminists, Friedan in particular, strove to show that the ideology of gender was precisely that, an ideology, a mere belief system. Likewise, the Black Is Beautiful movement also strove to expose racial ideology *as* ideology. These movements did not aim to emancipate their publics politically, as women and racial minorities had already obtained all legal rights. (The first wave of feminism, which began to operate in the mid-19th century, had already secured those rights for women, and African Americans obtained all civil rights in 1964, when the country became desegregated.) The main goal of these movements was to emancipate the *ideas, the imagination, the judgments, the affects, and the emotions of their publics*. These were the main fields of battle for these movements.

Feminists tried to help women see that the "femininity" promoted by the hegemonic cultural narrative (the feminine mystique), rather than being a supreme value, was an effective way of devaluing women. Feminists showed that being "feminine," as defined by the expectations of the time, was not only about being pretty, dainty, "intuitive," delicate, etc., but also about being financially dependent, less educated, and poorer. They showed that "femininity" often meant having the worse jobs—jobs that required less responsibility and more supervision, jobs that, therefore, paid less, that were less interesting, and were less likely to lead to a career. They showed that femininity also meant having less personal time, that it meant being less prepared for life and having less control over your own fate. The mystique said that ascribing to the given rules of femininity would give women a sense of self-realization. The second wave showed that this version of femininity was actually associated with mental health problems, such as depression, which were generational in scope.[4] The feminine mystique also said that a feminine attitude would not only help you find fulfillment but that it would help you fulfill the American dream. This ideology said that this dream was about being a modern housewife reigning over a good house full of modern appurtenances, taking care of a good husband and wonderful children, and all of what that implies: taking care of the cooking, the laundry, etc. The second wave, in turn, noted that this sort of femininity was anti-American, as the American tradition had actually pledged that Americans *would have a high degree of control over their lives and fate*. Recall that self-government was the professed mark of the American character. In contrast, the femininity advocated by the mystique discouraged women from living according to American values, such as self-government and self-reliance. This ideology also failed to uphold other American values, such as freedom and equality, as women were not really free to choose the jobs, careers, or lives they wanted, nor were they equal with respect to men.

The second wave showed, in summary, that femininity was not the ideal it was purported to be, particularly for women who—except for being tethered to the given ideas about their gender—had the potential to contribute effectively to their families and country in areas other than the domestic sphere as academics, politicians, scientists, doctors, businesswomen, etc.

The second wave and the Black Is Beautiful movements also sought to examine how societies come to produce certain ideas that, even if erroneous, become "commonsensical"—for example, the idea that

---

4   Indeed, these problems were widely acknowledged by the medical milieu (doctors had ready-made diagnoses for women: "housewife fatigue," "housewife syndrome," "housewife blight," etc. According to Miriam Joseph and Julian Durlacher, writers who have documented the lore and history of drugs consumed in the United States, 3.5 *billion* tablets of speed were manufactured in 1958 alone. Of course, these tablets were not prescribed exclusively to housewives, but the speed industry saw housewives as a key segment of this vast market, nonetheless. This staggering number suggests not only that this was a generation of women who were "ironing at the speed of light," as Joseph and Durlacher say, but also an unfulfilled generation, the bearers of an extra mental health burden. In the '60s, Friedan also reports, this problem had already "burst like a boil through the image of the happy American housewife" (Joseph & Durlacher, 2000).

women should stay away from public affairs. Ideas that, feminists also showed, push social groups or generations in a certain historical direction (for example, women in the 1950s were encouraged to go in the direction of the domestic sphere and away from the public sphere, away from business, politics, academia, science, etc.). And, importantly, these movements also sought to show that such inherited historical pathways could be altered, simply by altering the dominant "common sense." People involved in these movements thought that by creating new ideas, values, and experiences, they would thus create, as well, new futures for these groups. Both movements succeeded in both accounts. They transformed the dominant common sense about race and gender, and they thus succeeded in opening up new futures for racial minorities and women.

The success of feminists, in particular, has been breathtaking. Women in the United States and around the world began to see femininity, and their own feminine identities and natures, differently. So much so that, today, you don't have to be a feminist, or even know about feminism, to recognize the simple fact that average women lead very different lives than their mothers or grandmothers in the 1950s. And it is also easy to see that women today (and men as well) very seldom believe that femininity is naturally incompatible with such things as careers, high levels of responsibility, science, politics, etc. In fact, as discussed in previous chapters, today's generation of college-going women are outcompeting their male peers in almost every measure of success appropriate for their age, which simply could not have been possible without the sort of *ideology critique* launched, initially, by the second wave.[5]

Indeed, the lesson that this movement gave us is that when and if effective, ideology critiques can change not only the lives of individuals but also the course of history itself, the given order of things.

The job of this movement, in summary, was to help women see that "femininity" was not something inevitable, God-given, and thus timeless but a *created reality* that could be created anew. In turn, the job of the average woman was to see that gender is not something that one is simply born with, but something largely learned and acquired—and something that could also be achieved or accomplished. The task of the average woman was to understand that gender is a social convention that becomes alive in women and men, for better or for worse. (Sex, in contrast to gender, is what we are born with.) Simone de Beauvoir (2011), another iconic figure of the second wave, said, "One is not born, but rather becomes a woman." This is what many women eventually came to understand fully, and this insight changed not only their particular biographies but also, one person at a time, the world itself.

Obstacles Against Awareness

Yet let us note that such a task—decolonizing women's imaginations and affects—was not easy. It was, in fact, difficult, because many women had deeply internalized the ideology of the mystique and had therefore become their own their own censors, judging their own actions according to the given (and limiting) narrative.

Here is an illustrative example: Linda Lovelace was an icon in the pornography industry in the 1970s (although she eventually became a critic of this industry and an advocate for the second wave of feminism). In her autobiography (Lovelace, 2006), she reported that her husband, who was also her pimp, had threatened to kill her and her family if she failed to do his bidding. Imagine the scene

---

5   And let us add that this movement failed to do a proper analysis of non-white, non-middle-class, nonheterosexual women, whose particular circumstances were addressed by the third wave, which emerged in the early 1990s with its own agenda and its own kind of ideology critique.

when she talks about this to her mother, pleading for help. Frazzled, Linda told her mother, "Chuck has beaten me bloody":

> He has held a gun to my head and made me do awful things. He has forced me to have sex with women and other men. And now he is talking about making me have sex with animals. He has made me pose for dirty pictures and he is turning me into a prostitute. He is always threatening to kill me. He has even threatened to kill you and Daddy" (Lovelace, 2006, p. 86).

Her mother's answer? "But, Linda, he's your husband" (Lovelace, 2006, p. 86). Linda should just get over these "lover's quarrels" and, as a proper wife, show obedience to her husband. Lovelace's mother only knew, from day one, that kind of gender ideology, and she had therefore become blind to the reality of her daughter's problems and deaf to her words. Linda replied, "Mother, you are not hearing me. You are not hearing a word that I am saying."

For second-wave feminists, it was sometimes difficult to help women think outside this kind of ideological box, because some of them could not hear, either, what these activists were actually saying. Some of these reluctant women, confusing the dominant *culture* of femininity with the *nature of women,* regarded feminism as unnatural (likewise with many men). And they thus felt threatened *not* by the ideology of femininity, *not* by the mystique, but by the prospect of thinking outside this rigid ideological box.[6]

Total Domination

Let us now define one of the most important concepts in the sociology of domination, *symbolic violence,* which refers to the most effective form of oppression and social control (cf. Bourdieu, 1987, 1988).

This kind of violence, let us first say, is not exerted through force or through overt coercion, and in this sense, it does not seem to be violent to the victims themselves. Instead, both victims and oppressors see this sort of violence as not only normal, natural, and "commonsensical" but sometimes as honorable, and even as highly desirable. Linda Lovelace's mother, for example, is willing to defend a man who is threatening to kill her daughter, her husband, and herself—a man who has put a gun to her daughter's head and who plans to force Lynda to have sex with men, women, and animals just so he can make an extra dollar. This mother is clearly oppressed. But in defending this man and going against her daughter's pleading, she is not being morally blind and deaf, not in her own eyes. On the contrary, she thinks that she is acting out of decency. Linda's mother sees herself as defending moral principles and social institutions, such as the family, and family values, such as family cohesion and obedience. She is, for this reason, the perfect victim of a literally unspeakable form violence—unspeakable, indeed, because she cannot voice or articulate the violence that oppresses her *as violence.* She can only articulate it or voice it as something normal. This form of violence—exerted against her, her daughter, and women in general—is, for her, an aspect of a desirable order of things. Symbolic violence, to recapitulate,

---

6   Men also often had trouble understanding that "femininity" was an ideological construct, and they also earnestly felt that in attacking feminism they were defending a *natural,* not a cultural, order. It is not that these men simply enjoyed the privileges of their higher social status with respect to women and thus rejected feminism out of calculated and cynical convenience. Rather, many men also often became locked within ideology, taken by its hypnotic power, and thus genuinely saw their own superior status, and the inferior social status of women, as a mere result of a natural order.

a.   outsources policing and enforcing tasks to its own victims (e.g., Linda's mother); and

b.   outsources the task or reproducing the violence to those who ought to struggle to stop it. For example, Linda's mother sees that her job is, indeed, to "teach" Linda how to be a proper, "feminine" creature, which, in this context, means to be defenseless and subservient, a willing victim, willingly blind to the ideological reasons that justify her own mistreatment.

Let us quote Pierre Bourdieu, the sociologist who coined the term "symbolic violence." This form of oppression, Bourdieu wrote, "is hardly noticed, almost invisible for the victims on whom it is perpetrated; a violence which is exercised principally via [...] symbolic channels of [collective] communication and knowledge [and], in the final analysis, of feelings" (1988). Let me add that this is a *transformative* and, in a strict sense, *creative* form of violence, because, to meet its own ends, it transforms and creates the mental and emotional registers of its victims. It transforms and creates the ideas, values, and emotions of its victims so as to meet its own aims—namely, the domination and the submission of the victim in question. Hence, whereas domination by force or overt coercion can be fought against, this kind of total domination, which issues from symbolic violence, is very difficult to fight, precisely because it is seen as normal or even as desirable by the victims themselves.

Domination by Force

Let us consider a couple of examples pertaining to some of the most brutal forms of coercion to illustrate how even the most violent coercion is often, all things considered, less effectively coercive if compared to symbolic violence.

Imagine the following scenario: You live in the 19th century; you are a Ghanaian mother; you have spent the day tending your farm, and then you and your family eat supper and go to sleep. A couple of hours later, you are awoken in the dead of night by a gang of men there to kidnap you, your husband, and children. Screaming with terror, your family is chained and spirited away, and three days later, your entire system gripped by fear, you find yourself being pushed into a perfectly dark and nauseatingly fetid holding cell with hundreds of other men, women, and children, some of whom might be your own, although the noise, the cries, and the darkness make you initially unsure. This cell is also a latrine. And you are taken out of it seldom, once a week or so, and only to be used, sexually, by the men who have taken you there. After two or three months, you are branded, forced into a wooden ship, and taken as cargo along with hundreds of other captives, all of whom are chained to the floor of the cargo area such that you and the others cannot quite sit down. A foul stench also emanates from this area. Everyone around you is, of course, desperate, and many are sick or injured. You are fed gruel and are often given foul water. Some captives will die, so the mercenaries manning the ship will make their way to the cargo area to take out the dead, as well as those who are too ill to make it to the port of destination. They drag them out, and they throw them overboard, men, women, and children. This practice is so common that sharks in the Caribbean have learned to follow these ships.

Once you arrive at your destination, Virginia, Maryland, Barbados, Brazil, Lima, your psychical apparatus shattered, you are cleaned, oiled, and then auctioned to men who inspect your teeth (to make sure that you can eat the rough gruel they will give you), your hands (to make sure that you can work), and your body (as if they were inspecting the body of a mare that has to work and to reproduce). They then buy you to work you literally from dawn to dusk and to also breed their slaves, sometimes fathering these slaves themselves, children who might work side by side with you, their mother, or who might be sold to someone else. In this land, you have no rights and thus no legal recourse against any of this. Here your condition is often regarded as divinely ordained. And, as we saw, it is upheld by the most respected and influential citizens. This scenario closely approximates the experiences of hundreds of thousands, perhaps millions, of women who were traded as slaves during the 16th to the 19th centuries.

Let us quote from the autobiography of Frederick Douglass. In the following quote, he recalls one of his earlier memories as a young child living in a farm on Maryland:

> I have often been awakened at the dawn of day by the most heartrending shrieks of an own aunt of mine, whom [her master] use to tie to a joist, and whip upon her naked back until she was literally covered with blood. No words, no tears, no prayers from his gory victim seemed to move his iron heart from its bloody purpose. The louder she screamed, the harder he whipped; and where the blood ran fastest, there he whipped longest. He would whip her to make her scream, and whip her to make her hush; and not until overcome by fatigue, would he cease so swing the bloody clotted cowskin. This terrifying scene was the blood-stained gate, the entrance to the hell of slavery, through which I was about to pass. (Douglass, 2003, p. 20)

As a child, Douglass had "no shoes, no stockings, no jacket, no trousers, nothing on but a coarse linen shirt, reaching only to my knees." His feet were so "cracked with the frost, that the pen with which I am writing might be laid in the gashes" (Douglass, 2003, p. 37). He and other children were fed coarse boiled corn

> [that] was put into a large wooden tray or trough, and set down upon the ground. The children were then called, like so many pigs, and like so many pigs they would come and devour the mush; some with oyster-shells, others with pieces of shingle, some with naked hands, and none with spoons. He that ate fastest got most; he that was strongest secured the best place; and few left the trough satisfied (Douglass, 2003, p. 37).

This was a society where it was easier for slaveholders to remember the names of their horses than the names of their slaves, where schools legally denied access to black children and often taught white children that slavery was ordained by an all merciful God. Indeed, this society "took every pain to take everything away from its slaves"; not only such elemental aspects of life as parents, children, their sense of family, in general, but also the most elemental opportunities, their ability to decide for themselves, their ability to read, to add, to subtract (Narváez, 2012).

But here is something that the voracious American South could not take away from Frederick Douglass: his "capacity for indignation," to borrow the phrase from Alberto Flores Galindo, a Peruvian historian interested in colonization and the nature of the colonized mind. Douglass managed to keep this capacity to *understand* oppression, to *feel* the moral deficits of this system. This is the difference between coercive violence and symbolic violence: The former renders the dehumanizing nature of the system visible to its victims, and the latter, in contrast, makes this brutality invisible to them. Symbolic violence, let us insist on the key idea, removes the person's capacity to understand that oppression is, in fact, oppressive. It removes the person's capacity to *feel* the moral corruption that has dehumanized him or her, as the case of Linda's mother, for example, starkly illustrates.

Domination as Seduction

Consider now a very different example pertaining to slavery. The *St. Petersburg Times* (Garry, 2007) recounted the story of a "young slave from a Tennessee plantation named Louis Napoleon Nelson, who went to war as a teenager with the sons of his master"—fighting to defend the cause of the pro-slavery South. Louis Napoleon "cooked and looked out for the others." He foraged for food for his masters. "One time, he killed a mule, cut out a quarter and hauled it back to his comrades." Having memorized parts of the King James Bible, this illiterate slave served as a chaplain for mortally wounded confederate soldiers, thus laboring to absolve his oppressors and to grant them passage to heaven. He "saw action," the newspaper reports, "fighting with a rifle under the command of Confederate General Nathan Bedford Forrest," a slave trader, and probably the first Grand Wizard of the Ku Klux Klan. Upon dying, he bequeathed his confederate uniform to his grandson, as though encouraging the child to carry on with a tradition that had enslaved him.

Bourdieu notes that symbolic violence is a wrong interpretation of reality that is experienced as a truthful interpretation of reality, a process accompanied by the appropriate emotions and affects that tie the person to the erroneous interpretation. To paraphrase Bourdieu, the victim of symbolic violence is thus "seduced" by, and "espoused" to, the error. And in this sense, this person incarnates the error, brings it to life, as the error is expressed in his views, actions, desires. His desires are, of course, his own—but not strictly speaking, because they are rooted in an erroneous ideology that is not of his own making, a cultural narrative that is indeed designed to demean him. His desires are, in fact, his censors, and likewise with his worldview, his identity, his values: Their function is, above all, to keep him firmly in line, obedient to an oppressive order. Importantly, beyond individuals, symbolic violence can also affect groups, generations, and nations such that their collectively relevant values and motivations can also be disguised forms of oppression.

For these reasons, sometimes it is indeed a question of liberating the person from himself or herself, or liberating a group from its own internal dynamics, as Frantz Fanon, one of the most important contemporary black writers, has written. Reading the world, let us finally say, is sometimes a collective process that, often promoted by social movements or by awareness specialists, aims to liberate people from their own imaginations, from their own selves, from their own desires, from their own "common sense."

References

ABC International. (2018). El Helicoide de Caracas. *ABC Spain*. Retrived from https://www.abc.es/internacional/abci-helicoide-caracas-20181010225_video.html.

Akamatsu, R. (2010). *The Irish slaves*. New York, NY: Create Space.

Albright, M. (2018). *Fascism: A warning*. New York, NY: Harper.

Allcott, H., Braghieri, L., & Eichmeyer, S., & Gentzkow, M. (2019). The welfare effects of social media. *The National Bureau of Economic Research*. Retrieved from https://www.nber.org/papers/w25514

Allen, M. (2017). Sean Parker unloads on Facebook. Axios. Retrieved from https://www.axios.com/sean-parker-unloads-on-facebook-god-only-knows-what-its-doing-to-our-childrens-brains-1513306792-f855e7b4-4e99-4d60-8d51-2775559c2671.html

Al-Ghazali, H. (1963). *Incoherence of the philosophers* (S. A. Kamali, Trans.). Pakistan: Pakistan Philosophical Congress.

Al-Sharif, M. (2018, November 9). I'm a Saudi activist. Twitter put my life in danger. *The Washington Post*. Retrieved from https://www.washingtonpost.com/news/global-opinions/wp/2018/11/09/im-a-saudi-activist-twitter-put-my-life-in-danger/?utm_term=.ffd11bof4boa.

Alter, A. (2013). *Drunk tank pink: And other unexpected forces that shape how we think, feel, and behave*. New York, NY: Penguin Books.

American Anthropological Association. (1998). American Anthropological Association official statement on "race." Retrieved from http://www.aaanet.org/stmts/racepp.htm

Ansede, M. (2017, December 17). Ramon y Cajal contra "la superioritat del crani català." *El Pais*. Retrieved from https://www.cat.elpais.com/cat/2017/11/30/ciencia/1512040611_706407.html.

Arendt, H. (1977). *Eichmann in Jerusalem: A report on the banality of evil*. New York, NY: Penguin Books.

Asch, S. (1951). Effects of group pressure upon the modification and distortion of judgment. In H. Guetzkow (Ed.), *Groups, leadership and men* (pp. 177–190). Pittsburgh, PA: Carnegie Press.

Ashenburg, K. (2007). *The dirt on clean: An unsanitized history*. New York, NY: North Point Press.

Attenborough, D. (2018, December 3). United Nations climate summit speech, Katowice Poland. The Guardian. Retrieved from https://www.theguardian.com/environment/2018/dec/03/david-attenborough-collapse-civilisation-on-horizon-un-climate-summit

Bargh, J. A., Chen, M., & Burrows, L. (1996). Automaticity of social behavior: Direct effects of trait construct and stereotype activation on action. *Journal of Personality and Social Psychology, 71*(2), 230–244.

Basler, R., & Sandburg, C. (2001). *Lincoln: His speeches and writings*. Cambridge, MA: Da Capo Press.

Becker, H. (1963). *Outsiders: Studies in the sociology of deviance*. New York, NY: Macmillan Press.

Bernays, E. (1928). *Propaganda*. New York, NY: Liverlight.

Bernays, E. (2013). *Public relations*. Norman, OK: UO Press.

Baudrillard, J. (1995). *Simulacra and simulation* (S. F. Glaser, Trans.). Ann Arbor, MI: The University of Michigan Press.

Benjamin, W. (1968). *Illuminations: Essays and reflections* (H. Arendt, Ed., & H. Zohn, Trans.). New York, NY: Schocken Books, Inc.

Berger, J. (1980). *About looking*. New York, NY: Vintage International.

Berger, J. (1990). *Ways of seeing*. New York, NY: Penguin Books.

Berger, P. (1963). *Invitation to sociology: A humanistic perspective*. New York, NY: Anchor.

Berlin, B., & Kay, P. *(1969). Basic color terms: Their universality and evolution.* Berkeley, CA: University of California Press.

Black, W. (2014). *The best way to rob a bank is to own one: How corporate executives and politicians looted the S&L industry.* Austin, TX: University of Texas Press.

Blakeslee, S., & Blakeslee, M. (2008). *The body has a mind of its own: How body maps in your brain help you do (almost) everything better.* New York, NY: Random House.

Bogost, I. (2018). Cow clicker. Retrieved from http://bogost.com/games/cow_clicker/

Bollas, C. (2018). *Meaning and melancholia: Life in the age of bewilderment.* New York, NY: Routledge.

Borges, J. L. (2012). *Ficciones.* Madrid, Spain: Vintage.

Boulis, A., & Jacobs, J. (2008). *The changing face of medicine: Women doctors and the evolution of health care in America (the culture and politics of health care work).* New York, NY: Cornell University Press.

Bourdieu, P. (1987). *Distinction: A social critique of the judgment of taste.* Cambridge, MA: Harvard University Press.

Bourdieu, P. (1988). On male domination. *Le Monde diplomatique.* Retrieved from http://mondediplo.com/1998/10/10bourdieu.

Brailovskaia, J., & Margraf, J. (2019). Facebook addiction disorder (FAD) among German students: A longitudinal approach. *PloS ONE, 12*(12), e0189719.

Braun, K., Rhiannon, E., & Loftus, E. (2002). Make my memory: How advertising can change our memories of the past. *Psychology & Marketing, 19*(1), 1–23.

Bradley, M. (2009). *Colour and meaning in Ancient Rome.* Cambridge, MA: Cambridge University Press.

Bracken, P., Wachtler A., Panesar, R., & Lange, J. (2007). The road not taken: How traditional excreta and greywater management may point the way to a sustainable future. *Water Science and Technology: Water Supply, 7*(1),219.227.

Brodkin, K. (1998). *How Jews became white folks and what that says about race in America.* New Brunswick, New Jersey: Rutgers University Press.

Calafat, A., Ye, X., Wong, L-Y., Reidy, J., & Needham, L. (2008). Exposure of the U.S. population to bisphenol A and 4-*tertiary*-Octylphenol. Environmental Health Perspectives, *116,* (1), 39–44.

Campbell, C. (2006). *The China study: The most comprehensive study of nutrition ever conducted and the startling implications for diet, weight loss, and long-term health.* Dallas, TC: BenBella.

Caritas Venezuela. (2018). Monitoreo de la situación nutricional en niños menores de cinco años. *Caritas,* April–August 2017.

Carr, N. (2011). *The shallows: What the Internet is doing to our brains.* New York, NY: W. W. Norton & Company.

CDC. (2018). Adult obesity facts. Retrieved from https://www.cdc.gov/obesity/data/adult.html

Chaelin, R., Cho, J., & Stone, M., De La Cerda, J., Goldenson, N., Moroney, E., Tung, I., et al. (2018). Association of digital media use with subsequent symptoms of ADHD among adolescents. *JAMAL, 320*(3), 255–263.

Chang, K. (2009). Chronic pain: Cultural Sensitivity to Pain. In Eshun S. & Gurung, R. (Eds.) In *Culture and mental health: Sociocultural influences, theory and practice.* New York, NY: Wiley-Blackwell.

Caistor, N. (2000). *Mexico City: A cultural and literary companion.* New York, NY: Signal Books.

Chase, A. (1980). *The legacy of Malthus.* Champaign, IL: University of Illinois Press.

Chartrand, T., & Van Baaren, R. (2009). Human nonconscious mimicry. *Advances in Experimental Social Psychology, (*41) 219–274

Church, G., & Regis, E. (2012). *Regenesis: How synthetic biology will reinvent nature and ourselves.* New York, NY: Basic Books.

Cioran, E. (2004). *Tears and saints.* Chicago, IL: Chicago University Press.

Cox, B. (2008). *CERN's supercolider.* Ted Talks. Retrieved from https://www.ted.com/talks/brian_cox_on_cern_s_supercollider

Cummings, E. E. (1958). *Miscellany.* (G. Firmage, Ed.). New York, NY: October House.

Cycon, D. (2007). *Javatrekker: Dispatches from the world of fair trade coffee.* White River Junction, Vermont: Chelsea Green Publishing Company.

Damasio, A. (2005). *Descartes error: Emotion reason and the human brain.* New York, NY: Penguin Books.

Damasio, A. (2006). *The feeling of what happens: Body and emotion in the making of consciousness.* New York, NY: Mariner.

Darley, J., & Gross, P. (1983). A hypothesis-confirming bias in labeling effects. *Journal of Personality and Social Psychology, 44*(1), 20–33.

Dawkins, R. (2005). Why the universe seems so strange. Ted Talks. Retrieved from http://www.ted.com/talks/richard_dawkins_on_our_queer_universe

DeBell, M., & Chapman, C. (2006). *Computer and Internet use by students in 2003*. U.S. Department of Education. Washington, DC: National Center for Education Statistics.

De Beauvoir, S. (2011). *The second sex* (C. Borde and S. Malovany, Trans.). New York, NY: Vintage.

Descartes, R. (1988). *Selected philosophical writings*. Cambridge, MA: Cambridge University Press.

Dijksterhuis, A. (2005). Why we are social animals: The high road to imitation as social glue. In Hurley, S. & Chater, N. (Eds.), *Perspectives on imitation: From cognitive neuroscience to social science* (pp. 207–220). Cambridge, MA: MIT Press

Dorell, O. (2017, September 7). Alleged Russian political meddling documented in 27 countries since 2004. *USA Today*. Retrieved from https://eu.usatoday.com/story/news/world/2017/09/07/alleged-russian-political-meddling-documented-27-countries-since-2004/619056001/

Douglass, F. (2003). *Narrative of the life of Frederick Douglass, an American slave*. New York, NY: Barnes and Noble Classics.

Du Bois, W.E.B. (2011). *The souls of black folk*. New York, NY: Tribeca Books.

Durant, W., & Durant, A. (2011). *The age of Luis XIV: The story of civilization*. New York, NY: Simon & Schuster.

Durkheim, E. (1995). *The elementary forms of religious life*. (K. Fields, Trans.). New York, NY: Free Press.

Durkheim, E. (2007). *On suicide*. (R. Buss, Trans.). New York, NY: Penguin.

Elam, H. (2010). We wear the mask: Performance, social dramas, and race. In H. Markus & P. Moya (Eds.), *Doing race: 21 essays for the 21st* (pp. 554–562). New York, NY: W. W. Norton & Company.

Eliot, S. (2008, October 6). When doctors and even Santa endorsed tobacco. *The New York Times*. Retrieved from https://www.nytimes.com/2008/10/07/business/media/07adco.html.

Ellison, R. (1980). *The invisible man*. New York, NY: Vintage.

Encyclopedia of the New American Nation. (2015). Television: The Persian Gulf War. Retrieved from http://www.american-foreignrelations.com/O-W?Television-The-persian-gulf-war.html#b%23ixzzluKXkqB1I.

Fabri, A., Holand, T. J., & Bero, L. A. (2018). Food industry sponsorship of academic research: Investigating commercial bias in the research agenda. *Public Health Nutrition, 21* (18), 3422–3430.

Farzan, A. (2018, September 13). Florida State fraternity's "scumbag of the week" hazing tradition led to student's brain damage, lawsuit says. *The Washington Post*.

Fausto-Sterling, A. (1992). *Myths of gender*. New York, NY: Basic Books.

Festinger, L., Riecken, H., & Schachter S. (1956). *When prophecy fails*. Minneapolis, MN: University of Minnesota Press.

Fiennes, S. (Director). (2014). *The pervert's guide to ideology* [DVD]. London, England: British Film Institute and A P Guide /Blinder Films Production.

Fischler, C. (1990). *L'Homnivore*. Paris, France: Odile Jacob.

Flynn, J. (2012a). *Are we getting smarter? Rising IQ in the twenty-first century*. Cambridge, MA: Cambridge University Press.

Flynn, J. (2012b, August 20). The Flynn effect: Modernity made us smarter [Audio podcast]. Retrieved from http://www.scientificamerican.com/podcast/episode.cfm?id=the-flynn-effect-modernity-made-us-12-08-20

Foster, E., Jobling, P., Taylor, P., Donnelly, P., de Knijff, P., Mierement, R., Zeral, T., & Tyler-Smith, C. (1998). Jefferson fathered slave's last child. *Nature, 396,* 27–28.

Friedan, B. (2001). *The feminine mystique*. New York, NY: W. W. Norton & Company.

Fuller, R., & Warren, P., & Gaston, K. (2007). Daytime noise predicts nocturnal singing in urban robins. *Biology Letters, 3*(4), 368–370.

Fussell, S. (1991). *Muscle: Confessions of an unlikely bodybuilder*. New York, NY: Avon Books.

Gager, J. (1983). *The origins of anti-Semitism*. Oxford, UK: Oxford University Press.

Galeano, E. (1985). *Genesis*. (C. Belfrage, Trans.). New York, NY: W. W. Norton & Company.

Galeano, E. (1996, December 26). El Derecho de Soñar. *El Pais*. Retrieved from https://elpais.com/diario/1996/12/26/opinion/851554801_850215.html.

Galilei, G. (1997). *Il Sagiatore*. 1a Edizione Elettronica. Italy: Progetto Manuzio.

Garry, S. (2007, October 7). In defense of his confederate pride. *The St. Petersburg Times.*

Garcia-Sayan, Diego. (2019, January 29). ¡Dan vergüenza! *El Pais.* Retrieved from https://elpais.com/international/2019/01/24/america/1548370255_237317.html.

Gates, B. (2018). Reinvented toilet expo. Gates Foundation. Retrieved from https://www.gatesfoundation.org/Media-Center/Speeches/2018/11/Reinvented-Toilet-Expo

Georges, P., Bayle-Tourtoulou, A., & Badoc, M. (2013). *Neuromarketing in action: How to talk and sell to the brain.* London, England: Kogan Page.

Gino, F., Norton, M., & Ariely, D. (2010). The counterfeit self: The deceptive costs of faking it. *Psychological Science, 21*(5), 712–20.

Gombrich, E. H. (2002). *The story of art.* London, England: Phaidon Press.

Goodman, A. (2012). *Race: Are we so different.* Hoboken, NJ: Wiley-Blackwell.

Goodman, S. (2010). *Sonic warfare: Sound affect, and the ecology of fear.* Boston, MA: MIT Press.

Gopnik, A. (2000). *The philosophical baby.* New York, NY: Farrar, Strauss and Giroux.

Gore, A. (2008). *The assault on reason.* New York, NY: Penguin.

Gould, S. J. (2002). *The structure of evolutionary theory.* Cambridge, MA: The Belknap Press of Harvard University Press.

Grassian, S. (2006). *Psychiatric effects of solitary confinement. Washington University Journal of Law & Policy, 22,* (1), 325. Retrieved from http://digitalcommons.law.wustl.edu/wujlp/vol22/iss1/24.

Gray, K., & Wegner, D. (2008). The sting of intentional pain. *Psychological Science, 19*(12), 1260–1262.

Grzanka, P. (2014). *Intersectionality: A foundations and frontiers reader.* Philadelphia, PA: West View Press.

Halcomb, S. (2011). How Coca-Cola is gamifying vending machines in Japan. TechinAsia. Retrieved from https://www.techinasia.com/coca-cola-gamifies-its-vending-machines.

Haney Lopez, I. (2006). *White by law.* New York, NY: New York University Press.

Hanson, J., Hair, N., Chandra, A., Moss, E., Bhattacharya, J., Pollak, S., & Wolfe B. (2012). Brain development and poverty: A first look. In W. Barbara, W. Evans, & N. Adler (Eds.), *The biological consequences of socioeconomic inequalities* (pp. 187–214) New York, NY: Russel Sage.

Hartley, B., & Sutton, R. M. (2013). Stereotype threat account of boys' academic underachievement. *Child Development, 84*(5), 1716–1733.

Hatfield, E., Cacioppo, J., & Rapson, R. (1993). *Emotional contagion.* Cambridge, MA: Cambridge University Press.

Heng, G. (2011). The invention of race in the European Middle Ages. *Literature Compass, 8*(5), 258–274.

Herrero, A., & Casey, N. (2019, February 21). Ex Jefe de Inteligencia Militar Abandona a Maduro y Denuncia Narcotráfico y Corrupción en el Gobierno. *The New York Times, España.* Retrieved from https://www.nytimes.com/es/2019/02/21/venezuela-maduro-hugo-carvajal/

hooks, bell. (1996). *Killing rage: Ending racism.* New York, NY: Henry Holt and Company.

Hobbes, T. (2005). *The Oxford companion to philosophy.* (T. Honderich, Ed., 2015). Oxford, UK: Oxford University Press.

HUC. (2014, February 7). Report of the detailed findings of the commission of inquiry on human rights in the Democratic People's Republic of Korea. New York, NY: United Nations General Assembly.

Iacoboni, M. (2009). *Mirroring people: The science of empathy and how we connect with others.* New York, NY: Picador.

Ignatiev, N. (2008). *How the Irish became white.* Milton Park, UK: Routledge.

International Monetary Fund. (2018). *World economic outlook: Challenges to steady growth.* Washington DC: IMF Publication Services.

IPCC. (2018). Global warming of 1.5°C (V. Masson-Delmotte, H. O. Zhai, D. Portner, Roberts, D., Skea, J., Shukla, P.., Pirani, A., et al. (Eds.)). Retrieved from https://www.ipcc.ch/site/assets/uploads/sites/2/2019/02/SR15_Citation.pdf

Iwamoto, K., Cheng, A., Lee. C., Takamatsu, S., & Gordoin, D. (2011). "Man-ing" up and getting drunk: The role of masculine norms, alcohol intoxication and alcohol-related problems among college men. *Addiction Behavior, 36*(9), 906–911.

Jablonski, N. (2004). The evolution of human skin and skin color. *Annual Review of Anthropology, 33*(1), 585–623.

Jacobs, C. (2000). *Slavery in the 21st century.* London, England: Encyclopedia Britannica.

Jacobson, M. F. (1998). *Whiteness of a different color: European immigrants and the alchemy of race.* Cambridge, MA: Harvard University Press.

Johnson, S., Jabukek, A. B., Painter, M. S., Ellersieck, M. Welsh, T. Camacho, L., Lewis, S., et al. (2016). Effects of developmental exposure to Bisphenol A on spatial navigational learning and memory in rats. *Hormones and Behavior, 1* (80), 139–148.

Jordan, D., & Walsh, M. (2007). *White cargo: The forgotten history of Britain's white slaves in America.* New York, NY: New York University Press

Joseph, M., & Durlacher, J. (2000). *Speed: Its history and lore.* London, England: Carlton Books.

Jostmann, N., Lakens, D., & Schuber, T. (2009). Weight as an embodiment of importance. *Psychological Science, 20*(9), 1169–1174.

Kaimal, D., Teja Sajja, R., & Sasangohar, F. (2017). Investigating the effects of social media usage on sleep quality. *Proceedings of the Human Factors and Ergonomic Society, 2017 Meeting* (pp. 1–5).

Kenner, R. (Director). (2009). *Food Inc.* [DVD]. New York, NY: Magnolia Pictures.

Kenneth, C., & Mamie, C. (1939). Racial identification and preference in negro children. In E. L. Hartley (Ed.), *Readings in social psychology.* New York, NY: Holt, Reinhart, and Winston.

Kimmel, M. (2008). *Guyland: The perilous world where boys become men.* New York, NY: Harper Collins

King, B. (2002). *Biological anthropology: An evolutionary perspective* [DVD]. Chantilly, VA: The Teaching Company.

Kishiyama, M. M., Thomas Boyce, W., Jimenez, A. W., Perry, L. M., & Knight, R. T. (2009). Socioeconomic disparities affect prefrontal function in children. *Journal of Cognitive Neuroscience, 21*(6), 1106–1115.

Kosambi, D. (1967). Living prehistory in India. *Scientific American, 216*(2), 104–115.

Krauss, L. (2013). *A universe from nothing: Why there is something rather than nothing.* New York, NY: Atria Books.

Kristof, N. (2019, January 26). She wanted to drive, so Saudi Arabia's ruler imprisoned and tortured her. *The New York Times.* Retrieved from https://www.nytimes.com/2019/01/26/opinion/sunday/loujain-al-hathloul-saudi.html.

Kuran, T. (2018). Islam and economic performance: Historical and contemporary links. Journal of Economic Literature, 56(4), 1292–1359.

Lakoff, G., & Johnson, M. (1999). *Philosophy in the flesh: The embodied mind and its challenge to Western thought.* New York, NY: Basic Books.

Langer, E., Djikic, M., Pirson, M., Madenci, A., Donohue, R. (2010). Believing is seeing: Using mindlessness (mindfully) to improve visual acuity. *Psychological Science, 21*(5), 661–666.

Lautenbacher, S., & Fillingim, R. B. (Eds.) (2004). *Pathophysiology of pain perception.* New York, NY: Plenum Publishers.

Lazonick, W. (1990). *Competitive advantage in the shop floor.* Boston, MA: Harvard University Press.

Le Catron, M. (2017). *How to fall in love with anyone: A memoir in essays.* New York, NY: Simon and Shuster.

Lessing, D. (1987). *Prisons we choose to live inside.* New York, NY: Harper Collins

Lewontin, R. (1993). *Biology as ideology: The doctrine of DNA.* New York, NY: Harper.

Liederman, H. (1962). Man alone: Sensory deprivation and behavior change. *Correctional Psychiatry & Soc. Therapy, 1*(8), 64, 66.

Loftus, E. (1997). Creating false memories. *Scientific American, 277*(3), 70–75.

Lovelace, L. (2006). *Ordeal.* New York, NY: Kensington.

Lotzof, K. (2018). Cheddar man: Mesolithic Britain's blue eyed boy. Retrived from http://www.nhm.ac.uk/discover/cheddar-man-mesolithic-britain-blue-eyed-boy.html

Lozano, D. (2018, November 30). El estado de los hospitales en Venezuela. *El Mundo.* Retrieved from https://www.elmundo.es/internacional/2018/11/30/5c002e5ffdddff9506b461d.html.

Lozano, D. (2019, February 11). Radiografía medica de una catástrofe humanitaria. *El Mundo.* Retrieved from https://www.elmundo.es/internacional/2019/02/11/5c6070b8fdddff4f3c8b4582.html.

Lyons, M. A. (2004). *Fitzwilliam, Sir William (1526–1599), Oxford Dictionary of National Biography.* Oxford, UK: Oxford University Press. Retrieved from http://www.oxforddnb.com/view/article/9664

Manetto, F. (2018, December 12). La brecha social desangra Venezuela. *El Pais.* Retrieved from https:// elpais.com/international/2018/12/09/Colombia/1544392763_580355.html.

Marcus, H., & Moya, P. (Eds.) (2010). *Doing race: 21 essays for the 21st century.* New York, NY: W. W. Norton and Company.

Marías, J. (2018). *Cuando los tontos mandan*. Madrid, Spain: Alfaguara.

Marius, R. (2008, July 1). Saint Fiacre: Brief life of the gardener saint, 600–670. *Harvard Magazine*. Retrieved from https://harvardmagazine.com/1998/07/saint-fiacre.

Marks, J. (2002). *What it means to be 98% chimpanzee: Apes, people, and their genes*. Berkeley, CA: University of California Press.

Martin, D. (1995). *The Corinthian body*. New Heaven, CT: Yale University Press.

Masood, E. (2002). Arab science blooms in the desert. *Nature, 416* (6877), 120–122.

Maziak, W. (2017). Science, modernity, and the Muslim world. *EMBO Reports, 18* (2), 194–197.

McKoskey, D. (2004). On black Athena, Hippocratic medicine, and Roman imperial edicts: Egyptians and the problem of race in Classical antiquity. In R. Coates (Ed.), *Race and ethnicity across time, space, and* discipline (pp. 297–330) Leiden, the Netherlands: Brill.

Mead, G. H. (1934). *Mind, self, and society*. (C. W. Morris, Ed.). Chicago, IL: University of Chicago Press.

Meltzer, M. (1993). *Slavery: A world history*. New York, NY: Da Capo Press.

Merton, R. (1957). *Social theory and social structure*. Glencoe, IL: Free Press.

Meyer, I. (2003). Prejudice, social stress and mental health in lesbian, gay, and bisexual populations. *Psychological Bulletin, 129*(5), 674–697.

Melzack, R., & Casey, K. (1968). Sensory, motivational and central control determinants of chronic pain: A new conceptual model. In D. R. Kenshalo (Ed.), *The skin senses: Proceedings of the first International Symposium on the Skin Senses, Florida State University*. Springfield, IL: Charles C. Thomas Publisher.

Melzack, R. & Wall, P. (1996) *The challenge of pain*. London, UK: Penguin Books.

Meltzoff, A. N., & Moore, M. K. (1977). Imitation of facial and manual gestures by human neonates. *Science, 198*, 75–78.

Menchú, R. (2010). *I, Rigoberta Menchú: An Indian woman in Guatemala*. London, England: Verso.

Miles-Morillo, L. & Morillo, S. (2013). *Sources for frameworks of world history: Networks, hierarchies, culture*. Oxford, UK: Oxford University Press.

Milgram, S. (1975). *Obedience to authority: An experimental view*. New York, NY: Harper Perennial.

Morris, D. (1993). *The culture of pain*. Berkeley, CA: University of California Press.

Morrison, T. (1987). *Beloved*. New York, NY: Vintage.

Morrison, T. (1997). *The Bluest Eye*. New York, NY: Penguin.

Narváez, A. (2003). Cabeza y cola: Expresión de dualidad, religiosidad y poder en los Andes. (In L. Millones, H. Tomoeda, & T. Fujii (Eds.), *Senri ethnological reports* (pp. 27–68). Osaka, Japan: National Museum of Ethnology.

Narváez, R. (2012). *Embodied collective memory: The making and unmaking of human nature*. Lanham, MD: University Press of America.

Narváez, R. (2006). Embodiment, collective memory, and time. *Body and Society, 12*(3), 51–73.

National Human Genome Research Institute. (2005). The use of racial, ethnic, and ancestral categories in human genetics research. *American Journal of Human Genetics*, 77(4), 519–532.

National Institutes of Health. (2014). Talking glossary of genetic terms. National Human Genome Research Institute. Retrieved from http://www.genome.gov/glossary/

Neruda, P. (2018). *El libro de las preguntas*. Madrid, Spain: Seix Barral.

Nguyen, K., Glantz, S., Palmer, C., & Schmidt, L. (2019). Tobacco industry involvement in children's sugary drink market. *BMJ, 1*(2019),364:1736.

Nisbett, R., & Masuda, T. (2003). Culture and point of view. *Proceedings of the National Academy of Sciences of America, 100*(19), 11163–11170.

NYT Editorial Board. (2018, November 15). "Facebook cannot be trusted to regulate itself." *The New York Times*. Retrieved from https://www.newyorktimes.com/2018/11/15/opinion/facebook-data-congress-russia-election.html.

Ofek, H. (2011). Why the Arabic world turned away from science. *The New Atlantis, 30*(4), 3–23.

OHCHR. (2018a). Venezuela: Continued impunity amid dismal human rights situation. United Nations High Commissioner for Human Rights. Retrieved from https://www.ohchr.org/en/NewsEvents/Pages/DisplayNews.aspx?ID=23242&langID=E.

OHCHR. (2018b). Violaciones de los derechos humanos en la Republica Bolivariana de Venezuela (pp. 4–5). United Nations High Commissioner for Human Rights.

Palihapitiya, C. (2018). Money as an instrument of change. Stanford Business. Retrieved from https://www.youtube.com/watch?v=PMotykw0SIk

Palomino, E. (2018, March 16). Almagro comparte postura sobre Venezuela con Ciudadanos. *El Pais*. Retrieved from https://elpais.com/international/2018/03/16/actualidad/1521194779_281616.html.

Paoleti, J. (2012). *Pink and blue: Telling boys from girls in America*. Bloomington, Indiana: IU Press.

Parsons, T. (1968). *The structure of social action*. New York, NY: The Free Press.

Perea, J. (1996). *Immigrants out!: The new nativism and the anti-immigrant impulse in the United States*. New York, NY: New York University Press.

Pennycook, G., Cheyne, J., Barr, N., Koehler, D., & Fugelsang, J. (2015). On the reception and detection of pseudo-profound bullshit. *Judgment and Decision Making, 10*(6), 549–563.

Pereira-González, F. (2001). *Raza e alteridade. A reflexión sobre a diversidade humana na Galicia do século XIX*. A Coruña: Deputación da Coruña.

Pessoa, F. (2010). *O Guardador de rebanhos*. Sao Paolo, Brazil: Best Books Brazil.

Peters, W. (1971). *A class divided: Then and now*. New Haven, CT: Yale University Press.

Piaget, J. (1977). *The essential Piaget*. (H. E. Gruber & J. J. Voneche, Eds.). Jason Aronson New York, NY: Basic Books.

Pinker, S. (2018). *Enlightenment now: The case for reason, humanism, and progress*. London, England: Allen Lane.

Pinter, H. (2006). *The essential Pinter*. New York, NY: Groove Press.

Pounder, C. C. H, Adelman, L., Cheng, J., Herbes-Sommers, C., Strain, T. H., Llewellyn Smith, & Ragazzi, C. (2003). *Race the power of an illusion* [DVD]. San Francisco, CA: California Newsreel.

Press, E. (2012). *Beautiful souls: Breaking ranks and heeding the voice of conscience in dark times*. New York, Ny: Farrar, Straus and Giroux.

Plato. (1936). *The human soul in the myths of Plato*. (The Editors of the Shrine of Wisdom, Eds.). London, England: Hermon Hill.

Quillen, E., & Shriver, M. (2011). Unpacking human evolution to find the genetic determinants of human skin pigmentation. *Journal of Investigative Dermatology, 17*(131), E5–E7.

Rideout, V., Roberts, D., & Foehr, U. (2010). *Generation M2: Media in the lives of 8–18 year-olds*. Menlo Park, CA: Kaiser Family Foundation.

River, C. (2014). *American legends: The life of Jim Henson*. New York, NY: Create Space.

Rizzolatti, G., & Craighero, L. (2004). The mirror-neuron system. *Annual Review of Neuroscience, 27*(2004), 169–192.

Rollins v. State, No. 6 Div. 927. Court of Appeals of Alabama 18 Ala. App. 354; 92 So. 35; 1922 Ala. App. (1922).

Rosenthal, R., & Fode, K. (1963). The effect of experimenter bias on performance of the albino rat. *Behavioral Science, 8*, 183–189.

Rosenthal, R., & Jacobson, L. (1963). Teachers' expectancies: Determinants of pupils' IQ gains. *Psychological Reports, 1966* (19), 115–118.

Rositer, C., & Lane, J. (1963). *The essential Lippmann: A political philosophy for liberal democracy*. Cambridge, MA: Harvard University Press.

Roth, P. (2012, September 6). An open letter to Wikipedia. *The New Yorker*. Retrieved from https://www.newyorker.com/books/page-turner/an-open-letter-to-wikipedia.

Sartre, J. P. (1948). *Anti-Semite and Jew: An exploration of the etiology of hate*. New York, NY: Schocken Books.

Segall, M., Campbell, D., & Herskovits, M. (1966). The influence of culture on visual perception. In Touch, Hans, Clay (Eds.), *Social perception* (Ch.14). New York, NY: Van Nostrand Reinhold.

Seife, C. (2015). *Virtual unreality: The new era of digital deception*. New York, NY: Penguin Books.

Singer, P. (2007). *The ethics of what we eat*. New York, NY: Rodale Books.

Smith, A. (1994). *The wealth of nations*. New York, NY: Modern Library.

Seager, J. (2009). *The Penguin atlas of women in the world*. New York, NY: Penguin.

Slepian, M., Weisbuch, M., Rule, N. O., & Ambady, N. (2011). Tough and tender: Embodied categorization of gender. *Psychological Science, 22*(1), 26–28.

Sontag, S. (2001). *On photography*. New York, NY: Picador.

Sparrow, B. (2011). Google effects on memory: Cognitive consequences of having information at our fingertips. *Science, 333*(6043), 776–778.

Starr, F. (1977). *Apicius: Cookery and dinning in imperial Rome.* New York, NY: Dover.

Stauber, J., & Sheldom, R. (2002). *Toxic sludge is good for you: Lies, damn lies and the public relations industry.* Monroe, ME: Common Courage Press.

Steinberg, S. (1989). *The ethnic myth: Race ethnicity and class in America.* Boston, MA: Beacon Press.

Sturm, R. A., Teasdale, R. D., Box, N. F. (2001). Human pigmentation genes: Identification, structure and consequences of polymorphic variation. *Gene, 277*(1–2), 49–62.

Suh, E., Diener, E., Shigehiro, O., & Triandis, H. (1998). The shifting basis of life satisfaction judgments across cultures: emotions versus norms. *Journal of Personality and Social Psychology, 74*(2), 482–493.

Takaki, R. (2008). *A different mirror: A history of multicultural America.* New York, NY: Back Bay Books.

Thoreau, H. D. (2012). *Walden and civil disobedience.* New York, NY: Signet.

Tomatis, A. (1991). *The conscious ear.* Barrytown, NY: Station Hill Press.

Tocqueville, A. D. (2000). *Democracy in America.* Evanston, IL: University of Chicago Press.

Trading Economics. (2018). Hungary GDP. Retrieved from https://tradingeconomics.com/hungary/gdp

Transparency International. (2018). Corruption perception indexes 2017. Retrieved from https://www.transparency.org/news/feature/corruption_perceptions_index_2017.

Tranströmer, T. (2001). *The half-finished heaven: the best poems of Tomas Transtromer.* New York, NY: Graywolf Press.

Tufekci, Z. (2017). We are building a dystopia, just to make people click on ads. Ted Talks. Retrieved from https://www.ted.com/talks/zeynep_tufekci_we_re_building_a_dystopia_just_to_make_people_click_on_ads

UN Human Rights Council. (2015, May 12). Report of the special rapporteur on violence against women, its causes and consequences, Rashida Manjoo (pp. 3–5). UN General Assembly.

UN Human Rights Council. (2016, April 18). Report of the special rapporteur on violence against women, its causes and consequences on her mission to the Sudan (p. 8). UN General Assembly.

UN Human Rights Council. (2018, November 19). Concluding observations on the fifth periodic report of the Sudan (pp. 3–5) UN General Assembly.

University of Copenhagen. (2008). Blue-eyed humans have a single, common ancestor. *ScienceDaily.* Retrieved from www.sciencedaily.com/releases/2008/01/080130170343.htm.

U.S. Food and Drug Administration. (2018). The food defects action levels. Retrieved from https://www.fda.gov/Food/GuidanceRegulation/GuidanceDocumentsRegulatoryInformation/SanitationTransportation/ucm056174.htm

van Praet, D. (2014). *Unconscious branding: How neuroscience can empower (and inspire) marketing.* New York, NY: Palgrave MacMillan.

Vargas Llosa, M. (2012). *La civilización del espectáculo.* Madrid, Spain: Alfaguara.

von Ahn, L. (2008). Human computation. MIT. Retrieved from http://cci.mit.edu/presenters/vonAhn.html.

von Ahn, L. (2013). Human computation. CERN. Retrieved from https://indico.cern.ch/event/32943/

Wade, D. (1988). *Passage of darkness: The ethnobiology of the Haitian zombie.* Chapel Hill, NC: The University of North Carolina Press.

Wall, P. (2002). *Pain: The science of suffering.* New York, NY: Columbia University Press.

Ware, B. (2012). *The top five regrets of the dying: A life transformed by the dearly departing.* Carlsbad, CA: Hay House.

Weber, E. (1976). *Peasants into Frenchmen.* Stanford, CA: Stanford University Press.

Weber, M. (1958). *The Protestant ethic and the spirit of capitalism. (*T. Parsons, Trans.). New York, NY: Scribners.

Weinberg, S. (2007). A deadly certitude. *The Times Literary Supplement, 1*(5460), 5–6.

Wesby, J. (2018). Here is what is amazing about the Facebook Cambridge Analitica story. *Forbes.* Retrieved from https://www.forbes.com/sites/jodywestby/2018/03/27/what-is-amazing-about-the-facebook-cambridge-analytica-story/

West, C. (1999). *The Cornel West reader.* New York, NY: Basic Civitas Books.

Wilde, O. (2008). *The decay of lying.* Richmond, UK: Alma Classics.

Williams, L., & Bargh, J. (2008). Experiencing physical warmth promotes interpersonal warmth. *Science, 322*(5901), 606–607.

Winter, M. (2016). The taboo secrets of better health. Ted Talk. Retrieved from https://www.ted.com/talks/molly_winter_the_taboo_secret_to_healthier_plants_and_people#t-726199

World Health Organization. (2009). Noise. Retrieved from http://www.euro.who.int/en/health-topics/environment-and-health/noise

Wright, J. 2011. The mortal soul in ancient Israel and Pauline Christianity: Ramifications for modern medicine. *Journal of Religious Health, 50*(2), 447–4521.

X, Malcom. (1987). *The autobiography of Malcolm X: As told to Alex Haley.* New York, NY: Ballantine Publishing Group.

Zimbardo, P. G. (1971). *The power and pathology of imprisonment. Congressional Record, Ninety-Second Congress, First session on corrections, Part II, prisons, prison reform and prisoner's rights: California.* Washington, DC: U.S. Government Printing Office.

Zimbardo, P. G. (2007). Situational sources of evil—Part I. Retrieved from http://thesituationist.wordpress.com/2007/02/16/when-good-people-do-evil-%E2%80%93-part-i/

Zimbardo, P. G. (2011). The demise of guys. Ted Talk. Retrieved from http://www.ted.com/talks/zimchallenge

CPSIA information can be obtained
at www.ICGtesting.com
Printed in the USA
LVHW010340140722
723452LV00004B/37

9 781516 536528